"Fr. Steven Avella has produced a serious, thoughtful, and engaging history of the Diocese of Des Moines. As you will see, the story of the Catholic Church in southwest Iowa is filled with men and women of great faith who enriched the lives of all people in this region through selfless engagement in education, medical services, and countless other charitable endeavors. This book shows how the Catholic Church in the Diocese of Des Moines has offered the love of Jesus Christ to the poor, the immigrant, and the farmer for over one hundred years. After reading this compelling history of Catholics in southwest Iowa, one can only hope that future harvests will be just as fruitful!"

+Timothy Cardinal Dolan
Archdiocese of New York

"From the day Fr. Samuel Mazzuchelli first set foot on Iowa soil in the 1830s, Catholic bishops, priests, nuns, and laity have impacted the history of this state far beyond the number of the faithful. As Fr. Steven Avella has captured in this sweeping narrative of the Diocese of Des Moines, the moral impulses planted by those earliest religious pioneers would uplift generations. From its nineteenth-century origins, this exceptional twentieth-century legacy provided the foundation upon which Bishop Richard Pates would extend into the twenty-first century this tradition of peace and justice—the next chapter in Iowa's Catholic odyssey."

Ambassador Kenneth M. Quinn (ret.)
President, The World Food Prize

"Avella's history of the Diocese of Des Moines from 1911 emphasizes the interplay of the sacred and the secular. The lively spirit of Catholicism from Bishops Dowling to Dingman is broadly illustrated in this excellent contribution to US church and local history."

Mary Christine Athans, BVM, PhD
Professor Emerita, The Saint Paul Seminary School of Divinity
of the University of St. Thomas

"Fr. Steven Avella has produced an exceptional history of Catholicism in the American heartland. Based on rigorous, scholarly research and written in clear, compelling prose, Fr. Avella tells the story of the Diocese of Des Moines during the ten tumultuous decades of the twentieth century. This book will be of value not only to academic historians but also to general readers interested in the evolution of the Catholic Church in a diverse American diocese composed of small cities and big towns bound together by hundreds of bustling farms."

> Timothy Walch, PhD
> Author of *Parish School: The History of American Catholicism from Colonial Times to the Present*

"This fascinating and well-researched volume not only informs us of the history of the Catholic Church in southwest Iowa, but describes the growth of religion in the US heartland. Avella's history of the Diocese of Des Moines from 1911 emphasizes the interplay of the sacred and the secular."

> Most Rev. Jerome Hanus, OSB
> Archbishop Emeritus of Dubuque

The Catholic Church in Southwest Iowa

A History of the Diocese of Des Moines

Steven M. Avella

LITURGICAL PRESS

Collegeville, Minnesota

www.litpress.org

The production and printing of this book is a work made for hire between Liturgical Press and the Diocese of Des Moines.

Cover design by Monica Bokinskie. Cover art by James Downey.

Permission to use images in this book have been received from the collections of:

Library of Congress
Archives of the Sisters of St. Dominic of Sinsinawa
Archives of the Archdiocese of Dubuque
Des Moines Public Library
Historical Society of Des Moines
Council Bluffs Public Library
Archives of St. Benedict Abbey, Atchison
Archives of the Congregation of the Humility of Mary
Archives of the Diocese of Davenport
Archives and Special Collections of Marquette University
Catholic Church Extension Society
Archives of the Diocese of Peoria
Archives of the Sisters of Mercy of the Americas
Archives of the Sisters of St. Felix of Cantalice
Archives of the Dominican Sisters of Adrian
Mount Carmel Archives of the Sisters of Charity of the Blessed Virgin Mary
Archivio Vaticano Segreto
Archives of the School of Sisters of St. Francis

ISBN 978-0-8146-4471-3   ISBN 978-0-8146-8793-2 (e-book)

1	2	3	4	5	6	7	8	9

Library of Congress Cataloging-in-Publication Data

Names: Avella, Steven M., author.
Title: The Catholic Church in southwest Iowa : a history of the Diocese of Des Moines / Steven M. Avella.
Description: Collegeville, Minnesota : Liturgical Press, 2018. | Includes bibliographical references.
Identifiers: LCCN 2017055808 | ISBN 9780814644713
Subjects: LCSH: Catholic Church. Diocese of Des Moines (Iowa)—History. | Des Moines (Iowa)—Church history.
Classification: LCC BX1417.D47 A94 2018 | DDC 282/.7775—dc23
LC record available at https://lccn.loc.gov/2017055808

To
Bishop Richard E. Pates, Ninth Bishop of Des Moines
"Ut Unum Sint"

Contents

Foreword

There is the story that missionaries, probably black-robed Jesuits, were seen centuries ago at the confluence of what now are called the Des Moines and Raccoon Rivers. Observers asked, "Who are they?" The natives replied, "The Monks," which in French is *Des Moines.*

From that moment emerged the makings of the Diocese of Des Moines, embracing as territory the southwest quadrant of Iowa. It was a relatively long period of gestation to diocesan status as parishes and institutions began to be established through the mother dioceses of Dubuque and Davenport. There were also the normal intrigue and ecclesiastical "gerrymandering" by those to be affected by its establishment. Finally, on October 11, 1911, Pope St. Pius X decreed that the Diocese of Des Moines was an ecclesiastical jurisdiction in its own right.

The diocese gradually grew with a catalogue of events involving the activities of some remarkably dedicated clergy, vowed religious, and loyal laity. Over time, there arose a unique spirit and character embracing lively human interplay that incarnated itself into the Body of Christ in the twenty-three counties of Southwest Iowa.

A top priority marking the diocesan centennial in 2011 was the eventual publication of an academic history. Father Steven Avella, a highly regarded and experienced historian from the faculty of Marquette University, was recruited for the task. Father Avella has lived up to expectations. His text is carefully researched and, at the same time, captures the human spirit of those who made what is the history of the Diocese of Des Moines.

Also to be credited for essential assistance with the historical rendition are members of the diocese who were unstinting with gifts of memory and time. Many institutions opened their files and chests of memorabilia for this undertaking. Particularly noteworthy is the grant from the Edwin T. Meredith Foundation, under the leadership of Mell Meredith Frazier, E.T. Meredith IV, John Zieser, Cheri Cipperley, and Michael Frazier, which has made this publication possible. Appropriately, the parents of Mell Frazier and E.T. Meredith IV, Ted and Katie Meredith, played instrumental roles in the evolution of the diocese.

A bishop, as signified by his episcopal ring, is said to be married to his diocese. I was very fortunate to be matched with my bride—the Diocese of Des Moines. I am admittedly biased, but for my money, Des Moines is a great diocese. I hope you enjoy its history as captured in *The Catholic Church in Southwest Iowa* as much as I have.

Richard E. Pates
Ninth Bishop of Des Moines

Acknowledgments

I have accumulated many debts in putting together this history of the Diocese of Des Moines. First, my gratitude to His Excellency the Most Reverend Richard E. Pates for asking me to do this work. My invitation came through a mutual friend, Sister M. Christine Athans, BVM, a respected historian and theologian. Bishop Pates has been supportive and patient at every step of the way and generously shared the hospitality of his home with me. Within the bishop's office, diocesan chancellor Mr. Jason Kurth has been the go-to man for every need I have had. He has made the arrangements, opened the doors, and generously given me a tour of the Des Moines churches. When other duties overtook him, Mr. Adam Storey, vice chancellor, took over and helped see this book through to completion. Likewise, director of administrative services, Sister Jude Fitzpatrick, CHM, the overseer of the archives, has made the records available to me whenever I needed them. Sister Jude and the diocesan communications department were of great help in the selection of images for this book. The diocesan archivist, Ms. Lynn Wingert, has been on hand to help with questions. The cooperation and assistance I have had from everyone in the diocese has been outstanding.

I have received hospitality from Father Aquinas Nichols, Monsignor Frank Bognanno, Father John O. Bertogli, and Bishop Pates in Des Moines. Father Bertogli has been a good companion, often helping me to understand the "lay of the land" and taking time out of his busy schedule to enjoy an evening meal with me. In Peoria, I was the guest of the Conventual Franciscan Fathers, and in Atchison, Kansas, I enjoyed the hospitality of the guesthouse of St. Benedict's Abbey.

I have met and interviewed many priests: Monsignors Lawrence Beeson, Edward Pfeffer, Stephen Orr, and Frank Bognanno and Father David Polich, Father Daniel Kirby, and other pastors and permanent deacons who have opened doors for my visits. Father Kirby and Monsignor Beeson took precious time to give me a wonderful "heritage" tour of the diocese. Sister Mira Mosle, BVM, has been a wonderful source of information about the Dingman years. I had the opportunity to meet briefly with the former bishop, Joseph Charron. The late Father Jim Kiernan provided some important insights on my first draft. Monsignor Orr, Monsignor Beeson, and Sister M. Christine Athans, BVM, read this manuscript twice. My old friend and colleague, Dr. Joseph M. White, gave it a thorough reading and made many helpful suggestions. Timothy Walch, retired director of the Hoover Library and an old friend, also read the manuscript and provided a lot of encouragement. Mary Lou McGinn was a great help in matters related to the history of Council Bluffs. The maps and graphs were done by my former graduate student, Dr. Aaron Hyams, currently at Sam Houston State University in Texas. Sister Mira Mosle, BVM, Monsignor Bognanno, and my friend Douglas Firth Anderson of Northwestern College, read the second draft. Orr, Mosle, and Bognanno provided critical information about the papal visit and events during the term of Bishop Maurice Dingman. All of them offered helpful corrections, suggestions, and additional insights. I am deeply indebted to all of them.

I visited the following archives: the Archdiocese of Dubuque, where I had a chance to speak at length with now-retired Archbishop Jerome Hanus, OSB; the Diocese of Peoria, where my host was Sister Lea Stefancova, FSJB; the Diocese of Davenport, where I was warmly received by one of the best archivists I have ever met, Ms. Tyla Cole; the Archives of the Clerics of St. Viator, where Joan Sweeney was my contact. Sister Deanna Carr, BVM, and Jennifer Head of the BVM archives and Sister Joan Sheil of the Sisters of Humility provided important records from their archives. Sister Lois Hoh of the Sinsinawa Domincans always promptly responded to my e-mail requests. R.C. McDonald of the Archives of the Dominican Province of St. Joseph sent me some very important information on Bishop Daly's early years. Father Denis Meade, OSB, was my guide through the archives of the Benedictines of Atchison, Kansas. Monte Kniffen and his staff helped me access the materials in the Sisters of Mercy Archives in Omaha, Nebraska. I am also grateful to the Mercy Heritage Center in Belmont, North Carolina, for their help. At Marquette University, my academic home, I was able to access the papers of Monsignor Luigi Ligutti and the Catholic Worker Movement in Des Moines, thanks to the good offices of Phil Runkel and Amy Cooper Cary. I would also like to thank the Department of History at Marquette University for providing research assistance and technical help to produce this text. Special thanks to David Schenk for his statistical work.

The US Passionists sent me helpful material from their collection. In Rome, I found other materials related to the retreat of the Passionist Fathers in Des Moines. The staffs at the State Historical Center in Des Moines and the Secret Vatican Archives in Rome were always of great assistance.

In Des Moines, local historians were most helpful. These included Mr. Archie Cook, an independent historian and docent; Mr. Bill R. Douglas, also an independent historian; Mary Neiderbach, who graciously shared many important materials with me from her work with the Community Development Department of Des Moines; and Karl Althaus, property description clerk for the Polk County auditor. Carol Aina, registrar at Dowling Catholic High School, sent me important statistics.

I am, of course, grateful to Liturgical Press for producing the book, in particular to Hans Christofferson, Stephanie Lancour, Julie Surma, and Colleen Stiller. I also extend sincere thanks to the Rt. Rev. John Klassen, OSB, of Saint John's Abbey in Collegeville for his help in securing the services of Liturgical Press. Special thanks also goes to Cindy Coan who produced the index.

Nearly everywhere I went in Iowa and beyond I was received with courtesy and hospitality. Virtually everyone responded to my requests positively and helpfully. Overall, Iowa people really do live up to their reputation of being down-to-earth and friendly. Because of them, I learned a lot about Iowa during this project and grew in admiration for the work of the Catholic Church in that state. I am grateful to Bishop Pates for asking me to do this work. It has been difficult at times, but always a joy.

Introduction

Iowa is a lovely state with rolling hills, acres of corn, interesting cities, complicated politics, and a rich history. So many factors have contributed to the dense cultural fabric of the Hawkeye State. One of them is religion. Writing of the period before the turn of the twentieth century—but equally applicable today—Iowa historian Dorothy Schweider observed, the "social activities of Midwesterners, both rural and urban, centered around three institutions: family, church, and school."[1]

Indeed, people of faith—from native peoples down to recently arrived Asian and African refugees—have brought with them their religious beliefs, practices, and morality. They have left their imprint on the state by transforming open spaces in the city and the country into holy places: churches, synagogues, mosques, and temples. They not only provide spiritual comfort and support but also offer other critical services: schools, social welfare organizations, and health-care facilities. Although difficult to disentangle from other motivations, religious beliefs—individual or institutional—exercise an important and sometimes significant influence on the values and public actions of individuals and groups. One does not have to share these varied beliefs to acknowledge their presence. They are part of the cultural heritage of the State of Iowa. This book attempts to write religion more deeply into the social and cultural history of the state. It uses the Roman Catholic Church—principally the twenty-three southwestern counties encompassed by the Roman Catholic Diocese of Des Moines—as a case study of this influence.

Modern life makes sharp distinctions between the secular and the sacred, assigning them each respective spheres. But like any binary that tries to reduce what human beings do to simplistic divisions, this one often breaks down under deeper analysis. Sacred and secular, religion and society are really interdependent realities. The secular often touches on the sacred, while the sacred uses secular methods to accomplish its work. In pondering the history of a Roman Catholic diocese—a juridical entity that encompasses the lives of numerous people—one finds the opportunity to test the engagement of secular and sacred in a precise place, time, and set of events. The challenge of this book is to do just that. Rather than simply line up events and people chronologically, this text focuses on the impact of Catholicism in Iowa as a social, cultural, and spiritual force, particularly in the lives of the denizens of its twenty-three southwestern counties.

Catholicism in the territory encompassed by the Roman Catholic Diocese of Des Moines, as an institutional and spiritual force, was not as strong in this particular section of the state as in others. Indeed, when correlating the population statistics of these counties with the total Catholic population, it appears that Catholics were never more than 14 percent of the total population. Where people did claim a religious affiliation, they were predominately Methodists, Baptists, Lutherans, and occasionally Mormons. The following chart tracks the respective populations of the twenty-three counties and the Catholic Church from 1900 to 2000:

County	1900	1910	1920	1930	1940	1950	1960	1970	1980	1990	2000
Mills	16,764	15,811	15,422	15,866	15,064	14,064	13,050	11,832	13,406	13,202	14,547
Montgomery	17,803	16,604	17,048	16,752	15,697	15,685	14,467	12,781	13,413	12,076	11,771
Adair	16,192	14,420	14,259	13,891	13,196	12,292	10,893	9,487	9,509	8,409	8,243
Union	19,928	16,616	17,268	17,435	16,280	15,651	13,712	13,557	13,858	12,750	12,309
Clarke	12,440	10,736	10,506	10,384	10,233	9,369	8,222	7,581	8,618	8,287	9,133
Lucas	16,126	13,462	15,686	15,114	14,571	12,069	10,923	10,163	10,313	9,070	9,422
Harrison	25,597	23,162	24,488	24,897	22,767	19,560	17,600	16,240	16,348	14,730	15,666
Shelby	17,932	16,552	16,065	17,131	16,720	15,942	15,825	15,528	15,043	13,230	13,173
Audubon	13,626	12,671	12,520	12,264	11,790	11,579	10,919	9,595	8,559	7,344	6,830
Guthrie	18,729	17,374	17,596	17,324	17,210	15,197	13,607	12,243	11,983	10,935	11,353
Dallas	23,058	23,628	25,120	25,493	24,649	23,661	24,123	26,085	29,513	29,755	40,750
Polk	82,624	110,438	154,029	172,837	195,835	226,010	266,315	286,130	303,170	327,140	374,601
Pottawattamie	54,336	55,832	61,550	69,888	66,756	69,682	83,102	86,991	86,561	82,628	87,704
Cass	21,274	19,047	19,421	19,422	18,647	18,532	17,919	17,007	16,932	15,128	14,684
Madison	17,710	15,621	15,020	14,331	14,525	13,131	12,295	11,558	12,597	12,483	14,019
Warren	20,376	18,194	18,047	17,700	17,695	17,758	20,829	27,432	34,878	36,033	40,671
Taylor	18,784	16,312	15,514	14,859	14,258	12,420	10,288	8,790	8,353	7,114	6,958
Page	24,187	24,002	24,137	25,904	24,887	23,921	21,023	18,537	19,063	16,870	16,976
Adams	13,601	10,998	10,521	10,437	10,156	8,753	7,468	6,322	5,731	4,866	4,482
Fremont	18,546	15,623	15,447	15,533	14,645	12,323	10,282	9,282	9,401	8,226	8,010
Ringgold	15,325	12,904	12,919	11,966	11,137	9,528	7,910	6,373	6,112	5,420	5,469
Decatur	18,115	16,347	16,566	14,903	14,012	12,601	10,539	9,737	9,794	8,338	8,689
Wayne	17,491	16,184	15,378	13,787	13,308	11,737	9,800	8,405	8,199	7,067	6,730
TOTAL Pop.	520,564	512,538	564,527	588,118	594,038	601,465	631,111	641,656	671,354	671,101	742,190
Catholic total		25,000	36,370	37,959	41,090	50,154	72,050	80,106	80,059	95,180	96,492
% Catholic		5%	6%	6%	7%	8%	11%	12%	12%	14%	13%

Source: US Census and Official Catholic Directories

When dealing with the Catholic Church or religious bodies in general, however, numbers tell only a part of the story. Oftentimes, small religious groups, such as the Quakers or the Amish, exercise a wider social and cultural influence than their relative size would suggest. The Catholic Church has a strong institutional presence in the twenty-three southwestern counties of Iowa, and the Diocese of Des Moines today controls physical assets that are worth millions of dollars. Its human resources are probably greater in monetary value. It is also an economic force employing hundreds of men and women who administer churches, schools, hospitals, and other types of social provision. These bodies have budgets of various size and affect the local economy in significant ways. Through its institutional presence and its influence on the lives and imaginations of many inhabitants, the Catholic Church has a power to inspire, motivate, and significantly affect individuals and public life. Even people who formally leave or reject the church often carry the memories and thought-world of Catholicism.

I argue that Catholicism in southwest Iowa exercised a significant influence over this region despite its relatively small numbers. I further contend that Catholicism in southwest Iowa offers a case study of the impact of a visible religious minority on a wider environment. Other parts of America, for example, portions of the South, the Intermountain West, and the Pacific states (Oregon and Washington), have small Catholic populations but are equally visible and influential. The current population of Southwest Iowa is today concentrated in two urban centers—Des Moines and Council Bluffs—but its historic roots include a significant rural element.

Appreciating this history compels a delicate balancing act between the "internalist" and "externalist" dimensions of religious history. Explaining the Catholic Church as a social and cultural force demands a clear understanding of how the church understood what it was doing in the exercise of its presence and mission in the world. At the same time, it also requires some basic knowledge of how its practices were perceived by those outside its fold or even by its members. I have a rather clear understanding of the internals of Catholic life. I also appreciate how social and cultural historians provide another lens on these same developments and offer fascinating insights about gender, sexuality, race, and ethnicity—as well as power, memory, and global (transnational) concerns. Combining these two vantage points hopefully frames the people and events I describe in a wider context. It stresses that religious bodies of the size and significance of the Catholic Church do not exist in a vacuum but have a dialogic relationship with the world around them. This work demonstrates the scope and impact of Catholic agency in a geographically wide and culturally diverse area. Since the church is a case study, not every parish, Catholic group or activity, priest, sister, or layperson will be included here.

This is a different type of diocesan history. Instead of a yearbook-type narrative, it uses the church as a test case of the impact of religion on society. As such, it tries to avoid the exceptionalism of other diocesan texts, which write about the church as a self-contained entity. It attempts to place Catholicism in Southwest Iowa in a wider socio-cultural context, not only to help Catholics understand how their presence made a difference, but also to reach out to those who are interested in the role of religion in the history of the State of Iowa. It replicates traditional diocesan history by using the tenure of its bishops as chronological markers. While it acknowledges the significance of the men who held the office of bishop of Des Moines, they are, however, also considered in the same way we would examine the lives of political and economic figures of note. Local bishops have spiritual authority, but they also exercise a significant influence over personnel, finances, and institutional policies. In many instances, the typical American Catholic bishop has power greater than many CEOs of companies today.

The religious history of Iowa has influenced the state in significant and understudied ways. Native tribes practiced their religious traditions and customs long before Europeans came to this land beyond the Great River. Western religions entered the state in the seventeenth century, when French explorers brought with them Jesuit priests. The famous Father Jacques Marquette, the putative spiritual "founder" of many Midwestern communities, celebrated Mass in June 1673 on the banks of the Mississippi. Roman Catholics and Methodists took the lead in organizing religious institutions; in Dubuque, the Methodists opened a church in 1834, and a year later the Catholics did the same. Roman Catholic clerics such as Father Samuel Mazzuchelli, OP, and Father Charles Van Quickenborn organized the nucleus of what would become a strong Roman Catholic presence in the eastern portion of the state. Other religious groups, especially Methodists, but also Presbyterians, Congregationalists, Episcopalians, Lutherans, Baptists, and Disciples of Christ, created communities of faith in various parts of the state. Mormonism figured importantly on the Iowa religious landscape. Mormon pioneers pushing handcarts moved through Iowa and created enclaves in Lee County, Council Bluffs, and rural counties south of Des Moines. Dutch Reformed and Quaker settlements formed in the 1840s, as did the famous Amana Colonies, home of the Community of True Inspiration. Lutherans—who spoke Danish, Swedish, Norwegian, and German—came to Iowa, as did Jews and Muslims, in the nineteenth century. One of the nation's oldest mosques exists in Cedar Rapids.

Religion was always a force to be reckoned with in Iowa's history as more than 50 percent of Iowans consider themselves religious. Religious institutions and bodies have contributed to the sometimes contentious public debates over issues such as prohibition, divorce, care of the poor, abortion, homosexuality, and immigration. Religious forces make a strong showing as national presidential politics focus on the Iowa caucuses, and appeals to religious voting blocs become part of candidates' repertoires as they campaign for Iowans to put them on the road to the White House.[2]

Throughout its history, the Roman Catholic Church in Iowa has had a pervasive influence in the state. As of 2016, there are 454 Roman Catholic parishes in Iowa, with a Catholic population of nearly 500,000 people, or 16.5 percent of the total population. Historically, many of these churches first served various immigrant groups, and they reflect architecture, art, devotional life, and music of the groups that created them. Catholic sponsorship created schools, health-care institutions, childcare facilities, and other forms of social provision. In October 1979, in one of the major moments in state and US Catholic history, the Sovereign Pontiff of the Catholic Church, Pope John Paul II, visited Iowa—one of the largest single gatherings in the state's history. The records for social provision alone suggest that their influence goes beyond service to the Roman Catholic community, as schools and health-care institutions welcome people regardless of religious affiliation. At the present moment (2016) Catholics own or operate eighty-nine elementary schools attended by more than twenty-one thousand children and twenty-one high schools with over 6,700 students. There are five Roman Catholic colleges or universities in the state, which enroll 9,453 students. These include Briar Cliff University (Sioux City), Clarke University (Dubuque), Mount Mercy University (Cedar Rapids), Loras College (Dubuque), and St. Ambrose University (Davenport). There is also a school of health sciences associated with Mercy Hospital in Des Moines. Catholics also run sixteen hospitals, ten homes for the aged, and eighteen social service centers. There are also a number of individual parishes that operate food pantries around the state; assist Latin American, Asian, and African refugees; counsel women released from prison; and contribute to the support of homeless shelters.

Bishops and priests have been local leaders and men of influence in many communities—rural and urban. A pious legend suggests that Dominican Samuel Mazzuchelli helped design the buildings of the old capitol in Iowa City (not true), although we do know he built some of the first church buildings in Dubuque, Davenport, and Muscatine. Some clerics, like Bishop Mathias Loras, contributed to Iowa's settlement by encouraging Catholic settlers to come to the Hawkeye State in the nineteenth century. In rural Iowa, priests were at times the mainstay of many communities, where they often served for long periods of time. Some pastors built huge churches, schools, and social halls—reflecting the strong "brick and mortar" ethos of Catholic Christianity. Others were personal confidants, intervention counselors, sympathetic ears to their parishioners and a voice of authority that sometimes resolved family feuds. In urban settings, they frequently took their place with city elders who directed the economic, political, and social affairs of large communities. Des Moines bishops also played important public roles. In the 1930s and 1940s, Bishop Gerald Bergan opened channels to ministers of other faiths, which helped create civic harmony. Bishop Maurice Dingman, a visible leader during the Farm Crisis of the 1980s, took strong stands on controversial public issues, such as federal agriculture policy, nuclear war, American foreign policy in Latin America, and economic justice. He also headed a committee to help build a new jail for Polk County.

In Iowa, as in other places where the Catholic Church expanded, the bishop and his coworkers were responsible first and foremost for the preservation and transmission of the Catholic faith of the people in their jurisdiction. This meant making sure they had access to the Mass and the other sacraments (especially baptism, penance, and matrimony). This required financial resources, some of which came at first from generous European Catholics.

Catholicism in Iowa, as elsewhere in the United States, was transnational. It could not be otherwise. Indeed, many of the priests who gathered some of the first congregations for Mass, devotions, and other religious services were recruited from abroad, especially France and later Ireland and the German-speaking countries. A particularly strong cohort were Irish priests who would constitute one of the major sources of church personnel for years in Iowa and, along with Irish parishioners, imported not only Ireland's unique brand of Catholicism to Iowa's soil, but also sympathies for the home island's rocky road to independence. Irish Catholic tastes in church building, devotional practices, attitudes toward parochial schools, and public issues like prohibition were also transferred to the Iowa frontier.[3] Later, native-born clergy were raised up as the Catholic population grew, and institutions were created that encouraged and fostered vocations to the priesthood.

The work of vowed women religious played a critical role in Iowa's history. At a time when women were generally restricted from positions of higher authority in government and society, women religious effectively led and managed Catholic schools and colleges, built and administered large community operations, created healthcare institutions, and offered shelter to young working women living in large cities. Many sisters from various communities have served in Iowa. Among those who have their general headquarters in the state are the Sisters of St. Francis of the Holy Family (Dubuque), the Sisters of Charity of the Blessed Virgin Mary (Dubuque), the Presentation Sisters (Dubuque), Order of Cistercians of the Strict Observance (Trappistines) of Our Lady of the Mississippi (Dubuque), the Sisters of St. Francis (Clinton), and the Congregation of the Humility of Mary (Davenport)—all had houses of religious formation, colleges, and a significant institutional presence in the state. Other communities headquartered elsewhere included the Carmelite Sisters; Sisters of Mercy of Omaha, who ran hospitals and schools; and other educators, such as the School Sisters of St. Francis and the

Sisters of St. Francis of Assisi, both of Milwaukee; the Sisters of St. Dominic of Sinsinawa Mound, Wisconsin; the Sisters of St. Dominic of Adrian, Michigan; the Sisters of the Precious Blood from Missouri; and the Benedictine Sisters from Atchison, Kansas.

Religious orders of men ran schools, counseling centers, parishes, and centers for prayer and meditation. These included the Order of Preachers (Dominicans), the Order of St. Benedict (Benedictines, Atchison, Kansas), the Congregation of the Passion (Passionists), the Society of Jesus (Jesuits), the Society of the Divine Savior (Salvatorians), and the Order of Friars Minor (Franciscans). Dominicans, Passionists, Divine Word, and Salvatorians had training centers and ministries in Iowa. Irish Cistercians of the Strict Observance (Trappists) founded the Abbey of New Melleray in Peosta, Iowa, creating a large contemplative presence in the state and a place of spiritual rest for countless visitors. Trappists for many years were grain farmers. Today, they make caskets and sell caramels made by Trappistine nuns.

Apart from the human resources, the church contributed substantially to the built environment of Iowa. In a manner reminiscent of other places on ever-shifting Catholic frontiers, small houses of worship were built, which as time went on were replaced by "churches of suitable elegance"—many of them named for St. Patrick. Religious orders of women also were recruited to found schools, hospitals, and other institutions of social provision. Churches were often some of the most elegant structures in a community—many built in the neo-Gothic style that was favored in the nineteenth and early twentieth centuries. In several places, these church structures rivaled some of the finest European buildings. Churches like St. Raphael's in Dubuque, Sacred Heart Cathedral in Davenport, St. John's Basilica in Des Moines, All Saints in Stuart, St. Patrick's in Imogene, St. Joseph in Earling, and St. Ambrose Cathedral were or are places of artistic and architectural elegance. Many of these church structures occupy important space in urban or rural locations and function not only as houses of worship but also as meeting centers for groups of Catholics and others, where social and cultural events uplift and entertain communities.

In cities like Dubuque, Davenport, Sioux City, Cedar Rapids, Waterloo, Des Moines, and Council Bluffs, the church participated in the process of urbanization, erecting important structures that contributed to the urban landscape but also shoring up social stability and providing critical services to communities. Indeed, cities would be concentrated images of the permeable boundaries between sacred and secular—the city contributing land, resources, and deference to church figures, and the church advancing urban priorities of social and moral order and urban beautification.

The Catholic presence also offers a window into the fortunes of rural Iowa (territorially most of the diocese). Indeed, the church was a strong presence in rural communities, many of which were put on the map by the advance of the railroad through Iowa. In many counties, especially railroad hubs or repair centers or county seats, railroads generated employment and even donations of land, which made possible the building of churches and schools. These Catholic communities also provided the farming population with a gathering point for community activity, a place to celebrate the passages of life, and schools. The presence of priests and sisters in Shelby County provided inspiring role models for many young men and women who embraced religious life.

This growth was not warmly welcomed in all parts of the state. Iowa has also welcomed those with strong anti-Catholic feelings. In 1887, the city of Clinton, Iowa, was the national headquarters of the American Protective Association (APA), which flourished for a time nationally. The APA viewed with alarm the growing numbers of Catholic immigrants and raised public alarms about Catholics in publicly funded jobs, for example, school teachers, police, and fire departments. Portions of Iowa were also quite receptive to the virulently anti-Catholic publication of the APA, *The Menace*, filled with outlandish conspiracy stories about "Catholic power," and warmed-over invective from the Reformation era created problems for Catholics in various communities. The Ku Klux Klan also held sway in some of the southern counties of Iowa. They would be a direct threat to Catholic life in the Diocese of Des Moines.

Since the nineteenth century, southwest Iowa has always been in a state of social and economic flux. Business, commerce, and the links provided by state government or the railroad sustained its large cities. Catholicism flourished in these communities, fueled by the jobs and stability they offered. Rural areas and smaller towns managed to move forward as well. Other areas ministered to coal miners who dug into Iowa's once rich deposits and made livelihoods for themselves and their immigrant families. Both coal mining and farming, however, became imperiled. Farm distress had been a constant in Iowa history, creating some sympathy for Populist activity in the late 1890s. Farm prices were always unstable, especially after World War I, and farming as a career option began to slowly fade from the agendas of younger Iowans. What later became known as the "Farm Crisis" was a slow, steady retreat from the family farm or, as Bishop Maurice Dingman put it, deterioration from "agriculture to agribusiness," which became one of the accompanying factors of the story of Iowa Catholicism. As farm income and population declined, the church of Southwest Iowa became increasingly urban and suburban.

☙

This study was commissioned by Bishop Richard Pates as part of the celebration of the centenary of the Diocese of Des Moines in 2011. The bishop insisted the work be extensively researched and scholarly in approach. Broken into thematically arranged epochs, it uses the terms of various bishops as the gathering point for the myriad activities that comprised Des Moines's diocesan life. The narrative begins with the remote origins of Catholicism in Iowa and ends with the term of Bishop Maurice Dingman (1968–1987). Bishops William Bullock (1987–1993) and Joseph Charron, CPPS (1993–2007) are too close to present times to offer much historical perspective. This book's scope is defined by the sources available to the historian—hence it relies heavily on the archival collections in the diocesan chancery and other repositories; a careful reading of the diocesan and local newspapers, government records, and published sources; and substantial help from local historians, brother priests, women religious, and generous librarians and archivists. It covers the demographic growth of the diocese and the institutional response to that growth—especially the formation of new parishes and schools.

The author of this text is a Catholic priest and, as such, writes from both the assets and liabilities that status brings. On the one hand, the inner workings of the church are not strange or exotic to me. This is my "family" and I know the sometimes esoteric ways and inner realities of church life quite well. My perspective may, however, be influenced by a life of Catholic practice and identity—in ways that may not appreciate how others see or experience the church. I have relied on the art and craft of fellow historians to create a broader understanding of the materials I have gathered for this book. I have tried to remain faithful to the sources that I have discovered and the mandate given by the diocese that commissioned this book. As one reviewer observed, the text has a "masculine feel." Others have noted the lack of a lay voice. Of the former, I have tried to integrate the role and contributions of women, especially women religious, into the text. But the historical context of the diocese, at least until Bishop Dingman, sadly undervalued and underreported the role of women. This, of course, will not be the case when the sequel to this work is written, or an ambitious scholar decides to do a revision of this history. As for the lay voice, I have attempted to chronicle, where sources are available, the rise of important lay groups such as the Knights of Columbus, the Holy Name, and the Diocesan Council of Catholic Women. Nevertheless, records of Catholic lay organizations or even biographies of people who participated in major church events prior to Vatican II are not readily available. Stories in the Catholic press carry only announcements of fund-raisers, charity events, and public devotions. Some of these have been included in the text. But few journalists felt it necessary to ask about the faith and day-to-day life of the average Catholic. One could draw inferences from these reports, but without an actual person or persons to which I might attribute them, it would be nothing more than an educated guess.

The goal of this book attempts to do what historian William Cronon said of our profession: "Our core business [as historians] is resurrection; helping the past live again."[4] I also hope that local Catholics may develop another way of thinking about their history and the impact of their collective presence in Iowa. By the same token, I wish to contribute a perspective on the fascinating history of religion in Iowa and other parts of the Midwest. Paraphrasing Meredith Wilson, "I really did give Iowa a try."

Steven M. Avella

1

Building a Catholic Presence in the Hawkeye State

"You really ought to give Iowa a try"
—Meredith Wilson, *The Music Man*

Meredith Wilson's *The Music Man* has provided many Americans with their image of Iowa. Small towns, stubborn people, warm hospitality, and waving fields of corn (and other grain crops). In fact, Wilson, who based his story on Mason City, did capture some of Iowa's essence. It is the home of small-town America with communities such as Tipton, Colfax, Osceola, and Winterset. The lovely bridges of Madison County were made famous by novelist Robert James Waller and a film starring Clint Eastwood and Meryl Streep.

Its major cities—Cedar Rapids, Dubuque, Davenport, Iowa City, Sioux City, Waterloo, Des Moines, and Council Bluffs—are all in close proximity to each other, with each carrying its own unique charm: Dubuque and Davenport as Mississippi River communities (replete with riverboat gaming); Iowa City as the home to the state's first capital and flagship university; Council Bluffs, an old railroad center, rich with ethnic history; Cedar Rapids, today the second largest city in the state where many of the grains that come from Iowa farmlands are processed; Sioux City, a meatpacking center; and Des Moines, since 1857 the capital of the state. Iowa is home to many

1

popular American industries, including insurance, printing, and etha-nol. The state also provides most of the feed grain for the livestock we eat. At one time, Iowa mines produced loads of bituminous coal.

Iowa is part of the American Midwest, a particular region with somewhat amorphous borders that generates much debate about where it begins and ends. In the author's estimation, it is a diverse region—geographically and demographically—that stretches from Ohio in the east, across the mighty Mississippi and Missouri Rivers to the foothills of the Rocky Mountains. It spans north to south from the Canadian border to the Ohio River and the Northern and Central Great Plains. Geopolitically, it combines the old Northwest with the Louisiana Purchase lands. It was largely free of slavery, except for states like Kansas and Missouri that were afflicted by the "peculiar institution." This gave the lower portions of the region the look and feel of the South—and local racial relations a different twist.

The Midwest encompasses the Great Plains to the approaches to the Rocky Mountains. It is America's heartland, which has large cit-ies—some of them industrial giants like Chicago, Milwaukee, Detroit, Cleveland, or the Twin Cities of St. Paul and Minneapolis—and also small communities, many of them rural and agricultural. Over the years, it has attracted a medley of immigrant peoples. The Midwest has had diverse political sympathies over the course of US history, splitting political allegiances and loyalties over the years between Republicans and Democrats. Iowa shares many of the common characteristics of the Midwest—its farmland, its urban life, and it's evolving ethnic diversity, especially the growth of the Latino/a community.

Iowa's ancient glacial past, which carved out the rich Des Moines River Valley, the state's rolling hills, and few high elevations shaped its topography. Its prehistoric eras left it with especially rich farmland, providing a livelihood for its future inhabitants. Its population in 2014 was a mere three million people (contrasted with the 12.8 mil-lion in neighboring Illinois, 5.4 million in Minnesota, and 6 million in Missouri). Its people are mostly Caucasian (92 percent), with one of the smallest populations of African Americans in the United States: 3.3 percent. It is increasingly home to Hispanics (mostly Mexicans) who are 5.5 percent of the population. It also has African, Asian, and Pacific Island groups. One American president has come from Iowa, Herbert Clark Hoover, whose presidential library in rural

West Branch is a popular tourist attraction. Other famous Iowans of note—at least in birth—include Chief Blackhawk, Union Pacific railroad mogul Grenville Dodge, William Franklin Cody (aka "Buffalo Bill"), actors John Wayne and Donna Reed, band leader Glenn Miller, and First Lady Mamie Doud Eisenhower.

Native American people of the prairie plains culture resided in what would become Iowa. These tribes included the Dakota, Ho-Chunk, Otoe, Potawatomie, Fox, and Ioway (for whom the state was named). Later, one found the Illinewek, Meskwaki, Omaha, and Sauk.[1] These tribes settled on the fertile land, grew crops (especially corn), hunted, and fished. They also had their respective tribal religions, which marked the milestones of life and the cycles of the year.

European interaction with Indian peoples began in the seventeenth century, including their first experiences of Western Christianity. The iconic moment of these engagements came from the legendary Father Jacques Marquette, who celebrated Mass in Lee County at the Indian villages on the Des Moines River on June 15, 1673. The presence of Marquette in Iowa—as in other Midwestern states—did not signify the permanent planting of Catholicism in this region, but the accounts of these journeys crystallized (and embellished) in the minds of nineteenth- and twentieth-century Catholics the unique Catholic contribution to the development of the state and region.

President Thomas Jefferson secured the future state of Iowa from France in the famed Louisiana Purchase of 1803. This historic transaction transferred 828,000 square miles of territory to the United States—56,272 of those miles belonging to the future state of Iowa. The US government began to prepare it for settlement by formally extinguishing American Indian claims to land. A series of negotiated land cessions completed by 1824 effectively transferred most Indian populations out of the state. Iowa remained under a series of territorial governments between 1821 and 1834 until finally Iowa gained territorial status in 1838. By this time, more than twenty-two thousand people resided in the area—mostly along the eastern portion of the state along the Mississippi River.

By the end of 1846, Iowa attained statehood and the presence of a stable government encouraged greater settlement. By 1850, the state population had risen to 192,214 and thirty years later, there were 1.6

million residents.[2] Most of these were native inhabitants or migrants from other eastern states. A significant number of foreign-born people entered the state, however—many from German-speaking areas of Europe but also from Ireland and England.

Iowa's Religious Demographics

Iowa also developed a religious geography as part of its culture. Religious groups of all kinds settled in Iowa, establishing their churches, schools, and other institutions. In 1890, 1906, 1916, 1926, and 1936, the US government collected census statistics on religious communities in Iowa—assessing not only numbers of members but also church buildings, debt, and other relevant information about religious communities in the United States.

The Catholic population of Iowa grew rapidly during the nineteenth century. The religious census of 1890 notes that 22 percent claimed Methodism as their faith, followed closely by 20 percent who were Catholics. By 1906, five years before the founding of the Diocese of Des Moines, Methodists had slightly declined to 20.6 percent, Lutherans had increased to 14.9 percent, and Catholics had jumped to more than 26 percent of the total population of Iowa. Much of this Catholic growth was likely in the eastern part of the state, but new numbers in the western cities especially contributed to this steady increase. By 1926, Roman Catholics were the single largest denomination in the state, enumerating 287,000 members, followed by the Methodist Episcopal Church with slightly over 200,000 and Presbyterians at sixty-eight thousand. By 1936, the census found that the strongest growth in Iowa religious life had been the rise of evangelical groups who now exercise a significant influence in Iowa politics. By 2015 this group had risen to 30 percent of those who affiliated with religion, followed by mainline Protestants (28 percent). Catholics weigh in at 17 percent. Other religious traditions came in at single digits.

Thus, Iowa is a heavily Protestant state, perhaps the most Protestant of all the Midwestern states. It is heavily white in population, and its major growth since the 1980s has been in the cities of the state: Dubuque, Davenport, Cedar Rapids, Iowa City, Sioux City, Council Bluffs, and Des Moines, the state capital. Today, those who affiliate as

Catholics in Iowa are scattered in different locations throughout the state. In a region where Catholics are a numerical minority, it is important to note that their collective presence—larger than any other single religious rival—has had an important impact on the history of the state and the development of its local culture.

Catholic Visibility

Religious organizations, for the most part, have administrative units that assume responsibility for the temporal and spiritual affairs of a denomination. Methodists have state conferences, Baptists have districts, Lutherans have synods, Presbyterians have presbyteries, and Episcopalians and Catholics have dioceses. This particular type of Catholic organization is apparently borrowed from the divisions that the Roman emperor Diocletian made in his huge empire in the fourth century. Christianity adapted many Roman customs and organizational structures; hence, the Catholic and Episcopal (Church of England) churches have subdivided virtually the entire world into these diocesan jurisdictions. In Roman Catholicism, these boundaries are now drawn by the Holy See (the office of the pope, the bishop of Rome), and over the years many dioceses have undergone significant transition—reflecting demographic shifts and boundary clarification.

These organizational units are important to comprehending Catholic life and identity in any part of the world. In the United States, those diocesan boundaries overspread the map of the nation, encompassing state, county, and city jurisdictions. Each one is presided over by a chief executive office, a bishop, who is assisted by a cohort of middle managers: priests, deacons, women religious, and laypersons. As the state has a capital and each county a county seat, the central offices of diocesan administration (the chancery) are located in a "See" city (from the Latin *Sedes* or chair, the traditional symbol of the bishop's authority located in a cathedral). Here is located the general administrative headquarters of a local church, the repository of its legal records, and the home of its cathedral—often one of the most architecturally prominent buildings of the city. It is also the nerve center for a far-flung network of churches, missions, schools, and social welfare institutions (hospitals, orphanages, care centers).

The ultimate purpose of these diocesan structures is to support the worship and spiritual activities of Roman Catholics. Like the lines on maps that draw state, county, and city boundaries, diocesan maps represent significant clusters of people who create an important economic, social, and cultural presence where they are located. Diocesan boundaries point to a deeper set of social and cultural realities that coexist with political boundaries.

In the United States (as of 2017) there are currently 196 archdioceses and dioceses and one personal ordinariate. This includes 145 Latin Catholic dioceses, thirty-three Latin Catholic archdioceses, sixteen Eastern Catholic dioceses, two Eastern Catholic archdioceses, and one personal ordinariate of the Chair of St. Peter. These are arrayed in thirty-two ecclesiastical provinces usually, but not always, encompassing the boundaries of one state. Dioceses vary in territorial size and population, but each represents the collective expression of Catholicism in a particular area. All own property (some of it quite precious), all host an array of academic institutions from day care to universities, and virtually all have Catholic health care and social services in their boundaries.

The human assets of these institutions are the legions of laymen and laywomen (Catholic and non-Catholic) who frequent Catholic churches, schools, hospitals, shrines, and social welfare centers. Scores of trained church personnel, priests, and religious sisters are critical players in the Catholic impact on the local environment. The "professional" religious are the primary drivers of institutional expansion, raising funds, erecting buildings, contending with debt, warding off social and political hostility, and creating zones of authority for Catholic ideas and values.

A significant feature of this presence is the role of women religious or sisters. For many years, when the agency of women was rather closely circumscribed by law and custom in the United States, women religious (sisters) exercised a degree of autonomy and leadership over their lives that was significant and even remarkable for their times.

The cultural contributions of the Catholic Church are important. Many dioceses have church structures of great beauty and provide venues for the decorative and musical arts. Catholic buildings and public celebrations have become an important part of the fiber of rural and urban communities.

By the same token, the economic and political forces of a region have also shaped and made possible the Catholic presence. The work of entrepreneurs who created jobs and opportunities, the market demand for rural products, the impact of government on every level, infrastructure (roads, water, sewer and communication lines), and the tremendous boost the railroad and the local and super highways gave to state and local economies have been critical to the advance and spread of Catholicism. The church would not exist without the presence of people. Stable government, jobs, and transportation made this possible.

Western Iowa Development

Urban centers developed early in Iowa. The first settlements reached out from the Mississippi River—Dubuque, Clinton, Davenport, and Burlington. River commerce created thriving entrepôts, and rich farmlands provided products for transshipment to national and international markets. Fur traders of various nationalities had already settled in the Council Bluffs region in 1824. By 1838, a trading post and a log hut fort had been built, which became a subagency for the Pottawattamie Indians. Complex arrangements with various Indian tribes along the Missouri River affected the development of the region. Council Bluffs became a popular point of debarkation for those taking the Emigrant Trail or moving west, including many Latter Day Saints en route to their desert Zion. In 1846 it was named Kanesville, for a lobbyist of the Mormons. Later the name was changed to the more romantic-sounding Council Bluffs. This well-placed community, adjoining the Missouri River and in proximity to the growing city of Omaha, evolved into a thriving commercial center. To it eventually came the major rail lines that networked the eastern part of the nation, including the Transcontinental Railroad. Council Bluffs became a thriving community with a distinct urban culture. For Catholics, the relatively brief stay of the fabled Father Pierre Jean de Smet in 1838 and 1839 became an important source of local pride and ownership of the city's origins.

Des Moines began as a federal fort at the juncture of the Raccoon and Des Moines Rivers in 1843. It was used to monitor the Meswaki

(Mesquaki) and Sauk Indians. After they were removed in 1846, the fort was abandoned but remained the hub of an urban center and also a center of missionary activity. Also in 1846, it became the county seat of Polk County and in 1851 was incorporated as a city—dropping "Fort" from its title. In 1857, it became the capital of Iowa.[3] With the Des Moines River as the dividing line, the city developed an East Side–West Side culture. The two sides of the city competed with each other over the years to the benefit of Des Moines.

Both Council Bluffs and Des Moines developed local economies—most tied to the farming economy of the wider region. With these came retail outlets, entertainment centers, saloons, and city services. Urban governance took shape with elected officials directing the construction of public buildings and creating courts, fire and police departments, and other local services. Smaller farming communities also began to draw together to create social life on the agricultural frontier. The advent of the railroad made both Des Moines and Council Bluffs major centers but also contributed to the growth of small towns such as Leon, Earling, Creston, Corning, and Lenox.

This story focuses almost exclusively on the twenty-three counties of southwest Iowa, which were gathered together in 1911 as the Diocese of Des Moines. The diocesan boundaries encompassed an array of mostly rural counties, which were dependent on commercial agriculture. Some of these areas had mining communities with populations consisting of various ethnic groups. Most of these areas were linked by the railroad and the creation of county and later federal road systems. The cities of Council Bluffs and Des Moines remain the major posts of urbanization in the southwest, creating important business and government centers. Each of these locales created the seedbed for Catholic communities

Father Pierre Jean de Smet, SJ.
Credit: Library of Congress Prints and Photographs Division, Public Domain.

that built churches, schools, and hospitals and that exercised an influence over local life that, while not dominant, was certainly active and significant. Set across the backdrop of wider development in southwest Iowa, we see how a relatively small community transformed its environment.

Creating a Catholic Presence in Iowa

Iowa currently has four Roman Catholic dioceses: Dubuque, Davenport, Sioux City, and Des Moines. The most recently created is the Roman Catholic Diocese of Des Moines, established by a decree issued by the Sacred Consistorial Congregation and ratified by Pope St. Pius X on August 6, 1911.[4] By that time, Iowa had already been a state for ninety-five years and Des Moines its capital for fifty-four years. Catholic life in the new diocese built on the larger history of Catholicism in the state.

Eastern Iowa's initial Catholic contingent (many of them Irish lead miners around Galena, Illinois) was nurtured by Dominican Father Samuel Mazzuchelli.[5] An Italian missionary, Mazzuchelli began his service to the American church in 1828 in Ohio, then migrated from Mackinac, Michigan, to Green Bay, Wisconsin, and then to western Wisconsin. In 1835, he made his way to St. Louis, where he visited with Vincentian Bishop Joseph Rosati and discussed missionary needs of the rapidly filling upper Mississippi Valley.[6]

Mazzuchelli spent time between Dubuque and Galena observing the growth of Catholics in this prospering lead-mining region, and helped design and build churches in Dubuque, Davenport,

Father Samuel Mazzuchelli, OP, in Rome, 1825. Credit: Mazzuchelli Exhibit, Sinsinawa Archives, Sinsinawa, Wisconsin.

Muscatine, and Iowa City. Although the design of the old capitol buildings in Iowa City was the work of architect John Rague (an old friend of Abraham Lincoln who designed many landmark buildings in the Midwest), as noted earlier, there was an apocryphal belief that Father Samuel may have helped design the dome and the winding staircase in the buildings.[7] Other priests were sent by Rosati to minister to the far reaches of his diocese.

Ecclesiastical jurisdictions shifted constantly in this area. What became the state and ecclesiastical province of Iowa was alternately under six different dioceses in the nineteenth century. In 1837, at the urging of Bishop Rosati, the Third Provincial Council of Baltimore recommended to the Congregation of the Propaganda in Rome (the Roman office that created dioceses until 1908) that Dubuque be raised to diocesan status and that its territory take in all of Iowa, a large portion of Minnesota and portions of North and South Dakota. Responsibility for Galena, Illinois, and Prairie du Chien, Wisconsin, were also added on to the duties of the new diocese. On July 28, 1837, Rome created the Diocese (later archdiocese) of Dubuque, which encompassed all of Iowa and even portions of Minnesota and Wisconsin. Father Matthias Loras, a French-born missionary serving as vicar general in the Diocese of Mobile, Alabama, was chosen as the first bishop. In 1849, Propaganda scaled back the boundaries of the Diocese of Dubuque to the state of Iowa.

In 1850, Rome erected the Diocese of St. Paul (today the Archdiocese of St. Paul and Minneapolis), and the ties between St. Paul and Des Moines have been strong. Three of Des Moines's bishops would come from the Twin Cities (William Bullock, Joseph Charron, and Richard E. Pates), and a number of Des Moines priests would be educated at the St. Paul Seminary in St. Paul, Minnesota.

Parishes, schools, and other Catholic institutions grew in eastern Iowa in cities like Keokuk, Davenport, Clinton, and Fort Madison. This growth was nurtured by Bishop Loras, who traveled abroad to secure funds from European aid societies, the Propagation of the Faith in Lyons, the *Leopoldinen Stiftung* in Vienna, and the *Ludwig Missionsverein* in Munich. He also brought back several seminarians who would serve as priests in this far-flung jurisdiction. Loras also worked hard to evangelize Indian tribes in the region but spent even more time responding to the massive influx of immigrants flooding into Iowa in the latter 1830s and 1840s.

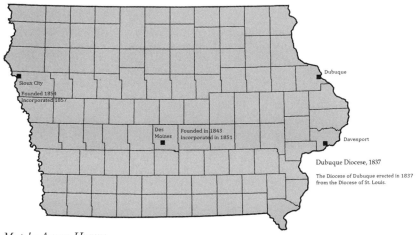

Map by Aaron Hyams

Demographic growth led to the foundation of the Diocese of Davenport in 1881 whose boundaries extended from the Mississippi River to the western boundary of Iowa (encompassing most of what would later become the Diocese of Des Moines). Similar growth in the northwestern portion of the state led to the creation of Diocese of Sioux City in 1902.

Map by Aaron Hyams

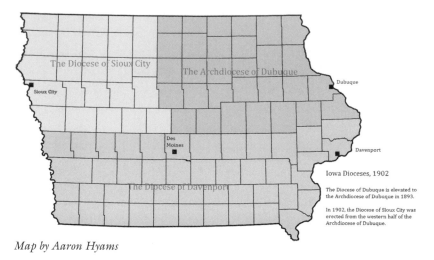

Map by Aaron Hyams

Even before Rome formally marked out the Diocese of Des Moines, this twenty-three-county section of Iowa already had twenty-five thousand Catholics and a visible infrastructure. By 1910, there were sixty-five diocesan priests and three from religious orders working in the future diocese. There were already fifty-four churches and twenty-five missions, sixteen grade schools and an academy for young girls. Three congregations of religious sisters, the Sisters of Mercy, the Sisters of Charity of the Blessed Virgin Mary (BVMs), and the Sisters of Humility, operated schools and health-care institutions.

Religious institutions grew as the nexus of economic and demographic opportunity and the spiritual needs and demands of religious people required them. Religious bodies also created a social sphere and had an impact on the wider environment.

Parishes as Creators of Catholic Space

The first need of a Catholic religious establishment is to create spaces for prayer and worship. For Roman Catholics, this involves the celebration of the Mass and the hearing of confessions, the most commonly celebrated sacraments in its religious repertoire. Early religious development was tied to the presence of devout laity who

were visited by itinerant clergy—a common form of religious formation for all Christian denominations in Iowa. Methodists in particular
excelled at this kind of ministry. Catholic missionary priests, traveling on horseback and later on railroad, brought the ministry of the
church to areas around southwest Iowa. As the body of Catholics
grew to a critical mass, they erected buildings of increasing sophis-
tication and beauty to accommodate the larger and larger groups of
communicants. These religious edifices created a Catholic space in
the wider environment—urban or rural—where centers of population required it.

Their location also served an urbanizing function. As one historian has observed, "Church buildings were very much about mar-
keting and from a locational standpoint the successful congregation
needed to have its church fronting on a major street and on a corner
location."[8] Churches were also built near other public buildings, for
example, schools or civic structures, clustering around city centers.
Churches often brought respectability and stability to a community.

The typical evolution of a church began in a local hall or con-
gregant household. This was followed by property acquisition,
fund-raising, and simple construction. Subsequent growth led to
larger buildings on the original site or a bigger parcel. For Catholic
churches, the buildings included a home for the clergy, a school, and
a residence for religious sisters. Resources for these initial foundations
came from local people and also the "parent" dioceses. The creation
of these churches was primarily a spiritual event, but they also had
significant economic, social, and cultural impact.

Catholic Seedlings

Father de Smet may have been an important memory in the
founding of Council Bluffs, but the actual creation of a steady church
presence there came from the mutual cooperation of local business
and ecclesiastical interests. This was evident in 1853 when a local
hotelier, Congregationalist Samuel Bayliss, the owner of the Pacific
House, a fine, brick, three-story hotel, and Philip J. McMahon, a
local physician (and a Mason), deeded over lots 1–4 on Main and
Pearl Streets to Bishop Loras for a new church. Fathers Matthias

Laurent and William Edmonds erected a temporary structure they named in honor of the Jesuit St. Francis Xavier to honor the memory of the Jesuit de Smet. In 1859 a new pastor began a new permanent church that was not completed until 1865. Thus began the first permanent Catholic space in Council Bluffs.

At another pioneer site, Loras sent an Irish priest, Timothy Mullen, to the Des Moines River Valley, and there he founded, with fifteen families, the church at Irish Settlement in 1852. St. Patrick was begun with a log chapel—a site commemorated by a monument in the middle of the current parish cemetery. Father Mullen served the small community gathered in Madison County, just slightly over the county line from the more populous Polk County. Itinerant priests served the small community of Irish farmers, and the lands they farmed were part of a forty-acre tract purchased by the real estate savvy Bishop Loras.

Pastors came and left over the years until Father Francis Mc-Cormick was appointed the first resident pastor in 1857. But even he apparently did not stay long, and priests from Des Moines attended Irish Settlement once a month. By 1868 the old log chapel had been outgrown and a new frame church was constructed under the direction of Father John Brazill, pastor of St. Ambrose in Des Moines. A new resident pastor came in 1872, and this small but tightly knit community continues to function to this day—although served now from Winterset.[9] This community welcomed Pope John Paul II, who visited Iowa in 1979.

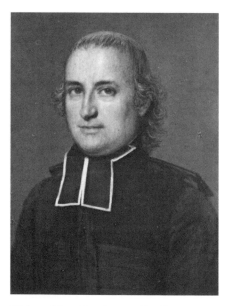

Bishop Matthias Loras. Credit: Archdiocese of Dubuque Archives.

Assisting the Urbanizing Process: Catholic Space in Des Moines

Des Moines was not much more than a fort when Father Alexander Hattenberger from Ottumwa traveled to this community in 1851 and 1852, saying Mass in a log home of a German Catholic in the old fort. Other traveling priests came and went (Fathers John Krekel and Philip Laurent), ministering to scattered Catholics in the western counties. Father Louis De Cailly, Loras's nephew, found only two Catholics when he visited Des Moines in 1855. (He couldn't have looked too hard; there were likely more.) That same year and at his uncle's direction, he purchased the first Catholic church property in Des Moines for seven hundred dollars at the corner of Sixth Avenue and Locust Street with Propagation of the Faith Funds on deposit in St. Louis.[10] In April 1860, Father George H. Plathe, a fifty-four-year-old German-born priest came from Westphalia, Germany. Described as "tall in figure, soldierly in bearing . . . a little severe against dancing and the like, but urbane, cultured, and loved by his people," he was the first resident pastor assigned to Des Moines.[11] He built a frame church named for St. Ambrose on the property purchased by De Cailly. This investment in land and building established the Catholic presence in the city. Later, this property would be sold to the Central National Bank, which built a seven-story building there in the 1960s.[12]

The building of the church corresponded to the fast-paced development of the city of Des Moines. Its population grew rapidly, starting with 127 people in 1846 and surging to nearly four thousand by 1860. In 1857, the city became Iowa's capital, and a neighboring community, East Des Moines, was joined with Des Moines to become one city. With its limits enlarged, it had five hundred dwellings, two newspapers, a few grocery stores, a post office, and a large number of real estate offices. Land speculation and development became critical to Des Moines's future. Once again, as with Bayliss in Council Bluffs, business and religious interests found a point of convergence.

This time, the catalyst was not a sympathetic businessman but a new Catholic priest, Father John F. Brazill, who arrived in 1863. He understood not only the growth imperative of his church but also how to integrate the church into the wider community of the burgeoning state capital. From the time of his arrival until his death in 1885, he was the most important cleric in the western part of the state and an important influence in the history of the city of Des Moines.[13] As early church historian Father John Kempker noted somewhat laconically, "Father Brazill . . . succeeded in awakening a wonderful interest in church matters in Des Moines."[14]

Clergy as Community Builders:
Father John Brazill—Shaper of Early Des Moines

Father Brazill was a significant force in the development of the city of Des Moines—and beyond. Born in County Clare, Ireland, on June 24, 1827, Brazill studied classics and one year of theology in his native Ireland and came to North America at the age of eighteen, residing first in Kingston, Canada. In Canada he attended the Sulpician College at Montreal and was ordained in 1851 in Wheeling, Virginia (today West Virginia), and served under the bishop of Richmond for a year.[15] He then moved to Iowa and affiliated himself with the Diocese of Dubuque and was tapped by then-Bishop Clement Smyth, OCSO (1859–1865), to serve as vicar general of the Dubuque diocese—which extended throughout the state.

Father John Brazill. Credit: Diocese of Des Moines Archives.

Brazill first came to Des Moines in 1861 as part of his general duties to oversee Catholic growth in the western part of the state. After a brief hiatus in Dubuque (substituting for Bishop Smyth who was away in Europe), he returned to Des Moines permanently in 1863 and threw himself into the work of church and community building. Brazill contributed to the rising tide of cultural development in the city by sharing his considerable erudition with rapt congregations and city audiences. A recollection of him notes: "The city became alive to the thoroughness of his lectures and sermons. He had a masterful command of the English language and was to a marked degree clear in expounding the great truths of the faith." The informant also notes: "Father Brazill was not unknown in coming to Des Moines and enjoyed an especially favorable acquaintance with some of the state officers."[16] A short biography of him in a book of Des Moines notables observes: "Though firm in his religious faith, he was tolerant toward all that would develop his theory of good government—education, industry, sobriety. He was . . . always diligent in advancing the welfare of his church, his schools and the city."[17]

Although there is some confusion about the date, by 1865 Brazill built a sturdier and larger stone church on the location of Father Plathe's small frame church—"recycling" the old building into a parish school run by the BVM sisters. Eventually, the growth of the parish continued, a new property at Sixth and Grand was purchased, and a three-story school was erected in 1872. This property eventually became the site of the Iowa Building and the Des Moines Theater, but it remained church property for many years, from which St. Ambrose Parish collected a large rent.[18]

Big, brawny, and shrewd, Brazill snapped up property around the growing city and in other areas. His connections with state government included playing a role in the completion of Iowa's magnificent state capitol building. According to one account, at the behest of his friend Representative John A. Kasson, Brazill helped find a hungover legislator on the banks of the Raccoon River who cast the deciding vote in 1871 for the completion of the project.[19] His eulogist, Father Thomas Lenehan, attested to his role as a city leader by noting that Brazill's "love for Des Moines and pride in the growth of the city [which] meant growth of the church."[20] In fact, when he lay dying, it was learned that his property acquisitions were valued at $250,000 in 1885 dollars.[21]

When Brazill died on August 25, 1885, he was honored by a five-hour long funeral that brought forty priests and turned out crowds of people who choked the streets and a funeral procession that stretched for many blocks.[22] Active in church planting in other parts of western Iowa, Brazill had acquired lands for the church, but also appeared to have commingled these purchases with his own personal land acquisitions. He acquired quite a real estate empire around Des Moines. When he drew up his will on his deathbed, he left most of his fortune to the church—a fact that led his brother and sisters to contest the will.[23]

Controversy must have dogged his later days, as his eulogist noted: "In his latter days he drank from the chalice of humiliation."[24] Others had to unravel his finances and straighten out the lines between his personal and church purchases. Despite his financial struggles, Father Brazill left the legacy of a strong and vibrant presence for the Catholics of Des Moines even though his personal debts hamstrung his successors and threatened the good reputation of the church. His successor, Monsignor Michael Flavin, later recalled that when he first came to Des Moines he spent a good deal of time "fighting and settling and paying Father Brazill's personal debts."[25]

Although Brazill had died cash-poor, he was property rich. His prime asset was a parcel of land he had purchased in 1883 through a local realtor on Sixth and High Streets. This property had once belonged to Dr. Francis Grimmel, a local physician who had come to Des Moines in 1846. Grimmel had purchased eighty acres of the future Des Moines and on the sight of the future cathedral had built the first timber frame house in the city. This property later became the site of St. Ambrose Cathedral—one of the most architecturally significant and beautiful church buildings in Des Moines.

Grimmel House at Sixth and High, Des Moines.
Credit: Diocese of Des Moines Archives.

Catholics and a Growing Des Moines

Real urban development took off in Des Moines during Brazill's years, and he was there to capitalize on it. The first railroad entered the city in 1866, and three years later the Rock Island Railroad completed its line across Iowa, connecting Des Moines and Council Bluffs to both Chicago on the east and lands west. Population shot up. By 1870, more than twelve thousand people lived in Des Moines, and, ten years later, the population skyrocketed to 22,408. The city's basic identity formed along the East Side–West Side realities created by the bisection of the Des Moines River. Initial suburban development had begun to the west and the north. Street paving had begun and Des Moines's economy expanded, fed by the work of coal mines, foundries, and machine shops and the manufacture of agricultural implements, furniture, pottery, woolen mills, brick, and carriages. The Equitable Life Insurance Company opened its headquarters in the city in 1867—the first of several insurance companies that would make the Iowa capital their home.

In 1870, a new capitol building was begun, an elegant gold-domed structure that would not be completed until 1886. In 1880, businessmen formed the Des Moines Improvement Association. This energetic group attracted new businesses, especially other insurance companies and printing and publishing firms, and sparked a building frenzy that lobbied for additional public schools, commercial buildings, and depots for the city's growing railroad traffic. They pushed for expanded public utilities and better streets and sewers. Indeed, they helped remake the face of the Iowa capital, which only forty years before had been a rural fort. In 1879 Des Moines became the site of the state fair, and elaborate new buildings for the annual event were constructed in 1885. In 1890, a major annexation of existing suburbs took place, extending the boundaries of the city—and its access to waterworks, electrical generation, and street railway.

Against this wider backdrop, the urban landscape in Des Moines began to fill with churches and other religious institutions. The Methodists, perhaps the most visible Christian denomination in southwest Iowa, had been in Des Moines since the 1850s. A Congregational church had begun in 1857 (Plymouth); Baptists inaugurated their ministry in 1850; Lutherans organized in 1854, as did

Des Moines churches, nineteenth century.
Credit: Souvenir of Des Moines, 1907 by L. H. Nelson Co.

the Episcopal Church; the Central Church of Christ organized in 1856; the United Presbyterians got a foothold in 1856 and 1857. It was not until 1873 that the first Jewish congregation was organized, B'nai Jeshurun, and a bit longer before they could build a permanent synagogue. Unitarians organized in 1880 and by 1882 had their first church. The most visible sign of church development was Des Moines's famous Piety Hill on the west side, which hosted seven houses of worship north of High Street, spanning from Sixth to Tenth Streets: First Methodist, Central Christian, First Baptist, Temple B'nai Jeshurun, Plymouth Congregational, and Central Presbyterian. The proliferation of these congregations worked in tandem with Des Moines's growing population, which spiked from 22,408 in 1880 to 50,093 in 1890. By 1900, Des Moines was a respectable city of 62,139.

East Des Moines was dominated by the state capitol building and grounds, civic buildings, and working-class neighborhoods. A number of churches were founded in this area, first situating themselves on major street corner locations, often near public transit and other major city buildings (e.g., public schools). Catholics were a minority in this part of town, but they soon found a toehold under the leadership of Father Joseph F. Nugent, a popular speaker (and later a foe of Father Michael Flavin), who bought lots on the corner of East Court and Seventh Street and founded Visitation Parish in 1882.

Here he built a small church and a school operated by the Sisters of Charity of the Blessed Virgin Mary.

Monsignor Flavin, who fretted that the Visitation Parish would cut into his revenues at St. Ambrose, hotly opposed its founding. He was even more alarmed when parishioners petitioned Bishop Henry Cosgrove to compel St. Ambrose to pay $20,000 to the parish as a reimbursement for the contributions they had made to St. Ambrose in the days of Father Brazill.[26] It is not known if they prevailed, but the church went forward. Visitation Parish played its part in the expansion of the striking new capitol building. In 1914, the expanding state capital requested the site of

Father Joseph Nugent, founder of Visitation Parish, Des Moines. Credit: Diocese of Des Moines Archives.

Visitation for its needs. By this time, a local bishop was in place, and he readily agreed. Church officials willingly collaborated with city officials to surrender the land and relocated the church. The new Visitation was built on the southwest corner of East Ninth and Garfield. Today it is called Our Lady of the Americas.

Catholic Health Care in Des Moines and Women Religious

Care of the sick and the indigent was an important priority for women religious who founded and developed a formidable network of Catholic hospitals across the country in the late nineteenth and early twentieth centuries.[27] The Diocese of Des Moines was a part of this wider expansion, especially in Iowa.[28] Although there were already two private hospitals in Des Moines, in the autumn of 1893 Bishop Cosgrove in Davenport recruited the Sisters of Mercy from Davenport to start a hospital in the state capital. In late November, Mother Mary Aloysia McLaughlin and Mother Mary Baptist Martin,

Early Mercy Hospital.
Credit: State Historical Society of Iowa.

together with four other Mercy sisters, arrived to make plans for the new foundation. The Hoyt Sherman estate was leased on December 8, 1893, and the first patient was admitted to this seven-bed institution. Mother Mary Baptist was to be the administrator of the hospitals in Davenport and Des Moines. Another sister, Mary Xavier Malloy, was also part of the founding contingent. Flavin helped the sisters find a property left to the church by Father Brazill at Fourth and Ascension Streets, and in June a new corporation—Sisters of Mercy Hospital, Des Moines—was formed and the property was purchased.

On July 3, 1894, ground was broken, and by February of the next year the sisters moved out of the Hoyt Sherman home and into their new structure, a four-story brick edifice on this spot that opened in April 1895. Additions to this structure were made in 1899, 1908, and 1912. A school of nursing was opened in 1899.[29] After a jurisdictional struggle with Des Moines Bishop Austin Dowling, administration of the hospital was transferred to the oversight of the Sisters of Mercy in Council Bluffs. The sisters also opened homes for young women: St. Mary's in Council Bluffs in 1901 and St. Catherine's in Des Moines in 1907. These institutions provided housing and a safe haven for young Catholic women who had often left the farms to work in the city.

Urban Beautification: St. Ambrose

The chief Catholic monument in Des Moines was St. Ambrose Church. This elaborate house of worship not only represented tremendous outlays of capital but also enhanced Des Moines's urban landscape while also providing a source of pride for the city's Catholics.

St. Ambrose was the brainchild of Father Michael Flavin, who, after the death of Brazill, came in 1884 to dominate Des Moines Catholicism for forty-one years until his death in 1926. Flavin was born in Waterford, Ireland, on October 31, 1841, and studied at Mount Melleray and Carlow seminaries. He was one of several family members "in religion" (two priest brothers, two BVM sisters, and three priest nephews). He came to the United States in 1869, finished his studies at St. Vincent's Seminary in Cape Girardeau, Missouri, and by happenstance was ordained in St. Ambrose Church by Bishop James Myles O'Gorman, vicar apostolic of Nebraska, on July 20, 1870, together with six other men who were to serve in Iowa.

Flavin functioned in a variety of assignments over the years before coming to Des Moines: St. Raphael's Cathedral in Dubuque, a parish in Cedar Falls (with five missions), and later pastor of St. Mary's Parish in Davenport. During his ten-year administration in Davenport he built a new rectory and church. In 1908, he became a monsignor (an honorific title conferred by the pope on a priest)—a rare papal honor in those days—and later a protonotary apostolic (allowing him to appear in episcopal regalia for solemn services but having no episcopal sacramental or jurisdictional powers—a "mule" bishop). Flavin became the major domo of Catholic life in Des Moines until the erection of the new diocese. Of him a fellow priest wrote: "A very gentlemanly priest, uniformly courteous to all, of tall and fine physique, a forceful speaker, strong in faith, he did not do much along social lines for the people." The scribe also noted inaccurately: "nor did he have a vision of greater things for the Church in Des Moines."[30] Nothing could be further from the truth.

Monsignor Flavin functioned as a kind of Catholic "boss" of Des Moines and steadfastly blocked—to the extent he could—any other parochial development there. He did this because he worried constantly about revenue (perhaps due to his experience of dealing with Brazill's tangled finances) and tried to keep parishioners and their donations coming in to St. Ambrose as long as he could. Flavin's concern for money was driven in part by his desire to build a new and even more glorious St. Ambrose Church when he realized that the stone church built by his predecessor was neither big enough nor elegant enough to keep a high Catholic profile in the state capital. Here he tangled with Bishop Cosgrove in Davenport, who kept a close eye on his plans.

When Flavin laid out the plans for the new St. Ambrose, Bishop Cosgrove continually questioned some of his administration of Brazill's estate. Cosgrove made some critical decisions that inflamed St. Ambrose parishioners: he sold the property of the old church, took the money, and insisted that the new St. Ambrose Church be built on the corner of Sixth and High on property that Father Brazill had purchased from the estate of Dr. Grimmel. He further insisted that the parish pay the diocese $25,000 for the site. This angered Flavin and his parishioners, who had paid the liens in excess of $10,000 on a lumberyard also owned by Brazill; Flavin and members of the congregation had set aside the revenues generated by the yard and the rents from another property to save for their new church. Cosgrove insisted that the site belonged to the diocese.[31]

Angry St. Ambrose parishioners petitioned the bishop to relinquish his claims, and Flavin himself begged for relief as well, claiming he was caught between obedience to the bishop and the demands of

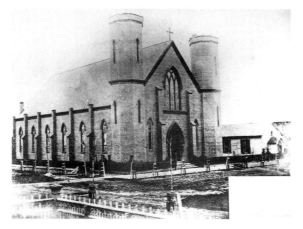

St. Ambrose Church, 1865–1891.
Credit: Diocese of Des Moines Archives.

his parishioners: "The chief aim of my life was to attend to my business and live in peace and harmony with my people and bishop, but if this claim be urged in an unreasonable manner I fear I'll find myself in the midst of a rebellion."[32] Cosgrove did not relent, however, and made Flavin scale back the size of the new church—although permitting them to expand the winter chapel and the baptistery.[33] (These would be reworked later.) Flavin protested, noting that a church in Clinton County of the same size and design of the new St. Ambrose had won the unqualified support of the bishop. His complaint was ignored.

In the spring of 1890, Flavin set to work to build a new St. Ambrose Church. Despite these tribulations (and promises from Cosgrove to help pay for the new church), the building went on. On May 28, 1890, Flavin reported a cost overrun: "We had to dig much deeper at the rear of the church. . . . The foundation will be finished I think about the 2nd week in June." Flavin moved his house to the property as the new church went up.[34]

Flavin went first class, employing the renowned architect James J. Egan of Chicago (who had also designed Sacred Heart Cathedral in Davenport, St. Mary of the Assumption Cathedral in San Francisco, and St. Paul Cathedral in Pittsburgh—as well as other prestigious church buildings in Chicago and other Iowa cities) to design a majestic Romanesque-style church. The new St. Ambrose would be faced with Bedford Stone and would measure 185 by 103 feet, costing nearly $120,000. No columns obstructed the view of the marble and gold altars, which were sent from Italy. Adorned with a huge campanile 120 feet high, sonorous church bells, and a seating capacity of about one thousand (later expanded to 1,300),

Monsignor Michael Flavin. Credit: Used with permission of the Diocese of Davenport Archives, Davenport, Iowa.

St. Ambrose Cathedral, approx. 1906.
Credit: Souvenir of Des Moines, 1907
by L. H. Nelson Co.

St. Ambrose would be a fitting Catholic temple for a new and burgeoning Des Moines. Around it would be built other large public buildings and rival churches.

The new St. Ambrose Church was dedicated in 1891, and the occasion not only brought out the top ecclesiastics of Iowa and beyond but also drew accolades from city leaders who praised the church of "suitable elegance" for the rising glory of Des Moines. The press account announcing the dedication noted: "Des Moines is already noted for its many fine churches, and the new St. Ambrose will materially add to that reputation. . . . Des Moines today is proud of St. Ambrose."[35] On the dedication day, the local press extolled the virtues of Flavin and his assistant, a Father Mackin.

Of the building, there were not enough superlatives about its design and its importance to the city: "Visitors from all over the United States have pronounced it one of the best churches they were ever in." "The Catholic people never do anything by halves," the paper proclaimed. "And the grand results of their efforts in this institute are a source of pride to them and every enterprising citizen of the city as well."[36] Flavin made the church a presence to be reckoned with in the city of Des Moines, and it was destined to become Des Moines's mother church. Other spectacular churches would adorn southwest Iowa.

Founding St. John's Church/Basilica, Des Moines, and All Saints, Stuart

Yet another diocesan church of extraordinary beauty would be built in the early twentieth century in the vicinity of Drake University. In 1905, Bishop Henry Cosgrove created St. John's Parish in

Des Moines, forming it from the northern portion of St. Ambrose. Daniel V. Mulvihill, a native of Irish Settlement, was appointed pastor. Previously he had been at St. John's in Adair.

Born January 16, 1865, Mulvihill attended St. Ambrose College in Davenport and Niagara University in New York. Mulvihill finished his seminary studies at Mount St. Mary of the West in Cincinnati and was ordained December 27, 1892, at Davenport. He taught at St. Ambrose in Davenport and served in pastorates in Williamsburg and Adair. He came to found St. John's in Des Moines in 1905 and remained until 1920, when he was appointed president of Des Moines College (later Dowling College) and then pastor of Visitation in Des Moines until his death in 1923. His clergy card noted: "A studious, hard-working, sincere priest, [who] did much work in building up the place where he was. In later years he was sickly and having a domineering nature somewhat self-willed he became irritable and flared up strongly at times. He died of heart trouble, not having risen much above the average, though a good average."[37]

Mulvihill purchased fourteen lots for St. John's between Nineteenth and Twentieth Streets (Harding Road) on University Avenue in Des Moines on June 7, 1905, for $8,000. Two other lots had already been purchased for $1,375. He first built a brick school with a large chapel on the second floor. The first Mass was celebrated on Christmas Day 1905. In September 1906, he opened a school with six BVM sisters and welcomed 164 pupils. In 1907, a high school opened, which continued until 1918, when all parochial high schools were closed to make way for Des Moines College and St. Joseph Academy. The future glorious St. John's would be built by Mulvihill's successor, who already had erected a church of "suitable elegance" in Stuart.

Father Martin S. McNamara was a native of County Clare, Ireland, born November 11, 1865, and was a grandnephew of Trappist bishop Clement Smyth of Dubuque, and his uncle Father T. F. Smyth was a priest of Davenport. Young McNamara came to live with his priestly uncle and finished school at Niagara University in New York and Mount St. Mary's of the West Seminary in Cincinnati. He was ordained for Davenport on June 24, 1893, and made pastor of a parish in Long Grove and later of Stuart. All Saints in Stuart had been founded in 1876 and was served by a frame church until Father McNamara arrived in 1905. Here, he built a spectacular Byzantine

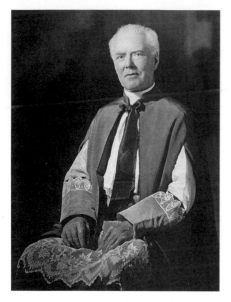

Father Martin McNamara. Credit:
Diocese of Des Moines Archives.

church at the cost of $75,000. Designed by the prestigious firm of McGinnis and Walsh, and imitating the magnificent St. Mark's in Venice, it included stained glass from Germany, marble from Italy, and a copper dome.[38] All Saints would be severely damaged by an act of arson in 1995.

On August 15, 1920, McNamara succeeded Mulvihill at St. John's. McNamara finished the church building, laying the cornerstone for a new upper church in September 1926. This magnificent structure also used the Roman basilica of St. Paul Outside the Walls as its model and once again drew on the talents of McGinnis and Walsh, who worked together with local architect John Normile. Set in a thriving neighborhood and very near Drake University, this structure cost $480,000 and could seat nine hundred people. Its exterior was Indiana limestone with a tile roof and bronze cross atop its bell tower. Its interior was plaster with a magnificent baldacchino similar in design to one used at the Eucharistic Congress in Chicago in 1926. The Conrad Pickel Studios of Waukesha, Wisconsin, produced forty-six stained-glass windows. It took until 1945 to eliminate its heavy debt, and McNamara, promoted to the rank of monsignor, died on February 2, 1949.[39] The building remains one of the most magnificent church structures in the Midwest and was raised to minor basilica status by Pope John Paul II on October 4, 1989.

Clergy as Community Builders:
Father McMenomy—A Father of Council Bluffs

Catholics also played a role in the shaping of Council Bluffs. This city's glory days began in earnest in the mid-nineteenth century as it became an important transportation hub for the expanding network of railroads. Three Iowa railroads terminated there, although the Union Pacific, planned and executed by Grenville Dodge, did not succeed in making the city the Western terminus. Instead, it ended at nearby Omaha.[40] Many of the workers were Catholics from various lands—a number of them Irish.

In 1869, another clerical giant, Father Bernard McMenomy (known by some as "Father Mack") was sent to Council Bluffs and served there continuously until his death in 1892. A church builder and urban pioneer, he understood, as did Brazill and Flavin, the relationship between the church and the growing city. Born in Donegal, Ireland, in 1830, he was educated at St. Columb's College, Londonderry, and immigrated to America in 1849. Affiliating himself with the Archdiocese of St. Louis, he was ordained there in 1854 and spent his first years of priesthood in northern Missouri. He came to Iowa and served at Georgetown (Monroe County) and built churches at Melrose, Chariton, Woodburn, and Leon. He was one of those who saw the importance of the railroad and built churches along the routes of the Chicago, Burlington, and Quincy railroads.

McMenomy contributed to the rise of Council Bluffs by elevating the status of Catholic space and providing a legacy of architectural distinction and opportunities for education to the growing city. Council Bluffs grew from 18,063 in 1880 to 21,474 in 1890 and to 25,802 in 1900. Already in 1888, these increased numbers pushed McMenomy to secure a larger property for the Catholic church on Fifth Avenue from Sixth to Seventh Street.

The cornerstone was laid on April 1887 with the grandiloquent Father Joseph Nugent of Visitation, Des Moines, preaching. Nugent's ringing sermons may have

Father Bernard McMenomy. Credit: Council Bluffs Public Library, Council Bluffs, Iowa.

spoken to a feeling of isolation by local Catholics who were a minority in the city by reassuring them that no other religion was true except the Catholic faith. "The speaker made an earnest appeal for Catholics to stand by their faith which has thus come down to them through the centuries from Christ himself." As Nugent spoke, a collection was taken up for the building of the new church, which was dedicated two years later.[41]

The day was marked by a huge civic parade, which included over two hundred members of the Ancient Order of Hibernians, a sixteen-piece band, and over one thousand marching in the streets from the old church to the new site. The new St. Francis Xavier Church, a magnificent Gothic structure, cost $50,000, and more than a thousand people pressed to get into the church on its dedication day in April 1889.[42] This structure was the mother church of the other Council Bluffs Catholic churches. It was demolished in 1975.

In 1871, McMenomy brought the BVM sisters to Council Bluffs to begin St. Francis Academy for girls. Led by Sister Mary Xavier O'Reilly, the sisters traveled by train from Dubuque and were warmly welcomed by the parishioners who had prepared for their arrival

by providing adequate living quarters.[43] McMenomy also founded St. Joseph's school for boys and was an important force in western Iowa Catholicism until his death on December 31, 1892. His large funeral was attended by many, and his strong impact on the wider community was noted by a newspaper reporter who wrote: "And thus will be laid to rest one of the kindest, truest, and best men, one who labored unceasingly, and was universally loved."[44] Like Brazill, he did not restrict his organizational skills to Council Bluffs alone. He was the first priest "to give regular service to Catholics in Glenwood, Pacific Junction, Plumer Settle-

St. Francis Xavier Church, Council Bluffs. Credit: Council Bluffs Public Library, Council Bluffs, Iowa.

ment in Mills County, Neola, and Honey Creek in Pottawattamie County and Shelby in Shelby County."[45]

Council Bluffs' diversity grew, and St. Peter's, a parish for German speakers in Council Bluffs, was founded on Bluff Street in 1887 (more on this later). Holy Family opened in 1908. The city relied heavily on its multiple rail lines, services for transferring mail and other goods, fruit packing, cut flowers, and some manufacturing, such as candy and railcar wheels. As nearby Omaha grew in size, Council Bluffs was drawn more into its orbit.[46]

Catholic Health Care in Council Bluffs and Women Religious

Father McMenomy was part of the decision to bring Catholic health care to Council Bluffs. In August 1887, two Sisters of Mercy, Mary Vincent McDermott and Mary Magdalen Bennett, arrived in Council Bluffs.[47] These sisters had quite tumultuous careers—leaving a convent in Minnesota as virtual refugees. They had been part of a Mercy community in the Archdiocese of St. Paul, which had been dissolved by Archbishop John Ireland. Both women were instrumental, however, in the creating a thriving Catholic presence in the field of health care. Sister Vincent, who had a brother-in-law in Council

St. Bernard's Hospital, Council Bluffs.
Credit: Council Bluffs Public Library, Council Bluffs, Iowa.

Bluffs, Dr. Francis Seybert, was herself an accomplished professional (a telegrapher and chief dispatcher for a Pennsylvania Railroad before entering the convent). Mother Vincent, as she would be known, was an exceptionally adept administrator and builder—perhaps one of the first women in Council Bluffs history to organize and direct an enterprise as complex and challenging as the health-care empire the sisters created in the city. Of her skills, the Council Bluffs *Nonpareil* noted: "No greater work has been accomplished by any half dozen or more industries in the city."[48]

The two homeless sisters met with McMenomy, who encouraged them to begin a hospital. On September 24, 1887, the feast of Our Lady of Mercy, they began St. Bernard's Hospital (named for McMenomy) in a rented house. Later, they moved into a more spacious old mansion, once owned by a local brewer, Conrad Geise, at Frank and Harmony Streets. The mansion had seventeen rooms and sat on three acres. The new St. Bernard's opened on May 24, 1888. Later, the sisters purchased additional land around the hospital, swelling their property to fifteen acres.

Local need and good fortune helped the enterprise move forward. In May 1890, the loyal Dr. Seybert helped convince the board of supervisors of Pottawattamie County to allow the sisters to take care

Mercy Hospital Council Bluffs.
Credit: Council Bluffs Public Library, Council Bluffs, Iowa.

of the "insane." A new 125-bed wing was added to the hospital, and in 1896 a school of nursing opened. Growth followed on growth as the needs of the community grew and the number of Sisters of Mercy increased. In 1902, the mental patients were separated from the general population and St. Bernard's was devoted exclusively to the mentally ill. Meanwhile, a new four-story, red brick building named Mercy Hospital was built in 1903, which included 135 beds. The two hospitals functioned as separate entities until the 1960s.

The success of the hospital endeavor gave birth to an independent community of Mercy sisters in Council Bluffs. In 1901, the sisters were able to realize a part of their founding charism—care for young women in big cities—and opened a residence for young working women. They purchased a home at 225 Harmony Street, near St. Bernard's, and began welcoming women. In 1905, the sisters purchased another mansion with an accompanying ten acres from Presbyterian Andrew Gilbert, a local ice and coal merchant. They called the new property Mount Loretto, where Mother Vincent had hoped to found a home for the aged. Instead, she opened an academy for boys, which ran until 1913, when the building became the novitiate of the Sisters of Mercy from 1913 until 1955, at which time the novices were transferred to Omaha. The building then became a girl's school that remained open until a new Catholic high school (St. Albert's) opened in Council Bluffs in 1964. The Mercy Sisters also formed a small academy for girls named Our Lady of Victory. They provided faculty for Holy Family School in Council Bluffs in 1916.

Mother Vincent and Sister Magdalen (who also became a superior at one point) were figures of great importance for Catholic life and the wider development of the region. Even people of the time saw them as more than sectarian figures or cloistered "China dolls." There seemed to be awareness that these women were more than passive "brides of Christ." As a 1910 article in the Council Bluffs *Nonpareil* noted: "Mother Vincent is known as one of the most capable executives of the church in the west, and in her work in this city has built up Catholic institutions from a small foundation to a series of institutions holding hundreds of thousands of dollars worth of property and doing work of much benefit to the city and patrons of the institution."[49]

Parish as Pioneer Memory

Another function of the Catholic Church in Iowa was its role in the creation of pioneer memories. Historical studies of Iowa, textbooks relating Iowa history and geography, and historical markers and memories began to define Iowa's sense of itself. Catholics in Iowa, as elsewhere, also claimed their share of the historic memory of the state. Memories may or may not be accurate, but their power to affect perceptions of the past are significant.

Perhaps the coveted title of "first Catholic" of Council Bluffs went to Billy Caldwell, a *metis* (Mohawk and Irish gentleman) who worked with the local Potawatomi Indians as a traveling agent.[50] His life was typical of the social fluidity of the frontier, and in his last days he settled with his third wife at Trader's Point (Council Bluffs) and was the most prominent local Catholic on hand to welcome Father Pierre Jean de Smet, SJ, who in the words of one historian "would become one of the most prominent figures in the nineteenth century West."[51]

With two other Jesuits, de Smet had chugged up the muddy Missouri River from St. Louis in 1838 to work with the recently relocated Potawatomi Indians and try to combat problems of alcoholism and public disorder in the tribe. De Smet wrote pessimistic letters about his work, and, eventually realizing his mission to the Potawatomi Indians was a failure, he left for points west. Despite his failure and abandonment of Council Bluffs, the memory of his short stay there passed into the lore of the town's history and the little mission founded in the donated block house became embedded as a foundational moment not only in Catholic annals but in the general retelling of the origins of the city of Council Bluffs.

As with other Catholic priests in various parts of the country (e.g., Jacques Marquette, Eusebio Kino, and Junipero Serra), the reputation of de Smet soon became legendary and integrated into the wider mythology of local foundings. De Smet, now subject to often critical reevaluation of his dealings with native peoples, has nonetheless been memorialized by his legendary travels across the Great Plains and into the Pacific Northwest, including a meeting with the Mormon Brigham Young that allegedly directed the Mormon chieftain toward the Valley of Wasatch in Utah.

Catholics and Ethnics: Accommodating the Irish, the Germans, the Italians

A significant number of Iowa Catholics were natives of Ireland. Irish priests were recruited to serve communities of their country-men in Iowa. For example, the little Irish settlement in Decatur County was an enclave of Irish farmers who created a small church and cemetery. Later, when a permanent settlement opened in Wood-land Township, predominantly Irish parishioners joined together to found a church there. Later, a new parish, named for St. Brendan, opened in Leon. Between 1881 and 1890, four parishes in honor of St. Patrick were opened: St. Patrick, Perry (1881); St. Patrick, Neola (1882); St. Patrick, Bayard (1882); and St. Patrick, Corning (1890). Altogether, the Diocese of Des Moines would have a number of churches named in honor of the patron saint of Ireland.

One source estimates that in 1911 about one-third of the priests in the newly created Diocese of Des Moines were Irish born. For a time, Irish clergy were the backbone of the presbyterate, travel-ing far from home to tend to the spiritual needs of Iowa Catholics. Bishop Thomas Drumm (1919–1933) continued to actively recruit priests from his native Ireland, and by 1937 there were forty-two foreign-born Irish priests working in the diocese. Taken all together, between 1911 and 1937, there were fifty-nine men of Irish national-ity who served as priests in the Diocese of Des Moines.[52] Hibernian Catholicism carried its own particular approach to pastoral ministry, devotional life, church architecture, and clerical culture. All this would be replicated in southwestern Iowa.

Typical of these Hibernian recruits was Father Francis O'Connell who became pastor of the cathedral in 1925. O'Connell, ordained in 1920, was the first Irish priest recruited by Bishop Drumm. O'Connell had originally been earmarked for the Diocese of Den-ver, Colorado, but had been wooed away to Iowa by Father James Troy, a friend of Bishop Austin Dowling (1912–1919), who came to Ireland seeking students. O'Connell recalled, "I was then in third theology [when] Fr. Troy asked me to transfer. I gave my consent. I knew no more except that Bishop Dowling made all the arrange-ments for incardination with Bishop Tihen [of Denver]."[53] After a year at Kenrick Seminary in St. Louis, Drumm ordained him. After a stint at the cathedral, he later went on to become the pastor of prestigious St. Augustin's in Des Moines.

Other Irish priests included Father John Judge, later pastor at Rosemount and Winterset, who was ordained in Ireland in 1920 and came to Des Moines, where he remained until his retirement in 1958. Father (later Monsignor) Michael Kelliher, who hailed from County Longford, was ordained in 1924 and served in a variety of parishes. Fathers Daniel O'Connell and John O'Connor, both from priest-rich County Kerry, served in a variety of diocesan assignments. The mixture of their Irish upbringing and education along with the cultural and existential realities of life in Iowa meant a great deal of change for these immigrant priests. The longer they stayed, the more they became adjusted to conditions in the United States and created for themselves a hybrid sort of Catholic experience—blending their inherited faith with the conditions in America. Irish clergy were English-speaking and perhaps more culturally attuned to American culture. They dominated the church scene in the state capital for many years. Other immigrants would not have it quite so easy.

Ethnic Accommodation: German-Speaking Catholics

German-speaking Catholics, a diverse but articulate group, were a major force in the American Midwest. In southwest Iowa, they had high visibility in Council Bluffs, Des Moines, and Shelby County. Possessed of their own distinctive ethnic Catholic culture and often quite prosperous, they were frequently organized and insistent enough to demand their own churches and schools.[54] Priests and women religious were also at hand in many places to create a successful parish and school. In allowing the Germans to have their own church, a German-speaking venue for their particular expression of religious faith, the church not only guarded the flock from Lutheran "poaching" but also served as an "ethnic broker."

Ethnic churches provided important spiritual and social functions, not only allowing Catholics of various nationalities to hear their own language in the pulpit, the confessional, and in devotional services (not the Mass, which was in Latin), but also offering important outposts for newcomers to adjust to American life. As some have argued, ethnic parishes preserved elements of the old country in prayer, song, and art that helped ground immigrants in a safe place as they coped with living in America. They also served at times as "way stations" to Americanization. These parishes were not organized territorially as most parishes were but drew people of their designated nationalities from all parts of the city and surrounding area. Their utility to the Catholic Church was obvious: they kept Catholics tethered to the church. Their usefulness to the city was important as well because they helped preserve a sense of order and stability in ethnic communities—providing needed space for newcomers to adjust and fit into the wider society. These parishes did not last forever, as immigrant numbers waned and generations became Americanized. Nevertheless, while these groups were still ethnically self-conscious they performed an important function in church and urban systems.

German Catholics in Des Moines and Council Bluffs founded German-speaking parishes for their ethnic group—interestingly, the only two national parishes erected in what would become the Diocese of Des Moines.[55] Father Aloysius Nicholas Sassel organized the first church in 1862 with twelve German-speaking families living in east Des Moines. Named St. Mary's, the first church was built on the banks of the Des Moines River with a simple frame structure, two stories and 20 by 22 feet. In 1877, a handsome Gothic-style church replaced the old structure. In 1871, a parish school was opened

St. Mary's Church, Des Moines, 1908. Credit: Photo Courtesy of St. Benedict's Abbey, Atchison, Kansas, KansasMonks.org.

St. Peter's Church, Council Bluffs, Iowa. Credit: Council Bluffs Public Library, Council Bluffs, Iowa.

under the Franciscan Sisters of Perpetual Adoration and later the Benedictine sisters of Atchison, Kansas.

When Sassel died at the age of thirty-nine in 1883, the German-speaking Atchison Benedictines sent Father Winifred Schmidt, OSB, to St. Mary's. He remained until 1911, when Father Alban Rudroff, OSB, succeeded him. In 1915, Father Dominic Weber, OSB, arrived and remained at St. Mary's until its closure and demolition in the early 1960s. In its heyday, the parish had a church, convent, rectory, and school.[56]

In Council Bluffs, German-speaking citizens were the second largest foreign-born group in the city, and parishioners grew restive worshiping together with people of other nationalities. In 1887, a German Catholic organization purchased land in Council Bluffs and, with the approval of authorities in Davenport, created St. Peter's Church. Later, the Atchison Benedictines would provide ministry to the church. A school was founded as well.

St. Mary's, by its presence, décor, and use of German language, provided a "middle ground" for the German Catholics of Des Moines. The parish abandoned the use of German in World War I and became more visibly "American" in its identity—also reflecting the changing character of the general Des Moines population. St. Peter's in Council Bluffs, also a pretty neo-Gothic church, designed by architect Matthias Schnell, was erected and a school opened. These first ethnic parishes not only served the Catholic German speakers but were of great assistance to the city in helping to negotiate the presence and identity of ethnic groups. The Catholic Church in Des Moines would repeat this experience with Italians, who came into the diocese in the early twentieth century.

Ethnic Accommodation: The Italians

Immigrants from Italy first began arriving in the 1870s. Luigi Jacopetti, who came from Vergemoili in Tuscany, is credited with being the first Italian to settle in the Iowa capital. After 1900, more Italians came, many from southern Italy. According to historians Barbara Benning and Patrice Bema, the migration of Italians to Des Moines had begun in the 1880s until, by 1915, about four thousand Italians worked in coal mines, in brickyards, and on railroads. Italians ran grocery stores, fruit stands, taverns, bakeries, and pasta shops. They eventually followed the streetcar line to the south side of town across the Raccoon River, and in 1898 a parish named in honor of St. Anthony was founded to serve them by Bishop Cosgrove. It consisted of sixty Catholic families in south Des Moines. Monsignor Francis Leonard was named pastor.[57] This first effort fell short, however, when the bishop's College of Consultors could not follow through with the new enterprise. The continuing influx of new Italian families into Des Moines added urgency to the cause, and a petition for a new parish was renewed. In 1906, Cosgrove procured the services of Father Victor Romanelli, a native of Naples, to attend to this new foundation.

The boundaries of the new parish consisted of all of the territory south of the Rock Island tracks, extending midway between Lacona, St. Mary's, Cumming, and West Des Moines (then called Valley Junction). Romanelli was no stranger to America. After he was ordained in Italy, he was sent to America to do missionary work among immigrant Italians in New York and then New Jersey (Madison, Morristown, Newark, Patterson, and Orange). In Orange, he built a church, school, and convent and opened a free hospital.

Arriving in Des Moines in 1906, Romanelli spoke and wrote English perfectly and knew his way around the business of land acquisition. He purchased an old firehouse at Southeast First and Columbus Streets. The first Mass at St. Anthony's was celebrated on August 19, 1906. Romanelli resided in a room in the rear of the old firehouse. He later purchased a piece of property at 18 Columbus Avenue, and a brick church was erected that same year. A few years later a second floor was attached to the building, and in 1912 St. Anthony's School opened under the direction of the Sisters of

Humility. By 1956, this became one of the largest Catholic grade schools in the diocese. Romanelli lived to see the creation of the Diocese of Des Moines but took ill in December 1915 and died the following April.

Romanelli's efforts no doubt helped Des Moines Italians navigate their way in the community and also within the wider Catholic community. The bilingual Romanelli conducted religious services (devotions) and heard confessions in Italian. He was on hand to explain to newcomers some of the realities of life in Iowa and remind them of the need to support the church (a different arrangement than existed in Italy). Although these immigrants did not leave many records, one can reasonably surmise that the Italian priest, as other ethnic priests, provided a bridge between the experience of the old world and the new.

Unexpected trouble came from Monsignor Michael Flavin, the pastor of St. Ambrose. Flavin was reluctant to let go of his canonical rights over the majority of Catholics in the city—or their donations. When the new parish was founded, he made it clear by word and deed that Romanelli's ministry was restricted just to "Eye-Talians" and St. Anthony's was an ethnic, not a territorial, parish—even though it had been designated as territorial by the bishop who founded it. Flavin insisted that every other person in that district who was not Italian had to contribute to St. Ambrose and receive their sacraments at his church. A letter to Bishop James Davis of Davenport in 1906 from J. J. Liter, a long-time Des Moines Catholic, protested this proprietary claim over the south side of the city and noted: "We have lived in this place for nearly 30 years and the Catholics here owe you a debt of gratitude for establishing a parish in south Des Moines." He praised Romanelli, whom he described "as kind and sympathetic," an excellent priest; "everyone here seems to be charmed with him."[58]

Liter also reported to Davis, however: "We regret to state that Father M. Flavin is throwing a wet blanket over St. Anthony's Parish. He has married about three couples living almost in the shadow of St. Anthony's Church. He has baptized and continues to baptize children from St. Anthony Parish as well as attend the sick. He tells south side Catholics that St. Ambrose is their parish and to attend no other. Bishop, we can scarcely believe this of Fr. Flavin but it is positively true. . . . In announcing the new parish to his congregation Father Flavin willfully, deliberately and intentionally misrepresented the facts. He said in substance that there is an Italian priest here who will establish a parish in So. Des Moines for the Italians of the city."[59] Romanelli followed with a letter the next day. He urged Davis to send him an altar stone because "The one I have now belongs to the Very Rev. Dean Flavin who expressly told me I should give it back to him when the cold weather sets in for he needs to have it placed in the altar of the chapel where Mass is said during Winter time." Romanelli too complained about Flavin's poaching on his parish territory, confusing people as to what parish they belonged to, and robbing him of revenue he needed to stay afloat: "Your intentions in establishing a new parish have been misrepresented to the people from the pulpit and public press with the ill-disguised purpose to have my work meet with failure. . . . I have been sleeping on a couch for two months in a damp and comfortless place and out of three marriages blessed during that time, two were taken away from me at the time I needed those $20 to pay for grocery bills having spent nearly $200 for coming over here myself and paying freight expenses for my library and personal belongs." He urged Bishop Davis to fix exact limits and to restrain the imperious Flavin from "such daring encroachment on other Pastor's jurisdictions."[60] No one except Nugent at Visitation, however, ever challenged or bothered Flavin until a bishop was appointed to Des Moines.

Urban areas were the best images of how the church impacted its community. The elegance of the buildings, the provision of schools, and the "way station" they often provided to foreign-language citizens were all important social functions of these institutions. Catholics also played a role in the development of rural areas—an important dimension of church activity in Iowa.

Creating a Rural Presence

Brazill and McMenomy also contributed to Catholic life in rural areas far from the more populous Des Moines and Council Bluffs communities. As local church historian John Kempker notes, one of the first discoveries Brazill made when arriving permanently in

Des Moines was a letter addressed to Father Plath requesting the services of a priest in the Guthrie County community of Panora.[61]

From his first assignment at Georgetown and even after his transfer to Council Bluffs, McMenomy maintained a steady pace of circuit riding that began a Catholic presence in a number of remote areas. McMenomy was responsible for Catholic beginnings in a number of locations in western Iowa. A partial list of them includes Walnut, Weston, Afton, Corning, Creston, Bedford, Maloy, Chariton, Woodbine, and Shenandoah. Brazill likewise contributed to new churches in Des Moines, Atlantic, Granger, Adel, Waukee, Guthrie Center, Perry, Panora, and Irish Settlement.

The presence of a Catholic church and sometimes a school in these heavily agricultural counties provided not only a place of worship but also a common ground for the widely scattered farmers and laborers to gather. Life for a priest in these rural communities was often difficult as long days of bad weather or the time between religious services left little to do. For example, Irish-born Father Charles O'Connor, who came to Chariton in 1924, frequently used his spare time to send angry letters to the *Des Moines Register*.[62]

Other parishes became the sites of modest but elegant building projects. St. Patrick Church in Corning was founded in 1869. In 1874, an old brick school house on Eighth and Adams was converted into a Catholic church. In 1883, the first resident pastor, Father Patrick Clarke, arrived and built a new church. In 1931, just as the Great Depression was wreaking havoc with already weak farm prices, Father Maurice Powers built an elegant Spanish-style church. The Felician sisters would eventually open Rosary Hospital there, which was later turned over to the Sisters of Mercy.[63]

St. Patrick in Missouri Valley was organized in 1877 by "a group of faithful parishioners" who built a church for Catholic families. In 1882, Father P. J. Moran became the first resident pastor and remained until 1890. A church was built in 1892 by Father T. J. Mullen, and a parochial school opened in 1915 under the aegis of the Dominican sisters.[64]

Other parishes soon appeared as population reached enough of a critical mass to warrant them.

Church	Town	Year Founded
St. Mary, Mediatrix of All Graces	Avoca	1882
St. Peter	Defiance	1882
St. Joseph	Earling	1882
St. Patrick	Walnut	1882
St. Timothy	Reno	1883
St. Columbanus	Weston	1883
St. Bernard	Osceola	1885
St. Mary	Portsmouth	1885

Catholics and Coal Country

Iowa's rich deposits of bituminous coal were a magnet for mining companies who recruited workers to dig and ship this popular fuel, primarily for railroads. The array of immigrants who came to work in these mines brought scores of Catholics in need of ministry. The Dallas County area contained coal deposits discovered in the late nineteenth century, and when the Scandia Mine opened, Iowa for a time became an important supplier of bituminous coal throughout the country. Granger's Assumption Church assisted the Catholics in the mining colonies. Within the boundaries of the parish were five coal mines, which together employed about 1,600 men. Workers were recruited from immigrant groups—Italians, Croatians, Eastern Europeans—all from Assumption Church.

Granger's Assumption Church began as a mission from the chapel at Fort Des Moines. Father Brazill had initially conducted Mass in the Radigan family home at Beaver Creek, and later Patrick and Walter Moran donated an acre to Bishop John Hennessy of Dubuque in 1872 for a church, St. Bridget's. When this church burned in 1902, its location was transferred to Granger, and a new church was built and renamed Assumption. Father Henry V. Malone became first resident priest in 1894. This would eventually become the parish of Iowa's most famous priest, Monsignor Luigi Ligutti.

There were five mining camps owned by the coal operators located at some distance from surrounding towns, and by 1926 Scandia had been abandoned. Still, mining camps at High Bridge, Zookspur, Dallas Camp, Gibbsville, and Moran continued to operate, and Catholic chapels were set up for their service. Coal deposits in Polk County near Ankeny also required a Catholic chapel for the workers in the area.

Another Factor in Rural Presence:
The Church and Railroad Symbiosis

Railroad expansion created modern Iowa. As historians Henning and Beam note, "The profound effects of railroad service upon a place would be difficult to overstate."[65] It linked the productivity of the agricultural areas with the markets and transfer points available in the cities. Railroad stops became small communities that could sustain and stabilize the population. Henning and Beam observe: "They brought land speculators, new town building, and general economic expansion wherever they went."[66] Railroads also brought Irish and German laborers, many of them Catholics who settled in the state. Catholic churches often flourished wherever there was a railroad stop. Railroad expansion obviously benefitted the larger metropolises of Des Moines and Council Bluffs, but railroads also made possible the expansion of a Catholic presence in rural areas as well.

The first railroad connection into Des Moines—linking the city with Keokuk—began August 29, 1866. The next year the Chicago, Rock Island, and Pacific Railroad steamed into town—providing jobs in repair shops and cross-country service. The repair shops eventually moved to Valley Junction in 1871. Four lines—eventually known as the Illinois Central, the Chicago and Northwestern, the Rock Island, and the Burlington Northern—thrust westward from various terminals on the Mississippi to Omaha, often via Des Moines and Council Bluffs. Return traffic connected all of Iowa with Chicago, the premier railroad hub in the Midwest. Railroads played a major role in the settling and shaping of western Iowa and brought people, lumber for construction, and wages that permitted people to earn a living.[67]

Railroads both indirectly and directly affected demographic patterns in Iowa and contributed to the development of social institutions for the people who clustered around rail hubs or who used railroads as a link in commercial agriculture. Churches of all denominations were the beneficiaries of this transportation pipeline. For example, Father McMenomy founded St. Mary's (later renamed Sacred Heart) in Chariton in Lucas County in 1869. Chariton grew as rail lines transformed the community, making it for a time an important transshipment center for livestock. A resident pastor was appointed in 1878 who also served Osceola, Woodburn, Leon, Olmitz, Tipperary, and Williamson. The church building was moved once and then a new church was built in 1915.

The chart below indicates the communities resulting from the railroads that ran through what would become the Diocese of Des Moines.

Railroad	Community Created	Year Founded
Rock Island Railroad	Atlantic	1868
	Avoca	1869
	Adair	1872
	Winterset	1849
Burlington Railroad	Creston	1869
	Cumberland	1884
	Lacona	1881
	Red Oak	1869
Chicago Northwestern Railroad	Earling	1885
	Panama	1882
	Westphalia	1874

The Social Impact of Rural Churches: The Case of Shelby County

Shelby County, a strong German enclave, became one of the most concentrated areas of Catholic life in southwest Iowa. Monsignor

Michael Schiltz, the pastor of St. Mary of the Assumption Parish in Panama, Shelby County, described the origins of this presence through a Catholic colonization project begun in 1872 in Westphalia Township, Shelby County. On land set aside by the Rock Island railway, three hundred Catholic families had settled in the area by 1882 and a parish was founded at Panama. In 1883, additional railroad growth by the Chicago, Milwaukee, and St. Paul railroad expanded into the northeast part of the county, creating the towns of Defiance, Earling, Panama, and Portsmouth. Local Catholics founded St. Peter in Defiance in 1882 and St. Joseph in Earling and St. Mary Portsmouth in 1885; St. Michael in Harlan was founded in 1888. Shelby County would, after Polk and Pottawattamie Counties, become one of the single largest concentrations of Catholics in southwest Iowa. It was heavily dominated by German-speaking Catholics who replicated their religious culture.

These communities were examples of the profound effect the Catholic community could have in these farming communities. Perpetuating their German heritage, all of these parishes erected majestic churches—still gems even today—and five Catholic grade and high schools run by either the Benedictines or the School Sisters of St. Francis educated more than one thousand pupils. During the first seventy-four years of Catholic presence, Shelby County parishes sent more than two hundred young people to religious life. St. Boniface

St. Joseph Church, Earling, Shelby County.
Credit: Diocese of Des Moines Archives.

in Westphalia alone provided seventy-eight young people. St. Joseph in Earling sent forty-three girls to convents and thirteen boys to the priesthood and four to the Alexian Brothers—totaling sixty religious vocations. Most of the boys became diocesan priests, although some men from this county also joined the Jesuits, the Divine Word Fathers, and the Benedictines. A large number of the girls joined the Milwaukee-based School Sisters of St. Francis.[68]

Clergy as Community Builders: Father Edmund Hayes of Imogene

Beautiful churches were not reserved for well-heeled urban congregations. A magnificent church was built in the little community of Imogene, Iowa, in Fremont County. This small farming community in the state's southwestern corner near the Nebraska and Missouri borders was settled by Irish farmers who were enticed to buy land in the Monroe Township of Imogene, which was founded in 1879. A rail line from Council Bluffs to St. Louis brought some vitality to the area and Catholic life was stirred into existence. Imogene was at first a ministry of Trappists from New Melleray Abbey in Peosta (many of them Irish and from the same area as many of the original settlers). One of the brothers, Bernard Murphy, ran a cattle ranch that helped support the abbey. He attracted a cohort of Irish settlers and the area was known as Little Ireland. By the early 1870s a first Mass was held in a private home by the ubiquitous Father McMenomy. In 1876, Father Gerald Stack came and a parish was organized by 1880. At first it was a mission of the more populous Shenandoah but detached from it in 1888.

Father Edmund Hayes, St. Patrick's Church, Imogene. Credit: Diocese of Des Moines Archives

Its most famous pastor was Father Edmund Hayes, who was born in County Cork, Ireland, was educated by Christian Brothers in San Francisco, studied theology at Grande Seminaire in Montreal, and was ordained in 1878. Hayes was independently wealthy and traveled extensively. His wealth came from the large fortune he had inherited from his brother who had silver mines in Ely, Nevada, as well as gold and oil holdings in California; he had also invested heavily in the Omaha Stockyards, Union Pacific stock, and Iowa farmland. Hayes was perhaps the most influential force in the development of Imogene and tried to attract Irish settlers to the community by reselling good farmland at reasonable prices.

A splendid speaker with an outsized personality, he was eulogized as "probably the best known Catholic priest in Iowa" and "probably the best known minister of any denomination in southwestern Iowa."[69] Hayes is also one of the best examples of the permeable boundaries between secular and sacred. In addition to being a very devout and cultured clergyman, he was a true city developer of Imogene. Not only did he try to attract more people to Imogene, but his wealth enabled him to contribute to the electrification of the city, donate money to fund street lighting, and contribute substantially to the town's waterworks and library. Hayes died in 1928 and was deeply mourned.

His primary contribution was the erection in 1892 of a magnificent Gothic-style church, which burned in 1915. Hayes rebuilt the church in an even more magnificent style, erecting a splendid Gothic/Romanesque revival church with an eight-story bell tower, a ceiling that rose sixty-five feet, exquisite stained glass from Munich, a marble sanctuary from Italy (ordered twice because the ship carrying the original was sunk by a German mine) crowned with a statue of St. Patrick, and even an episcopal throne.[70] Today the church is a tourist attraction in the area. Hayes began a school, St. Patrick's Academy, in 1906, directed by the Sisters of Mercy. In 1920, the Sinsinawa Dominicans replaced the Mercy sisters. Although Imogene never took off like Des Moines and Council Bluffs (current population at this writing is sixty-nine), Hayes showed how clerical leadership could go beyond denominational boundaries and work the church into the development of an area.

A Glimpse of Catholic Life

While the story of parish formation essentially repeats the fairly constant pattern of church foundations (land acquisition, temporary and later permanent building, pastoral leadership, women religious and schools), the experience of the "ordinary" Catholic is never explored in great detail. To find this, one needs to examine the accounts of parish organizations: sodalities, altar societies, pious organizations, and pictures of popular religious events such as First Communions, the anniversaries of the parish or the pastor, and the occasional first Mass of a young parishioner who became a priest. Many parish histories contain lists of priest sons and young women who became sisters. Some include names of parish members (sometimes with their annual contributions listed next to their names). The Catholic press carries accounts of parish celebrations, parties, fund-raisers, devotional celebrations, and confirmations.

Although these have too often been generic, from time-to-time stories of Catholic experience of those early years were incorporated into them. One account was of Barbara Reis, who in 1961 at the age of eighty-nine was still the sacristan (and occasional Mass server) for St. John's Parish in Greenfield, Adair County. Reis, "of a devout German family," grew up on a farm near Bridgewater and recalled the ministry of itinerant priests who came irregularly. When there was no priest, Barbara's father or one of her uncles would lead Catholic neighbors in Sunday devotions in a part of the Reis home set up as a chapel. They would read through the Mass for the day, review the faith, and reflect on written meditations. Reis recalled that some families came from a distance to attend these services.

The first priests who made regular stops at Bridgewater were the Benedictines of Creston. When they came, the Reis house was cleaned from top to bottom. The monks quizzed the children on catechism, baptized, solemnized marriages, heard confessions, and offered Mass in the Reis home. On occasion the bishop of Davenport, Henry Cosgrove, would visit and confirm candidates in the small community. Reis herself never married, as she could not find a Catholic man for a spouse, and never considered becoming a sister, as she had never seen a nun and only read about them in books.[71] No doubt there were many like Barbara's family who kept the Catholic faith alive through private devotion and mindfulness of God even when the Eucharist was not easily or regularly available.

Women Religious: Sisters and Their Schools

Education was a critical hallmark of local development. Schools were often among the first institutions founded when local governments were established on the city and county level. Cities like Des Moines began the first public schools in 1846 with subscription schools. A school district was organized in 1849, and in 1851 the first tax for the building of a school was imposed, resulting in the construction of the Third Ward School at Ninth and Locust. As the years went on, school building took place in both west and east Des Moines as a growing population demanded it. Des Moines created one of the best high schools in the state.[72] Catholics would also erect schools with many of their parishes. These competed with the more numerous and better endowed public institutions. Catholic schools were never as robust as in other parts of the state, for example, in Dubuque or Davenport, because the Catholic population was small and the number of sisters free to work in them were limited.

Nevertheless, the Catholic schools, as with the hospitals, offer a good opportunity to examine the agency of women religious (sisters) in southwest Iowa. As with the hospital sisters, the autonomous activities of these women stood out significantly from the traditional roles assigned to women during the nineteenth and early twentieth centuries. Noting of the several Iowa sisterhoods—the Sisters of Charity of the Blessed Virgin Mary, the Sisters of Mercy, and the Presentation Sisters (all Irish in origins)—Helen Marie Burns notes: "Women religious participated in the establishment of Catholic culture in their frontier environment in much the same way that women in general served as conduits of civilization and tradition in the larger cultural process. They created homes for young children; tended to the sick, the dying, and the elderly; educated young persons and others in the rituals, customs, and doctrine of Roman Catholicism." She further notes, "active women religious engaged also in 'men's work'—finances, administration, building, construction, property development, and business travel."[73]

Burns accentuates a dimension of the agency of women religious in Iowa (and elsewhere) that, because they were dispersed far from their motherhouses, they were obliged to become self-supporting in local settings "as soon as possible [which] . . . fostered local autonomy and mobility" and decision making necessary to direct their lives and operations, an autonomy other women of the time did not share.

The Sisters of Charity of the Blessed Virgin Mary (BVM), founded by Mother Mary Frances Clarke in 1833, offers an excellent case study. Clarke had moved the headquarters of her community from Philadelphia to Dubuque in 1843 at the invitation of Bishop Matthias Loras. Clarke and her advisers (together with co-founder Father Terence Donaghoe, also their spiritual director) directed their own affairs, often negotiated property and building arrangements, and organized functional elementary (and even secondary) schools in remote and urban areas.

Historical geographer Rachel Daack Riley insists that the history of these schools and the impact of the teachers (most of them religious sisters, but also laywomen) has been seriously understudied.[74] Riley examines the history of the BVM sisters—noting how they took care of their own internal affairs—even at times keeping at bay local bishops and priests. This included Des Moines's Father

Sisters of Charity of the Blessed Virgin Mary.
Credit: Used with permission of Mount Carmel Archives of the Sisters of Charity of the Blessed Virgin Mary, Dubuque, Iowa.

Mother Mary Frances Clarke, BVM.
Credit: Used with permission of
Mount Carmel Archives of the Sisters
of Charity of the Blessed Virgin Mary,
Dubuque, Iowa.

Brazill who insisted on seeing the sisters' accounts only to be informed by Mother Frances Clarke (politely but firmly) that that was not going to happen. "Very Rev. Father, you wish to examine the Sister's accounts. It is the first time that any Gentleman not even our Right Rev. Bishops required that. Therefore you will excuse me for positively and finally declining."[75]

Riley also notes the pragmatic dimension of Mother Clarke's administration. Spiritual values were to dominate, but Catholic schoolteachers were to be equipped with the best knowledge and teach the "profane" subjects with accuracy and excellence. She exhorted her sisters, "Let us then acquire and impart secular knowledge . . . keep our schools progressive with the time in which we live."[76] Clarke insisted that teachers keep their pedagogical skills up-to-date and recommended books for her sisters to read.

Curriculum and moral formation were important tasks; religious sisters were also trained to be land managers, tending to acquisitions, building costs, and renovation efforts and taking note of adequate living spaces for sisters and their boarders and school rooms for children. As Riley and others have noted, the BVMs "managed large budgets, supported all of the buildings and lands they owned, the school operating funds, and living costs for each member."[77] While the sisters maintained boundaries of religious life—separation from aspects of the "world," the religious habit, acquisition of personal money and effects, and prohibitions on certain types of "worldly" behavior—the ability to negotiate between spiritual and sacred realities was an integral factor in their survival and the general success of their work.

St. Joseph Academy. Credit: Used with permission of Mount Carmel Archives of the Sisters of Charity of the Blessed Virgin Mary, Dubuque, Iowa.

BVM sisters opened their first Catholic school at St. Ambrose at the invitation of Father Brazill. The first contingent of sisters to come, led by Sister Mary Michael Nihil, nearly met with disaster as the train on which they were traveling derailed and their car slid down an embankment. The sisters plowed on to Des Moines in a blinding snowstorm, cajoling a stagecoach driver with promises of more money to bring them to the state capital.[78] They opened their school on November 1, 1865. The same sisters opened St. Francis Xavier School in Council Bluffs in 1871, and a school at Visitation Church in 1881, and St. John's School in Des Moines in 1906. St. Joseph Academy, run by the BVMs, began in 1884 when two girls enrolled in a building that had been purchased by the sisters from W. H. Welch, the owner and editor of the *Des Moines Leader.* The building, known as the Grandview Place, was located in a heavily wooded area beyond the end of the car line—a fine old two-story Victorian-style building. An addition was made in 1896, and the old mansion known as Villa Maria was set back on the property in 1906. The academy accommodated both day and boarding students until the boarding program was discontinued in 1951. The academy grew slowly but steadily, taking in many new boarding girls when the boarding department of Council Bluffs' St. Francis Academy closed in 1908.[79] In 1918, Bishop Dowling designated St. Joseph's as the central high school for the Catholic girls of the city. Boarders came from all over the country to attend. In 1910, the school added a commercial department, and, in 1914, scientific and domestic classes, as well as a Normal School, were incorporated. The school merged with Dowling High School and St. Joseph Education Center in 1972.

The Benedictine Sisters of Atchison, Kansas, were also an important presence. Benedictine Mother Evangelista Kremeter came to Atchison, Kansas, at the behest of the Benedictine monks and founded a convent called Mount Scholastica. Eventually seven other sisters joined her, and in 1888 a group of these sisters joined the Benedictine monks at St. Malachy's in Creston and St. Peter's in Council Bluffs, where they staffed parish schools. Later, groups of Benedictine sisters administered schools at St. Mary in Des Moines, St. Mary in Portsmouth, St. Peter in Defiance, and St. Mary in Panama.[80]

The Congregation of the Humility of Mary—founded in Dommartin, France, in 1854—first sent a contingent of sisters to America in 1864 at the invitation of Bishop Amadeus Rappe of Cleveland. In 1870 at the invitation of Bishop John Hogan, several sisters served in schools in northwest Missouri. In 1877, under the leadership of Mother Mary of the Angels Maujean, the Congregation of the Humility of Mary separated from the Sisters of Humility in the east, became an independent community, and established their motherhouse and novitiate in Ottumwa, Iowa. In 1925 they opened Ottumwa Heights College. The CHMs began staffing schools in Des Moines, Neola, Dunlap, and Stuart. Later, the sisters would take over the Christ Child Home in Des Moines.[81]

Mother Mary of the Angels Maujean
1828-1902

Mother Mary of the Angels Maujean, foundress of the Congregation of the Humility of Mary. Credit: Archives of the Congregation of the Humility of Mary.

The School Sisters of St. Francis, founded in Milwaukee, specialized in ministry to German-speaking Catholics. These sisters came to the area in 1872 and staffed several schools: St. Joseph's grade and high schools in Earling; St. Boniface grade and high schools in Westphalia; and St. Mary's grade school in Rosemount.

In 1920, the Dominicans of Sinsinawa came to Imogene. The Franciscan Sisters of Penance and Charity, another group founded in Milwaukee, arrived in the diocese in 1944 to staff the parish school at Granger. Sisters of the Precious Blood came to St. Joseph School in Des Moines in 1949. Other communities included Franciscans from Clinton, Iowa, and the Adrian Dominicans.

The proliferation of schools took place apace. The location of these schools indicated the growing presence of the Catholic community. Polk County had four schools: St. Ambrose, St. John's, St. Mary, and Visitation. Pottawattamie County (Council Bluffs) had three schools: St. Francis Xavier, St. Joseph, St. Peter and St. Patrick in Neola. Shelby County had Earling's St. Joseph as well as St. Mary in Portsmouth and St. Boniface in Westphalia. Warren County had St. Mary in Lacona, and Audubon County had St. Boniface in Exira.

&

By 1911, the impact of the Catholic Church on conditions in southwest Iowa was significant. Although not numerically large, this part of the state enjoyed the presence of elegant churches and functioning schools and health-care facilities. Priests like Monsignor Flavin and Father McNamara had contributed substantially to the beauty of Des Moines. The Atchison Benedictine monks and Father Romanelli at St. Anthony kept ethnic groups loyal to the church. The two Mercy hospitals were continuing to grow. Women religious like Mother Vincent proved to be capable and farsighted leaders. Des Moines especially was a city of prominence, with a magnificent capitol building, handsome public structures, public transit, electrical current, and businesses of substance. The railroads continued to bring passengers and freight into the cities and an emerging road system would begin to accommodate the growing reliance on the automobile. Calls for a new diocese in Western Iowa were, to a large extent, an affirmation of the accumulated social and cultural development of the region.

2

The Politics of Catholic Space

Carving a Niche in Southwest Iowa

Creating new dioceses is an administrative decision ultimately made on the highest levels of the Roman Catholic Church. It is a process roughly akin to forming a new congressional district or administrative unit. Until 1908, the decision to create a new diocese came from a formal request of the American bishops to the Congregation for the Propagation of the Faith in Rome. Local authorities sketched out boundaries and offered proof that such a new jurisdiction could support a bishop, a cathedral, and the other agencies of church life. After 1908, when the United States was no longer considered a mission territory, the decision was passed on to the Sacred Congregation of the Consistory (also known as the Consistorial Congregation). Local information and issues of financial viability also came from US sources and was affirmed by the pope's representative in the United States, the apostolic delegate. Sometimes these decisions would be discussed and pondered over many years.

For Catholics, the diocese has various levels of importance. First and foremost, it is a spiritual reality—a manifestation of the local church, with a critical mass of Catholics assembled under the leadership of a bishop, a spiritual "successor to the apostles" and the sponsoring authority for parish churches and other Catholic institutions. Dioceses have their origins in ancient Catholic practice—going back to the fourth century—and their spiritual significance is affirmed at different times in the church's calendar, especially when there are large common celebrations with the local bishop, for example, the annual blessing of the oils used in sacramental ceremonies (the Mass of Chrism).

Dioceses are also socio-economic entities, in many ways resembling large businesses or corporations. Like them, dioceses require the gathering and dispersing of resources and the allocation of personnel. They also collect revenue to sustain the central offices and the institutions deemed important to the local area. A diocese creates new concentrations of people, money, and influence. Bishops are the primary spiritual leaders for tens of thousands of Catholics, but they also have extensive control over the welfare of churches, schools, hospitals, and cemeteries—each of which requires public space, creation of a built environment, and controls millions of dollars of investment as well as untold hours of sweat equity. Dioceses provide revenue for local businesses and raise up people who can affect the direction of local development and even politics. On many levels, diocesan creation is reflective of the interplay between the secular and the sacred. Iowa today has four Roman Catholic dioceses.

The creation of the Diocese of Des Moines came when the growing pastoral and administrative needs of the southwestern twenty-three counties of Iowa reached a critical point. The increase in population required local leadership and more immediate pastoral care of the Catholics in the region. The increase in population also created the potential for the economic stability to underwrite church projects: churches, schools, health care, and other forms of social provision.

In Catholic organizational theory, the formation of dioceses is also a manifestation of "subsidiarity"—a cherished Catholic principle that valorizes local control of church affairs. By 1911, Des Moines and Council Bluffs, although still under the jurisdiction of the bishop of Davenport, were now at a stage where they required more direct contact and direction by a local bishop and greater local oversight over their own affairs. The path to this decision was not easy.

The decision to create this new diocese was a protracted process, which is difficult to understand because Des Moines was not only the state capital, but also the largest city in the state since the 1890s. The reason for this long delay was primarily financial. Since early in the twentieth century, it was required that diocesan boundaries be conformed to county boundaries (rather than rivers or other natural boundaries), setting up a contest between those who lost and who gained counties, almost the equivalent of gerrymandering struggles for state congressional districts. This was because not all counties were equal in Catholic populations, church buildings, and other institutions. Most important, they were not equal in their capacity to generate revenue to support the central administration of the diocese. There were other reasons that delayed the decision to create the Diocese of Des Moines, but, in the end, the "parent" Diocese of Davenport was apprehensive about the economic loss. What follows is a description of the lengthy process that went on to create the Diocese of Des Moines in 1911.

The first open discussions of creating a diocese in southwest Iowa were briefly held by clergy of Iowa as early as 1881, the same year the Diocese of Davenport was created. This question was rejoined by the consultors (the board of priests who advised the bishop) of the Diocese of Davenport in 1886, when they were petitioned to found new parishes in Council Bluffs and Des Moines. The priests agreed to establish a new German church in Council Bluffs (St. Peter). Financial concerns, however, stayed the hand of any future parishes in Des Moines "until debts on the property there be paid and the deeds of all the property be made to the bishop."[1] They did acknowledge "a probability of the establishment of a new See at Des Moines," but the time was not yet. As a kind of interim step in the process of creating a new diocese, the bishop and his consultors created a deanery (an administrative subunit of a diocese) headquartered at Des Moines, giving jurisdiction to the dean (the presiding cleric) over more than twenty-three counties—many of them later transferred to Des Moines.[2]

The erection of a new and imposing St. Ambrose Church on Sixth and High Streets in Des Moines in 1891 also seemed to presage a certain prominence for the Des Moines church (although its builder, Michael Flavin, was against the creation of a new diocese for some time). In 1891, when Archbishop John Hennessy celebrated his twenty-fifth anniversary as archbishop of Dubuque, the topic of a new diocese was again brought up—and dropped—again likely until the new St. Ambrose debt was retired. Start-up costs for a diocese

Diomede Falconio. Credit: Canadian Copyright Collection of the British Library (found on Wikicommons).

would sap too much money from the necessary funds to start a new diocese. Therefore, although Des Moines was bursting with growth, for the remainder of the century, the city and southwest Iowa remained under the jurisdiction of the Diocese of Davenport. As time went on managing the needs of this vast expanse became problematic. Stasis was not, however, an option for too much longer.

In 1902, western Iowa got its first new diocese when Rome created the new Diocese of Sioux City out of the twenty-four counties of northwestern Iowa, with Philip Garrigan as its first bishop.[3] After the creation of the Diocese of Sioux City, John J. Keane, archbishop of Dubuque, convened a gathering of the Province of Dubuque in December 1902. This included the bishops (suffragans) of Davenport, Iowa; Omaha and Lincoln, Nebraska; and Cheyenne, Wyoming. At this meeting, the prospect of raising Omaha to archdiocesan status was discussed and with it the prospect of creating a new diocese in the southwest of Iowa. Keane and his suffragans voted to create a new diocese headquartered at Des Moines. This petition was forwarded to Archbishop Diomede Falconio, the apostolic delegate to the United States.[4] Archbishop Falconio's task was to gather the required information and forward it to the Congregation of Propaganda in Rome where the boundaries would be settled and a new bishop selected.

But this action was stopped in its tracks when Davenport bishop Henry Cosgrove, who had earlier expressed support for the new diocese, began to have qualms. Cosgrove had at first been glad to detach the western counties of his diocese. Father John Kempker (a historian of Catholicism in Polk County) recalled in 1903 driving Bishop Cosgrove to county-line divisions between Bauer and Rosemont, Iowa: "He [Cosgrove] informed me that this was the division line for the new diocese of Des Moines."[5] Indeed, the long distances required for travel to administer confirmation and tend to local issues in the western part of the state had become too much after a while. Moreover, he was ill. To Keane's consternation, Cosgrove unexpectedly withdrew his endorsement of the petition of the previous December. Rather than split the diocese, he instead requested a coadjutor (an assistant bishop) who could help with the pastoral ministry.[6] Cosgrove's switch was motivated in part by his priests and others who worried that detaching the western part of the diocese would deprive the diocese of funds necessary to build up the diocese's St. Ambrose College in Davenport.

Keane reluctantly endorsed the proposal for a coadjutor and wrote to apostolic delegate Diomede Falconio: "Last week I saw Bishop Cosgrove at his home in Davenport. It is quite evident that his work is ended. The appointment of a coadjutor is an urgent necessity. . . . He begs that this permission be obtained as speedily as possible." But when Falconio pressed as to why Cosgrove withdrew his approval of a new diocese, Keane demurred: "As to his petition that the appointment of a Bishop for Des Moines be postponed, I do not venture to pass judgment on his request, but leave that to the wisdom of the Holy See."[7]

Bishop Henry Cosgrove of Davenport. Credit: Used with permission of the Diocese of Davenport Archives, Davenport, Iowa.

Falconio sought Keane's estimation. Keane replied that although Cosgrove felt that a new young bishop could more easily attend to the needs of the far-flung diocese, he (Keane) still felt a new diocese was necessary: "It is . . . my conviction and that of the other Bishops and Archbishops whom I have heard speak of the matter, that the interests of religion in the Western portion of the Diocese of Davenport would be very greatly promoted by the creation of a new diocese with its See at Des Moines. Such a division of the Diocese of Dubuque has proved very beneficial."[8]

Falconio pressed Cosgrove who hedged: "The principal reason I had for asking to have the diocese divided was to lessen the work on account of my advanced age and failing health, and I hoped some time ago a division of the diocese would enable me to administer the affairs of a smaller place without such a coadjutor." He also noted, however, "Should Rome see fit to give me a coadjutor and at the same time divide the diocese and appoint a bishop for Des Moines, I will be perfectly satisfied and will receive the decision in humble obedience."[9] When Falconio asked Bishop Philip Garrigan of the recently created Diocese of Sioux City, he demurred, claiming he was "not familiar enough with the territory or the conditions that obtain in the southern part of the state to give an intelligent opinion on the contemplated move." But he did point out the need for greater Catholic visibility in the western part of the state: "Had a bishop been sent to this City ten years ago, the Church would have made much progress and would be in a far more flourishing condition than it is now."[10]

Bishop Richard Scannell of Omaha, who lived "next door" to Iowa, and who wished to see Omaha raised to archdiocesan status (and himself made an archbishop), wrote most forcefully to the delegate about the delay, noting that the western territory, "extending for 300 miles to the Missouri River, being remote from episcopal supervision, was neglected and Catholic settlers avoided it." He further insisted: "It would be a fatal mistake to wait until these vast territories are settled, for then the field would be occupied by non-Catholics. . . . The Bishop of Davenport does not need Western Iowa. . . . Des Moines is the capital of the state and a very large and rich city with at least three churches, one of them a very fine one, so that the new bishop would have a fine cathedral ready to receive him. I believe the new Bishop would, in five years, find himself at the head of a most prosperous diocese."

Scannell also revealed a more venal reason for the delay—this one originating from among the priests of Des Moines who worried that a new diocese would "freeze them in place" and did not want to do all the work to build up new diocesan institutions in the western part of the state: "Some of the priests of western Iowa are opposed to the establishment of the new See on selfish ground, as they admit, as they have helped to build up diocesan institutions in Davenport, they do not want to be taxed for others at Des Moines."

Nevertheless, he observed: "But it is unnecessary to point out that such a principle, if acted upon, would prove disastrous to the best interest of religion, at least in the West."[11]

Michael Flavin, rector of St. Ambrose Church, the dean of the area, tried to discourage the split: "As I have resided in this city for nearly twenty years and know the territory that would be included in the new diocese as well as the sentiments of the priests in that territory to this contemplated division, I deem it my duty in behalf of the priests of this deanery and at their express request to convey to Your Eminence . . . the following facts which should be seriously considered in making this division."

Flavin noted the paucity of Catholics in southwest Iowa, their poverty and inability to contribute much toward the salaries of priests and the upkeep of the church. He painted a bleak picture of future economic prospects: "For the land is all taken and cannot be purchased for less than $100 to $150 an acre." He informed the delegate "that pastors in this territory knowing all this and realizing their inability to contribute to the maintenance of a Bishop and the building of his Cathedral and other diocesan institutions are opposed to this division."[12]

Flavin, long the "king of the hill" in Des Moines, did not want any "interference." Bishop Cosgrove had come every three years for confirmation and that was enough. "I suppose our Rt. Rev. Bishop will get a coadjutor and in the meantime should his diocese be divided we would have three bishops in this small corner of southwest Iowa which would seem to be altogether unnecessary."[13]

The only dissenter in the deanery was Father Joseph F. Nugent, pastor of Des Moines's Visitation Parish and a nemesis of Flavin. Nugent highlighted the tremendous growth of the city and how Catholics lagged behind, noting how the one Catholic school enrolled three hundred students while close to five hundred Catholic students attended public schools. He pointed out that St. Ambrose Church was flush with money due to the rise in property values; "to this was added several large bequests." Indirectly indicting Flavin, he wrote, "The history of the church shows that wealth and ease generally produce, in the church what is known in the body as . . . the fatty degeneration of the heart."

He further suggested that poor and ailing Bishop Cosgrove had been outmaneuvered by his priests. "Each time he made an effort in this direction, he was out figured." Nugent also scorned the careerist ambitions of the younger priests and noted that Flavin made "direct appeals to the cupidity of younger members of the clergy. They are made to understand that their time for promotion is near at hand and better chances will soon open in the Eastern portion of the diocese and that in case of a division, their chances for better parishes would be greatly diminished."[14] Nugent's clergy rivals were quick to protest his characterization of them, ridiculing his tiny church, his poor school, and his heavy debts. Snarled one: "He considers himself the great orator of Iowa and gives lectures all over the country, leaving his congregation to the charity of neighboring priests to attend their sick calls and spiritual wants."[15] The matter stood still as long as Cosgrove was still in power.

When Cosgrove's health took a sharp decline, a coadjutor was appointed to help him—Irish-born Father James Davis, rector of the cathedral and vicar general of the diocese. The *Des Moines Register* carried an August 29, 1904, article detailing the selection of a coadjutor (it would be either Davis or Flavin) but also noting the still-confused state of the question regarding the formation of the new diocese. The paper accurately noted that Cosgrove was the main opponent but that, when he passed from the scene, a new diocese would be carved out of western Iowa.[16]

Bishop James Davis of Davenport. Credit: Used with permission of the Diocese of Davenport Archives, Davenport, Iowa.

Davis, a native of County Kilkenny, Ireland, came from a large religious family (all of his siblings were either priests or religious). Ordained a priest for Dubuque in 1878, he was a successful pastor, building a new cathedral for the Davenport diocese. In September 1904, he was appointed coadjutor bishop of Davenport and consecrated in Sacred Heart Cathedral on November 30,

1904. Cosgrove died in 1906, and Davis assumed complete control of the diocese. On Davis's accession, the pressure for a new See at Des Moines resumed. On Christmas Eve 1906, the *Des Moines Register* opined: "The belief among the Catholics of Des Moines is that the time is ripe for further agitation of the matters. Des Moines is the logical seat of a new diocese." The *Register* reported further that the churches of Des Moines were among the strongest in the state and that the two clerical panjandrums of the city, Flavin, despite his earlier opposition, and Nugent, favored the new diocese.[17] It would be five more years, after some hard bargaining, that Davis would agree to let go of the western part of his statewide See.

The final stimulus came when discussions were resumed about raising Omaha to archdiocesan status, and the issue of the western part of Iowa came into focus again. Dubuque's province extended well into Nebraska (encompassing the dioceses of Omaha and Lincoln, Nebraska, and Cheyenne, Wyoming), and the archbishop of Dubuque was interested in restricting his sphere to the state of Iowa.

Reluctantly, Davis took up the question of a new diocese at Des Moines with his consultors in early 1907, writing to Falconio of his misgivings about it. Once again, he insisted he could not let the "rich" counties of southwest Iowa go because he still needed cash for an addition to St. Ambrose College in Davenport. The priests of the western portion of the diocese were unwilling to contribute, "owing to persistent rumors circulated in the newspapers that the Diocese of Davenport was to be divided in the near future." He noted to the delegate that priests of the diocese felt "no need of any division since the spiritual wants of the various parishes can be attended to conveniently under present circumstances."

Davis rehashed the indecision of his predecessor, claiming he was "influenced by the Bishops of the Province to consent to the division of the diocese" because they wanted the Province of Dubuque within the border of Iowa—and had plans to raise Omaha to Metropolitan status. "Afterward, Bishop Cosgrove, learning of the opposition of the priests and the detriment the division would be to the diocesan college [St. Ambrose] (which is supported in great measure by the western portion of the diocese) . . . he realized that such a decision as he agreed to, would not be in the interests of religion."[18]

Davis seemed to know, though, that he was staving off the inevitable and began to drive a hard bargain with Dubuque to make sure his diocese would remain fiscally and demographically solvent after a split. In February 1907, Davis and his consultors and the irremovable rectors sent a petition to Falconio, protesting "against any division of said diocese under conditions indicated by rumors." They explained that cutting off the western portion of the diocese "would impoverish both dioceses and materially interfere with the progress and work of religion." They pointed out that "an exact split would give Davenport 35,000 people and 65 priests while Des Moines would have 25 priests and not more than 20,000 people."[19] The petition noted that Dubuque was surfeited with priests (231) and a Catholic population of 109,000. Sioux City, detached from its western turf, had 109 priests and fifty thousand Catholics.

To right this obvious imbalance, Davis and the priests insisted, "Dubuque ought to give to the Diocese of Davenport the counties immediately bordering upon it, and the Diocese of Sioux City ought to give the Diocese of Des Moines the territory bordering it. That would be a proportionately fair division." Davis, Flavin, and five other priests signed the petition.[20] But this would be the last time the plans would be delayed. Things were changing, especially in Des Moines.

DES MOINES NAMED SEE CITY BY POPE

Confirmation of News of Division of Davenport Diocese Received at Omaha.

FLAVIN FOR BISHOP?

Rumored His Name Will Be Considered—Elevation of Des Moines Means Erection of Many Buildings.

Headline of the establishment of the Diocese of Des Moines. Credit: Des Moines Public Library.

Des Moines: A City on the Move

Since the 1880s, Des Moines had been one of the flagship urban centers of Iowa and by that same year slightly edged out Dubuque, and Davenport was the state's largest city (22,408).[21] It had grown thanks to the presence of the state capital and the railroads. Its expanding population was 19 percent foreign-born by 1880, and half of the citizens were women. In 1880, only 9 percent of the population was Catholic but that number was growing. Telegraph and later telephone communication was advancing, as was bridge-building technology that allowed the community to ford the Raccoon and Des Moines Rivers. Electricity came to Des Moines in 1881.[22]

The city had also developed a booster cadre who waded into the issue. The Commercial Club, founded in 1880, was a group of citizens, both Protestant and Catholic, who had been a major force in beautifying and upgrading the quality of life in the city: roads, water purification, schools, and elegant buildings. The club had also pushed for the establishment of commission-style municipal governance in the state capital, advancing a reform that soon swept the nation.[23] The leadership of the club also wrote to Bishop Davis, urging the creation of a new diocesan center at Des Moines.

Clearly, they believed that making Des Moines the center of a new Catholic jurisdiction would be yet another jewel in the city's crown. With some exaggeration they informed Davis: "Des Moines is a city of 100,000 inhabitants, centrally located in the great state of Iowa. . . . There are seventeen radiating lines of the railroad including branches. There are five interurban or electric lines extending out into that portion of the state that would contain within its limits the new diocese. Of the 99 county seats within the state, 74 are reached by direct train service." The Commercial Club men decried the lack of Catholic institutions: "Outside of four parochial schools, the Catholics have only one academy for the education of young ladies."

Pointing out other assets of the community and urged by Catholic members of the club, they resolved to "use our influence to have this city receive the honor of an Episcopal See." They sent a copy of this letter to Falconio.[24] Davis and Falconio also heard from Senator Albert Cummins, who also urged the honor for Des Moines and promised to "do anything in my power to help them accomplish their desires," even offering to acquaint Falconio, who resided in Washington, DC, "with the glories and strengths of Des Moines."[25]

Realizing that this time he could not finesse the issue, Davis now began to bargain. "I have no objections to a new Bishopric at Des Moines. As however, a new See in Des Moines involves a division of the Diocese of Davenport, I cannot in justice submit to an unreasonable division. . . . A new See in Des Moines means to Davenport the loss of twenty-five counties [*sic*], almost half the number of clergy . . . and the loyalty and generosity of a devoted laity. To compensate at least in a small measure for this enormous loss, the Clergy and Laity demand at least six counties above be attached to the Diocese of Davenport."[26] Davis repeated the demands of 1907 in a note to Falconio—indicating that he wanted the counties of Clinton, Jones, Linn, Benton, Tama, and Marshall annexed to Davenport.

The New Diocese Becomes a Reality

On May 23, 1911, the bishops of the province met in Omaha, and the first concrete steps toward the creation of the Diocese of Des Moines were taken. After this meeting the bishops formally petitioned Cardinal Gaetano De Lai, prefect of the Sacred Consistorial Congregation, to raise Des Moines to the rank of a See city and include in its jurisdiction the counties of Harrison, Shelby, Audubon, Guthrie, Dallas, Polk, Pottawattamie, Cass, Adair, Madison, Warren, Mills, Montgomery, Adams, Union, Clark, Lucas, Fremont, Page, Taylor, Ringgold, Decatur, and Wayne. They appended a map of Iowa to explain this to Roman authorities.

Of Davenport's demands for the lower tier of Dubuque, Davis was willing to settle for only one: Clinton County—a territory that included five churches and schools.[27] Falconio wrote back quickly, returning the petition and asking for additional details: the Catholic population of the proposed diocese, the church to be used as a cathedral, the proposed episcopal residence, information about debts on either structure, and the amount to be considered for the *cathedraticum*—or the tax on parishes for the support of the new diocese.[28] St. Ambrose Church would of course be the cathedral; the rest of the information was provided by Davis and Flavin, the dean.

With this information in hand, Falconio then sent off the formal petition to Rome sometime in June 1911.[29] On August 6, 1911, the pope formally ratified the recommendation of the Consistorial Congregation and approved the formation of the new diocese. On August 14, 1911, Cardinal De Lai informed Falconio that the petition had been accepted and that the bulls of erection would be issued.[30] On August 31, 1911, Falconio informed Davis of the decision of Rome and directed him to pay the taxes for the bulls that were the official documents of the transition. At the same time, Bishop James J. Keane, formerly of Cheyenne (and who had been opposed to the multiplication of dioceses), was transferred to Dubuque, where he now had a new member of his metropolitan province.[31] The thirteen priests of Clinton County entered a protest against their transfer to Davenport—to no avail.[32] By November, the bulls had arrived and the formal announcement of the diocese could be made. Davis was appointed administrator, but the diocese waited anxiously for its new bishop—who would be announced the following January.

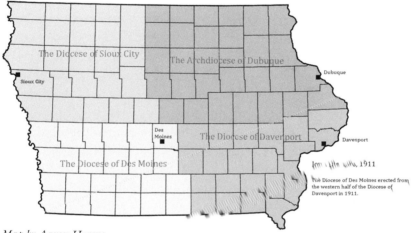

Map by Aaron Hyams

The New Diocese: Implications

What is the larger significance of the creation of a diocese? In the case of Des Moines, this halting and sometimes contentious process lays bare the complex network of dynamics that exists in Roman Catholic administration. While seemingly at odds with the spiritual priorities of the church, money was a crucial factor. The Diocese of Davenport had already developed a network of important institutions—schools, orphanages, and St. Ambrose College (University)—

which required large outlays of money to exist and serve the people. Losing the revenue from Des Moines and Council Bluffs with their growing Catholic populations was a blow.

The needs of southwest Iowa Catholics grew to a critical mass, however, and the ability of Davenport to manage and direct church affairs grew increasingly tenuous. Even with rail lines, the trip to the western part of the state was difficult. Local pride as well played a role. Critical to this process was the nudge given to church administrators by influential people in Des Moines and elsewhere. Few of them were Catholics, but all of them understood that a Catholic diocese conferred a status on the city that it felt, especially in this moment of its expansion, it needed and deserved. The presence of a diocese would be written into the booster materials that advertised the city to potential businesses and residents. Catholic churches and institutions contributed to the general welfare and upbuilding of the city.

Diocesan formation was to some degree like the creation of a new business in this part of the state. The new diocese would recruit more church personnel, manage the diverse ethnic realities of the community, build new churches, found new schools, and provide for social needs. The church would consume local goods and purchase land on which to build churches and schools. The prestige and stability of a diocese would enhance the ability of local Catholics to interact with the local community and to contribute to it. It also would add a new star to the constellation of community and regional leadership: a local bishop who would outrank and speak with more authority than any individual priest could. Although Des Moines bishops would be of quite diverse temperaments and approach issues confronting the church differently, they would be the most visible symbol of Catholic views and presence in this area.

The Diocese of Des Moines was created in a particularly interesting period in Catholic history. The formation of the diocese built on the actions and achievements of previous generations—so it was not created *ex nihilo*. But currents within church life were going to have an impact on Catholic developments. For example, the forces of Catholic associations would be felt. The Knights of Columbus, a fraternal/insurance organization founded in Connecticut in 1881, would find a receptive field in the diocese. Even though Des Moines itself would become a major insurance company center in the Midwest, the fraternal activities and public presence of the Knights, who combined their love of church with American patriotism, would be a force in diocesan life. The Knights would provide spiritual and financial support to many Des Moines activities and offer services to military men and women who were stationed in Iowa. Catholic women would find outlets for their creative energies not only in religious congregations but also in parish societies that helped with financial and social concerns.

Few Catholics related regularly with larger diocesan matters—lay participation being strongly regulated by clerical rule. But for most Catholics the church was their home parish. There, changes mandated by the Holy See would begin to transform their lives. Already in 1903, Pope Pius X's decree *Tra le Sollecitudine* called for the revival of Gregorian chant and encouraged more active participation of the faithful in praying at Mass. In 1905, the pontiff issued the *Sacra Tridentina Synodus,* which lowered the age of First Communion to the "age of reason" (considered to be seven years of age). It also urged frequent communion by the faithful—overcoming earlier patterns of receiving the Eucharist only on rare occasions. Both of these decrees and papal calls for "Catholic Action" to bring Christ into the "marketplace" would have a profound effect on Catholic laity and the condition of the church in the Diocese of Des Moines.

The leader in implementing these and other church directives would be the local bishop. For many years, "outsiders" would be called in to rule over the Diocese of Des Moines. The first of the bishops, Austin Dowling, came from the farthest part of the country to a land of "green pastures."

3

"In a Place of Pasture He Hath Settled Me"

Austin Dowling and a New Diocese

May 1912 was a tempestuous time for America and the world. The great ocean liner *Titanic* had sunk only a month before, killing thousands of passengers—including an English Catholic priest, Father Thomas Byles. Former President Theodore Roosevelt was struggling to wrest the Republican presidential nomination from the incumbent, his former friend, William Howard Taft. Beryl F. Carroll, a local hero for rescuing important documents in a fire, was in his last year as Iowa's governor. At the same time, probes were underway on the conditions of child labor in Iowa's mining camps.

Amid all this, on May 12, 1912, the Rock Island train chugged into Des Moines carrying the newly consecrated Austin Dowling and an entourage of clerical friends from his home diocese of Providence, Rhode Island.[1] The train had earlier stopped in Davenport, where Archbishop James John "Hickory" Keane of Dubuque; Bishop Peter Muldoon of Rockford, Illinois; Bishop Philip Garrigan of Sioux City; and Bishop James O'Reilly of Fargo, North Dakota, boarded. When the train entered the Des Moines station, the crowd went up in cheers.

The religious significance of this event was evident to any practicing Catholic.[2] Welcoming Dowling were some of Des Moines's most influential citizens and representatives of the state legislature.

73

DOWLING CREATED HEAD OF DIOCESE

Induction Into High Office Marked by Impressive Ceremonies.

Headline of Bishop Dowling installation. Credit: Des Moines Public Library.

These included L. H. Kurtz, the hardware store merchant who had so strongly urged the creation of the new diocese; R. O. Brennan, a well-known local attorney; and Republican state Senator John B. Sullivan, a Catholic from Des Moines.

The new bishop emerged from the train car and "doffed his soft hat and bowed gracefully and smilingly right and left." A clipping from the Catholic newspaper *Western World* reported: "Bishop Dowling is a man of rather less than medium height [he was 5'5" tall] and of dark complexion. Perhaps the most striking outward characteristics noted by those who see him for the first time are the amiable or benevolent expression of his countenance, the brilliancy of his dark eyes, his alert glance and the intellectual power indicated by his broad forehead and massive head." The paper also mentioned "the modesty and unobtrusiveness of his general demeanor."[3]

The streets of Des Moines were alive with Catholic pride. A huge parade assembled to escort him to the newly designated St. Ambrose Cathedral. Two hundred men from the Ancient Order of Hibernians (a fraternal organization for Irish Catholic men), 150 from the city's Italian organizations, 350 Knights of Columbus (thirty alone in the full regalia: capes of fourth-degree members, plumed hats, capes, and swords) accompanied him as he processed toward St. Ambrose, where a standing-room-only crowd strained to see him.

Keane noted that bishops of the province "listened some time ago to the long and earnest prayer of Des Moines for the establishment of a new See in southwestern Iowa. . . . I am glad that the metropolitan city of Iowa, the capital of this great state has been so favored. I am glad that the church has taken a more secure position here by the halls of legislation."[4]

Monsignor Michael Flavin, who for years had opposed the creation of the diocese, now took the podium to herald the civic implications of Dowling's appointment and its meaning for the burgeoning city of Des Moines. He more than any other speaker appreciated the significance of the moment and announced a "new era in the history of the Catholic church in the state of Iowa." He lauded the can-do ethos of Des Moines: "Des Moines, the capital of this great state is a progressive and prosperous city and will . . . benefit by your residence here. Our motto is 'Des Moines does things' but one of the best things that Des Moines has done for many years or rather that has been done to promote the growth and prosperity of the city is the establishment of an episcopal See here, marking this city for the future [as] the very center of Catholic activity."

Flavin noted proudly the social impact of the Catholic Church over which he had presided since he first came to St. Ambrose in 1884: "Through its energy and activity and influence [the church] will grow up gradually institutions of education, charity, and benevolence that will advertise this city most favorably and secure many to come and dwell in it."[5] The next day he began helping the new bishop find a suitable dwelling.

A Bishop for Des Moines:
Spiritual and Secular Considerations

Why was the advent of a Catholic bishop important? For Catholics, he was the local leader of their faith and their linkage to the universal church. The devout regarded him as a "successor to the apostles"—carrying on the ministry entrusted by Jesus Christ himself to the twelve apostles. This office evolved in the long history of Christianity to a position of unique theological significance: the bishop was the source of spiritual authority, the presider over the most significant rites of Catholicism, and the chief teacher of the people entrusted to his care.

In fact, the chair or *sede* in his cathedral was the symbol of his teaching authority. He was garbed with medieval attire—a miter (a pointed hat) and a crosier (a shepherd's crook)—and wore a ring symbolic of his authority. The faithful kissed that ring with a genuflection to indicate their deference to his person and his office. Des Moines bishops differed in their personalities and their understanding of the requirements of their office. But they were a force to be reckoned with, especially by clergy and religious, but also by the laity and the wider community.

The bishop was also a temporal leader. He had significant managerial and often legal responsibilities over large numbers of "employees," land, and civic affairs. Although he did not actually own church properties, he had a say in how they were acquired, maintained, staffed, and sold. He did not have the key to every parish church, school, convent, or diocesan social welfare agency, but his decisions affected them directly. His most direct authority over people extended to the priests of his diocese, who had vowed to him obedience and respect. He could move them, reward them, punish them, and order them about. He could even remove them from ministry if the reasons were grave enough.

Over women religious and priests and brothers of religious orders, he had a more indirect sway. Each of these groups had its own rules and superiors to whom they were primarily accountable. But a bishop could also affect the internal dimensions of the institutions run by these communities. Over laypersons, he had extensive spiritual authority. He could make rules for the proper observance of their religious duties and assign them priests and religious to tend to their needs. His power over them was, however, primarily suasive, not coercive. Religion in America was a voluntaristic enterprise. People were, nonetheless, disposed to support, help, and assist the church.

The local bishop had many other responsibilities. He was ultimately responsible for the financial affairs of the diocese—and even those of individual parishes (although those financial obligations fell mostly on the local pastor). He was the chief representative for Catholic affairs when they intersected with wider secular interests. He was the final authority in any kind of legal or corporate organization. Depending on his personality, he was an important bridge to other people of his rank in society and at times could be a civic leader.

In short, the powers and duties of the bishop were akin to (and perhaps even exceeded) that of a local businessman or even government leader. Although the public sphere acknowledged his spiritual leadership, few compared with his sway of authority over people and money to other corporate and government leaders. Yet there were many similarities. Des Moines's bishops enjoyed all of these prerogatives. Some used them in a very modest way and kept closely to a church sphere. Others actively engaged local civic and regional issues.

Dowling entered Des Moines at a propitious moment. During his tenure, from 1912 to 1919, the city population would swell from 86,000 to 126,000. The general status of Catholics in the twenty-three counties was still small. As this chart indicates, the percentage of Catholics when measured against the total population of the twenty-three counties was a paltry 5 percent, but under Dowling they would be a meaningful part of life in this part of Iowa.

County	1910	1920
Mills	15,811	15,422
Montgomery	16,604	17,048
Adair	14,420	14,259
Union	16,616	17,268
Clarke	10,736	10,506
Lucas	13,462	15,686
Harrison	23,162	24,488
Shelby	16,552	16,065
Audubon	12,671	12,520
Guthrie	17,374	17,596
Dallas	23,628	25,120
Polk	110,438	154,029
Pottawattamie	55,832	61,550
Cass	19,047	19,421
Madison	15,621	15,020
Warren	18,194	18,047
Taylor	16,312	15,514
Page	24,002	24,137
Adams	10,998	10,521
Fremont	15,623	15,447
Ringgold	12,904	12,919
Decatur	16,347	16,566
Wayne	16,184	15,378
TOTAL Population	512,538	564,527
Catholic total	25,000	36,370
% Catholics	5%	6%

Source: US Census and Official Catholic Directories

Dowling the Man

The Eastern-bred Dowling was not a native of Iowa or even the Midwest. Until a trip to Omaha a few years earlier, he had never been west of the Mississippi River. Of his early years, we know little except what can be gleaned from an adoring mini-biography written by his sister, M. Antonine Dowling, a Sister of Mercy in Providence, Rhode Island.[6] He was born Daniel Austin Dowling in New York on April 6, 1868, one of four children and the only son of Daniel and Mary Santry Dowling. His father was a native of Kilkenny, Ireland, and his mother was from London. Mary Santry Dowling, according to her daughter, "possessed a great love of books and was blessed with a retentive memory." She read to her children and introduced them to the joys of reading—including Bible history and lives of the saints, "particularly St. Augustine and St. Francis de Sales."[7]

When Daniel Austin was three, the family moved to Newport, Rhode Island. Here he attended an academy run by the Sisters of Mercy. At a time when First Communion was deferred to adolescence, young Austin made his at the age of ten. An early interest in the priesthood was stoked by the sisters of his school and his parish priest. The Dowlings attended Newport's only Catholic Church, St. Mary's (where many years later John F. Kennedy married Jacqueline Bouvier). The parish had a long and storied history, but the dominant figure at the parish was its longtime pastor (1868–1898), Father Philip Grace, known as the "Doctor." Grace cleared away older debts, added to the parish property, and had the joy of seeing his debt-free church solemnly consecrated on August 15, 1884, with young Dowling no doubt in attendance.

In 1884 Dowling continued his education at Manhattan College, run by the Christian Brothers. Located at 130th and Broadway in Manhattan, Austin boarded at the school. It was already a New York institution of note, having opened in 1853 when five LaSalle Christian Brothers moved to a small school on Canal Street to the section of New York City called Manhattanville. College-level courses (today what we would call high school) were added in 1859. In 1861, this part of the school called itself "Manhattan College." As its course catalogue put it, Manhattan College combined the "advantages of a first-class college and Polytechnic Institute." The college would produce a host of distinguished alumni over the years, including entertainers (e.g., Dennis Day), two mayors of New York (Hugh J. Grant and Rudolph Giuliani), and, in addition to Dowling, two future bishops (Patrick Hayes of New York and George William Mundelein of Chicago; both became cardinals).

Dowling chose the more academically demanding Classical Department and enhanced his facility with Greek and Latin. He graduated in June 1887 and was awarded the alumni gold medal for the best English essay and two special awards given to top students of the college: the Quinn gold medal for philosophy and the Develin gold medal for classics. Dowling always savored a love for the classics and continued pursuing this interest in Des Moines, occasionally dining with professors from Drake University who taught in this field.

In 1887, he entered St. John's Seminary in Brighton, Massachusetts. Designed by Maginnis and Walsh (who would design some prominent Des Moines churches), St. John's was "of Norman chateau style with towered corners" and "it stood out like a medieval castle" from its Brighton location.[8] Here, Dowling came into contact with the redoubtable Father John J. Hogan, SS, one of the most accomplished scholars of the Society of St. Sulpice who were the seminary professors.[9] The Society of St. Sulpice, a community founded in the seventeenth century, consisted of diocesan priests released for service by their bishops to serve as seminary educators. Hogan, who had taught in the Society's seminary in Paris for many years, was known as the "Abbe" and was particularly concerned that Boston seminarians be well educated, especially in Sacred Scripture and church history.

Hogan favored greater cultural adaptation to American realities: separation of church and state, freedom of the press, religious toleration, and the like. Dowling himself later eulogized Hogan at a memorial Mass after his death in 1901: "Father Hogan had the rare gift of filling the student's mind with the unrest of inquiry." Reflecting on an experience he likely had with the Abbe, he noted: "From the moment that, primed with pride of success at college, still odorous with bouquets of commencement, still delighted with the vigorous applause of our friends, we crossed his path to find our degrees discounted, our judgments questioned, our definitions qualified, and all our prestige gone . . . we rarely left him without feeling the ambition and obligation of looking up some question further."

Dowling also recalled, "He was forever whetting our appetite for knowledge. . . . It was his business to set us thinking. . . . Often he would seem to go to the very limit of daring in the vigor with which he plied us with objections, annihilated our arguments, and then walked off without vouchsafing an answer to our difficulties."[10] His admiration for his teacher and mentor was deep: Hogan "did not think that truth had anything to fear from investigation."[11]

The feeder for the Boston seminary system was the Jesuit-operated Boston College, which regularly sent a cohort of young men to St. John's seminary. After entering, the men studied an additional six years—two years of philosophy and four of theology—until they were admitted to the priesthood.[12] Unlike other American seminaries, St. John's students were allowed to read newspapers and other current periodicals.

Two years into the seminary course, Austin became ill just prior to his ordination to subdiaconate, then a step into what were called "major orders." Illness of this sort was often the death-blow to a priestly vocation. Dowling was also underage for ordination (he was not yet twenty-five). Nonetheless, his bishop, Matthew Harkins, allowed Dowling to pursue priestly studies at the recently founded Catholic University of America. Only a year before, Abbe Hogan himself had been sent to head up the new Divinity College of the Catholic University of America, where he presided as superior and spiritual director over a strict seminary-like regime of young priests who resided at Caldwell Hall.

At Catholic University, Dowling became closely attached to John J. "Sugar" Keane, the first rector of the university and later archbishop of Dubuque. As we have noted, Keane was one of those who helped create the Diocese of Des Moines. Dowling worked in church history with another future bishop and later president of Catholic University of America, Thomas J. Shahan.

Bishop Matthew Harkins of Providence ordained Dowling on June 24, 1891, together with John F. Sullivan, Peter Malone, and Edward Colgan, in what was the first ordination in the new cathedral of Ss. Peter and Paul in Providence. Dowling would later become rector of this magnificent church. After his ordination, he returned to Catholic University to earn a licentiate in sacred theology, but his deepest love was for history. As his first biographer, Father Marvin O'Connell, noted, he was "a man who was by taste, habit, and profession an historian; he could not set about finding solutions to problems facing him until he examined those problems in the light of the past."[13]

After priestly ordination, Dowling served briefly as a curate under Father John Hart at Sacred Heart Parish in East Providence. Sacred Heart was just thirteen years old when Dowling arrived and had two missions, one at Rumford and another at Riverside. His parish experience lasted briefly. In 1893, Hogan's successor, Father Charles Rex, invited Dowling to return to St. John's Seminary to teach church history, which he did until called back to his diocese in February 1896.[14] Dowling's years on the faculty afforded him time to read, prepare lectures and sermons, and otherwise intellectually prepare himself for a life of learning.[15]

In 1896, Bishop Harkins appointed him editor of the *Providence Visitor*, where his writing was characterized by "clearness of style, depth of thought, and a dash of humor that easily charmed the reader and endeared him to men of letters."[16] Dowling's writings in the *Visitor* were often instructive, and he loved to dwell on historical themes and topics, demonstrating a commanding knowledge of the history of the United States.

He was withdrawn from the *Visitor* in 1898 to begin work on a history of the Diocese of Providence. This was actually a contribution to a compendium of histories written about four dioceses in New England, edited by Father William Byrne, DD, and published by the Hurd and Everts Company of Boston.[17] Dowling's piece on Providence was a skillfully written essay of the historical development of the diocese and brief sketches of each of the parishes.

In 1899, he was sent as an assistant to St. Joseph's Parish in Providence, where he served until 1902, when he was once again stricken with illness. Going abroad to recover, he spent time in England and then six months at Fribourg, Switzerland, where he learned German. Dowling was happy in the German-speaking areas of Europe. He would later declare in a speech promoting Catholic patriotism: "I yield to no man in my love and admiration of the German people. I know them in their homes as my friends. I know them in their literature as my masters."[18]

In 1904 he returned to Rhode Island and was eventually assigned to the pastorate of St. Mary's in Warren, an old whaling town that had reinvented itself as a center for textile manufacturing. Dowling's sister, Mary Antonine, noted that Warren was a poor place with lots of working-class Portuguese and Polish immigrants, but she somewhat defensively observed of her brother's commitment in his one year in the parish, "Warren was never a stepping stone to him. It was his home and he was father of his flock."[19]

Despite Sister Antonine's comment about "stepping stones," it seemed to many that the erudite and kindly Dowling was moving up the ecclesiastical ladder: meriting plum assignments, very little sustained parish work or teaching, and rather amazing European travel for a person of his time and social class. In 1905 he was transferred to the Cathedral of Ss. Peter and Paul. This large Romanesque structure, begun in 1878, was not completed until 1889. It was the backdrop for Dowling's longest period of parish activity. In addition to the run of pastoral work, he added a new system of lighting, erected a distinctive baptistery near the entrance of the church, and installed a chancel organ. Here too, he likely learned the administrative habits that would serve him well in Des Moines and St. Paul.

Going to Iowa

It was to the Providence cathedral that Apostolic Delegate Archbishop Diomede Falconio sent notice of Dowling's appointment to the new See of Des Moines in January 1912. The creation of the new diocese had not been on Dowling's radar when it took place the previous August—nor had anyone tipped him off, even indirectly, that his name was on the list of three (the *terna*) submitted to Rome. Hence when newspaper men descended on him for a comment, he admitted somewhat sheepishly: "Why, I do not know where Des Moines is on the map." (On further reflection, he recalled later that he had actually traveled through Iowa en route to a celebration in Omaha.) He had an easterner's view of the Midwest as a land filled with corn fields and livestock. He chose as his motto a verse adapted from Psalm 22, "In a Place of Pasture He Hath Settled Me" (*In Loco Pascuae Me Collocavit*). His selection likely may have been arranged by his former professor and Catholic University superior, Archbishop Keane, who a few years earlier had brought another of his Catholic University colleagues, Philip Garrigan, to found the Diocese of Sioux City.

Dowling was consecrated a bishop in the Providence Cathedral on April 25, 1912, with Matthew Harkins of Providence as his principal consecrator and James Davis of Davenport and one of his seminary professors, Bishop Louis Sebastian Walsh of Portland, Maine, as co-consecrators. He "took possession" of the new diocese in St. Ambrose Church on May 1, 1912.

In a diffident initial interview Dowling parried with a bemused *Des Moines Daily News* reporter who noted, "The bishop didn't want to be interviewed so he took refuge in trying to ask questions himself." He tried to joke with the reporter, at one point assuring him

Austin Dowling as bishop. Credit: Diocese of Des Moines Archives.

that he wasn't a vegetarian and didn't live in a tree. "I live my life as a priest. I have few fads. I am not especially an outdoors man though I like fresh air. I am not a vegetarian though I eat them when the notion suits me."

When the reporter managed to get through one serious question: "What do you think of women's suffrage?" Dowling stifled "the faintest beginning of a yawn. 'Suffrage is alright if the women want it, I suppose. It is not a vital issue. I cannot see any reason why the women shouldn't have it if they want it. But what do they want with it? Half of the men don't want to vote as it is." He concluded the interview, "I'm sorry I don't make more interesting material for a story."[20]

Pious, scholarly, erudite, Dowling's family background, Irish heritage, and priestly formation equipped him with the confidence and stamina for the work ahead. His unquestioning Catholic faith and his familiarity with Catholic institutions provided a blueprint to expand and develop the church in southwest Iowa. His goal was spiritual—to create a religious home for what he hoped would be a strong Catholic presence in this part of Iowa—but his actions also pressed the church to become a more engaged social and cultural institution in the region. He created parishes, searched for native-born priests, and built a major and still surviving Catholic secondary school, all of which created a positive place for the church in Des Moines and contributed substantially to the ongoing improvement of Des Moines's social and cultural development. Dowling also sought friends in the city's civic elites, spent engaging evenings with professors from Drake University, and cajoled generous local citizens and others to contribute to his causes.

Dowling was, above all, aware of the minority status of the church. In a retrospective on his years in Des Moines, Dowling wrote of the challenges facing him, especially the strong Protestant presence, which made difficult the prospect of "making converts from heresy to the true faith" because of "the prejudice and ignorance of the Protestant farmer who is frequently a Lutheran from Denmark or Sweden, or who, when he is of American origin reads anti-Catholic papers like the *Menace* [the anti-Catholic paper of the American Protective Association]."[21]

Indeed, anti-Catholicism seemed to flourish in rural areas. "There are schools everywhere, but people are not educated. They are very readily aroused by slanders and charges against the church. Though many of the non-Catholics do not go to church, they are still in sympathy with Protestant prejudices. When they are not bigoted, they are liberal." He noted, "The church in the United States is strong in cities but weak in rural districts. Yet it is rural districts that have preponderating influence in the various legislatures of the Country and as the Church is poorly represented in them, there are frequently laws passed that are inimical to the interests of the Church and are not representative of the feelings of the majority of people."[22]

Unwilling to accept second-rate status for Catholics in the heavily Protestant and rural counties, he urged his priests and laity to "push back" against the traditional hegemony enjoyed by Methodists and Baptists in some areas. Dowling was first and foremost a bishop. But he was also a city builder, a financier, and a public presence of prominence not only in Des Moines but all over the southwestern counties of the state.

Bringing New Internal Order to the Church

Dowling lived in temporary quarters for two weeks until he bought a Queen Anne–style house at 2000 Grand Avenue in Des Moines. This acquisition was no doubt aided by Flavin, but the proceeds to purchase came out of Dowling's pocket and the home was titled in his name. He furnished the house with his own possessions from Providence. This house, which still stands, was built in 1881 for Jefferson A. Polk, a Kentucky-born lawyer and railroad entrepreneur who owned the Des Moines Railway Company. Polk was a major contributor to the prosperity of Des Moines through his creation of interurban railways, which stretched from Des Moines to Fort Dodge in Webster County. Polk died in 1907, and when his heirs sold the rambling old mansion to the new diocese (likely at a reduced price) they added the proviso that it remain in the hands of the Catholic Church for twenty-five years.

Set on five acres, the house had fourteen rooms and hardwood floors. It was known as Herndon Hall—named after the family of Polk's wife Julia. This structure would be the center of diocesan administration up to the era of Bishop Gerald Bergan (1934–1948). It was within walking distance of St. Joseph Academy, the central high school for all Catholic girls run by the BVM sisters. Dowling loved the girls' academy, which was close to his home on Grand Avenue. He frequently walked to visit the school to chat with the sisters and students.

Adding to the Catholic Infrastructure

As we have seen, Dowling inherited a fairly decent Catholic infrastructure, built up over the years when southwest Iowa was under the jurisdiction of either Dubuque or Davenport. The new See had sixty-five priests, fifty-four parishes, sixteen Catholic schools, and roughly twenty-five thousand Catholics. There were only three priests from religious orders (the Benedictines of Atchison) and a little more than 1,500 students in Catholic schools. Many parishes still had missions attached, meaning travel for the padres who ran them. The bulk of Catholics lived in the cities of Des Moines and Council Bluffs.

Catholic Space in Des Moines, IA, 1919

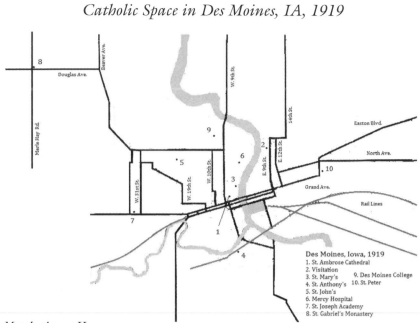

Des Moines, Iowa, 1919
1. St. Ambrose Cathedral
2. Visitation
3. St. Mary's   9. Des Moines College
4. St. Anthony's   10. St. Peter
5. St. John's
6. Mercy Hospital
7. St. Joseph Academy
8. St. Gabriel's Monastery

Map by Aaron Hyams

Catholic Space in Council Bluffs, IA, 1919

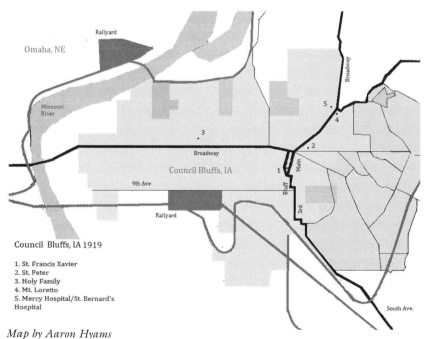

Council Bluffs, IA 1919

1. St. Francis Xavier
2. St. Peter
3. Holy Family
4. Mt. Loretto
5. Mercy Hospital/St. Bernard's
Hospital

Map by Aaron Hyams

Nevertheless, railroad communities (often also the county seats) had respectable populations. Elementary education was a priority for parishes that could afford it; St. Joseph's Academy for girls in Des Moines enrolled about 150 students annually. Council Bluffs had a formation house for the Sisters of Mercy, and St. Francis Xavier Parish had an academy for girls.

By the time Dowling departed for the See of St. Paul in 1919, the number of priests had risen to seventy-five (some from Ireland), and additional religious order priests (Passionists) had also come to help. The number of Catholics had surged as well, rising to thirty-five thousand. In comparison with the other dioceses of Iowa, however, Des Moines was still the junior See of the state.[23] The number of parishes was growly slowly—only fifty-seven by 1919—and the number of missions rose to thirty-one. Dowling's single most important legacy was the founding of a Catholic secondary school for boys.

Creating a New School

From the outset Dowling planned a secondary school for Catholic men. This was part of a larger trend among US Catholic dioceses to amalgamate small existing high schools (such as the one at St. John's Basilica) into larger, high-profile secondary schools. This institution, first known as Des Moines Catholic College—later Dowling High School—was and is one of the most important Catholic institutions in the city of Des Moines. Its immediate purpose was to recruit local young men for the priesthood.

The diocese began with a healthy contingent of priests, many recruited by the bishops of Davenport from Ireland. Dowling recalled, "There have been few vocations to the priesthood in the diocese and the candidates who have been ordained in the last few years have come for the most part either from Ireland or from the largest cities of the East where Catholics are numerous." He noted sadly, "They are sent when young into [the] country towns where sometimes the priest is the only Catholic resident and where they readily become discouraged."[24]

Dowling had already sent one of his friends, Irish-born Father James Troy, to Ireland to recruit priests. But urged by the apostolic delegate and others, he was pressed to find priests from among the people of Iowa. The need to raise up native vocations had no doubt been impressed on Dowling when he was appointed, and he likely needed no prodding as he himself was the product of a domestic seminary. He ordained three men to the priesthood in his first years: one native of Iowa, Francis Ostdiek, and two other priests from Ireland. (Ostdiek in later correspondence with Dowling often referred to himself as "the first born.") Providing a school that would encourage priestly vocations was critical.

The Founding of Des Moines Catholic College

By 1911, Des Moines already had two public high schools (East and West). A third, Theodore Roosevelt, would open in 1923. Just before Dowling's arrival, St. John's Parish in Des Moines had begun a high school program in its building.

In 1914, Dowling began planning and fund-raising for a new post-elementary school for the diocese: "In order to develop vocations and to increase the interest of the diocesan priests in educational matters. . . . The college [academy] is the hope of the future, first by providing vocations to the priesthood, next by educating Catholic laymen to understand and proclaim Catholic principles."[25] In 1917 he finally launched a $250,000 general fund drive throughout the diocese for the new school. This was an act of faith, because the Catholic population of Des Moines was relatively small and the wages of most Catholics were probably paltry.

Monsignor Luigi Ligutti, one of the original staff of the new college, recalled in 1970: "I remember that the year I was ordained [1917] Bishop Dowling was running all over the diocese trying to raise money to buy the old Baptist College."[26] The results were astounding. Dowling personally solicited much of the money, and received a huge sum from the priests, "who themselves first gave large sums to the Bishop and then helped him to collect in various parishes of the diocese, so that through donations, collections, and legacies the Diocesan College received over a year a sum of money not far short of $225,000."[27]

The nature of this was very personal. As he explained to his successor Bishop Drumm: "As I collected them and solicited them and managed them, I kept them in my hands."[28] Some of the fund-raising was uniquely Catholic and might be considered simonaical today.[29] One particularly unique source was "endowed Masses." Those who gave the princely sum of $1,000 were considered "Founders" and were promised two Masses every week in perpetuity for their intentions.[30] In a move that would have made the Baptist pioneers in that building turn over in their graves, Dowling in effect "sold" grace.[31]

Dowling set his sights on an old Northern Baptist College on Ninth Street and College. It had been founded in 1866 but moved to this site in 1884. This college had always struggled but died in 1916. In July 1917, Dowling bought the property for $170,000 (roughly $1.5 million in today's money) and took possession of the cluster of buildings in 1918—locating the first classrooms in a structure built in 1884 and later named Flavin Hall. Dowling even took a hand in preparing the building for its first students—even to cleaning out a particularly filthy lavatory in one of the buildings (he was rescued from this task by faculty members Luigi Ligutti and John Boylan, who were also working to shape up the building).[32]

Flavin Hall at Des Moines Catholic College.
Credit: Diocese of Des Moines Archives.

Charming the Benefactors

Dowling's personal charm and sincere appeal managed to raise large sums from the priests and also from generous benefactors for whom he named the halls. In March 1918, he wrote to one of his priests in studies, "I am busy trying to get funds—beating the air a bit, but also raising some cash. We've taken in so far $9,300 plus. . . . I shall have to get $55,000 more by that time to pay cash for it."[33] This involved cultivating moneyed people.

One such family was that of William Coolbaugh. Born in 1821, Coolbaugh hailed from Pennsylvania and began his life working on a farm. In 1842 he moved to Burlington, Iowa, where he began a general store, which was quite successful. He amassed a substantial fortune and became active in the wholesale grocery business. He then became a banker under the name of Coolbaugh and Brooks, located in Burlington. In May 1862 he moved his family to Chicago, where he opened a banking office. Coolbaugh had four children and died in 1877.

Two of his daughters, Wilhelmine Coolbaugh and her sister Adelaide Coolbaugh Brown, donated $5,000 toward the project and altogether gave $12,000. Dowling corresponded often with both Wilhelmine and Adelaide Coolbaugh who lived in Santa Barbara, California, at the time of their donation.[34] "Miss Coolbaugh is a woman in middle age," he wrote, "rather sickly but very devout. She gave this money, the two thousand I mean, without the knowledge of her sister."[35]

A conscientious fund-raiser, Dowling urged his successor to pay attention to the hypersensitive Coolbaugh sisters: "You should cultivate Mrs. A. C. Brown and Miss Wilhelmine Coolbaugh. They are willing to continue their gifts if noticed. I met them only twice, but I wrote them frequently. Don't trust [this] to the College. Nobody there would say thank you if you gave the college $10,000. These ladies are not rich but they are interested in Des Moines. . . . You must attend to this yourself if you wish to keep up what they have begun."[36]

Another friend of Dowling, William Shaw, generously donated $40,000, which, combined with the donations from clergy and laity, made possible the purchase of the buildings. Shaw had been born near Farrar, Iowa, in 1872 and, with his brother John, became a prosperous farmer. Shaw died in 1915 in Albuquerque but left substantial funds to Des Moines Catholic causes on which Dowling could draw once he got the school project underway.[37] Finally, the redoubtable and very wealthy Monsignor Michael Flavin, who had "presided" over the Des Moines clergy, donated the huge sum of $100,000. A building was named for him after his death in 1926.

The School Is Launched

Dowling was as diligent in recruiting a competent faculty as in fund-raising. One of his protégés, Luigi Ligutti, was given special training. "Latin will be your branch," Dowling wrote to Ligutti. "I wish you . . . to address yourself to the study of Latin as thoroughly as may be."[38] As the date of the college's opening drew near, Dowling realized that his faculty would have to be flexible. "As to your work, it is extremely difficult for us to plan it with necessary definiteness. . . . You are to be one of our pioneers and in a psychological way *paratus ad omnia* [ready for anything]."

Dowling worried about the number and quality of students and the big risk he had taken in beginning with all four years of high school when he insisted on closing a boys' school that Father Mulvihill had already opened at St. John's.[39] The college opened in September 1918 with Father George Toher as the first president. It was originally called Des Moines Catholic College. About eighty students enrolled in this first year.

In the first graduating class of Des Moines College in 1919 were young men who would become bankers, a physician, attorneys, a dentist, an engineer, a farmer, a district court judge, and two priests. Indeed, many of Des Moines's priests would have their first training at the college, which would be renamed Dowling after the prelate's death in November 1930. Ligutti recalled: "I was the first registrar. I occupied a room just inside Coolbaugh Hall and registered the young men as they came in. . . . The first year enrollment for the schools was over 80. . . . We had boarders also in Shaw Hall." Ligutti recalled further: "Bishop Dowling took great interest in the school. He would come sit in on the classes and criticize the teachers afterwards if they needed to be criticized. On occasion, if one of

Early Des Moines College. Credit: State Historical Society of Iowa.

them were sick, Bishop Dowling would come and take the class."[40] In 1922, Father Daniel Mulvihill succeeded Toher, and a junior college program was opened. Father John Boylan succeeded Mulvihill.[41]

The creation of Des Moines Catholic College was the high point of Dowling's accomplishments in Des Moines. He viewed it as a specific asset not only to the Des Moines Catholic community but also to the city. When Bishop Gerald Bergan renamed the school in Dowling's honor, he noted the institution's civic impact: "He [Dowling] regarded it as one of Des Moines's great agencies for good, and he rejoiced in the thought he had thus been able to contribute materially to the welfare of his adopted city."[42] Founding Des Moines College also provided Dowling with important experience he was able to transfer to the Archdiocese of St. Paul, where he founded Nazareth Hall, a minor seminary.

Schools, especially Des Moines College, were Dowling's chief priority. Before he left the city in 1919, he summoned all of the children of the city's Catholic schools to the cathedral to bid them farewell: "It seems only yesterday since I first entered this Cathedral, though it is seven years. What a change in seven years. How it has changed you physically, mentally, spiritually. Seven years from now hardly any of you will be children. You will have become men and women living in your community and living in this diocese. . . . For this reason your parents and pastors have striven and labored in poverty and with difficulties to erect schools so that now right here in the city of Des Moines, we have not one or two, we have six schools."[43] Indeed, the schools began to educate generations of Des Moines children—and the college eventually became the source of a number of vocations to the priesthood and religious life.

Negotiating Space in the State Capitol

Catholic churches, as we have seen, played an important role in the shaping of Des Moines's urban space. The Catholic presence on Des Moines's East Side was limited to Visitation Parish, located at the southwest corner of East Tenth and Walnut. Although the original capitol buildings had been completed in 1886, another round of expansion was necessary in 1914. As with many state capitols, the state of Iowa could extend its power over local lands—a process that relied on providing a good price for the land and reciprocal goodwill on the part of the donor.

As noted earlier, Visitation Parish, pastored by the eloquent Father Joseph F. Nugent, had been founded when Nugent celebrated the first Mass on July 2, 1882, the feast of the Visitation in Hoberger's Hall on East Locust Street in Des Moines. A small frame church was constructed on Seventh and Court Avenue, and by early July Visitation had its first church at the East Tenth and Walnut site. One of Nugent's early parishioners, Luigi Ligutti, remembered that the pastor was a good friend of the populist-minded and Democratic presidential nominee William Jennings Bryan and, like the "Great Commoner," was a distinguished speaker and preacher. Ligutti also recalled that Nugent loved the psalms and invoked them regularly in his sermons. Nugent would later preach at the future priest Ligutti's first Mass.[44]

Visitation Parish was also part of a local contest for urban space when it stood in the path of expanding state capitol buildings. Bishop Dowling determined early on to make the decision to move the parish and accommodate the state capitol expansion. Sensitive to the significance of parish boundaries (and its fund-raising and duty-related matters), he wrote to Nugent: "I am putting before you the subject of dividing lines. My intention is to make a division of Visitation Parish that is the old parish should retain the majority of the families and of the purchase money. For the sake of discussion, I suggested that there should be a north-south parish, the north to be the division to receive $20,000, the south to be the Visitation Parish to receive $60,000. . . . This will give you something to dispute or allow on Friday morning when I hope to see you. If you have an alternative proposition bring it along and let us finish this thing then."[45]

The "new" Visitation was relocated to Ninth and Garfield, where a new church and school were erected. In 1924, Father (later Monsignor) Joseph M. Hanson, ordained in 1897, became pastor. He arrived at Visitation on a cold winter's day and later joked that his first task was convincing his parishioners he was not Swedish. He remained at Visitation for thirty-five years, dying in 1958 at the age of ninety-two.[46] In 1915, the movement of Catholics to the north side of Des Moines brought the foundation of St. Peter's Church, with the newly appointed pastor, George Toher, purchasing lots at East Eighteenth and Des Moines Streets where he built a combination church-school.[47]

Tending to the Spanish-Speaking in Council Bluffs

Accommodating and working with immigrants continued to be part of the church's mission in southwest Iowa. The next group requiring these services was Mexican Catholics fleeing north to escape the revolutionary turmoil that had engulfed their homeland since 1911. Pastoral care for the thousands of Spanish-speaking refugees had been assumed by the bishops of the United States and Catholic groups like the Knights of Columbus. While mostly huddled in the Southwest and California, a number of Mexicans went to the Midwest, and in 1917 members of the Catholic Woman's League in Council Bluffs discovered a colony of them living along a set of railroad tracks. With the help of a local pastor and the blessing of Bishop Dowling, a generous railroad executive donated a boxcar where they began weekly religious instructions for the children.

After four years, the same man who had lent the boxcar donated a small parcel of land, and St. Francis Xavier Church donated an old building. The building was disassembled and hauled to the site where a contractor reassembled it. Funds to underwrite this mission came from the Knights of Columbus, the Catholic Daughters of America, and the Ladies Auxiliary of the Ancient Order of Hibernians—with an especially generous benefaction from a Ms. Anne Mithen. The little chapel was dedicated in 1925 and tended to by the priests from St. Francis Xavier who celebrated Mass there weekly. Donations of church goods came from St. Francis and Holy Family churches. Pews were donated from Mercy Hospital and sacred vessels purchased by the Knights of Columbus. Over the altar hung an image of Our Lady of Guadalupe.[48] This chapel was still functioning in 1946.

Creating More Sacred Space: A Passionist Retreat

All churches and sanctuaries of the Catholic community were intended to be places of spiritual refreshment. In larger dioceses, however, orders of religious men or women often ran retreat centers or opened their chapels to visitors. The intent was to create a spiritual oasis where there would be silence and the opportunity for confession and prayer. Des Moines lacked this kind of facility until a very important religious community decided to make it home.

The Passionists (Congregation of the Passion) had been founded in Italy between 1720 and 1725. Their work consisted in giving spiritual renewals to Catholic parishes—revivals of sort—that would tone up the quality of Catholic faith. They lived lives of penance and austerity in monasteries called "retreats," from which they sent missionaries to visit parishes and other religious houses. Their presence was always welcomed. They had come to America in 1852, first settling in Pittsburgh, Pennsylvania, and later forming their first general headquarters in that city. By 1906 they had founded a "western province," headquartered in Chicago. These black-robed priests and brothers had a distinctive black-and-white badge and tried to live a self-sufficient life on their properties.

Once settled in Chicago, they accepted missions in various Iowa parishes. Their initial entrance into Des Moines was rocky. Bishop Dowling was first interested in them because they promised foreign-language priests who could help with ethnic Catholics, and in 1914 the bishop approved the entry of five members of the Passionist Order into Des Moines. As Dowling explained to his successor in 1920, it was, however, a case of "bait and switch." "They were very eager to come, but I was moved to permit them to come because they promised to send a priest who understood Italian and Slavic language and would be useful in the Mining Camps. I was to pay him $50 a month. When they came, they brought a broken, lifeless priest who had spent a few months in Italy but didn't know Italian and hated Italians and of course didn't know a word of any Slavic tongue. I offered them Highland Park, but they said it was against their rule to take parishes and on three occasions declined a parochial charge. They have not been of any great help to Des Moines though of course they were often good in an emergency help-out. They did not keep their contract with me though they expected me to pay $50 a month which I declined to do."[49]

Despite this rocky beginning, these pioneers under the leadership of Father Benedict of the Seven Dolors Hanley leased an eleven-room house at 1715 Ninth Street in Des Moines. Dowling granted permission for them to raise money to start their house. While they waited for furniture from Chicago, they lived with the Sisters of Mercy, who provided bed and board and also generously supplied free medical care for several of their ailing members. A Passionist-authored account of the first days of the community notes that a Brother Louis arrived from Chicago on March 19, 1915, and set up a chapel at the Ninth Street monastery, and on March 21, Passion

Passionist Monastery in Des Moines. Credit: State Historical Society of Iowa.

Sunday, the Passionists sang their first Mass with nearly eighty people in attendance and a choir from All Saints Church in Highland Park. Afterward, prayers and intercessions were offered for peace as Pope Benedict XV had instructed on that day to beg for an end to World War I (Peace Sunday). Within two weeks the new monastery was furnished, and a small community assembled.[50]

The Passionists then put down roots in Des Moines. Already in 1914, they purchased twenty-four acres northwest of Des Moines called Indian Lookout. Discovering later that this property sat on a deposit of coal and anticipating "future difficulties" (one of their other houses in Scranton had also had a bad experience as it too sat on coal land), they sold the property for $20,157. In 1915, the Western Province purchased fifty acres at Douglas Avenue and Fifty-Eighth Street. Later, Fifty-Eighth Street was renamed in honor of Merle Hay, one of the first three US World War I deaths.

The Passionists remodeled a hundred-by-forty-foot hut once owned by the Knights of Columbus from nearby Camp Dodge into a monastery and moved from their Ninth Street house by the end of November 1920. By 1922, the new Passionist Retreat was designed by the local firm of Boyd and Moore. On August 5, 1922, the feast of Our Lady of Snows, building began. The new monastery was named in honor of the recently canonized Passionist saint, Gabriel of Our Lady of Sorrows. The $122,000 building was dedicated by Bishop Thomas Drumm one year later on August 6, 1923.[51]

St. Gabriel's monastery was a place of peace and repose—as well as a religious tourist site in Des Moines. In 1929, Pope Pius XI urged laity to make retreats in his encyclical *Mens Nostra*, which added to the popularity of the practice. The Passionists offered retreats and a prayer center for locals, but, most important, it provided theological and spiritual formation for young Passionists in their final years of preparation for the priesthood. In 1936, the students were transferred from St. Gabriel's, and for twelve years St. Gabriel's was a training house for Passionist home missions. In 1948, the house welcomed students again, this time for their course of philosophy.

The Passionists were faithful help-out priests, willing to take parishes for priests who took long vacations or home visits abroad. Indeed, at one point Bishop Bergan (who often used the Passionist facilities for retreats and clergy conferences) scolded the local clergy, telling them "that the inmates of St. Gabriel's consider their principal work the giving of missions and retreats, etc., not merely to help with Sunday work."[52] Their grounds were a spiritual center for Des Moines residents, and the grotto the brothers built held a popular crèche that attracted crowds at Christmas. They also came for fresh eggs raised by the brood of chickens kept by one of the brothers. The grounds themselves were kept up by the groups of young men who came there for study and prayer. Bells rang ten times a day to summon the Passionists to prayer—the first hour at two o'clock in the morning. The brothers took care of their own needs from the revenues of their missionaries, operating a tailor shop, and the sale of eggs. At one report, one of the brothers raised three hundred chicks. Another brother made beautiful vestments, which "attracted the attention of the city's clergy."[53] For many years, Des Moines Catholics and others seeking a bit of refuge from the "world" would come to the monastery for prayer and reflection.

St. Gabriel's continued as a Des Moines institution until it was sold in 1956. Ironically, it had been sold because, as Passionist superior Father Ignatius Bechtold informed the press, it held "only" fifty men and they needed more space. A Chicago developer paid more than $550,000 for the land. Anticipating a change, the Passionists had already purchased 160 acres of land for a new monastery north of Grimes, Iowa.[54] The Passionists remained in the old building for a time until it was demolished, and a new shopping mall nearby was erected. After the old monastery closed, a contingent of Passionists remained in Des Moines in a residence on Sixty-Third Street. The Grimes foundation never developed, and in 1971 the Sixty-Third Street home was sold to a Raymond Hailer, a carpenter who converted the house chapel into a living room.[55]

The Travail of Mercy Hospital

The beginnings of Des Moines's Mercy Hospital in 1893 were auspicious—a good contingent of sisters, a parcel of available land, and a solid building augured well for the future of Catholic health care in the state capital. But there were problems. One set came from the local superior Sister Mary Xavier Malloy, whom the Mercy historian characterized as "quite a controversial character and the apparent source of many problems experienced by the Des Moines hospital in later years."[56] The hospital was under the direction of the Mercy superiors in Davenport, and this did not sit well with city physicians and the redoubtable Sister Xavier, who wanted more local control and hence separation from the motherhouse.

Sister Xavier had engaged in a noisy dispute with her superiors over the scope and expense of an 1897 expansion of the hospital and, when she was overruled, complained bitterly to local medical and commercial benefactors. Historian Kathleen O'Brien notes that local businessmen, like hardware merchant L. H. Kurtz, were not happy with the relative lack of autonomy the hospital had. Writing to Bishop Cosgrove of Davenport, he observed: "The city of Des Moines, as you well know, is a thriving go-ahead town, and the citizens of this community feel that the sooner independence is granted Mercy Hospital the better it will be for all concerned."[57]

Kurtz also suggested that Mercy Hospital might have Protestant rivals, and if it were not given autonomy local doctors would affiliate with them and leave Mercy in the lurch. O'Brien notes that the inspiration for this and other letters of warning was Sister Xavier, who had been unwilling to step down as local superior. Even after she was removed from office in 1901, Sister Xavier apparently stirred the pot by inducing local doctors and businesspeople to intercede for her. This perturbed Father Flavin of St. Ambrose, who wrote Cosgrove about Xavier's activities and related a discussion he had with the apostolic delegate regarding her removal.[58] Sister Xavier, however, managed to return to Des Moines in 1904 and all went smoothly until Des Moines became a diocese.

The erection of the new diocese activated a provision in the original 1894 charter that if Des Moines became a diocese, the hospital would be separated legally and canonically from the jurisdiction of Davenport. Bishop Dowling decided to pursue the issue, insisting that a religious community like the Sisters of Mercy should be under his jurisdiction and not that of either the bishop of Davenport or the Sisters of Mercy of Davenport. Moreover, Dowling had more than a passing knowledge of how Mercy sisters ought to live and the structures of their governance—thanks to his own sister who was herself a superior in the east. From the sisters' confessor, he received alarming reports of laxity in community observances, of scandalous freedom to come and go, and of a general lassitude concerning the observance of the essential elements of religious life.

Dowling became increasingly inquisitive about the state of internal discipline among the Des Moines sisters. By 1915, Dowling proposed to Bishop James Davis (who had replaced Bishop Cosgrove in 1904) that the local community be placed under his (Dowling's) direct jurisdiction or that Mercy Hospital cease to consider itself a Catholic institution. A separation would allow him and his delegates to establish a clear chain of command among the Des Moines sisters—who rarely if ever heard from or met their Davenport superiors.

Meetings with Bishop Davis and Mother Aloysia, the Davenport superior, and Dowling were to no avail. On April 25, 1915, Dowling intended to separate the two communities by fiat. When the sisters appealed to the apostolic delegate, Archbishop John Bonzano, protesting Dowling's move, Dowling informed Bonzano that he was taking this step because the sisters were living a far too lax life and that order needed to be restored. In the end, the separation was granted, and the Davenport sisters working at the hospital were withdrawn—except Sister Xavier and Sister M. Anthony Reilly.

Bitter negotiations over finances ensued once the separation began. Dowling offered them $50,000 for the "divorce" from Davenport. By November 1916, the matter was finalized, and until 1922 the hospital was independent, receiving various Mercy sisters from other places to help staff the hospital. Dowling spent a lot of time micromanaging the internal affairs of the sisters, corresponding occasionally with the apostolic delegate about such matters as the length of a novitiate and also financial issues related to the sisters' indebtedness.[59] Dowling had intimated to the apostolic delegate that he wanted to merge the Des Moines community with the more stable group of sisters in Council Bluffs and even reported that this was an accomplished fact in a report to Rome in 1919.[60] The sisters in Council Bluffs, however, were not eager to take on the hospital because of its debt, so the matter lapsed.

Dowling departed from Des Moines in 1919, leaving the task of reorganizing the community to his successor, Thomas W. Drumm. On January 31, 1922, the Des Moines sisters voted to amalgamate with Council Bluffs, and this became effective on June 4, 1922. Conditions at the hospital had deteriorated, but the plant was in good shape and the number of admissions steady. Sister (now Mother) Xavier continued to be a problem for the local sisters and for Bishop Drumm, whose relations with the forceful Mother Xavier were not always pleasant. She still felt miffed by the alignment of the hospital with Council Bluffs and placed obstacles in the path of amalgamation. Drumm grew increasingly angry with her obstruction of his efforts to straighten out the affairs of the hospital and the sisters, but in the end he prevailed. After the affair was over, Mercy would survive and prosper, becoming a health-care giant in Des Moines.

The First World War

The Great War took its toll on Iowa. Camp Dodge, a short distance northwest of Des Moines was a major training facility for inductees. Over 500,000 Iowans registered for the draft, and 115,000 actually served in the military, among them many Catholic young men who volunteered for service. Only two Catholic priests from Des Moines served as military chaplains: Fathers Patrick McDermott and James A. Troy. McDermott, a native of Ireland, had been ordained in 1908 and was serving as pastor of St. Patrick's Church in Massena. McDermott was an ardent patriot, writing later: "As a boy in Ireland I merely existed, but when I first sited the skyscrapers of New York I began to live and was so excited to be a part of this great country that within five days after landing I had my first citizenship papers."[61]

He volunteered for service in 1917 and served first as chaplain to nearby Fort Dodge, where he teamed with the Knights of Columbus to stage a weekly boxing show. Here he also became friends with other chaplains, including a Baptist minister who later became an organizer for the Ku Klux Klan.[62] McDermott joined the American Expeditionary Force with the Third Battalion of the Ninetieth Division, conducting services for the famous "Lost Battalion" at the bloody battle of the Argonne. Discharged in 1919, he was a chaplain to the American Legion and the Iowa National Guard and was eventually assigned to Ss. Peter and Paul Church in Atlantic, Iowa, in 1920 where he served until his death in 1963.[63]

The other chaplain was James A. Troy. Troy was born in Listowel, Ireland, July 29, 1883. He completed his theological studies at Carlow College, and the bishop of Kildare ordained him on June 9, 1907. He came to the United States in 1908 and was admitted to the Diocese of Davenport.[64] He served in parishes in Farmington, Winterset, and Lenox. At Lenox he left behind beautiful stained-glass windows in a magnificent, sturdy brick church before going into the chaplain corps of the US Army in 1917 when the United States entered World War I. Troy was something of a tortured genius. His brother was a priest of Davenport, and Troy himself had worked in the Davenport diocese for a time as a kind of missionary to Lee and Davis Counties. He toyed with the idea of joining the Graymoor Friars in order to preach missions, but he disliked community life and wanted to offer a type of mission that blended good singing, Carthusian penitential practices, and his own florid rhetoric.[65] Later, after the war, he would have a chance to put some of those plans into action.

In the army he had an exciting career, traveling with the troops and working to see that their spiritual and material needs were met. He remained in Europe until 1921, in the end serving the American occupation force at Coblenz, Germany. There he wrote a controversial report decrying the lack of attention to the social and spiritual needs of the American troops. His superior officers wanted him to remain in the army. By this time, Troy's patron and friend, Austin Dowling, had been transferred, and a new bishop, Thomas Drumm, was at the helm. Drumm was willing to allow it, but Troy agonized over a return to parish life.[66] Eventually, however, he changed his mind and returned. Drumm welcomed him home and sent him to Dunlap, right into the midst of a bitterly feuding parish.

Father James Troy. Credit: Diocese of Des Moines Archives.

Transit for Dowling

By the time Troy was returning, Dowling was already gone to a new assignment. In September 1918, the great "Consecrated Blizzard of the Northwest," Archbishop John Ireland of St. Paul, died. A brief *sede vacante* was followed by the surprise announcement that Des Moines's first bishop was now to head north to Minnesota. The school and other initiatives of Dowling's years were to be advanced by his successor, a Dubuque priest of Irish birth—Thomas W. Drumm.

At a March 3, 1919, farewell banquet, Father Charles O'Connor acknowledged Dowling's role in raising the profile of the Catholic community of southwestern Iowa. Although still a minority of the population of the twenty-three counties, Catholics were better organized and capable of leaving an imprint on this section of Iowa, in particular on the two largest cities: Des Moines and Council Bluffs. He also left behind a more confident local church: "The rights of the Catholic body . . . more clearly defined, and confidence and prudent self-assertion inspired in all."[67]

Dowling proposed a bit of retrospective wisdom: "A diocese should have been made in this center of Central Iowa thirty years ago when land was cheap" for the settling of Catholic immigrants. "Even now however, the erection of the diocese has been a blessing for it has aroused our Catholic people who are always generous to surpass themselves in their donations to the church and it has given them courage to face their opponents." While optimistic about the church in the city and the future of Catholic education, he worried about the "isolation of our priests in country places who live far from one another and have not enough to do."[68] Nonetheless, he quickly moved north, and on March 25 he was installed in St. Paul. A successor would soon appear and with him a new leap forward for the Catholic community of southwest Iowa.

"That I May Squeeze a Small Part in Your Hearts and Affections"

Thomas Drumm and Vital Expansion

In the aftermath of the Great War, Iowa settled into an uneasy period. In the cities, there was continued growth and development. The nation was roiled with noisy and divisive public controversies. The first major "Red Scare" raised the specter of Bolshevik-inspired radicalism threatening the nation's institutions—including organized religion. The forces of immigration restriction, which had been building before the war, finally achieved their goals with two major pieces of legislation (1921 and 1924) that severely curtailed the number of immigrants allowed in the United States, especially from southern and eastern Europe. Racialist, anti-Catholic, and anti-Semitic overtones accompanied the reasoning behind these restrictions. The Ku Klux Klan surged in power and influence during the 1920s, using anti-Catholic prejudice and support for prohibition as lynchpins of their appeal. At the same time, however, Mexican migrant workers began to come north to help plant and harvest crops and do other work. In rural areas, however, it was only the beginning of stress. Hawkeye agriculture had known a golden age from 1909 through World War I. But once the war's demands for agricultural products ended in 1918, Iowa farming had begun to decline, and crop prices fared badly during the 1920s. This steady collapse in farm prices left farmers struggling.[1] Rural churches suffered a decline in membership and revenue, and, while they continued to serve, many of them consolidated their headquarters into towns. Iowans began to purchase automobiles, but roads in rural areas were still difficult. At the beginning of this era, Rome appointed a man with experience in both the rural and urban experience of Iowa Catholicism: Irish-born Thomas W. Drumm, a priest of the Archdiocese of Dubuque.

Even though he was foreign-born, Drumm understood the meridian of life in Iowa better than his predecessor. Born on July 12, 1871, Drumm was a native of Fore, Castlepollard, West Meath, Ireland, one of three children of Thomas Drumm and Mary Cullen. His father owned a pub called The Seven Wonders, which referred to sites of devotion in the area, including two holy wells frequented by pilgrims to this small community.

When he was sixteen years old, young Thomas went to work with his uncle Patrick Drumm who owned a farm near Rockwell, Iowa. Rockwell, a rural community in Cerro Gordo County, is located about eleven miles south of Mason City. Here he helped on the farm and acquired a lifelong affection for agricultural life. Even during his years as bishop of Des Moines, he raised barnyard animals at the episcopal mansion, did small repairs, and dressed like a farmer whenever he could. But the occasional country-bumpkin routine belied a sharp-minded, shrewd, and hard-working, if occasionally eccentric, leader. His heart was always in the country, but the lion's share of his activities were for the growing church in the cities.

In 1893, Drumm began studies for the priesthood at St. Joseph's College, the preparatory seminary (today Loras College). The curriculum included philosophy, elocution, composition, natural sciences, mathematics, bookkeeping, Latin, Hebrew, French, and German.[2] Drumm's program took five years to complete. He later demonstrated an enviable ability to distill this material into popular talks and sermons.[3] In 1898, he was sent to the Sulpician-run Grande Seminaire in Montreal, Canada, where he received intellectual and spiritual formation at the hands of the Sulpicians. Montreal Archbishop Paul Bruchesi ordained him on December 21, 1901. He left the Montreal seminary with a bachelor's degree in theology (STB) and canon law (JCB). Drumm was not the scholar or writer that Dowling was, but he was considered talented enough to be sent to

Catholic University for advanced studies in 1903. Here he spent only one year.[4]

Drumm spent a brief period in New York, where he honed his skills as a preacher. Archbishop John Keane formed a Mission Band—a mobile cohort of priests who gave parish missions, days of recollections, and spiritual talks year-round in the archdiocese. Drumm served for twelve years on this band. He was well known in every corner of the archdiocese and even in Des Moines, where he once preached a well-received mission at St. Ambrose. This gift for pulpitry never left him, and later Drumm became one of Des Moines's first

Bishop Thomas W. Drumm. Credit: Diocese of Des Moines Archives.

"radio priests," when, beginning in 1924, he was regularly heard over the airwaves from radio station WHO. At the end of 1914, he came off the mission circuit and was appointed the pastor of St. Patrick's Church in Cedar Rapids.[5]

Rome did not tarry long. From a *terna* that included fellow priests Francis Joseph Leonard and William Patrick Shanahan, Rome picked Drumm. The bishop-elect was at Cedar Rapids when he heard the news of his elevation to Des Moines, which was announced in Rome on March 28, 1919. On March 30, 1919, the *Des Moines Register* ran a flattering story on Drumm, extolling his humble origins. Stressing his rags to riches rise to episcopal office and common touch, Drumm was seen as a man of the people. Of his term as pastor in Cedar Rapids, the paper noted, "It has not been uncommon to see the pastor playing with the children or dressed in overalls making necessary repairs and improvements to the property. . . . He rejoices in America, the land of liberty and opportunity where an immigrant in thirty years can become a bishop in the capital city of Iowa—and it may be noted that in Iowa this whole evolution took place."[6] Drumm's ability to bridge the gap between his foreign birth and the needs of a local community served him well in advancing the presence and prominence of the Catholic Church in southwest Iowa.

Taking Charge

As soon as he heard the news of his successor, Dowling extended his congratulations and offered avuncular advice to the bishop-elect: "Don't lose any time in being consecrated. As soon as you get your outfit, go there. The sooner the better. If you can spare time to come and see me I shall be glad to tell you about the diocese and to help you in every way."[7] A second letter followed up informing Drumm of the procedures and costs of procuring the papal bulls certifying his selection and urging him to get his entire episcopal garb. "I told Msgr. Flavin he should buy you your things. He probably won't offer to do so. But take my advice and sweetly but firmly just go ahead and send him the bills. Tell him you're going to. Remember he has the revenue of the best parish in the diocese. . . . Go to Des Moines and superintend your house cleaning or you'll be sorry. . . . Don't be too deferential or you'll get walked over. You're going to like Des Moines and Des Moines will like you."[8]

Drumm was consecrated in Dubuque's St. Raphael Cathedral on May 21, 1919, by Archbishop James John Keane, with Bishop James Davis of Davenport and Edmond Heelan, auxiliary bishop of Sioux City, as co-consecrators. On May 23, he arrived in Des Moines and was enthroned in St. Ambrose Cathedral by Archbishop Keane. Drumm spoke warmly to the crowds assembled to welcome him: "My heart, hopes and efforts are entirely at your disposal," he noted, "and my only trust is that I may be able to serve in such a way that I may squeeze a small place in your hearts and affections." Dowling was on hand to praise his successor, assuring the people that, unlike him, "he knows Iowa" and predicting that his successor would "bring a new source of inspiration and idealism."[9] The stately, forty-seven-year-old Drumm, with his wavy hair, soon took over and began to move the diocese forward. On arriving in Des Moines, Drumm found seventy-six diocesan priests and seven religious order priests. He began with fifty-six parishes and thirty-one missions serving thirty-five thousand Catholics. By the time of his death in

1933, Des Moines had ninety-nine diocesan priests and seventeen religious. The number of parishes founded climbed from fifty-six to sixty-three and missions actually decreased by one to thirty. These parishes served nearly forty thousand Catholics.

Drumm the Man

Drumm was an energetic and zealous bishop, but as time went on he became more eccentric and irascible. His eccentricities displayed themselves conspicuously during a diocesan synod he convoked in 1923 when he reconfigured the diocesan curia using terminology from American civil government. The Officialis was dubbed the Chief Justice; the other canonical judges, Associate Justices; the promoter of justice, the Attorney General; and the college of consultors, the Senate.[10]

There were personality conflicts as well. One of the priests with whom Drumm clashed was Father James Troy, whom he tried to remove from a pastorate in Dunlap. Troy reported the matter to Apostolic Delegate Pietro Fumasoni-Biondi and related a bizarre experience of visiting the bishop at his home: "As without collar or cassock in his shirt sleeve and pants and sometimes in overalls he opens the door of the episcopal residence to all comers, so I am not surprised when he is equally informal in canonical procedure. His house is a bedlam of squawking parrots, racing dogs, rabbits, goats, and amid these distractions he has to compose his mind for passing sentence on poor priests like me. . . . The night he came to Dunlap in preparation for his extraordinary investigation of me, he entertained me with the story of his goats and especially one called Nubia which was about to have kids. At 10 o'clock at night his housekeeper called by long distance to inform him that Nubia had two kids." Troy wryly observed: "I could not disassociate my discomfiture from his amazing interest in birds and beasts, and refrain from the thought that if he were to be my judge, my chance of favorable consideration would be better if I had four legs than if I had two."[11]

Apostolic Delegate Pietro Fumasoni-Biondi visited the diocese in 1931 and saw in person what Troy had related several years before. He noted in his report of the diocese that Drumm was "un uomo retto, zelante, e di pronto ingegno" (a righteous and zealous man with a ready wit). But, he also added, the bishop was "considerato curioso" (odd) because of his deficient knowledge of canon law and his having spent most of his priesthood giving missions.[12]

As Drumm grew older, he often lashed out at priests whom he believed were disobedient to his sometimes unrealistic demands. For example, in the Dunlap controversy, he had ordered Troy to take to the hustings for the diocesan Mission Band—and then criticized him for being away from his post for periods of time. When he sent Father Francis William Doyle to St. Patrick's in Imogene, a parish that had spent a lot of money to build a new church and school, he set the new priest on a path that would surely make his position among the people less secure:

> My chief reason for delay in appointing was due to the fear that you were not strong enough [not physically] to counteract the influences for isolation that have grown up among the people of that parish for years and guide them securely and quickly to the acceptance of the fact that they must, to be Catholic, become a real part of the Diocese and the Church. . . . These people have never been a part of the diocese; have contributed nothing towards the erection of the Diocese, nothing to the purchase of the Bishop's House, nothing to the college, nothing to the Christ Child Home, and little at any time to the collections for any activities in the Diocese. I figure they owe since the foundation of the Diocese some $22,000. I am pleased to note, however that last year you raised the parish from Nos. 49 and 47 and less of previous years to No. 22.[13]

When Father George J. Toher, pastor of All Saints in Stuart, could not keep up with diocesan assessments during the Great Depression, Drumm sent a nasty letter to which Toher replied in April 1933:

> I have just finished reading your threatening letter and want to say I am about ready to throw up my hands. If after all the sacrifices I have made to keep this place going during this depression you feel toward me as your letter implies my efforts to keep this parish from becoming hopelessly involved in debt have been as you say "a serious mistake." Please Bishop, advert to these facts: My regular income had dropped from about $8,000 to $3,000, my expenses have not dropped in proportion. . . . Since September the sisters have had no salary other

than the food I had to supply. In your letter you threaten me because I have not sent you money. Bishop, while I could go without salary and ask the sisters to do the same, neither the sisters, nor the school children, nor myself could go without fuel. . . . You will notice that I have not taken any vacation the last two or three years. I have not the money. In addition to being deprived of my salary, I went without mass stipends for long periods of time. The five dollars I receive in the Sunday collection is used to pay a housekeeper and if there is food on the table it is because I still have a few hundred dollars left from the times when I drew a salary. If my income has dropped from $8,000 to $3,000 it is because the farmers are bankrupt and one cannot expect a great deal of help from people who are going without the necessities of life. . . . In closing I want to say that I resent the threat of punishment and the charge of having made "a serious mistake" while I was making sacrifices for religion which others were unwilling to make.[14]

Drumm's persecution of his clerical enemies and rivals was noted by Father William Appleby, who blamed his departure from the priesthood on Drumm's treatment of priests:

I know your Lordship is impulsive and hasty. I know you have few friends in the diocese and few outside—so I have heard. Why? Please let me tell you!! Because you have been too autocratic, too hasty both in judgment and action. You have sycophants—that's true, what Bishop has not? It is not his fault nor his seeking—sycophants are not—never have been friends. As a rule, they are the first to criticize."[15] When Appleby informed Drumm he was not returning to the diocese or the Catholic faith, he blasted the bishop: "Remember Bishop . . . it was your own conduct that finally made me decide against that Faith that once I would have died to defend [especially], your treatment of excellent priests, Father Troy and Father Ostdiek and others.[16]

Priests in the Drumm Years

Drumm was hard on his priests. But he also gave them some leeway to innovate to respond to local pastoral needs.

Monsignor Vitus Stoll. Credit: Diocese of Des Moines Archives.

One of his closest associates was his chancellor and vicar general, Monsignor Vitus Stoll. Born and baptized in Westphalia, Iowa, in August 1889, Stoll was a champion athlete. While a student at Campion College in Prairie du Chien, Wisconsin, in 1909, he struck out eighteen Detroit Tigers during an exhibition game. This feat won him a spot in the famous "Ripley's Believe It or Not" column—along with a cow that had what appeared to be a swastika on its forehead and a man who spoke one hundred languages. In his official diocesan roles, Stoll was efficient and loyal but appeared to have carte blanche to administer harsh discipline to the clergy. Stoll had a dim view of his brother priests, and priests' files are full of note cards written or typed by Stoll that often contain tart and acerbic comments. Drumm and Stoll had a falling out sometime before Drumm's death, and Stoll would spend his final years of priestly ministry in the railroad town of Creston. Not all Des Moines priests were like the cynical Stoll.

Innovative Priests on the Iowa Landscape: Luigi Ligutti and Hubert Duren

Catholic priests were first of all spiritual leaders of church communities, but in certain areas of Iowa they exercised a wider influence. Many of them were family counselors, adjudicators of quarrels, and marriage brokers—bringing together Catholic young people in a way replicated by dating databases in the twenty-first century. Local issues brought forth a wealth of creativity from Catholic priests. Two men who stood out as genuine local and even regional leaders were Fathers Luigi Ligutti and Hubert Duren.[17] Of them both, Ligutti would become one of the best-known priests from the Diocese of Des Moines.

Luigi Ligutti was born March 21, 1895, in the province of Udine in Italy. His mother was well connected with the church, having an uncle who was a cardinal bishop of Padua and a brother who was a priest of the Archdiocese of Udine. Members of his family began to migrate to America—first his sister and then two brothers—coming eventually to Iowa. His father joined with them for a brief time but returned to Italy, where he died.

In 1911, Luigi entered the seminary in his native Italy. In 1912, after the death of his father, he, his mother, and a sister came to Des Moines. Father Romanelli of the Italian St. Anthony Parish took the family under his care and saw to it that Luigi was enrolled in Davenport's Ambrose College. After his graduation in 1914, he asked Dowling if he could be accepted for priestly studies by the Diocese of Des Moines. Dowling agreed and sent him to St. Mary's Seminary in Baltimore, and the Ligutti family became parishioners at Visitation Parish in Des Moines, where Father Joseph F. Nugent provided an important role model for the young cleric.[18]

The intellectually gifted Ligutti so excelled at the seminary that the Sulpicians who ran the school invited him to join the community and go on for further studies. But Bishop Dowling turned him down: "Had I great abundance of priests, I should gladly encourage you to go to the Sulpicians . . . but in great measure I am planting the church in this district and I need young priests to help me. This is a land of sacrifice where success is not assured and where there is no hint of the self-denial one may have to practice." Dowling revealed how much he had spent on Ligutti from his own pocket and gently

Young Luigi Ligutti. Credit: Courtesy of the Department of Special Collections and University Archives, Marquette University Libraries.

reminded him of the sacrifices he had made for the young cleric. He told him that he would be willing to release him to the Sulpicians "after a few years of service" at the new school he was planning.[19]

On September 22, 1917, Dowling ordained Ligutti to the priesthood. Dowling then sent him back to the east to study at the Catholic University of America, where he specialized in classics.[20] The linguistically gifted Ligutti had hoped to procure a doctorate in the classics but was called back to serve at the new Des Moines College, where Dowling appointed him to the faculty and made him librarian.

Although a gifted teacher and voracious reader, Ligutti transitioned to full-time pastoral work in 1920, when his financially strapped mother needed support. She agreed to move in and help care for the household, and Bishop Drumm assigned him to Sacred Heart Church in Woodbine, with the mission of St. Bridget of Erin Parish in Magnolia, one of the oldest parishes in Iowa. Later, he also served at St. Ann's Parish in Logan.

At Woodbine and Magnolia, Ligutti developed a lifelong interest in rural Catholicism and traveled to the mostly Irish congregation of Magnolia on dirt roads by bicycle, motorcycle, and foot to seek out and minister to his parishioners. At Sacred Heart he was able to finish a church begun by his predecessor. Rural parish life required an adjustment. Ligutti had a restless intellect and was full of energy; to stave off boredom he also became an avid hunter, stalking game of various kinds.

Ligutti believed that proper education was the key to keeping the faith alive in rural areas and launched a series of religious education classes to acquaint people with Catholicism and rebut falsehoods. Drumm himself came to Logan, Iowa, to deliver a series of lectures, and Ligutti took out ads in local newspapers to advertise these presentations. At Magnolia, he began summertime religious education program (under a huge elm tree), starting what became a very popular tradition of religious vacation schools in Iowa. The school drew in children from Mondamin, Modale, Logan, and Pisgah. Dominican sisters assisted him with these programs.

He did run into the recalcitrance of local parishioners who were not financially supportive of the parish, lamenting to one priest colleague: "Another lovely occupation is that of Pew Rent collector. Am not so proficient at that as hunting."[21] Ligutti then became one of the first to replace the old (and increasingly unenforceable) pew-rent system with collection envelopes for church support. In his spare time, Ligutti wrote numerous letters to Catholic periodicals and to the editors of Catholic newspapers. His biographer noted one of his more famous letters to the *Woodbine Twine*, "A Reply to the Klan," where he criticized a Ku Klux Klan speaker who had attacked Catholics during a speech in the city park.[22]

In April 1926, Bishop Drumm transferred him to the struggling parish of the Assumption in Granger, Polk County. Assumption church had been founded in August 1900 in an area composed of farms run by Irish, but there were five bituminous coal mines in the parish territory, each employing nearly 1,600 men living in mining camps owned by the coal companies. A number of these coal miners were of various ethnic nationalities (mostly Italians and Slavs) that were traditionally Catholic. Many resided in High Bridge, Zookspur, Dallas Camp, and Gibbsville.

Ligutti set to work, building on the techniques he had used in Woodbine and expanded religious education via the Confraternity of Christian Doctrine (CCD), a religious education program designed for rural areas without Catholic schools.[23] He also founded a parish school (closed in 2016), which catered to rural youth from primary grades through high school. Large numbers of children flocked to the religious education classes, which also had summer sessions taught by nuns and seminarians.

Assumption High School, founded by Ligutti, mirrored the success that rural high schools had in those days—attracting small numbers of students (most attended public school) but producing a respectable array of professionals: priests, sisters, doctors,

Portrait of Monsignor Luigi Ligutti, ca. 1935. Credit: Courtesy of the Department of Special Collections and University Archives, Marquette University Libraries.

lawyers, businesspeople, and in particular farmers and farmers' wives. Ligutti devised a course of studies that taught a variety of very practical classes for future farmers. For example, young women were taught domestic skills that would assist in the maintenance of the family farm. The school quickened the pace of life in the community with athletic events, fairs, boxing, and other social events. Ligutti's expertise in rural Catholic issues linked him with national concerns and organizations. His skills as a writer propelled him more and more into the public eye. His contributions to Catholic rural life and his efforts to end world hunger will be discussed later.

Father Hubert Duren and the Westphalia Cooperative

Father Hubert E. Duren was quite a different character than Luigi Ligutti. A big man, six foot six, 250 pounds, Duren had worked as a lumberjack in his early years. But in his own way he became a larger-than-life figure in the Shelby County community of Westphalia when he took an eclectic amalgam of ideas about cooperatives and put them into action.

Duren was born in 1892 in Cazenovia, Wisconsin, one of fourteen children of a parish organist and a saintly mother. Hubert learned the rudiments of music from his father and was a skilled instrumentalist, composer, choir director, and organizer. He attended St. Lawrence Seminary at Mount Calvary, Wisconsin, and St. Francis de Sales Seminary in Milwaukee. Duren had a hard time breaking into the priesthood. One of his problems was his uncle, Stephen Duren, a priest of the Diocese of La Crosse, who sent intemperate letters to the La Crosse bishop, James Schwebach. In addition, Duren's father was accused of public intoxication by some of the parish priests in the diocese.

But the big issue was language—still a hot topic in early twentieth-century Wisconsin. Although of German parentage, Duren was opposed to German-language instruction and was the leader of a cadre of students at St. Francis Seminary who worked against the use of German in hymnody at the seminary. His pastor at Cazenovia, "one of the pro-German types," heard of the fracas (which did not amuse many of the members of the St. Francis Seminary faculty, including

Father Hubert E. Duren. Credit: Diocese of Des Moines Archives.

the Austrian-born rector, Monsignor Joseph Rainer) and roused other German priests of the diocese to block Duren's ordination. English-speaking priests rallied around him. The result was that he was permitted to be ordained, but it could not be in his native diocese of La Crosse. Drumm adopted him and by some quirk (likely bishops' schedules) he was ordained July 9, 1922, in Davenport. He then was assigned to the cathedral at Des Moines, where Drumm made him diocesan director of music and allowed him to teach music at Des Moines College.

In 1926, he was assigned to St. Boniface Church in the Shelby County community of Westphalia and remained there for the rest of his life, becoming one of the most influential community figures in the area. In 1927, he erected a $100,000 grade and high school. When the Depression hit and crashed an already struggling farm economy, Duren took to heart the exhortation of Pope Pius XI in *Quadragesimo Anno*, 1931, to help people make a living in a just and charitable way and to overcome the individualism of rural life. He discovered a cooperative enterprise in Rochdale, England, and implemented the principles of this experiment in Westphalia, forming the Westphalia Consumers Cooperative Association in 1937.

Through his dynamic and somewhat eccentric personality, he made the parish the spark plug for the community's recreation needs, building a baseball diamond and a recreation center called St. Hubert's Club, where there was a space for card playing, board games, dances, and other entertainment—but no liquor. In 1939, he began a parish credit union, a cooperative local store, and a gasoline station and built a new convent and a refrigeration plant—all to fit into what Duren called the Complete Life program, which sought to unify religion, education, recreation, commerce, and credit.[24]

In October 1939, Westphalia commemorated the centenary of Rochdale principles with a huge celebration, drawing thousands of people to the little town to inspect what Duren had done. Among the attendees was Bishop Edwin Vincent O'Hara and Monsignor Luigi Ligutti, both of the National Catholic Rural Life Conference. (Ligutti had become closely associated with this organization even during his Granger pastorate.)

One of Duren's most helpful accomplishments was a plan to allow people to own houses by recruiting local residents to pool their labor. These "Villa Nova" homes were lengthy barracks-like structures that had three bedrooms. He made a point of using the wood of Catalpa trees—considered a "weed tree" but proving to be useful for studs, joints, and rafters. The wood also could be used for making varnish. Six families and a professional carpenter were necessary to erect the homes, which required cash outlay of only $5,000 and a pledge to work with other families to build the homes after hours at a regular job.[25]

Duren also painted large murals, including one called "The Pride of Iowa," depicting commerce, agriculture, and manufacturing in the Hawkeye State. He composed songs, directed choirs, and at one point had the entire church congregation singing rather than collectively reciting the rosary.[26] Duren's love of the spectacle enlivened the course of the year in Shelby County. One old parishioner recalled the Corpus Christi procession, which took place on the first Thursday after Trinity Sunday each year. This was a popular procession that involved hundreds of people marching according to ranks. At the rear was a priest who carried the Blessed Sacrament in a monstrance, flanked by servers, bell ringers, candle bearers, and, over his head, a mobile canopy carried by parish men. At three different altars set up in the parish cemetery, he would pause and bless the people with the sacred host. When the procession reached the altar and Benediction of the Blessed Sacrament was given, three parish-owned cannons "manned by enthusiastic cannoneers . . . were fired at the principal parts of the Mass and again at the Benedictions given at each chapel. The burst of cannon was accompanied by a spontaneous outcry of all the babies present."[27]

In May and October, he organized rosary processions, a popular form of intercessory prayer at the time. Duren's Marian devotion was attested to by School Sister of St. Francis Romaine Muskat, who spent nine years teaching in Westphalia. Duren, Muskat noted, "had a deep love for Mary. During May and October the rosary was recited at the outdoor shrine of Mary by Fr. Duren, the Sisters and any of the town people who would come at 7 P.M." On October 7, the feast of the Holy Rosary (or the Sunday closest to this feast), the whole parish turned out to sing the rosary as they marched down the main street of Westphalia. "Each family brought their large rosary from home and carried it draped on a wooden-type beam. Father Duren led the rosary from a microphone near the church grounds." Duren's most popular song, "Mother Dearest St. Mary," was always sung on this occasion.[28] One person remembered that Duren always scheduled the October devotion during the World Series game "to test the faith of his flock." The impact of all of this was quite significant. In all, fifty-seven women entered the School Sisters of St. Francis from Westphalia—and others entered other orders.

Ligutti and Duren were two very different people. But the impact they made on their rural communities was long-lasting.

An Organizational Revolution: Diocesan Synod and the Rationalization of Catholic Charities

Bishop Drumm shored up his authority and clarified diocesan policies in a number of areas, especially by convoking a diocesan synod in 1923. His predecessor had held such a meeting in 1912 that may have laid down basic diocesan policy in critical areas of sacramental and administrative life.[29] After the promulgation of the Code of Canon Law in 1918, Rome required the holding of a synod every ten years in a diocese. Here were presented for formal clerical approval local requirements regarding church governance, administration of the sacraments, church building, the liturgical year, and catechetics. Priest representatives met with Drumm at the chapel of Des Moines

College on June 15, 1923, and formally approved a prewritten set of rules and regulations that governed Catholic life in Des Moines. These rules laid out specific applications of the common law of the church. The deliberations of this synod were printed and bound within a sturdy blue cover and distributed to pastors. The typical Des Moines pastor had a compendium of these rules and regulations at his fingertips for many years.[30] Bishop Gerald Bergan would update these statutes in the 1930s. How many priests actually consulted them on a regular basis is not known.

Catholic Charities

Drumm's organizational revolution extended to the field of social service and the delivery of welfare. As many Midwestern states, Iowa passed laws governing the administration of public charity and creating a more rationalized and ordered system for the dispersal of public services to the needy. The Catholic Church, which had well-developed networks of social provision (hospitals, nursing homes, orphanages, etc.) followed suit, and Catholic Charities became a much more structured and well-run operation. In 1924, the St. Vincent de Paul Society, a lay organization that delivered direct aid to the needy and poor (e.g., food, clothing, bedding, even housing), began a particular council to oversee charities in twelve parishes.

On the national level, the delivery of Catholic social services (care for orphans, the disabled, unwed mothers, and poverty cases) was reworked according to new ideas that were changing social services nationwide during the Progressive Era (1900–1920). Monsignor William Kerby of the sociology department of the Catholic University of America formed the National Conference of Catholic Charities and founded the school of social work on the campus. On May 11, 1925, Bishop Drumm formally organized the office of Diocesan Catholic Charities Bureau to coordinate the charitable outreach of the diocese. "The Des Moines Catholic Charities is the official head of all Catholic welfare agencies in the diocese and the line of cooperation with all other welfare agencies. . . . It is meant . . . to coordinate, knit up and systematize existing charity activities, to organize, and promote the establishment of new welfare work when and where this is deemed advisable." Father (later Monsignor) Michael Schiltz became its first director.

One of the first acts of this newly created diocesan agency was to establish a much-needed diocesan orphanage, the Christ Child Home, in March 1925. Bishop Drumm purchased a home, located on 2910 Grand Avenue in Des Moines, and three German Dominican sisters came to tend to the new operation. When they returned to Germany in 1935, Bishop Bergan replaced them with the Sisters of Humility from Ottumwa. Licensed to care for at least thirty children from infancy to the age of six, the home was filled to capacity for many years.[31] The successful orphanage lasted until about 1955, when foster care replaced institutional care for dependent children. The reduction in state financing made the orphanage financially untenable, and it closed in 1966.

Christ Child Home and Sister of Humility. Credit:
Archives of the Congregation of the Humility of Mary.

Enhancing the Catholic Presence in Des Moines: Upgrading St. Ambrose Cathedral

In October 1922, Drumm sent Francis J. O'Connell along with Father Lester V. Lyons to assist the faltering Flavin. "I will look to you . . . young men to assist the pastor and build up the Cathedral services so as to attract the people. Intelligence in preaching so as to do all the people good, affability in the matter of confessions and sick calls and 'cases' and at the same time storing your minds with study and observant experience—these ought to make for mutual good for all concerned."[32] When Flavin died on October 12, 1926, Drumm appointed O'Connell administrator and eventually rector of the cathedral.[33]

O'Connell, a man of exquisite tastes, oversaw major changes to the cathedral property during his eleven years of service. In 1927 he built the adjoining cathedral rectory using the same exterior stone as the cathedral. The residence, today the home of Des Moines's bishops, with its distinctive turret carries the coat of arms of Bishop Drumm. On the upper floor of his residence off the turret was a small private chapel that the bishop could use for his personal prayer and private Masses.

Drumm and O'Connell spent $90,000 upgrading the sanctuary, providing a new episcopal throne of inlaid marble, a new communion rail, and a new pulpit. They also added on to the existing small chapel in the cathedral by creating additional space for as many as three hundred people. Arches were cut into the sanctuary wall, set off by attractive wrought iron grilles, enhancing the new space. The expanded chapel had new pews, a new altar, and a tabernacle set against a blue and gold tapestry and surmounted by a crucifix carved by artisans from the famous German community of Oberammergau, Bavaria. Adjoining the chapel was a new baptistery with a font of green marble with a bronze cover.[34]

In 1929, O'Connell installed a new pipe organ with chimes, specifically designed for the cathedral, and Professor V. G. Magin held a magnificent recital with a huge mixed choir of adults, a vested boys group, and a girls choir. A renowned organist from Oak Park, Illinois, Dr. Francis Hemington, also performed organ pieces at the recital as he accompanied voices in song.[35] Des Moines's most important Catholic church was now ready for a new generation of service to its large congregation.

Parish Builder:
Claiming More Urban Space in Des Moines

Drumm expanded the visible presence of the church as no other bishop before or since has done. During the prosperous 1920s, he authorized the construction of twenty-nine churches and founded seven parishes during his tenure—the most palpable mark of the growth of Catholic life in southwest Iowa. Among the most important church foundings was St. Augustin's Parish in Des Moines.

Father John T. Noonan, who founded St. Augustin's Parish in 1920, was a native son of Iowa born in 1876. Ordained May 7, 1899, he taught at St. Ambrose College, Davenport, and was pastor at Lenox for five years. Despite opposition from the local Benedictines, Noonan founded a second parish in Creston (Immaculate Conception) and built a magnificent church there. He was next transferred to St. Anthony's Parish in Des Moines, where he became the savior of the financially troubled parish. When Drumm appointed him to found a new parish "South of Grand Avenue," an upscale portion of the city, he explained to his consultors: "He is a splendid administrator, a good student, a close reasoned, fine preacher, and prudent advisor. . . . I know of no other priest who can place the teaching and philosophy of the church more kindly and yet more convincingly to intelligent non-Catholics, with whom he has wide contact and influence."[36] Indeed, Noonan's ability to work across denominational lines and impress others with his business savvy, his fiscal prudence, and his elegant tastes made him an important bridge between Catholics and moneyed people in Des Moines.

Remaining true to the character of the neighborhood in which he planted a Catholic church, Noonan spared no expense in designing St. Augustin's Church, contracting the prestigious architectural firm of Maginnis and Walsh of Boston to draw up plans. The parish would add an array of spectacular stained-glass windows in 1935. St. Augustin's is, to this day, a gem set among the exquisite homes and architecture along Grand Avenue. Fitting into the neighborhood

Father Francis Ostdiek. Credit: Diocese of Des Moines Archives.

and enhancing its value by the elegance of the buildings reflected the symbiosis of Catholic space and neighborhood concerns.

For the working class, Drumm sent the purposeful (but at times irascible) Francis Ostdiek to found Holy Trinity Parish in the growing Beaver Park neighborhood of Des Moines. Ostdiek set to work like a man on fire, erecting in less than a year a two-story brick edifice that included a church and a school staffed by the Sisters of Mercy. Shrewdly keeping his eye on coveted parcels in the neighborhood, he kept expanding the property and adding to the school, which rapidly grew. Local real estate entrepreneurs noted how Ostdiek's new parish directly enhanced the attractiveness of the neighborhood to residents. Indeed, as the real estate agent B. C. Hopkins noted in his advertising that the "beautiful residence district" of Beaver Park was "free from the smoke and gas of the city," and he touted "the new Holy Trinity Church and Parochial School" as one of the assets of this "new, healthy, and progressive district."[37]

At one point the sometimes undiplomatic Ostdiek annoyed the equally cantankerous Drumm, who wanted to transfer him. Ostdiek defended himself and his parish turf like a medieval lord. A tough-talking man who had a hard time concealing his heart of gold, Ostdiek inspired deep devotion from his people—even the school-children whom he would wrap in his big clerical cloak on cold winter days. In fact, he became a neighborhood institution. Ostdiek probably frightened some people with his blunt-spoken opinions, but his bark was far worse than his bite. He was not a mover and shaker in moneyed or elite circles, but his example and encouragement induced a significant number of men to consider the priesthood. He encouraged nearly fifty young men to enter the ranks of the clergy. If he had been an army recruiter, he might have created his own regiment.[38]

Less flamboyant but memorable figures were enlisted to expand the church. In the summer of 1924 Father Francis P. Larkin was appointed as founding pastor of St. Joseph Church in Des Moines. Des Moines was expanding eastward into undeveloped lands. The new church lot was purchased at East Thirty-Third and Easton Boulevard, then the main road out of the city, which "included three lots, barn sheds, and a brick farm house. . . . It lay amid many farms in a vast farming area."[39] A portable sectional building served as the first church, dedicated on October 13, 1924. Later, a brick veneer was added and more lots purchased.

Father (later Monsignor) Maurice Aspinwall. Credit: Diocese of Des Moines Archives.

The church had its frontage on Easton. In 1929, the parish built a social hall.

Larkin was later transferred to St. Ambrose Cathedral, and in July 1933 Father Maurice Aspinwall took over as pastor. A native of Cedar Rapids, he attended seminary in Baltimore with classmate and future cathedral rector Lester V. Lyons and had assignments in rural areas (Harlan, Audubon, Exira). By 1943, St. Joseph was free of debt, and in 1949 a school opened. Aspinwall served long enough to build a new church in 1955 and retired after thirty-six years of service in 1969, having expanded the church to a square block. Somewhat melodramatic in his pulpit oratory, one priest recalled his macabre habit of knocking on the lid of the coffin of the deceased at a funeral as a way of dramatizing the passing of the deceased. Like Ostdiek, Aspinwall was known among his flock and his efforts to help Des Moines's worried citizens through World War II were much appreciated. Ostdiek and Aspinwall were important links in a wider environment of urbanizing Des Moines.

Catholic Space in Des Moines, IA, 1933

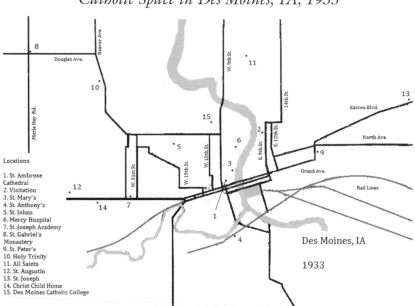

Locations

1. St. Ambrose Cathedral
2. Visitation
3. St. Mary's
4. St. Anthony's
5. St. Johns
6. Mercy Hospital
7. St. Joseph Academy
8. St. Gabriel's Monastery
9. St. Peter's
10. Holy Trinity
11. All Saints
12. St. Augustin
13. St. Joseph
14. Christ Child Home
15. Des Moines Catholic College

Des Moines, IA

1933

Map by Aaron Hyams

Catholic Space in Council Bluffs, IA, 1930

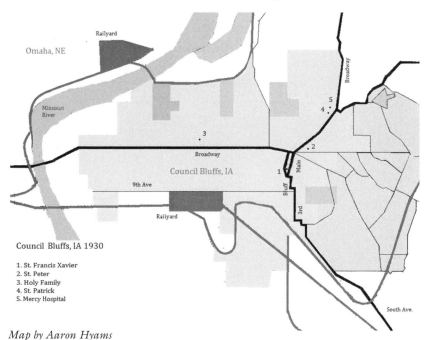

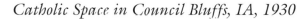

Council Bluffs, IA 1930

1. St. Francis Xavier
2. St. Peter
3. Holy Family
4. St. Patrick
5. Mercy Hospital

Map by Aaron Hyams

Serving the Rural Communities

City growth and development would dominate Catholic activities in southwest Iowa. Rural areas, however, faced a slow but steady decline in population, as evidenced by the statistics in this chart.

County	1920	1930
Mills	15,422	15,866
Montgomery	17,048	16,752
Adair	14,259	13,891
Union	17,268	17,435
Clarke	10,506	10,384
Lucas	15,686	15,114
Harrison	24,488	24,897
Shelby	16,065	17,131
Audubon	12,520	12,264
Guthrie	17,596	17,324
Dallas	25,120	25,493
Polk	154,029	172,837
Pottawattamie	61,550	69,888
Cass	19,421	19,422
Madison	15,020	14,331
Warren	18,047	17,700
Taylor	15,514	14,859
Page	24,137	25,904
Adams	10,521	10,437
Fremont	15,447	15,533
Ringgold	12,919	11,966
Decatur	16,566	14,903
Wayne	15,378	13,787
TOTAL	564,527	588,118
Catholic total	36,370	37,959
Percentage of Catholics	6%	6%

Source: US Census and Official Catholic Directory

Nonetheless, many rural areas were still vital centers of Catholic presence and influence. Such was the case of Shelby County in the northernmost tier of the counties of the diocese, and one of the most Catholic areas in southwest Iowa. As we have seen, Father Hubert Duren had taken Westphalia by storm.

The Strange Case of St. Joseph in Earling

Another outpost, St. Joseph Parish in Earling (named for Albert Earling, a division superintendent of the Chicago, Milwaukee, and St. Paul railroad), was founded in 1886 and had its first resident pastor in 1887. St. Joseph's Church, even today, is one of the neo-Gothic monuments of the Midwest. Erected between 1891 and 1892, it was designed by Mathias Schnell of Rock Island, Illinois (who also had dealings with the Texas state capitol) and was the gift of the labors and donations of local families. St. Joseph's provided a place of exquisite beauty for the farmers and workers in the area. The School Sisters of St. Francis from Milwaukee accepted the task of staffing the large parish grade school and also a high school, which lasted for many years. Under the pastorate of Father Joseph Steiger, who served from 1917 to 1938, the parish prospered.

Father Theophilus Riesinger, OFM Cap. Credit: Diocese of Des Moines Archives.

Steiger was born in Altoetting, Bavaria (home of a famous Black Madonna Shrine frequently visited by Pope Benedict XVI). He came to America when he was only sixteen years old and finished studies for the priesthood at St. Meinrad Seminary in southern Indiana. He was ordained in June 1914 and pastored various churches in the diocese. In May 1917, Dowling appointed him to Earling. Steiger was an indefatigable builder and opened a Catholic high school in the fall of 1918 (the parish already had a thriving grade school), which peaked at more than four hundred students until the high school closed in 1967. Like many rural pastors, he fell behind in paying the salary of the sisters (and other parish bills) during the Great Depression. The mother general of the School Sisters of St. Francis, Sister Stanislaus Hegner, generously canceled his debts.[40]

One of the strangest episodes in diocesan history took place at the Earling parish during Steiger's pastorate—the rite of exorcism. The subject was a woman, Anna or Emma Ecklund, who had been sexually abused by her father at the age of fourteen and also "cursed" by her Aunt Mina who had been having an affair with her father. Capuchin Father Theophilus Riesinger, a bilingual (German and English), affable friar who gave missions around the Midwest, had also cultivated a reputation as an exorcist and was called in 1908 and again in 1912 to pray over Ecklund, who evidenced a peculiar aversion and hostility to religious objects and churches.

Riesinger had apparently driven demons out of the woman in 1912, but in 1928 she was again afflicted at the age of forty and required yet another exorcism. The noises and shrieks that accompanied this process required a remote location so that people would not be frightened. Riesinger was an old friend of Steiger's and also hailed from Altoetting. The Capuchin petitioned Steiger for permission to exorcise the woman at the convent of the Earling parish. Although he admired Riesinger, Steiger was reluctant and sought permission from Drumm, who warned him about the perils and tumult it would cause him and the parish. Nonetheless, he gave approval and Riesinger went forward.

The exorcism went through three stages: August 18–26, 1928; September 13–20, 1928; and December 15–23, 1928. The rites were performed in the convent with a few strong nuns holding Ecklund down as both Riesinger and Steiger said the prayers. Shrieks, wails, curses, vomit, and allegedly even levitation accompanied the action. Finally, the demon left two days before Christmas in 1928—to the relief of Steiger and his housekeeper who grew anxious about the entire operation.

An account of the interaction with the various demons possessing the woman is related in a popular pamphlet by a German priest, Father

Carl Vogl, and was translated into English by a German Benedictine, Celestine Kapsner.[41] In this rendition of the account, Steiger only reluctantly allowed Riesinger to perform the exorcism, and even Drumm warned about the toll it would take on the pastor's health. It also contained a "validation" account from a Milwaukee physician and a brief testimony from Steiger's housekeeper, who also knew of the episode. A brief account of it emerged in *Time Magazine* in 1936.[42]

What can one make of this episode? It is hard to tell, because most of the "evidence" of the case is contained in files that were sent to Rome. Riesinger, Steiger, and the sisters who allegedly witnessed the spectacle never spoke publicly about it, and no documentation exists in the files of the sisters who were there. Riesinger sent all the documentation to Rome, where it is under lock and key. Riesinger himself seems trustworthy; his very positive obituary drafted by his provincial relates that he was a fine religious with a good reputation but also makes clear that his exorcism ministry found skeptics and critics among the members of his Capuchin province. Riesinger died in 1941. After Steiger died in 1938, Father Peter Bissen took over and served until 1972.[43]

A Minority Fights Back, Confronting the Klan, and the 1924 Chapel Car Escapade

Bishop Drumm's issues over the support of the school notwithstanding, Des Moines College continued to grow. One memorable priest assigned there was Father Albert Shaw, another native of Ireland, ordained in 1925. Assigned to Des Moines College in 1926, he remained on the staff until his transfer to Winterset in 1942. Shaw, an abstemious teetotaler, took advantage of the national craze for Prohibition and introduced a branch of the Pioneer Total Abstinence Society in the school. Described as a strict disciplinarian during his years at Des Moines College, he nonetheless convinced many a young man to foreswear alcohol until they came of age. Taking note of the poverty descending on Des Moines in the "terrible thirties," he also began a branch of the St. Vincent de Paul Society in the high school as well.[44]

The temperate Shaw might have been a great candidate for Drumm's effort to reach out to the church in the southern counties of his diocese, an area where support for Prohibition ran high. These communities were very small, and the minority status of Catholics was greatly accentuated. Catholics were often anti-Prohibition and, especially in rural counties, subject to a great deal of anti-Catholic bias. This prejudice was usually of the "soft" kind—disparaging remarks, minor insults to clergy, and typical Protestant accusations of infidelity to the Gospel. It also had a violent component. In the 1920s the southern counties of Iowa were also a breeding ground for a revived Ku Klux Klan. Most Catholics put their heads down when confronted by these frightening bigots, but Drumm was not inclined to let this go unchallenged, and, in fact, the diocese did push back against Klan threats. Catholics were not passive.

Much has been written about the so-called Second Klan, which grew exponentially among whites not only in southern and rural areas but even became popular in cities.[45] The putative origins of the Second Klan are attributed to the first feature-length movie, *The Birth of a Nation*, produced in 1915. A romantic adaptation of the novel *The Clansman* by Thomas Dixon, it portrayed the hooded "knights" as the valiant protectors of white womanhood from rapacious African Americans. The movie's popularity, along with the rise of Jim Crow "legal" segregation and subordination of African Americans, inspired entreprencurial types to organize and refound the Klan, pitching its appeal to Americans tired of social turmoil and suspicious of African Americans. Added to this list of undresirables were Jews, foreigners, and Catholics. In fact, anti-Catholicism became one of the major attractions of the organization. Klan members were also supporters (and enforcers) of Prohibition, which became the law of the land in 1920 after the passage of the Eighteenth Amendment. Klan strength manifested itself in marches, rallies, acts of intimidation, and also as an unofficial enforcement posse for Prohibition laws. The Klan flourished in various parts of the Midwest and in Iowa but particularly in the southern counties of the state. Few Catholics lived in these counties. Some had fallen away from the church. Dowling was one of the first to note this about some places in his diocese.

Drumm likewise believed that much of this anti-Catholic animus flourished because of sheer ignorance and handed-down prejudices against "Romanism." He also felt that education and debate were the best tools to use to tackle these negative perceptions and might also lure back the "fallen-aways." Drumm appealed to the Catholic Church

Extension Society, which gave hundreds of thousands of dollars to rural churches to underwrite this project. He then recruited several of his braver and more articulate priests who volunteered to go into these unsafe (at least for Catholics) locales to proclaim the Catholic message. Father Shaw, prohibition's staunchest supporter, was not included on this mission to Klan strongholds in southern Iowa.

The Chicago-based Church Extension Society had at its disposal chapel railway cars—mobile evangelical units. Quaintly named St. Peter and St. Paul, they were fully equipped with a chapel and place for literature and discussion, as well as living quarters for a priest or two who managed the car. Working with the local railway lines, the cars could be attached to trains going into remote areas and there unhitched for a time, providing a pulpit for the Catholic missionaries. A typical chapel car experience lasted at least a week and involved advertising, evening lectures, handouts of literature, and even Mass and devotions aboard the car.

Drumm managed to secure the St. Paul for use in the late spring of 1924 and wrote to the pastors of parishes in the southern part of the diocese—Bedford, Clarinda, Shenandoah, and Sidney—for suggestions as to where it might stop to good advantage. Pastors from six counties responded affirmatively and enthusiastically, advising Drumm of local conditions and suggesting that the best time for presentations would be later in the day when the farm work was done. Pastors like J. C. Maher of Leon wrote back enthusiastically, "I'll do all in my power to help and make the chapel car a success in this neglected community."[46]

The pastor of Immaculate Conception in Maloy recommended that the car go to Mount Ayr, "a fairly large town with very few Catholics and with a number of people who should be Catholics." He also urged the car to stop at Diagonal: "There are quite a number of Bohemians there who are not Catholic—except in name—and it is very difficult to do anything with them." Many, he noted, were "uninstructed and unbaptized and quite indifferent. I am of the opinion that we may be able to get them back." He also urged a visit to his own parish in Maloy, where he noted there were many good Catholics but that the "bigoted" non-Catholics might find the car a novelty "and pay us a visit." He urged the car to come after corn planting was done at the end of May.[47]

To staff the car, Drumm eventually selected Father William Appleby, who courageously led the car for its first plunge into Wayne County. Appleby dutifully recorded statistics of the numbers of Catholics and fallen-aways he found and the number of people who came to his lectures or received literature. The challenge was daunting. At Corydon in Wayne County, Appleby noted in his report that there were about four Catholics but that fifteen had attended his mission. Fifteen non-Catholics also attended. He was the object of repeated insults and noted pessimistically, "In Corydon high feeling against the Church. Very 'Black' town and little if anything was accomplished. Even the literature was in most cases spurned. The Business people refused to display posters with three exceptions."[48] He noted the strong opposition of local Methodists and the refusal of Methodist spouses of Catholics to consider validating their marriages in the church. Appleby next traveled to Humeston, also in Wayne County. Here he found more interest in the chapel car in the town of 1,200, but he also noted in a letter to Chancellor Vitus Stoll: "Last night there was a large K.K.K. demonstration, and quite a number, I hear, were initiated into its mysteries. Nothing was said against anyone or anything, save the Catholic Church." That particular rally had more than one thousand participants. Appleby hoped that the Klansman would rouse enough curiosity "to see and hear so strange a monster as a priest."[49]

St. Paul Chapel Car, Church Extension Society. Credit: Photo courtesy of Catholic Extension.

In Humeston, Appleby had greater success with non-Catholics, averaging sixty-nine Protestants per night during his evening presentations—and one night alone more than 140. Appleby described a spectrum of reactions to his presence, some including mere curiosity, including a farmer and his wife and four children who took him on a ride in the county because they had never spoken to a Catholic priest before. Rumors soon spread that Appleby's mission was nothing more than a stalking horse for the presidential candidacy of Governor Al Smith of New York in 1924. On the Friday night of his stay in Humeston, the local Klan organizer "honored me with a visit. He is now Pastor of the Christian Church at Chariton." After Appleby's presentation, he asked permission to speak and then launched into a diatribe against the Catholic Church. Appleby responded calmly but firmly, wondering how "a pastor could so be uneducated in simple matters." The pastor slipped away, but "he returned wishing God to bless me and immediately to show his good faith, I suppose, SET FIRE TO A CROSS, no more than 12 yards away from the Chapel Car." Appleby took the incident in stride and after someone yelled that this would make him go, he simply announced, "Service at the usual time tomorrow night—all are cordially invited."[50]

The next day, some men came to apologize for the action of the Klan.[51] The experience in Humeston left Appleby depressed and feeling out on a limb. He complained of his plight and wrote to Vitus Stoll, who assured him of Drumm's support. Appleby wrote back: "Your kind words about his Lordship's appreciation have touched me much." He described in greater detail the harassment he had suffered in the small town from the Klansmen and their intimidation of local townsfolks: "Last night my audience was perceptibly scared and many refusing to come inside [the chapel car]." He also spoke of his loneliness but also of "the colored boy" to whom he was giving instructions as also being badly scared. "He fears the Klan. His one topic of conversation night after night is 'suppose we are killed by the Ku Klux.'" Appleby told him to study his catechism and prepare for baptism and even if they should be killed, "he would go straight to heaven." But, replied the young man, "I don't want to go yet!"[52]

In June, Drumm wrote cordially to the beleaguered Appleby, encouraging him to view these counties as foreign mission territory. Appleby replied: "You say truly, we have China and Africa right here. But only one who actually passes through the midst of these modern pagans can ascertain with certainty how deep, how dark is the shadow of ignorance, unbelief and prejudice and hate in which these poor unfortunates live and move. The bitter hate for the Church I had never dreamt—could be so extensive, so universal and so dreadful."

Appleby learned to his horror that "a plot was being hatched to blow the car to pieces. Indeed, I had lived during that week and also during my stay in Humeston in perfect dread that some calamity would happen." Appleby spoke piously of a "martyr's death," yet "human nature being what it is, fear naturally arises in the breast, not a cowardly fear, but one nevertheless that bring with a feeling no less pleasant. . . . I have had little sleep."[53] Appleby went forward on the car, scheduling stops during the month of June in Davis City, Kellerton, Mount Ayr, Bedford, Gravity, Clarinda, Villisca, and Sidney.

The experience of this escapade and his own personal issues were the beginning of a downward spiral for the eloquent and intelligent Appleby. He became pastor of Bayard, but in 1926, he sought a leave of absence to go to New York to write plays. Ultimately, he left the priesthood and joined the Episcopal church, married, and toyed with converting to Judaism. He relocated to California, where he approached the Los Angeles chancery with a plan to be reconciled, but died in 1963, still outside of the church.

At Mount Ayr, Father Cornelius Lalley of St. Anthony Parish replaced him on the car. Lalley too worried about the Klan but met no direct opposition from it in Mount Ayr or Bedford, although he referred to the latter as his "time of exile among the K.K.K.'s." Like Appleby, he placed fliers in store windows advertising chapel car services and lectures, sought out fallen-away Catholics, and validated marriages. But as the weather grew warmer and the car became uncomfortable, Lalley requested Father James Troy to take it over for a couple of weeks, and then he promised to return to take another two weeks. Troy, who had seen combat in World War I, was unintimidated by Klan threats and demonstrations. He represented the strongest voice of those who were not willing to stand down because they were in the minority.

Troy plunged into the work with gusto. He had already authored a paper called the "Rural Problem" and believed that the challenges to Catholicism could be met by a strong program of positive public relations. He even expressed admiration for the Klan in the way they advertised their activities widely. "We must advertise extensively if we are to have crowds."[54] At the little town of Gravity in Taylor County, he met Klansmen who not only burned a cross a little way from the chapel but also set off small dynamite explosions for several hours at the conclusion of the service.

As the car spent the hot months of June and July in Clarinda, Villisca, and Sydney, Troy believed that the work of the mission car needed a strong follow up. Recommending Clarinda as the hub, he urged an ongoing effort involving subscriptions to the *Sunday Visitor* and the erection of a small chapel.[55] Troy made a fulsome report of the chapel car experience and sent it to the apostolic delegate: "Not many realize that the southern tier of counties of Iowa from Van Buren County on the East to Fremont on the West—there is scarcely a parish of any size, and not one county seat that has a resident pastor. These fine towns through this territory, some of six thousand population have perhaps two or three Catholic families and a distance of twenty-five and thirty miles from a church is not unusual."

He praised the potential of the chapel car, noting he believed it was "destined to accomplish very much more than we can realize." Decrying, as did his colleagues, "the dense ignorance about the church," he did not blame the people "who are fair minded and willing to listen to a reasonable exposition of Catholic belief and practice, but ourselves that we have done so very little to reach these good people who have been fed on the putrid carrion of Maria Monk's diseased mind and similar stuff."[56] Minority status notwithstanding, Drumm and Troy were willing to push back.

Catholic Education: Creating a Catholic Enclave

Drumm sincerely believed that the best antidote to anti-Catholicism was education, and he devoted the bulk of his energies to expanding and stabilizing the Catholic schools of the diocese. When he took over, there were sixteen schools instructing more than 2,400 students. Enrollment in St. Joseph's Academy stood at 250 young women, while Des Moines Catholic College already had 107 young men. By the time he died in 1933, the number of Catholic schools had grown to twenty-eight, with more than 4,500 students. St. Joseph Academy had declined a bit to 214, but Des Moines Catholic College enrollment had surged to 231.[57]

The Catholic education of youth needed more, as Drumm discovered when he received the results of a census of Catholics in Des Moines in 1930, carried out by the Diocesan Council of Catholic

Women.[58] This study revealed that there were only 12,983 Catholics in Des Moines compared to 11,141 in 1921. In addition to noting a decline in baptisms and an increase in mixed marriages, the survey revealed that a significant number of Catholic children were enrolled in public schools. This, he believed, would crimp plans for local vocations to the priesthood and religious life.

In June 1931, after digesting and thinking about the results of the census, he first lauded the growth of Catholic schools: "We have nine Catholic grade schools in the City, supplied and operated at tremendous sacrifice by parishes; trained and devoted teachers win the love of the children, and 2,400 are taught as we Catholics believe all children should be taught; interested pastors watch over them with jealous care; the schools are filled. The work is beyond praise. Thank God. So far, so good." But he worried that "more than 1,400 Catholic children [are] in the public schools of the City, most of them in the grades." He wondered, "What is being done for these children? What are we doing to teach them the Christian religion? . . . The City is doing its duty well in giving them a secular training, so well indeed that we sometimes complain that today the minds of both parents and children are set on success in material affairs, to the exclusion of all else." Drumm noted, "We could command you to build bigger schools and supply more teachers . . . but that would be thought impractical just now." Instead, in September 1931, he expanded the religious education for children who could not or would not attend Catholic schools. At a meeting of young ladies in a Knights of Columbus Hall he organized the Confraternity of Christian Doctrine to be started in the diocese. He noted that "one hundred [teachers] are offering themselves for this blessed service."[59]

Promoting and Funding a Prosperous Des Moines Catholic College

At the flagship institution, Des Moines Catholic College, Drumm brought back Father John J. Boylan as president in 1923. Boylan, a native of New York, had been educated at Mount St. Mary's Seminary in Emmitsburg, Maryland, and then at St. Bernard's Seminary in Rochester, New York. He was ordained in Providence, Rhode Island, for the Diocese of Des Moines in 1915 and spent a brief time as a curate at St. Francis Xavier in Council Bluffs. He attended the Catholic University of America and received a degree in canon law.

Boylan joined the Des Moines College faculty in 1918 and became vice president of the school the next year. The financial difficulties that attended the opening of the college plus his duties as a school disciplinarian drove him to distraction, and he somehow managed to alienate faculty members. To escape the tension, Boylan was permitted to study in Rome in 1921, and he remained there until late 1922. Boylan was not keen on returning to the school and questioned Drumm's plan of

Father (later Bishop) John J. Boylan. Credit: Diocese of Des Moines Archives.

adding a two-year college. He reopened channels with faculty mate Luigi Ligutti, to whom he wrote when Ligutti asked if he was coming back: "In fact, I am full of doubts! Doubtful about the money, doubtful about the fact as to whether or not it is a good thing to have secular priests teaching the high school grades to youngsters of that wild age. . . . Of course I am doubtful about the college department." He suggested that he would not return, "You ask if I shall return to D.M.? An honest response consists in this: 'Never if I can possibly help it!'"[60]

Boylan, however, was subject to Drumm, who insisted on opening the college department. He called Boylan back and appointed him dean of the college. When Boylan learned of this he wrote to Drumm: "In your article in the *Western World* you state: 'after prayer and consultation' you have decided to open the College Department immediately. That settles what was an open question and now it is our part to 'pitch in' and do whatever we can to make the college the best possible college not only in Iowa but in the country." But Boylan begged not to have any part in administration, "I could do more for the institution at present if I had nothing to do with management. . . . I'm not a 'persona grata' with most of the members of the faculty and I want to be; because successful work in a college demands unity. The college is only as strong as its faculty. . . . If my mind is clear I can make up with the various members of the faculty. If not I'm done for!"[61]

Drumm helped him overcome his misgivings. When Boylan came back in 1923, he took over the presidency of Des Moines Catholic College and rose in prominence and prestige in the city and the diocese, performing a number of other jobs, including vicar general. Drumm worked hard to keep the school alive, assigning priests to serve on the faculty and allowing the scholarly Boylan a free hand in administration. Boylan remained as head of the college (later renamed Dowling College in the 1930s and later high school) until 1943, when the Holy See selected him to be the bishop of Rockford, Illinois.

Drumm no doubt enticed the reluctant Boylan back by promising to help shoulder the financial burden. Dowling had told him when he took office: "You'll get some hard luck stories about the poor people but you need not be impressed by them. There's plenty of money and good will besides and everything I am sure will be very agreeable to you."[62] Indeed Drumm proved to be a formidable fundraiser, increasing the school's endowment so it could keep pace with faculty salaries (many of them low) and the upkeep of the buildings.

In October 1920, an impressed Dowling had written to his successor: "You are to be congratulated on the funds you have in hand for the College. Many a long established institution has no such nest egg. Campaigning is rough work and expensive. We have a mailing list of 65,000 and we are using the mails three times in this campaign. I will have them send you what we are getting out. Three sermons in every Church in the diocese on the subject go together with publicity."[63] But by January 1931 the Great Depression had dented the income of most Iowa Catholics, and Drumm's earlier successes could not be replicated.

Saving Des Moines Catholic College

The school began to hemorrhage money, eating through the reserves Drumm had built up in the 1920s. To relieve the burden, in January 1931, Drumm shifted a heavy portion of the financial responsibility for the school to the parishes that were assessed each month on the basis of the number of students they had in the school. This did not go over well with pastors who were struggling themselves to make ends meet during the Great Depression. In September 1932, Boylan reported to the board of trustees that bills totaling nearly $5,000 had gone unpaid. Moreover, tuition payments from the parishes also lagged by $5,200. To save money, Boylan planned to chop the wages of the priests on the faculty, reducing the monthly pay according to years of ordination (those ordained fewer years got less money).[64] Reductions in the athletic program followed as well.

The college barely balanced its budget and had to keep bill collectors waiting. A barrage of criticism flowed into the college during the last months of 1932, mostly from the unhappy pastors who began to cast a dim eye on the expenses of the college. Boylan lashed out at this sniping in a January 1933 letter: "For the past four months there has been a whispering and a murmuring that has only lately become audible and common gossip of the old wives' variety and degree of intelligence which is lugubriously uttered as a doleful ditty that runs somewhat like this: 'They burn too many lights at the College'—'The College is going bankrupt'—'They leave too many doors open at the College'—'The College must close'—'They are woefully extravagant at the College'—'The College will not reopen', and so on ad nauseam."

Boylan insisted that the college's indebtedness was not insurmountable, praised Drumm's January 1931 decision to place the responsibility for supporting the college on the parishes as well as his desire to upgrade the academic quality of the faculty and secure accreditation from the North Central Association, and insisted that the school was vital to the future of the diocese in many ways.[65]

But opposition persisted. In a May 1, 1933, meeting of the board, Drumm declared that he had "repeatedly mentioned the matter of payment of College dues by the parishes, but that he cannot get results. He wondered whether it was because of opposition on the part of the pastors to his regulations or because they could not get the money." He concluded "that he had done all he could do barring the extreme measure of removal of pastors, which he felt he could not do."[66] Boylan and Father Peter Bissen tried to find a compromise between the demands of the school and the resistance of the pastors.

Every proposal offered to ratchet down the tensions was swatted down by Drumm. Nonetheless, the board voted for a more realistic assessment program, and Drumm agreed to "speak to the pastors on the matter of College finances." Boylan warned: "Money would have to be provided now to pay the bills else he could not keep the College open."[67]

In May 1933, Drumm informed the pastors that the once strong $400,000 endowment fund had dwindled to $1,600 and that he had to borrow $10,000 to pay the bills of the school. He threatened to close the school unless the pastors stepped forward to help fund it. Father Hanson of Visitation Parish in Des Moines protested that his allotment was too heavy. He took up a new phase in the battle between the east- and west-side parishes by urging that St. Ambrose Parish pay a heavier share, since the parish had rents from an old property that came to about $10,000 of added income per year.

But Drumm would not hear of it. To keep the place open, the priests on the faculty agreed to salary reductions for the upcoming year.[68] While this edified the bishop, Drumm used a graduation speech in the cathedral on June 6, 1933, to warn the graduates (both academies and the Mercy School of Nursing) that he had decided to close the college and high school owing to the disloyalty and lack of support on the part of the pastors but that the faculty had helped save the place by renouncing their salaries.

A traveling salesman who often went to Mass at St. Ambrose when he was in Des Moines happened to be in the cathedral, where he heard this tirade. He wrote to the apostolic delegate that he had often heard uncomplimentary things about Drumm when he visited Des Moines and related how his informants called the bishop "shanty Irish" and "fool" and even questioned his sanity. He was appalled to hear Drumm denounce the pastors and threaten them with removal "if they did not pay up." The correspondent noted: "I have always tried to defend him, but since June 6th [the day of the St. Ambrose address] I would believe most anything I would hear about him."[69]

Drumm followed up in July 1933, when he wrote in a letter to be read from the pulpit on August 6 to the Des Moines parishes complaining that in some of the city parishes "no effort was made by pastors to get all their high school boys to the College and no effort was made to collect for the boys in the College High School.

Hence the College had to borrow $10,000 to finish the year. . . . There was no reason for that, and there is no reason for it if the pastors and people do their share."[70]

Drumm reminded the hearers of the letter of what he had said in his commencement speech the previous June: "I will insist on City parishes maintaining their central high school. I insist further now that our City parishes must be provided with pastors who believe in maintaining their central high school." He lectured: "You have one of the very best high schools for our boys in the state of Iowa; our people are proud of it; it is now fully accredited by the North Central Accrediting Association, and it must be so maintained." He noted that some of the professors had agreed to work without salary. "We insisted that it is not required and refuse to consider it. They work hard, have fitted themselves with summer schools, and should not be punished when parishes can pay."[71] This provoked a torrent of opposition from the clergy, who protested to the apostolic delegate, Archbishop Amleto Cicognani (in letters likely read by his Dominican secretary and future Des Moines bishop, Edward Daly).

One of the first to weigh in was Father Joseph Hanson of Visitation Parish, who complained that the support of the college had been transferred to parishes just as the Depression was cutting the income of parishioners and parishes. The assessment also took money away from paying off the debts of virtually every church in Des Moines that had built or improved their facilities during the prosperity of the 1920s. Hanson repeated all of these events in a lengthy letter to the apostolic delegate, noting that Drumm had "belched out . . . all this ludicrous and slanderous rubbish . . . before the promiscuous gathering [the June 6th graduation]." Drumm had already carried

Archbishop Amleto Cicognani. Credit: Library of Congress Prints and Photographs Catalogue.

out his threats to remove the "disloyal," Hanson noted, including "his vicar general who [*sic*] he replaced with his Chancellor, a man as well fitted for the office as would be a South Sea Islander." Hanson, who also feared being removed, concluded with a résumé of his own school and church building activities and his pastoral efforts.[72]

Francis Ostdiek, who had already defied Drumm's efforts to move him, also defended his unwillingness to contribute to the central high school "because we have not the means" and worried that "paying to the Central High School means closing my parochial school." He begged Cicognani to keep his complaint confidential, "for I have worked under his jurisdiction fourteen years and I know how vindictive he is."[73] Drumm never carried through on his threat, but by this time, many knew that the bishop was capable of retribution and known for writing threatening letters to his priests.

In the end, what saved Des Moines Catholic College from financial ruin was the death of Drumm in October 1933. In his will, the generous Drumm bequeathed $10,000 in burses (funds for Masses), a 120-acre farm (value: $15,000), and $6,000 for a burse of his own.[74] In June 1935, the board voted to rename Des Moines Catholic College "Dowling." Given his generosity and full-throated support of the school, perhaps it should have been Drumm High School.

Drumm's efforts to rescue the faltering school were critical to its survival. Dowling's hopes and Drumm's strong insistence on keeping the school open and the use of diocesan priests paid a handsome dividend to the local church. The beneficiary was the Diocese of Des Moines. Thanks to the union with St. Joseph's Academy, this school has had over eighteen thousand graduates. Of these, 110 graduates became priests, and three became permanent deacons. The city's other Catholic high school, St. Joseph Academy, also produced its share of religious vocations with over 130 graduates becoming religious.

Bishop Drumm's Last Days

The Depression years were very difficult for Drumm, as he faced serious financial problems and resistance from priests for his insistence on propping up Des Moines College. His irascibility and propensity to unload sharp insults and accusations on his priests in hotly written letters grew worse over time. As one priest's memoir suggests, "In the last few years of his life, Bishop Drumm suffered from intense high blood pressure, which made him unpredictable in his reactions, and his condition became a great distress to all who knew him."[75] In October 1933, a case of food poisoning and a stroke waylaid the once vigorous bishop. He lingered for a time but then died on October 24, 1933. He was only sixty-two years old.

Drumm's years were of great consequence for the Catholic presence in southwest Iowa. He had formed new parishes in Des Moines and Council Bluffs, increased the number of priests, at least temporarily stabilized the troubled finances of the Des Moines Catholic College, confronted the Klan, and kept the church in the public eye by radio broadcasts and expansion of the school system. His interactions with civic and state leaders were limited. Nonetheless, Catholicism was stronger, more visible, and more assertive in this part of Iowa. Drumm's successor, Gerald Bergan, would not appear until the next year.

Bishop Thomas W. Drumm in his later years.
Credit: Diocese of Des Moines Archives.

5

"I Know I Shall Be the Happiest Bishop in America"

Gerald Bergan during Depression, War, Recovery

The Great Depression was hard on Iowa. The agricultural crisis of the 1920s got even worse as the Depression pushed prices even lower and intensified the suffering in the farming sector. Farm income plummeted even more sharply and mortgages for farmland, often based on inflated prices, caused serious distress for Iowa farmers during the 1920s and especially the 1930s. Indeed, the value of Iowa farms slipped dramatically between 1920 and 1940, from $7.6 million to $2.6 million.

The Roosevelt administration appointed Iowan Henry Wallace to the post of secretary of agriculture in 1933, and his team produced the Agricultural Adjustment Act/Administration (AAA), which sought to benefit farmers by reducing agricultural surpluses. Relief checks began to fill the demand for cash needed by farmers. Although some balked at aspects of the program, grousing about government "interference," a survey determined that 75 percent of Iowa farm operators entered the AAA in 1940 while 11 percent stayed out and 14 percent were "undecided." Despite grumbling about "socialism" and the federal policies under Henry Wallace, one farmer in Truro summed up what many felt: "Wallace is all right. I think he has done us a lot of good. A lot of farmers kick on him—they kick, but they like to get those checks."[1]

145

This steep decline in agricultural prices had a ripple effect on other aspects of Iowa life. For example, local banking, the life-blood of the capitalist economy, suffered as well. Since many of these banks held mortgages on Iowa farms, their vitality—or lack thereof—provided a significant indicator of local prosperity. The declining farm economy, the loss of farmland, and the restrictions on credit to farmers greatly distressed the condition of the church in its agricultural counties. The steady decline of the family farm and the unsteady economic conditions in rural southwest Iowa had a corresponding impact on the vitality and financial health of local Catholic churches and schools.

When industries also began to falter early in the 1930s, President Herbert Hoover exhorted business and community leaders to rally public morale and urge businesses not to lay off workers. Not surprisingly, Des Moines Catholic leaders participated in this "cheerleading" exercise. Drumm wrote to his clergy in September 1931, "The Secretary of the U.S. Department of Labor writes us that 'The pastors of the Diocese of Des Moines can be of great aid in relieving the unemployment situation' by cheerful references from the pulpit, urging employers to retain their help, getting others to employ another worker, getting jobs for willing workers, etc. as their experiences will suggest. The Charity Office . . . has an employment department, and should be used much more than it is in getting jobs for workers and workers for jobs." He added, "Here let me add in days of depression a Catholic should be the last to be depressed, our religion teaches us to be cheerful and happy, and we do not depend for happiness on worldly goods."[2] Hoover's "cheerleading" strategy was doomed to failure, as was Drumm's injunction to put on a happy face. Priests in the field were not so sanguine about rhetorical efforts to meliorate the effects of the Depression.

Hunger stalked Des Moines as St. Peter pastor Father Thomas P. Murphy wrote to Drumm in January 1933: "There is hardly a person in the parish working. A lot of them are living in sheds and garages. They can't give a thing. In fact, I have given between $500 and $600 myself to feed and clothe them in the last six months. There is real poverty right now *here*."[3] Murphy worked closely with the poor, encouraging devotion to the recently canonized St. Thérèse of Lisieux. He had erected a shrine to her in 1928.[4]

Some noted the effects of the Depression but blamed them on personal failure. Such was Father Jeremiah O'Sullivan, pastor of St. Mary's in Guthrie Center, who wrote to Drumm, "As every bank in Guthrie Center and Panora has been closed within the past year and are closed, our Catholic people are in straitened circumstances." But O'Sullivan noted sourly: "However, it is not the financial conditions so much as the local prevailing tide of irreligion and paganism that are whittling away the spiritual life of Panora. There is no shortage of money when it comes to gratifications."

The pain of the Depression was often echoed in the letters of Catholic priests to the bishop. Father James Judge from St. Mary of Perpetual Help in Rosemount experienced so much financial trouble that he felt compelled to close the school. He wrote to Mother Stanislaus Hegner of the School Sisters of St. Francis at the end of summer in 1932: "Yesterday I held a meeting of the Congregation and we decided to close the school for the coming year. This being so, there will not be any need to send Sisters. All summer long I have tried to collect money for the school, but could not do so. Nowadays, all one hears is farmers loosing [*sic*] their farms. If conditions do not change soon I fear we will be compelled to close the church."[5]

Hegner graciously agreed to allow the sisters to remain without any compensation save room and board. In 1934, a new pastor, Father Michael Corcoran, implored the new bishop, Gerald Bergan, for another reprieve. "While farm conditions have been exceedingly bad in the Rosemount parish, the new pastor, filled with the enthusiasm of youth and who is also most anxious that the school be kept open, feels that before the end of this year, he will be able with his good people, to better the condition of the Sisters."[6] Corcoran's efforts appear to have worked, because the school remained open and the sisters remained until 1968.

One pastor, Father W. J. Kleffman of St. Patrick's in Neola implored Bishop Bergan for permission to stop paying a former pastor $15 a month, a deal negotiated to get him to resign the parish. Kleffman tried to keep up the payments but lamented:

> Then the Depression came which further depressed farm prices. The farmers received 10 cents a bushel for corn; less than it cost them to produce it. It was then that Church income naturally

> dropped. . . . Then what came was worse, the drought, seven
> years of it, when my people received from nothing to about
> one-fourth crop. Prosperity which had existed among my people
> obviously ceased; debts accumulated, interest and payment on
> farms were impossible and the farms were eventually lost. . . .
> At present I have less than 200 families in the parish. About
> 100 of them are farmers; however I don't think 10 of them are
> land owners. These [land owners] of the parish consists either
> of WPA [Works Progress Administration] or old age pension
> families.[7]

Bergan refused the permission.

Des Moines Catholics, caught in the grip of the Depression, found a voice of hope in the broadcasts of "Radio Priest," Father Charles E. Coughlin of Michigan, who broadcast every Sunday on radio station WOC–WHO at three o'clock in the afternoon. Coughlin often blasted the "forces of greed" that had brought America to its knees and urged with increasing insistence a greater inflation of the currency through silver. Coughlin traveled to Des Moines in 1934 to address the National Farm Holiday Association, which met in the city. While in the Iowa capital, he stayed at St. Augustin's rectory with Monsignor Vitus Stoll and Father Francis O'Connell. Later, he gave a condensed version of his address at the local radio studio; large crowds of Catholic residents and others crammed the studio and its reception hall to hear and catch a glimpse of their hero.

Coughlin regularly invoked a version of Catholic social thought to address his view of the causes of the Great Depression. Later, he became a virulent critic of the Roosevelt administration and in the end had to be silenced by his archbishop for indulging in wild conspiracy theories and anti-Semitism. Despite Coughlin, American bishops kept up a steady stream of messages and statements on social issues. They warmly embraced Pope Pius XI's request for "Catholic Action"—a call for an energized laity and clergy to advance Catholic social principles in the wider society. Bishops Drumm and Gerald Bergan were sympathetic to these movements, but it is unclear if they participated in the seminars and conferences sponsored by the bishops' agency, the National Catholic Welfare Conference.

New Leadership

The nation was wrapped in gloom by 1933, facing 25 percent unemployment, starvation in some areas, terrible agricultural distress, and distressing urban poverty. In that year, Franklin D. Roosevelt, jaunty and optimistic despite the gloom, took over in Washington. In the next year, Des Moines received its new bishop: Gerald Thomas Bergan. Like FDR, this third Des Moines bishop was a warm-hearted and much-loved figure in the Iowa capital and in southwestern Iowa. For eighteen years he fulfilled the tasks of episcopal leadership, but, perhaps more than his predecessor, and certainly more than his immediate successor, Edward Daly, Bergan built bridges of friendship beyond the Catholic community. He reached out to people of other religious traditions, to civic and state leaders, and to the "ordinary Catholics" in the pews who loved his sense of humor, his approachable manner, and his engagement with the various social and cultural issues of his day.

Bergan was born July 26, 1892, in Peoria, Illinois, one of five children of William and Mary Elizabeth O'Connor Bergan. He grew up in St. Mark's Parish in Peoria, where he claimed that his pastor,

Young Gerald Bergan. Credit: Archives of the Diocese of Peoria.

Father James Shannon, was the inspiration for his priestly vocation. Young Bergan attended the Spalding Institute in Peoria, which was conducted by the Brothers of Mary, and in 1909 enrolled in St. Viator's College in Bourbannais, Illinois. This small and struggling institution, run by the Clerics of St. Viator, had many prominent alumni, including the historian John Tracy Ellis and Catholic televangelist Fulton J. Sheen. His low-income parents had a hard time scraping together the tuition, but the kindly Viatorians waived many of the fees. Later, when he was bishop, he tried to repay the debt by placing the Viatorians on the Dowling College faculty and welcoming them to preach and collect money in both his dioceses (Des Moines and later Omaha).

At St. Viator's he stood out for his academic excellence, and despite his short stature and somewhat pudgy physique, he played basketball and participated in other sports. Here he cultivated his gifts as a speaker, was known as a first-rate debater, and was chosen by the school to give the class valedictory address. Given this strong academic record, when he asked to be admitted as a candidate for the priesthood for the Peoria diocese, Bishop Edmund Dunne readily accepted him.

Dunne was a blunt-spoken prelate who looked with amusement on working-class boys who affected airs of nobility, especially if they became bishops. Bergan recalled of Dunne when interviewed by the local press: "Being a frank and honest gentleman, he stated that if American bishops were honest, they would place on their coats-of-arms a pick and shovel and wheelbarrow to denote their lineage."[8] Indeed, Bergan was from a working-class family, and Dunne was fortunate not to see how this favorite son developed a great affection for episcopal regalia, for example, long trains, the ermine collared *cappa magna*, and other *pontificalia*.[9] Although Bergan later claimed to be happy when all of this episcopal plumage was abolished or simplified after Vatican II, those who knew him best noted that he missed it. One of his priests in Omaha observed: "He was in his glory every time he made an appearance in his *cappa magna*."[10]

After graduation from St. Viator's, Bergan was selected to study for the priesthood in Rome, a singular honor for a working-class boy from Peoria. He resided at the old North American College on Via dell'Umiltà and took classes at the Urban College of the Propaganda. Among his classmates in the ordination class of 1916 were future bishops Francis Spellman (New York) and Robert Lucey (San Antonio). Bergan savored his time in the Eternal City, even meeting occasionally with Pope Pius X (allegedly having a long private conversation with the Holy Father in 1914, just before the pontiff's death) and spending the hot Roman summers in the cooler Alban Hills at the Villa Catarina, a summer home for the North American seminarians. In the Eternal City he was enthralled with the majestic ceremonies of the church and met ecclesiastical dignitaries like Cardinal Rafael Merry del Val, the cardinal secretary of state, and others.

Bergan appreciated being in "the hub of Christendom" and absorbed the spirit of *Romanita* intended by a Roman education. Cardinal Basilio Pompilj ordained him (ahead of his classmates) on October 28, 1915. Three weeks before his ordination, his father had died at the age of forty-nine.

Bergan returned to Peoria in July 1916. He celebrated his first Mass at St. Mark's and was appointed assistant pastor at St. Mary's Cathedral, where he remained for eighteen years. In 1926, Bishop Dunne appointed him chancellor of the diocese and rector of the cathedral. In 1928, he was named vicar general. Of the multiple tasks assigned, Ber-

Bergan as a diocesan priest in Peoria. Credit: Archives of the Diocese of Peoria.

gan later recalled: "During my 18 years at the cathedral I not only performed parish work but most of the Chancery work of the diocese. This work was lighter in those days than at present, and it didn't take too much of one's time. One priest could very well fill both positions."[11] He likely filled in for Dunne where he could since the bishop often took off on extended trips where he could not be reached. When Dunne died on October 4, 1929, Bergan was appointed administrator of the Peoria diocese until Bishop Joseph Henry Leo Schlarman arrived in April 1930. Schlarman extended Bergan's assignment as rector and had him promoted to the honorary rank of domestic prelate, or monsignor.[12]

After the death of Drumm, Rome deliberated for a while, pondering Bergan, St. Ambrose College professor William Lawrence Adrian (later bishop of Nashville), and a Father Michael Tarrent as potential candidates for the vacant See. In the end, Bergan won the nod and was appointed to Des Moines on March 24, 1934, and on June 13 Cardinal George Mundelein consecrated him as bishop at St. Mary's Cathedral in Peoria. He was assisted by Bishops

Joseph Henry Schlarman of Peoria and Henry Rohlman of Davenport. Secular commentators noted Bergen's tender affection for his mother, observing that after his consecration he "stepped down from the altar and crossed to the front pew in which sat his white-haired mother. . . . Bending to her beaming face amid all the splendor of the occasion and in full view of the church's gathered faithful, he kissed her." Bishop Bernard Sheil, auxiliary of Chicago, preached at the occasion, but his address alluded only briefly to the duties of a bishop (the traditional subject matter for such a sermon) and veered off into a ringing endorsement of the advances of organized labor.[13]

Bergan arrived in Des Moines on the rainy evening of June 20, 1934. Despite the weather, thousands turned out to greet him, the Moose Club band pumped out airs, and a procession of one hundred cars formed to escort him from the train depot to his new residence. The rain let up just as Bergan made his way through the streets. He joked with the crowd gathered on his lawn, "You have seen my power," he said laughingly, "I brought the rain and I made

Right to left: Bishop Bergan,
Monsignor Lester Lyons. Credit:
Diocese of Des Moines Archives.

it stop just before I arrived." The crowd chuckled, "However, I will not risk becoming a false prophet by telling you whether or not it will rain again!"[14]

On the steps of the episcopal mansion (no doubt cleared of Drumm's farm menagerie), Bergan, dressed in a black frock coat and tall silk hat, waved to the crowd: "My dear people of Des Moines," he shouted, "it was not easy to leave Peoria, but if the people who came to meet me today are a sample of the people in my new diocese, I know that I shall be the happiest bishop in America!"[15] At his installation, he noted: "I only know one way to govern a diocese; it is the same way in which I ruled my parish: with love and affection for my children; and in return receiving loyalty, helpfulness, and cooperation and responsiveness."[16] Indeed, until he departed for Omaha in 1948, Bergan's jovial ways, his kind-heartedness, and his openness to local culture made his tenure one of the happiest of all the bishops of Des Moines.

Bergan caught the attention of the entire city because he never thought it beneath his dignity to make people laugh—even in church. His trademark humor was on display at the huge civic reception given him at the Shrine Auditorium. Before a crowd of two thousand people, he pledged his allegiance to the teetotaling culture of the Iowa capital: "As proof positive I have separated myself from Peoria, I will do something no loyal Peorian will do after he is seven years old." Bergan then poured and drank a glass of water—to the howls of the crowd. He also quipped about his residence: "In spite of the Depression, I think I have done pretty well in Des Moines, starting out at 2000 Grand [the address of his home]."[17]

The Catholic newspaper noted near Christmas in 1937 that *Des Moines Tribune* columnist Elizabeth Clarkson Zwart reported, after hearing about Bergan's appearance at a public event, "I'm hearing from all sides that the life of the party, the belle of the ball, the wow of the evening . . . was the most Reverend Gerald T. Bergan, Bishop of the Des Moines Diocese. . . . The bishop it seems 'rolled them in the aisles.' Not the first time either."[18]

Bergan did not have to wait long to exercise his newly acquired episcopal powers. On June 24, 1934, he ordained John Gorman and John Higgins to the priesthood at St. Ambrose Cathedral. Father Michael Schwarte recalled that on that first ordination day Bergan smiled widely and swayed on his crosier, noting: "This proves that Iowa can produce something more than corn and cattle and grain and hogs."[19] "The bishop said he was extremely happy on this morning, one that he would always remember, for these were his first children."[20]

Bergan's gift was opening wider a space for Catholics in the broader community—much of which was Protestant. Dominican theologian Thomas O'Meara, whose father became a good friend of the bishop, recalled that Bergan

> had the reputation of being an extraordinarily witty public speaker. Des Moines at that time had a small Catholic population in the center of a largely Protestant state. In the 1930s, anti-Catholicism had been prominent; Protestant churches advertised lectures by ex-priests; the Ku Klux Klan was strong in southern Iowa; some country clubs were closed to Catholics. The charming and funny young bishop became a frequently sought-after speaker for any function, secular or religious. Through humor he worked against prejudice and changed the climate for Catholics in Iowa. . . . I sometimes rode along with my father when he drove Bishop Bergan to a parish dinner, a confirmation, or to the exciting Rock Island Railroad Station. But my memories of him preaching come from Confirmations and other church events. . . . His energy and humor lit up the church. Like a good public speaker he never spoke long, and his ideas were focused. There was always a joke or two, but in the sermon they illustrated some aspect of Christianity at work in people's live at that moment. People left the liturgy with the impression that the Christian faith was happy, vital, and practical.[21]

Bergan's jokes made him the Bob Hope of the speaking circuit. One of his standards was the old saw: "I'll most likely die the same way Christ did, between two thieves—my doctor on one side of me and my lawyer on the other."[22]

Others saw a less flattering side to the prelate. Historian Stephen Szmrecsanyi wrote that some saw Bergan as a bit narcissistic, never laughing at others' jokes, and loving to be the center of attention. He also noted that "at times he could be biting and sarcastic and while he was always friendly, he was not kindly." Yet others who knew him well attested to his basic concern for his priests and people and the lengths he was willing to go through to help them. Defending his love of ecclesiastical regalia, they observed that he was always a formal man and dismissed accusations of pomposity, insisting instead the he was a man of the church in the best sense.[23] Bergan was astute enough to insist on controlling his official affairs. He retained Monsignor John J. Boylan as his vicar general and made Father William McMahon his chancellor.

Assisting the Poor: Bergan, Ligutti, and Rural Life

Coal mining had been one of the staples of Iowa life for many years. Rich deposits of bituminous coal in Polk and Dallas Counties attracted a medley of ethnic miners who worked and lived in company towns near the mines; however, coal mining took a big hit during the Great Depression, and many of the miners faced poverty and homelessness. Ligutti, now pastor in Granger, had the pastoral care of some of these mining communities. Here, a Catholic priest, acting under the inspiration of Catholic social teaching (particularly its emphasis on distributive justice), decided to do something about poverty conditions.

In 1933, the famous Hundred Days' Congress passed one of Roosevelt's key initiatives, the National Industrial Recovery Act. The law itself dealt primarily with the stabilization of industrial prices, but it had riders and amendments that addressed other needs. One of them was housing. A section of the bill created the Subsistence Homesteads Division. This provision provided homes for the impoverished in rural communities. Thousands of communities applied for funding, including Ligutti who petitioned for fifty houses to be built on 225 acres of farmland a half mile out of Granger. These simple but comfortable homes were intended for the families living in squalor near the mining camps. Like many rural life enthusiasts of this period, Ligutti believed that country living and agricultural labor had a cleansing power for the human body and spirit. The family farm and these homesteads, which had about three acres for cultivation, provided not only a home but a spiritual experience for their inhabitants.

In January 1934, Ligutti traveled to Washington to lobby for the Granger homesteads. Aided by the future founder of the Glenmary

E. Roosevelt's visit to Granger Homesteads, June 1936.
Credit: Courtesy of the Department of Special Collections and University Archives, Marquette University Libraries.

Home Missioners, Father Howard Bishop, and the chairman of the Rural Life Committee of the National Catholic Welfare Conference, Father Edgar Schmiedler, OSB (a monk of Atchison), Ligutti tirelessly touched base with every Catholic politician, ambassador, and cabinet officer he could and also enlisted the help of the National Catholic Welfare Conference. The diligence paid off. In March 1935, secretary of the interior, Harold Ickes, announced that Granger would be a site for the proposed subsistence homesteads. Although the Subsistence Homesteads Division officially managed the project, Ligutti had extensive influence over the project.

By October 1935, the homes were built and fifty families of various nationalities moved into them, thirty-three of them Catholics. The families had thirty years to pay for the land at a 3 percent interest rate. Although the home program was discontinued in the 1950s, many recalled special memories of Ligutti and his many efforts.[24] Like Duren in Westphalia and other Catholic agrarians, Ligutti helped form cooperatives for buying, selling, and manufacturing, as well as for the ownership of expensive heavy machinery.[25] He also founded a credit union that persisted long after the project ended.

In June 1936, these successful homesteads won the attention of Eleanor Roosevelt, who personally came out to inspect the community with Ligutti as her tour guide. Later, Frances Perkins, secretary of labor, visited as well. Other visitors from around the nation and world—and even the Vatican—stopped to see the homes. Ligutti gave the residents his special care and inquired about them even after he left Granger in 1940 to assume full-time leadership of the National Catholic Rural Life Conference (NCRLC).

Ligutti became the most visible priest in the history of the Des Moines diocese as he continued to write on agricultural issues. He formed an extensive network of friends and associates that was international in scope and was frequently called on to speak on the topics dear to his heart in various parts of the country. After World War II, he became a renowned global expert on a variety of agriculture-related subjects—including irrigation and the distribution of food. Among his many contacts were agricultural luminaries in many nations as well as Monsignor Giovanni Battista Montini, then working in the Vatican Secretariat of State, afterward the archbishop of Milan, and later Pope Paul VI. The pontiff drew on his expertise in drafting encyclical letters.

In 1938, Bergan made Ligutti a monsignor (a title the priest publicly disdained but privately loved). He became connected to a number of rural bishops: Peter Bartholome of St. Cloud, Minnesota; Aloysius Muench of Fargo, North Dakota; and Joseph Schlarmann of Peoria, Illinois. He was also quite active in the NCRLC, serving as president in 1937 and again in 1939. In May 1939, Ligutti became executive secretary of the NCRLC. In late 1939, when plans were being floated about moving the conference headquarters to Washington, DC, nearer the National Catholic Welfare Conference (NCWC) Ligutti sought advice about what to do. Bergan urged him to either be a pastor or devote full-time efforts to the work of the conference. When the bishops rejected efforts to move the NCRLC to the nation's capital, Ligutti convinced them to locate in Des Moines, and on January 1, 1941, he bade farewell to Granger, turning the parish over to Father John Gorman.

Monsignor Ligutti at NCRLC headquarters, 1967. Credit: Courtesy of the Department of Special Collections and University Archives, Marquette University Libraries.

Ligutti took up residence in Des Moines and eventually purchased a headquarters at 3801 Grand Avenue, where the conference remained until 1979. On the top floor he created a small chapel named in honor of St. Isidore, the patron of farmers. To the rear of the house, he planted a garden, which a young grade schooler and future chancellor, Stephen Orr, passed each day, eventually summoning up courage to speak with Ligutti about a vocation to the priesthood. Later, Orr and Ligutti became close friends while in Rome together—the younger priest helping his Des Moines colleague with social obligations. From his Des Moines headquarters Ligutti traveled far and wide, produced myriad books and pamphlets extolling the virtues of the land, and offering advice about the food supply and population issues. Historian David Bovee records the wide stretch of Ligutti's activities, chronicles the evolution of the Catholic Rural Life movement to a broader international movement, and notes the priest's home-spun appeal to audiences around America and the world.[26] Ligutti flourished under Bergan's benign rule.

Postwar Growth

Due to the restraints on family growth and migration caused by the Great Depression and the Second World War, the number of Catholics grew only modestly under Bergan, inching up from 39,250 to 43,500 between in 1934 and 1948. As the chart suggests, rural counties continued to lose population while the two most heavily urbanized areas, Polk and Pottawattamie Counties, registered increases.

County	1940	1950
Mills	15,064	14,064
Montgomery	15,697	15,685
Adair	13,196	12,292
Union	16,280	15,651
Clarke	10,233	9,369
Lucas	14,571	12,069
Harrison	22,767	19,560
Shelby	16,720	15,942
Audubon	11,790	11,579
Guthrie	17,210	15,197
Dallas	24,649	23,661
Polk	195,835	226,010
Pottawattamie	66,756	69,682
Cass	18,647	18,532
Madison	14,525	13,131
Warren	17,695	17,758
Taylor	14,258	12,420
Page	24,887	23,921
Adams	10,156	8,753
Fremont	14,645	12,323
Ringgold	11,137	9,528
Decatur	14,012	12,601
Wayne	13,308	11,737
TOTAL	594,038	601,465
Catholic total	41,090	50,154
Percentage of total	7%	8%

Source: US Census and Official Catholic Directory

Saving the Catholic High School

Growth in the educational work of the diocese occurred primarily in Catholic schools as the number of schools surged between 1934 and 1948 from twenty-eight to forty-one—the latter growth the pent-up expansion stymied by Depression and war. The numbers of students likewise increased from 5,330 to 8,640. Only three new parishes were founded, lifting that total from sixty-three to sixty-six, while the number of missions remained constant at thirty. Enrollment at St. Joseph Academy rose from 350 to 468 during that period.

Growth surged at Des Moines College from 250 to 418, and the school even found the money to build a new gym.[27] Its teaching corps was primarily diocesan priests, but handling teaching and student discipline was always challenging.[28] Few of the priests on the Dowling staff were lifelong educators and were eventually needed to serve in parishes.

In 1935 Bergan renamed the school Dowling College (later high school), in honor of the recently deceased first bishop of Des Moines and its founder. More important, despite its rising enrollments, Bergan faced financial issues with the high school as well as challenges staffing it with diocesan priests who could function as teachers and who could work with adolescents.

Saving the High School—The Viatorian Gambit

As the chief personnel officer of the diocese, Bergan was facing a shortage of trained people. The flow of Irish-born priests declined somewhat with the Depression and World War II, which made travel and finances difficult. Fewer priests stretched resources greatly. This was particularly true with Dowling High School, whose priest staff was important to the school's Catholic identity. They were often in short supply, however, particularly in the fields of mathematics and science. President John Boylan had noted this already in 1933, when he complained of the "woeful deficiency of priest instructors—in the departments of Natural Science and Mathematics."[29]

In addition, once the war started, many Des Moines padres were anxious to become military chaplains. Hiring lay faculty, even at low wages, became problematic for the school's shaky finances. Boylan pressed hard to get rid of the college program—in part because teachers were not properly trained to teach college-level material. Moreover, this would save the still financially struggling institution, which was still dependent on large transfusions of cash from the diocese.

While thumbing through a copy of the Chicago *New World* in 1939, Bergan noted that the Clerics of St. Viator, the teachers of his youth, had just ordained eight priests. In early March, two Viatorians—James Maguire and Timothy Rowan—were visiting in the diocese, and Bergan broached the idea of having the community come to Des Moines. With their encouragement he dashed off a letter to Viatorian Provincial John P. O'Mahoney, who apparently knew Bergan during his school days, congratulating him on the new priests: "I do not know the number of applications you have for their services, but would be most happy to have two of them if you could spare them. We would give them teaching positons in our high school—375 boys—and I know they would be happy here in Des Moines."[30] To Bergan's great delight, O'Mahoney responded positively to the request, promising to bring it up with his council and asking questions about length of service and the remuneration.[31] Bergan then became more specific: "If we could have two priests who could teach high school English and a little history; or if one might know some commercial work, we would welcome them." Bergan was looking for a long-time commitment and promised to pay them $500 for an academic year and also include room, board, and laundry.[32]

Bishop Bergan was even more delighted when O'Mahoney sent him three priests: Michael Malone, Redmond Burke, and Francis J. Larkin. The work apparently went so well that Bergan proposed in 1942 to a new Viatorian provincial, Father Richard J. French, the prospect of handing over the entire administration of the school to the Viatorians. "Msgr. Boylan [the school president] and I have talked over the matter many times. Would your Order be interested in taking Dowling College? . . . The school is quite a problem for a small diocese like ours with secular priests."[33]

Father French responded positively, asking for an opportunity to meet with Bergan. The bishop quickly convened a meeting of the board of trustees of Dowling and explained the prospects of the Viatorians coming on full time. He noted the dearth of qualified diocesan priests and laity to take over faculty positions and, most important, finances. "Because of the cost of operating Dowling under present arrangements, an excessive drain on the financial resources of this diocese . . . cannot be continued indefinitely." The board approved the negotiations.[34] Getting Dowling off the diocesan books soon became a priority—one the Viatorians were quick to apprehend.

After hearing more details, French met with his council and reported back to Bergan in mid-April, "I held a meeting with my Council yesterday in Chicago, and presented your great and magnanimous offer to them, and I hasten to add that it was readily accepted." French noted, however, "there was a little trepidation in my Council about the financing of the College."[35]

The Viatorians had just lost their college in Bourbannais, Illinois, in 1939 and were skittish about financial matters related to educational institutions. French was sure the matter could be worked out, but he sent Father Christopher Marzano, the provincial treasurer, to take a survey of the situation. French urged Bergan to keep the priests and lay teachers for a year and anticipated putting in a full faculty during the 1943–1944 school year.[36] The devil would be in the details. As the proposal matured, the Viatorians made it clear that they wanted the title to the Dowling property—for their own security and assurance that they would truly be in charge of the institution.

But Bergan balked at this, remembering that it had been purchased with the money of the priests and people of the Diocese of Des Moines. Bergan instead wanted to lease the debt-free buildings (which now included a newly built gymnasium) to the Viatorians for a dollar a year. They would assume complete control of the school but also be responsible for the upkeep of the property as well as the various insurance payments. They would also have to maintain a salary scale commensurate with their accredited status by the North Central Association.

Misgivings about the deal began immediately. One of the Viatorians on the faculty, Joseph Ryan, reported conversations that suggested the diocese was "dumping" Dowling on the Viatorian community. Without owning it, the Viatorians would be liable for all its fixed costs (e.g., insurance and maintenance) and inevitably left with a white elephant of a building with limited means of supporting itself. Marzano's report to his superiors had also warned of the financial pitfalls of taking on the school lock, stock, and barrel. Bergan now began to hear rumors that the Viatorians were not coming. "We have had no word from you," he wrote worriedly to Father French. "We are a bit anxious because the Superior of your men at Davenport is broadcasting *urbi et orbi* that the Viatorians are not coming to Dowling." He also sought to allay Marzano's and French's fears that the school could not produce enough revenue to support itself.[37]

Bergan handed over precise details of the transfer to the diocesan attorney, Judge Thomas J. Guthrie. As the bargain moved into the final stages, Viatorian attorney Lowell Lawson weighed in and, like Marzano, urged the community not to accept the care and financing of the buildings but instead to merely offer to staff the school.[38] Bergan was now caught short-handed. He had counted on the Viatorians to come through and had begun to transfer the diocesan priests off the faculty: "I have sent my professors into the Army and Navy and also other vacancies in the diocese," he lamented. Repeatedly he tried to convince the Viatorians that "the place is theirs, except for strict legal title," and that the lease would work better for them in case they decided to get out. Marzano had reported that the community would need $17,000 to $20,000 a year to meet the payments. Bergan agreed to cover that for three years and once again tried to sell the high school as "the finest proposition they ever received." He rejected a staffing-only solution, however, admitting with a tone of sadness: "We might just as well continue as we are." In begging for help, he promised that he was "not handing them [the Viatorians] any lemon." But he insisted, "My reason for the change is that the school has grown too large for this small diocese to handle. I have no teachers of science, math, and commerce. My coming Ordinandi are few and the diocese is growing."[39]

But French and his Council were not moved. "We could not accept a lease, we do not want a lease. . . . It would be suicidal for us." French worried that taking teachers away from posts that paid them $1,000 per year (a large salary for professed religious in those days) and sending them to Dowling, "where financial sources are so dubious," would be hurtful to the future of the community. Speaking to Bergan's appeal to a community he loved and respected, French wrote, "I know and realize your great love for us and for your great diocese. . . . I know only of the failures of St. Viator College and of the good things we now enjoy, and I cannot jeopardize these. . . . A lease project would never be acceptable." French hoped for a "satisfactory conclusion," but to no avail.[40] The remaining Viatorians eventually left Dowling, and the faculty remained diocesan priests and laymen. To save money during the war, the college program was suspended. Efforts to restore it after the war were studied by Bishop Edward Daly and Father Thomas Costin. By 1951, the prospect of reopening the college was a dead letter.[41]

A Blessing in Disguise

Even though Bergan was disappointed, the Viatorian refusal ultimately worked to the good of the Diocese of Des Moines. This personnel flap revealed just how important the high school had become to the local church and to the wider community. Keeping diocesan priests on staff at Dowling meant that the boys had regular role models of priests who could encourage their vocation to the priesthood. As Bishop Dowling had hoped, the number of Dowling graduates who went to the seminary increased. Diocesan priests were about 101 in number in 1933 but had jumped to 115 by the time Bergan departed for Omaha in 1948. The number of priests from religious orders (mostly Passionists) had declined a bit from twenty-eight to twenty-six.

After the war, a vocation boom began that tipped the balance in favor of a native clergy. A number of former servicemen discovered their vocation on the battlefield or had deferred earlier plans in order to serve the nation. In 1946, twenty-six men were preparing for the diocesan priesthood—attending a variety of seminaries.[42] Page after page of the Catholic newspaper carried accounts of the ordinations and first Masses of many sons of the diocese, diocesan and religious priests.[43] Rural communities, especially those whose parishes sponsored high schools, also produced vocations. At least into the 1960s, Dowling produced a cadre of local priests who served the diocese well.

Creating Catholic Culture by a Catholic Press

Maturation and growth of the Catholic community required even more efforts to maintain a Catholic culture. Bishop Bergan used a local and regional Catholic newspaper to create a common pool of information for the far-flung diocese. The papers covered not only local Catholic events but also Catholic news from around the world. Catholics could keep in touch with what the pope was doing or significant developments in American Catholic life. Parishes often provided these papers free of charge to parishioners.

Since its inception, the diocese had been served by regional Catholic newspapers. The news of the area was covered until 1923 by the independently owned *Western World*. The *Davenport Catholic Messenger*, a successor, covered all of southern Iowa and included a page of Des Moines news. Under the tutelage and with the support of the Davenport journal, Des Moines produced its own Catholic newspaper in October 1936, called *The Catholic Register*, edited by Father John J. Molyneaux, who provided a healthy brio of local stories about the Des Moines church, mostly events in the city. Molyneaux, a native of Listowel, Ireland, was born in 1893. After completing his philosophy studies in Ireland, he finished his seminary training at St. Viator's College in Illinois, where he likely knew of Gerald Bergan. He was ordained in 1916 and did graduate work at Columbia University in New York. He came to Des Moines, where he served in various parishes and taught English at Des Moines College. Bergan appointed him editor in 1936 and also made him chaplain at St. Joseph's Academy.[44]

Yet another paper—this one produced at Dowling—called *The Aquin* was published by one C. S. Andrus, who also owned *The Catholic Register*, and included a good bit of diocesan news delivered to parishes on Sunday mornings. In 1939 Father Robert A. Walsh replaced Molyneaux, and Bergan bought *The Catholic Register* from Andrus. In September 1941, faced with high expenses, Bergan joined the paper to the Denver *Register* chain of Catholic newspapers (not to be confused with the above-named *Register*), which he promised would "furnish a splendid 8 page newspaper for our diocese." Father Raymond Conley, ordained in 1936, was appointed as the editor. Conley was dispatched to Denver, where he spent six weeks learning the trade and the particular techniques of the *Register* chain. Urbane, at times acerbic, but always competent, Conley would edit the paper until 1962.[45]

Experiencing World War II through Catholic Eyes

American entry into World War II (1941) took a toll on the state as 276,000 Iowans marched off to battlefields in Europe and the Pacific. The state went on wartime footing as workers from dormant factories and starving farmers received orders that pulled them out of the Great Depression. On the farms, the "Food for Freedom"

Father (later Monsignor) Raymond J. Conley. Credit: Diocese of Des Moines Archives.

campaign was launched and the restricted production of the first Agricultural Adjustment Act–era gave way to a demand for all-out production that in turn enriched the distressed farming frontier.[46] The state implemented rationing, blackouts, and other civilian defense procedures, and local military installations, such as nearby Camp Dodge in Johnston, Iowa, soon experienced huge booms in population.

Production also went into high gear. Des Moines's eleven industrial plants received defense contracts that flowed into the state, producing "everything from gears to clothes to corrugated boxes to mud lugs for tanks."[47] Des Moines's Boyt Harness Company made haversacks, gun covers, and cartridge belts.[48] The only aircraft factory in Iowa was the Solar Plant in Des Moines. When the US government E awards lauded the plant's contributions to the war effort, Bishop Bergan himself praised the Solar workers who, "without benefit of publicity, praise, glamour of battle have done a good job and remained devoted servants of God."[49] Ankeny, ten miles north of Des Moines, hosted a small-arms ammunition plant and a rifle range built on a clover field. The company employed twenty thousand workers at its peak, including African Americans and women.[50] By the time it closed in August 1945, this plant produced billions of .30 and .50 caliber bullets. Des Moines provided labor and transportation for these new war industries; Ankeny's Catholic population would continue to grow, soon bursting the small chapel that had been built for the coal miners of the area.

Catholics patriotically supported the war effort. Catholic children saved scrap metal and other items needed for war (e.g., baking grease). The Catholic press published information about the various War Bond drives, which the local priests endorsed. Catholic sisters and high school students participated in Red Cross training, rolled bandages, and sent gifts to troops abroad or en route to debarkation points east and west that rumbled through Council Bluffs and Des Moines. Chief among the duties of the clergy was consoling the families of fallen soldiers and calming the anxieties of those who worried about their sons and daughters abroad. While it brought back prosperity, the war also demanded payment in blood. The number of Iowa's war dead was one of the highest per capita in the United States, with more than five thousand going to their graves by early 1945.[51]

In all, fourteen Des Moines priests volunteered for chaplain duty, some of them serving in dangerous combat locations and even being captured by the enemy.[52] These chaplains wrote as often as they could to Bishop Bergan and revealed an important contribution of the Iowa Catholic commitment to America's victory in World War II. Seeing the war through their eyes adds another layer to our understanding of the war's impact on Iowans.

Father Albert Davidsaver joined the army as a way of helping his father pay his debts: "My dad is still way in debt. I have tried my best to help him, but he is still far in the red. Here would be an opportunity to get him back on his feet."[53] But the experience of the service was eye-opening for many. Davidsaver was sent for a time to Fort Bliss, near the Mexican border, where he attempted to learn how to ride a horse.

By August 1943 he was in Australia: "Am learning after much experimenting that the best way to get the men to the Sacraments is by actually going into each troop and bringing the sacraments to them. I finally hit on this solution and so now I explain to each troop

Father (later Monsignor) Albert Davidsaver. Credit: Diocese of Des Moines Archives.

ahead of time, hear confessions the night before and have Mass just before supper so they can receive Holy Communion and not miss a meal. . . . Have had to say Mass in the open with altars of various shades and designs, including the front of a jeep, the back of a command car, mess tables. Have heard confessions right out in the open on Mother Earth, on the trunk of a tree, inside tents, behind a tree, in storage rooms, in kitchens. Talk about improvise! We do it. 'Sacramenta propter homines' [sacraments are for people]."[54]

Davidsaver was with the first cavalry and was seriously wounded in an encounter with a Japanese soldier in the Los Negros Islands.[55] He was awarded the Bronze Star and the Purple Heart and achieved the rank of colonel in the army reserve before he returned to the diocese in 1946. Likewise, Father Richard Carberry of Panora, Iowa, although a priest of the Archdiocese of Portland, survived the siege of Bataan and later succumbed to malaria. He was awarded a Silver Star and Oak Leaf Cluster for his gallantry.

Davidsaver learned about the flexibility of Catholic practice created by battlefield conditions. Other priests found that even good Catholic soldiers could sometimes misbehave when wartime dynamics loosened traditional morality. For example, Father Joseph Devlin wrote to Bishop Bergan in 1944 after participating in a war-bond auction in Kansas City: "At the monthly show held in the officer's club, a young girl billed as being from the Art Institute in Kansas City was placed on the stage. An auction of her clothing was then held. The officer who bid the highest in war bonds received the article of her clothing; he also removed it from the girl's body. It finally reached a point where the girl had only the last two essential articles left on her body. The Base Commanding Officer bought and removed one; the Bomb commanding officers bought and removed the other. (For this we fight and buy war bonds.)"[56] Poor Father Devlin must have found all this quite taxing.

POWs: Catholic Priests as Prisoners of War

Sadder cases followed. Father Thomas Barrett entered the army in July 1942 and joined the troops in Burma, where he was chaplain to Merrill's Marauders. He died of typhus while on duty.[57] Some Des Moines priests endured the privations of being prisoners of war. Father Stephen Kane with the Thirty-Fourth Army Division in Tunisia provided the most exciting news of the war. Born August 30, 1908, in County Longford, Ireland, and ordained in 1933, he served in various rural parishes. His last stateside appointment was St. Bernard's Parish in Osceola, and in 1940 he became chaplain of the Iowa National Guard and was stationed at Camp Claiborne in Louisiana.

Kane joined the first contingents of American soldiers sent to North Africa in 1942 to dislodge the Germans. He wrote to Bergan in 1942, "We are in Algeria at the moment, after an eventful cruise and exciting arrival. . . . The horrors of war could never be imagined, all description is beggared. . . . Modern war too strikes quickly and with all the efficiency of scientific destruction. Des Moines's own first battalion was first to set foot on African soil and with them I found a spot in the overcrowded landing craft."[58]

One group that was with Kane, Company M from Red Oak, had received an emotional farewell from the hometown folks. This group would be part of a bloody engagement with the Germans at Kasserine Pass, where 311 Iowa soldiers out of 814 were reported missing. Indeed, one-half of Iowa's casualties were from the southwestern region of the state. In the battle of Kasserine Pass in early 1943, Red Oak took forty-five casualties; Atlantic, forty-six; Shenandoah, twenty-three; and Clarinda, forty-one. "War Hits Red Oak" was the title of a grim *Life* magazine story in May 1943.[59] One observer noted that the losses in Red Oak would be seventeen thousand men if compared to the population of New York City.

Kane described the first phase of the operation: "I came ashore in the second wave of assault landing craft; I made the entire crossing

Father Stephen Kane. Credit: Diocese of Des Moines Archives.

with the Des Moines Battalion. They were the first ashore and they certainly did a great job. Capt. Ed Bird of Visitation Parish was by far the outstanding hero of the now famous D-Day [not to be confused with the famous landing at Normandy, which took place in June 1944]. Capt. Frank Conway of St. Ambrose, Capt. Tim Gillespie, Capt. Bob Brown, Lt. Frank Noonan—all Dowling grads and worthy leaders did a great job."[60]

On February 17, 1943, while crossing a minefield in Tunisia to retrieve the body of a fallen comrade, Kane was captured and reported missing. He was taken to a prisoner of war camp in Germany.[61]

Bergan finally heard from Kane on September 3, 1943: "Death or capture or safe return is all to the hands of Providence. But here the priest is most filled with the importance of his mission. How our boys lived and fought and died is a credit to faith and the state. . . . Here despite petty tyrannies, the constant goodwill of our men for one another is remarkable."[62]

In another letter to Bergan, Kane related: "Thank God I am all in one piece. . . . The group included very many of your friends: you recall Red Oak, Jefferson, Clarinda, Atlantic, Shenandoah, and the Bluffs boys; they all suffered my fate. . . . I have not requested repatriation with the medics as I feel my obligation is with my boys through these days of sorrow especially. . . . Indeed . . . 1943 had brought me the experiences of a hundred lives. Prison life may be one of petty tyrannies, but it is assuredly one of good fellowship. There is a hidden wealth in humans that only suffering will reveal. This life is not one of jaded emptiness and hours passed recapturing the past and planning for the future. Here men are most themselves, so poor creatures of circumstance in defiant, patient waiting the dawn of the

Father Francis Sampson, chaplain.
Credit: Diocese of Des Moines Archives.

Great Day."[63] In all, Kane spent twenty-eight months in captivity, which he jokingly referred to as a "long retreat." He was released in the spring of 1945 and returned to Des Moines that June.[64] He went on to serve in the Korean War as well.

Des Moines also had the heroic Father Francis Sampson, who published his exploits in a book titled *Look Out Below*, later updated as *Paratrooper Padre*. Ordained in 1941, Sampson was an assistant at St. Patrick's in Neola and joined the service in 1942. He went to England and in June 1944 jumped with the 101st Airborne Division as the Normandy invasion began. He landed in a river and was so caught up in his parachute he nearly drowned. Freed by one of his colleagues, he swam back and retrieved his three hundred–pound backpack, which included his liturgical vessels and even a pyx with the Blessed Sacrament. He cared for the wounded and braved machine gun fire to tend to the dying. He was briefly captured but forty-eight hours later escaped to England. He then rejoined the men at the front and was himself wounded. He was captured once again near Bastogne by the Germans and freed by the Russians in April 1945. Sampson wrote of his exploits in the Normandy invasion, reassuring folks at home by telling them that many of the men went to confession and Communion before they parachuted behind German lines.[65]

Prisoner-of-War Camps in Iowa

As Catholic priests were held prisoner, Iowa also had prisoner-of-war camps. The main encampment was first at Algona and then at Clarinda. Father John Patrick Cody, chancellor of the Diocese of Kansas City, Missouri (later cardinal-archbishop of Chicago), informed Bergan in 1944 that three hundred Italian prisoners were being sent to do farm work in the diocese. Cody wrote: "The colonel invited me to sit in on a meeting of the officers and he instructed the captain who is in charge of the transfer of these men to communicate at once with the local parish priest of the church at Shenandoah, Iowa regarding the spiritual assistance given these men. . . . There are some three hundred and they will arrive on Sunday. This information, I am given to understand is a strict military secret."[66]

Des Moines priest Father Paul Marasco went to this camp near Clarinda and recruited priests from Shenandoah and Conception Abbey to help tend to the prisoners—initially a mixture of Italians, Japanese, and Germans. A Maryknoll missionary who could speak Japanese also arrived to assist in the work. Many of the 1,200 Japanese were from Nagasaki. Marasco devoted a lot of time to the camp and brought his mother and sisters to sing a high Mass for the Italians and to speak to them in their own language. Bergan came to the camp to greet the prisoners and asked them to lay aside hate. At the end of 1944, most of the German POWs were transferred to a camp at Algona, Iowa. Another camp at Tabor, Iowa, received most of the Italians. The pastors of Shenandoah and Hamburg assumed care of them.[67]

The Toll on Catholic Men

Father Sampson lived to fight another day after Normandy. Such was not the fate of Ernest A. Block of Earling (Shelby County), who also landed on D-Day and was reported missing on July 29, 1944, and whose death was officially confirmed on February 16, 1945.[68] The small community grieved the loss, and funeral services held at the majestic Earling church helped give his family some comfort. Sadness also visited the Schram family of Earling. They had two sons: Theodore who went missing in 1942 and Edward who was killed in 1944. Later it was discovered that Theodore was a POW of the Japanese held in Burma.[69]

Reports of the men and women who served in the military were also reported—as well as tragic casualties. A young Dowling graduate, Captain Edward Clarke of the Marine Corps, died in the invasion of Saipan and left his family grieving at St. Augustin's Church.[70] Indeed, every parish in the diocese was affected by the war. In 1944, the Catholic press reported that 4,203 men and women from the diocese were in the armed forces. Sampling the parishes, they reported that the largest contingent came from Des Moines parishes, 400 from St. Anthony's Parish, 320 from St. John's, 248 from St. Ambrose, and 239 from St. Augustin's. In Council Bluffs, 295 came from St. Francis Xavier, 96 from Assumption in Granger, 91 from St. Patrick's in Perry, and 55 from All Saints in Stuart. The largest number of Catholic enlistees (2,812) were in the US Army; 1,040 in the US Navy; and 229 in the US Marines. Sixty-six women joined, among them fifty-four nurses.

By early 1944, thirty-four Catholic service members from Des Moines had been killed and another twenty had been wounded.[71] After the war was over, the Catholic newspaper stated that more than 5,600 from the diocese had served in the armed forces. Forty-four of the diocese's sixty-six parishes had fatalities. St. John's Parish in Des Moines suffered the most with nineteen casualties. St. Anthony's, St. Ambrose, and St. Augustin's each had thirteen, while St. Francis in Council Bluffs lost twelve.[72] As painful as these were, the loss of life in the smaller communities of Red Oak and Shenandoah left a deep wound on those small communities.

Fighting the War at Home: Catholics and Local Mobilization

Des Moines Catholics swung firmly behind the war effort. At Dowling College preparedness coursework had already been in place before Pearl Harbor. Father Charles McAniff, a noncommissioned officer of the US Army, offered courses in electricity, architectural drawing, aerial photography, and military communications to the Dowling men. Sgt. Oscar McPherson, chief radio technician of Fort Des Moines, taught courses in radio-telegraphy. A civilian pilot-training course had already trained seventy-five students by early 1942, many of whom enlisted in the service once war was declared.[73] Red Cross instructors schooled Dowling students in life-saving techniques while fundraisers for the organization were held in the school's new gymnasium. Similar classes were also offered in a variety of parish halls under the auspices of the National Council of Catholic Women. Red Cross instructors also came to St. Joseph Academy and taught the girls to roll bandages. The academy participated in bond drives, and helped conservation efforts to win the war.

Spiritual consolation was the primary focus of diocesan efforts, which gave comfort and, above all, hope to worried parents and spouses who sent their sons and husbands overseas. To cope with this, Des Moines priests and Bishop Bergan became skilled at offering consolation and providing comfort at memorial Masses. In Earling, a novena was held in honor of the parish patron, St. Joseph, in March 1942 for the men in service.[74] Meanwhile, St. Joseph's Church in Des Moines was packed every Friday for the popular Sorrowful Mother Novena that had been promoted by the Servites of Chicago. "Countless thousands attend," wrote the Catholic newspaper, "to pray for victory and peace and the safe return of people in the military service all over the world."[75] Father Hubert Duren of Westphalia rose to the occasion by composing a Victory Song: "Right makes might. Right makes might," warbled the school-children of the parish. "Get us right—We're all in this fight. . . . We are ready one and all, the world to save from old Japan and the rest of the Axis Clan."[76]

Men and women from landlocked Iowa found themselves in parts of the world they had only read about in *National Geographic* or seen in movie theater travelogues. Father Davidsaver described the flora and fauna of the Pacific Islands, which must have intrigued Bergan and those who read the chaplain's letters. Corporal Frederic McDermott, formerly the postmaster of Wiota, Iowa, was among the contingent of US soldiers that were involved in the liberation of Rome in 1944. McDermott gaped in awe at the sights and sent back vivid descriptions of the Eternal City and of St. Peter's Basilica.[77]

When the war finally ended in August 1945, thanksgiving services were held all over the diocese. At the public celebration in Des Moines, three thousand gathered at the Shrine Auditorium, where a group of ministers, including Father Maurice Aspinwall, spoke of the dawn of peace. Aspinwall reminded the listeners: "If your loved one has been spared from the carnage of this world slaughter, think prayerfully of thousands of homes which never again hear the familiar step bouncing through the door."[78]

Americanizing St. Ambrose Cathedral

At the very time that the American war effort was heating up, Bergan used the cathedral to accentuate the patriotism of local Catholics. Father Lester Vincent Patrick Lyons was now in charge of the church. A native of Chicago, he had been ordained by Drumm on June 15, 1922, and appointed an assistant at St. Ambrose. He later became diocesan superintendent of schools.[79] On September 14, 1935, Bergan appointed him rector of St. Ambrose Cathedral and in 1943 vicar general of the diocese. Lyons tackled some of the structural problems of the cathedral, including its poor acoustics. The local Catholic newspaper had noted in its sassy column "Grist" that "the Westminster Cathedral in London is testing amplifiers and suggests that St.

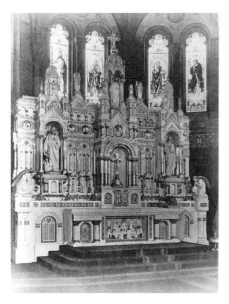

Renovations of St. Ambrose Cathedral, Old High Altar. Credit: Diocese of Des Moines Archives.

Ambrose might do the same—with much profit all around."[80]

When it was time to replace the nave windows in the church, Bergan worked with Lyons to create a patriotic tableau that linked the church with the cause of America. At Bergan's direction, six windows—three on each side of the nave—depicted not biblical or pietistic scenes but historical events of the Catholic Church in America and Iowa. These windows included and celebrated a particular Catholic take on the history of the country. The subjects included the landing of Columbus; Cecil Calvert sending his brother to Maryland; the martyrdom of the North American martyrs; images of

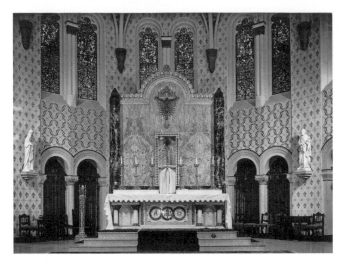

Renovations of St. Ambrose Cathedral, New High Altar.
Credit: Diocese of Des Moines Archives.

Francisco Coronado and Hernando de Soto, who roamed around
the interior of North America; the consecration of the first American
bishop, John Carroll; an image of Father Pierre Jean de Smet, who
was a traditionally historic figure in Iowa's Catholic history. These
windows and thirty-four others consisted of translucent mosaics held
together by lead. The cathedral rector, Father Lyons, commented:
"Bishop Bergan thought that since the cathedral is in the capital city
of the state and is the mother church of the Des Moines diocese, it
would be appropriate to have something of historical interest in it."[81]

Bergan also made extensive renovations to the sanctuary. The high
altar already had a magnificent *mensa* (table), a copy of an altar designed by the famous Tiffany Company of New York and first displayed
at the 1893 Columbian Exposition in Chicago. Monsignor Flavin had
seen the model and had a copy made for St. Ambrose. Later, he hoped
to construct a matching altar platform and steps and a suitable reredos
to complement the beautiful altar. This was finally accomplished by
Bergan and Lyons, who constructed a harmonious eighteen-foot altar
reredos through the efforts of the Milwaukee-based Conrad Schmitt
Studios. A bronze cross and a wooden corpus were added to the new
framework. Bergan and Lyons completed this work in time for the
Christmas celebrations of 1944.[82] Bergan loved the cathedral and pre-

sided often at the high Mass at eleven o'clock on Sunday mornings, which had Father Byron Nail directing the choir and Professor V. G. Magin at the organ. A packed house often met the bishop, who, as noted earlier, was an engaging and often humorous preacher.

War-Time Prosperity: An Unexpected Escape from Debt

Since the war reignited the local economy and put people back to work, Iowa's economic life perked up considerably. By 1940, Iowa ranked nineteenth among states in factory output. Des Moines was among the six major cities that led in the value of their manufactured products. By 1940 as well, Des Moines was the largest city in the state, with a population of 159,819. Increased donations began to flood into parish coffers, and a number of parishes were able to reduce or eliminate their indebtedness. The Catholic press reported that the cut in parish debt "reflects the war-time prosperity in the corn-belt area."[83] St. Augustin's shaved $108,000 off its debt while St. Peter's in Defiance paid off $26,000. In June 1943, St. Joseph's Parish in Des Moines paid off the last $11,000 on its mortgage, and in August All Saints in Stuart paid off $21,500 in debts.[84] In 1944, twenty-seven more parishes reduced their collective indebtedness by $177,000—the largest pay-downs were from St. Anthony and St. Augustin Parishes.[85] In fact, St. Anthony's not only paid off its debt but made an additional $20,000 in improvements and petitioned Bishop Bergan for the unique privilege of being consecrated (as opposed to blessed or dedicated) according to a unique ritual of the Roman church. Bergan conducted the four-hour ceremony on December 19, 1946.[86] Only forty years before, Father Romanelli had struggled to start the parish. Less than a year later, St. Augustin's wiped out its $293,000 debt, and Bergan consecrated it as well.[87]

Institutional Expansion

War-time restrictions on building crimped the ability of the diocese to expand its presence. There were only three new parishes founded under Bishop Bergan. One of the pressing needs was on the growing south side, where St. Anthony's had been the only parish for years. Growth in this part of the city, beyond Watrous Street, required a new worship space to accommodate Catholic servicemen and their families, the Civilian Conservation Corps, which had a facility in that area, and families living beyond Watrous Street. Mass was celebrated for a time at the nondenominational chapel at Fort Des Moines, about two blocks north of the army post. By 1935, St. Anthony's had three thousand parishioners and Bishop Bergan had already purchased a 2.5-acre parcel bordered by Wall Street, a dirt road, and SW Ninth Street, a two-lane paved road. Around the new acreage were truck farms and small farm acreages. In 1939, Christ the King Parish in Des Moines was split off from St. Anthony Parish; it encompassed everything south of Watrous Avenue and was known for a time as the Fort Des Moines church. Father Thomas Moriarty, previously the business manager at Dowling College, became its pastor on April 19, 1940. Moriarty launched Christ the King Parish

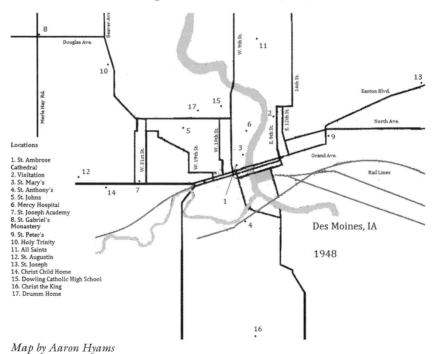

Catholic Space in Des Moines, IA, 1948

Locations

1. St. Ambrose Cathedral
2. Visitation
3. St. Mary's
4. St. Anthony's
5. St. Johns
6. Mercy Hospital
7. St. Joseph Academy
8. St. Gabriel's Monastery
9. St. Peter's
10. Holy Trinity
11. All Saints
12. St. Augustin
13. St. Joseph
14. Christ Child Home
15. Dowling Catholic High School
16. Christ the King
17. Drumm Home

Des Moines, IA

1948

Map by Aaron Hyams

using the services of diocesan architect John Normile to design a new church for $40,000. Moriarty left the parish in 1953.[88]

Father John Aldera, a native of Cleggio, Italy (although of German and Spanish ancestry), succeeded Moriarty. Ordained on July 28, 1928, the energetic Aldera founded a school, a convent, and added to the still-growing church.[89] Aldera was at one time noted for his engagement in early ecumenical efforts in the diocese.

Bishop Bergan also created the new parish of St. Clare in Clarinda with a mission at Villisca. This church was founded on July 1, 1942, by Father Paul Marasco, a native of Des Moines who had attended West High School and Dowling and completed his seminary work at St. Paul in Minnesota. He was ordained to the priesthood in 1930 and served at Clarinda for ten years.[90]

The community of Clarinda was named after Clarinda Buck, the niece of a prominent pioneer who actually lived in Portland, Oregon. Clarinda also had a large mental institution, which required religious ministry. Marasco traveled to the new parish with his mother and sisters, Margaret and Mary. He recalled of the parish origins in 1971:

> Bishop Bergan appointed me to open a new parish in Clarinda, Villisca Mission, and be chaplain to the Mental Hospital. Someone was to get a rented home for us, but failed to do so, and we had to hunt, while the furniture van waited three hours.
>
> There were supposed to have been 21 families, but only five turned out to the first Sunday Mass in the Odd Fellows Hall. Sixteen were fallen aways. Every one of those families were brought back to the church except two. We were much pressed for finances from the very start which continued for ten years. The Diocese sent $25.00 per month, the State Hospital, $20.00 per month, very little from the poor five families—including plate collection each week, $5.40 or less. Mary and mother supplied something each week for groceries and Margaret sent $70 each month. Our house rent was $56.00 for a month.[91]

Marasco found a temporary structure for the church and held a vacation Bible school with the help of the Sisters of Mercy. Clarinda grew largely due to government jobs. Marasco lived with his sisters, who helped him negotiate the purchase of an old house and four lots at 200 East Lincoln from a Mrs. Charles Hobson. Two Civilian

Front row, far left: Father Paul Marasco.
Credit: Diocese of Des Moines Archives.

Conservation Corps barracks were moved to the property in 1944, and, with lumber from other barracks, a church was erected. Bergan came to dedicate it on June 1944.[92] He would return in October 1945 for confirmation and to visit the POW camp.

Bergan also founded St. Joseph in Villisca in 1942, which he attached as a mission to Clarinda. Eventually Villisca constructed a new church for its growing members.[93] Among the distinctive features of the Villisca church was the original artwork of Father Paul Marasco's brother, newspaper artist Frank Marasco, who produced a painting of the Holy Family for the small community. Frank Marasco's work would be an important part of the church's cultural heritage.[94] Bishop Bergan also raised St. Columbanus in Weston to parochial status and assigned a full-time priest there.

The Sisters of Mercy opened a facility for the elderly named the Drumm Home, located on Des Moines's north side. Begun in 1939 with a $25,000 gift from the Catholic Women's League, the sisters had purchased an old Congregational Hospital at 1409 Clarke Street and invested another $25,000 to get the building operating. The facility soon reached capacity and required significant additions in 1947 and again in 1957. Later, in 1965, a chapel was added.[95]

This modest program of expansion included purchasing a new home for Bergan. In mid-summer 1946, the diocese purchased the spacious home of the recently deceased Senator Clyde L. Herring at 180 Thirty-Seventh Street at a cost of $31,500—although it had been assessed at $43,755. The new brick house "of English type" had been built in 1911.[96] This twenty-three-room mansion remained the episcopal residence until Bishop Maurice Dingman sold it in 1980.[97]

Bergan the Ecumenist: A Bridge to the Wider Community

In what was a clear innovation in his day, Bishop Bergan developed warm personal and professional relations with the clergy of other faith traditions. Perhaps no other action of his term signaled Bergan's desire to carve a responsible and cooperative stance for the Catholic Church in Des Moines and the rest of the diocese. Other Catholic priests like Monsignor Vitus Stoll had interacted with local ministers on an infrequent basis. Although there would be no *communicatio in sacris* (joint participation in worship services), priests could and did give talks on "neutral" topics in Protestant churches.

Bergan was at first alarmed by this. When he discovered on the pages of the *Des Moines Register* that Luigi Ligutti was going to the Euclid Avenue Methodist Church to speak on the Homestead Project, he wrote asking Ligutti to "cancel your engagement." He noted, "I do not wish to be unreasonable, but I know from experience what is the attitude in Rome in priests appearing in Protestant churches." He recalled an experience when he was administrator in Peoria when a priest had preached at a Thanksgiving Day event in a Protestant church and news of it had reached the apostolic delegate who had "asked for an explanation." He noted, "I do not wish Rome to remove my miter so shortly, but they are bitterly opposed to such procedure."[98]

Ligutti canceled the appearance but informed Bergan that he had only accepted "because of previous traditions existing in our diocese," noting that "some few of our priests did speak from Protestant and Jewish pulpits."[99] Bergan eventually softened his tone and ultimately took the lead in establishing warm personal relationships with ministers and rabbis in town. Here he was able to tap into the ecumenical interfaith activities of a group called the Des Moines Round Table or the Good Will Team of Des Moines. This group originated in the aftermath of the bitterly divisive election of 1928, when the issue of New York Governor Alfred E. Smith's Catholicism had played a role in the election's outcome.

In Des Moines, the Round Table consisted of Rabbi Eugene Mannheimer of Temple B'nai Jeshurun; Reverend Stoddard Lane of Plymouth Congregational Church; Willard Johnson, then executive director of the local chapter of the National Conference of Christians and Jews; and Father Robert Walsh, a teacher at Dowling High School. This group traveled and gave talks and presentations around Iowa, touting toleration and emphasizing common values. Walsh eventually dropped out because of mental illness, even for a time, being ousted from the priesthood.

Bishop Bergan soon provided the Catholic presence in the Round Table. Mannheimer, a native of New York, represented the Reform Jewish tradition and was a familiar face in Des Moines's intellectual and civic circles that held services on Sunday mornings. Bergan often recalled that among his first visitors in Des Moines were Eugene and Irma Mannheimer, who lived in the same neighborhood as the bishop. Mannheimer was long active in interfaith activities and helped rekindle interest in joint Thanksgiving services. In 1938, Bergan overcame his anxiety about "losing his miter" and preached at a Thanksgiving service at the Shrine Temple in Des Moines.

Stoddard Lane had arrived in Des Moines in 1929 and quickly became friends with Mannheimer. An ardent progressive, Lane was also a committed pacifist (even after Pearl Harbor) and a staunch friend of organized labor. With Bergan, these men formed a close personal and professional bond that "did more to break down misunderstanding than anything else." They spoke to each other's groups and in churches. At one point someone teased Bergan about speaking so often before a Jewish men's club: "Are you going to take over the synagogue?" To which Bergan quipped, "Not until the debt is paid off."[100]

Monsignor John McIlhon recalled on the occasion of Bergan's fiftieth anniversary of priesthood in 1965, "Back in the days when the word ecumenism was unheard of, let alone correctly pronounced, he was practicing it. Jewish and Protestant groups in Des Moines and elsewhere regularly featured Bishop Bergan as the main speaker for various functions. During his fourteen years in Des Moines, he made many close friends among those not of the Catholic faith."[101]

Out of this, Des Moines formed a branch of the National Conference of Christians and Jews and urged greater civility and mutual understanding among people of different faiths. Bergan became closely involved with the National Conference of Christians and Jews, and offered financial support. These initiatives came to a halt under Bishop Daly, who regarded them with great suspicion. Years later, when Bishop Maurice Dingman appointed a priest (Father Jacob Weiss) to serve as a staff associate with the Des Moines Area Council of Churches, he noted Bergan's contribution to common church action to confront urban issues. "I am conscious of the fact that what is happening today is in no small measure due to the pioneering efforts of [Bergan] in establishing fine interfaith efforts in this community."[102]

Transitioning Out

Bishop Bergan, although extremely popular with priests and laity in Des Moines, and well known to the business and ecumenical communities, must have started feeling restive in Des Moines. He had the benefit of a long-term friendship with the kingmaker of the American Catholic hierarchy at that time, Archbishop Francis Spellman of New York. The two men had maintained their closeness over the years, even as many regarded Spellman with a combination of envy and awe as his prestige and influence grew.

The New York cardinal was close to Pope Pius XII, whom he had known from work in Rome in the 1920s. He had even escorted the future pontiff across the United States in a famous 1936 tour. These good deeds had won him an auxiliary bishop's spot in his native Boston. Then in 1939, when Pacelli became Pope Pius XII, he elevated Spellman to the prestigious See of New York, and in 1946 he created him a cardinal. Spellman was one of the most visible American prelates of his era, and as head of the Military Ordinariate (the Catholic authority for chaplains and ministry to servicemen and servicewomen), he worked closely with various presidential administrations and also took trips to combat zones during the war while also overseeing chaplains.

Bergan had been a steady friend and was among the handful of fellow bishops who accompanied Spellman to Rome for the consistory of 1946 when he became a cardinal. In 1947, on a general swing of the Midwest and West, Spellman visited Des Moines and stayed with Bergan for a couple of days. He went to see local charitable groups and presided at a packed Mass at St. Ambrose that welcomed two thousand participants.[103] With Bergan in tow, he praised the work of local Des Moines chaplain Father Stephen Kane. Spellman, ever the ambitious ecclesiastical chess player, may have wanted to "do something" for his old classmate and loyal friend. Perhaps only a coincidence, but within a year of Spellman's flying trip to Des Moines Bergan would be transferred to the Metropolitan See of Omaha and the archiepiscopal pallium would be placed on his shoulders.

Bergan had received notice of this on January 28, 1948, and the news was kept secret until February 13, when Bergan was in Texas in the company of Dr. Henry G. Harmon, president of Drake University, on a trip to inspect some Texas oil lands near Pecos, given to the university and to Mercy Hospital. Bergan's statement conveyed his sadness at leaving Des Moines and its people, "both Catholic and non-Catholic." But in his own pleasant way, he assured his now former flock that he would not be "far away from the place where I have been Bishop for fourteen years."[104]

Before he departed, Bergan officiated one last time at Holy Week services in St. Ambrose Cathedral. Even before he took leave, the Holy See announced that Dominican Father Edward C. Daly, a long-time staffer at the apostolic delegation was to be appointed his successor.[105] Bergan asked for no farewell ceremonies and sent his final message to Catholics via his Easter Sunday sermon, which was broadcast over station KSO. At a farewell luncheon hosted during Holy Week by the priests at the Hotel Des Moines, both the oldest (Jeremiah Costello) and the youngest (Joseph Sondag, recently ordained) rose to pay him tribute.[106]

The farewells were numerous and heartfelt. Isaac Metcalf, the local leader of the National Conference of Christians and Jews, congratulated Bergan, but added, "I almost want to weep when I think of the loss it means to Des Moines, and particularly for the National Conference of Christians and Jews. I trust you will implore all the saints to help in securing a bishop for Des Moines who will be as cooperative as you have been."[107] Rabbi Martin Weitz of Des Moines's Temple B'nai Jeshurun wrote: "We of the House of Israel, deeply feel honored by your promotion, for you are as great a Rabbi as we have ever known, for your ministry has helped bring order out of chaos and understanding in the midst of misunderstanding, wherever you have served. . . . 'Sholom. . . . Peace be unto you.'"[108]

Father Joseph Hanson of Visitation Parish couldn't resist the urge to bash the long-dead Drumm, who had threatened to remove him from his pastorate. Of Bergan he wrote: "Your coming soon dissipated the gloom and ill feeling with which incompetence and stubbornness had permeated the diocese. Your stay with us has meant nearly fourteen years of peace and good will among priests and people and a real advance and uplift in the things of religion."[109] Even a lowly chancery official in Davenport, Father Maurice Dingman, sent his best: "We will be sorry to see Your Excellency leave the state of Iowa, but we rejoice that the Holy Father has graciously placed you near our border."[110] Bergan departed Des Moines on March 30 and was installed March 31, 1948, in Omaha's St. Cecilia's Cathedral. Des Moines then prepared to host the first episcopal consecration in its history.

&

The Bergan years had been full of the challenges of the Depression and War—two circumstances that severely taxed the resources of the Catholics in southwest Iowa. Perhaps the single biggest effect of the Depression was to undercut church revenues; weekly collections were the lifeblood of church, and they disappeared in many places. The war provided another unique opportunity for the church to make its mark. Encouraging patriotic activity, providing a measure of pastoral care on the home front and the battlefield—all contributed to helping the state of Iowa cope with its many casualties. Shenandoah and Red Oak, communities particularly hit hard by the war, also had strong Catholic communities. The postwar religious boom was only beginning before Bergan departed for Omaha. But the groundwork was in place to welcome a new generation of priests, thanks in part to the presence of diocesan priests on the faculty of Dowling and elsewhere. But Bergan also captured the postwar irenicism of religious traditions—often balkanized in their respective spheres—especially the Catholic Church, which embraced a form of religious exceptionalism that made Catholics fearful for their souls if they engaged with their Protestant and Jewish neighbors. Bergan at least began the kind of social outreach to fellow believers that contributed to civic amity and may have laid the groundwork for common approaches to communal problems.

"It Is Good to Have a Home in Iowa"

Edward Daly and Maturation and Mobility

The period after World War II down through the 1960s was an era of growth and expansion for Iowa and the Catholic Church. In 1950 the state registered a population of 2.6 million. By 1970, it had increased slightly to 2.8 million. The Catholic population of southwest Iowa surged dramatically from forty-five thousand in 1948 to seventy-seven thousand by 1964—many people living in the Des Moines metropolitan area or Council Bluffs. With new members and greater resources, Catholics entered into a new epoch of visibility and institutional expansion that expanded the wider social and economic presence of the church. For many, looking back nostalgically, this was a golden era of Des Moines Catholic life.

The Farming Economy

Lisa Lynn Ossian notes the qualitative changes that took place in Iowa's farming communities in the postwar era. Good prices on crops during the war gave many farmers the resources to improve their homes (e.g., indoor plumbing, central heating, refrigeration).

Likewise, lifting war-time restrictions on building materials and resuming consumer manufacturing helped the farmers as well.

A new embrace of farm mechanization increased agricultural output. Although farm prices tapered off a bit after the war, thanks to government supports they did not crash as severely as they did in the 1920s and 1930s. Nevertheless, Iowa's agricultural sector witnessed a steady reduction in the number of farms and a growing increase in their acreage and mechanization.[1] Corporate agriculture began to dominate the state's agricultural economy.

A More Robust Industrial Order and Population Growth

Postwar industrial development pivoted away from war-time production. One example of this is that Des Moines businesses began to lay off women by mid-July 1945, sending them to "traditional" jobs as maids, telephone operators, and secretaries. Some war factories were reconverted, however, and thrived. After the war, the Reconstruction Finance Corporation—a government agency—purchased the Ankeny ordnance plant and later sold a portion of it to the John Deere Company in February 1948. From making bombs and bullets, the plant now manufactured cotton pickers and sprayers.[2] Demographically, postwar Iowa changed significantly. Urban areas increased dramatically while rural communities declined.

Thanks in part to the GI Bill thousands of Iowa veterans returned to college and professional schools and, by enhancing their levels of education, were able to participate in the consumer culture of the period. The advent of television, the proliferation of automobiles, independent home ownership (with the help of Veteran's Home Loans and the Federal Housing Authority)—all contributed to the growing numbers of children and began to reshape the minds, hearts, and expectations of the "good life" for Iowans. Cities like Des Moines and Council Bluffs began to expand into undeveloped areas, creating a wider metropolitan community. As population shifted to the peripheries of these cities, a corresponding decline in urban communities occurred. Once-thriving urban neighborhoods were either left behind or bulldozed to make room for freeway construction or urban renewal. The Catholic Church was caught up in this fast-paced change.

County	1960	1970	1980	1990
Adair	10,893	9,487	9,509	8,409
Adams	7,468	6,322	5,731	4,866
Audubon	10,919	9,595	8,559	7,344
Cass	17,919	17,007	16,932	15,128
Clarke	8,222	7,581	8,618	8,287
Dallas	24,123	26,085	29,513	29,755
Decatur	10,539	9,737	9,794	8,338
Fremont	10,282	9,282	9,401	8,226
Guthrie	13,607	12,243	11,983	10,935
Harrison	17,600	16,240	16,348	14,730
Lucas	10,923	10,163	10,313	9,070
Madison	12,295	11,558	12,597	12,483
Mills	13,050	11,832	13,406	13,202
Montgomery	14,467	12,781	13,413	12,076
Page	21,023	18,537	19,063	16,870
Polk	266,315	286,130	303,170	327,140
Pottawattamie	83,102	86,991	86,561	82,628
Ringgold	7,910	6,373	6,112	5,420
Shelby	15,825	15,528	15,043	13,230
Taylor	10,288	8,790	8,353	7,114
Union	13,712	13,557	13,858	12,750
Warren	20,829	27,432	34,878	36,033
Wayne	9,800	8,405	8,199	7,067
TOTAL	631,111	641,656	671,354	671,101
Catholic Total	72,050	80,106	80,059	95,180
Percentage of pop.	11%	12%	12%	14%

Source: US Census and Official Catholic Directory

Extending the Catholic Social Safety Net

All Catholic institutions grew to meet the demands of the expand-ing population. This was felt particularly in health care as medical technology advanced and the need for more maternity wards, hospital beds, and surgical centers grew. Federal concern for health-care facili-ties brought about the passage of the Hill-Burton Act of 1949, which made grants for hospital expansion all over the country. This law and other innovations in medical technology directly affected the medical establishment pioneered by the Sisters of Mercy in Des Moines.

Building expansion of Mercy Hospital had slowed with the De-pression and war-time shortages of building materials. In 1946, how-ever, Mercy built a new nursing school. Subsequent additions to the hospital and consistent technological improvement transformed the sisters' hospital into a major medical resource for Polk County. The Hill-Burton grant for Mercy was $166,000. With that money the sisters could leverage loans and run successful fund drives that made expansion possible. In the 1950s, Mercy Hospital in Des Moines announced a $2.7 million addition to their existing facility—the first such expansion in thirty years, adding one hundred more hospital beds for the growing health-care needs of the community. This ad-dition tapped local resources and received a hefty grant from the

Mercy Hospital in 1959. Credit: Institute of the Sisters of Mercy of the Americas, Mercy Heritage Center.

Ford Foundation and the US government. Steady improvements in health-care technology and needs demanded continual adaptation by the sisters. The nursing school underwent significant improvement by 1957, opened a new facility, and received accreditation.

Development continued as health care and the delivery of medical services underwent dramatic changes. The advent of health insurance and the creation of Medicare and Medicaid changed the world of healthcare. Mercy grew and expanded to become one of the premier health-care sites in the state of Iowa. Property for expansion was acquired by Sister Anita Paul, and by 1959 a new wing of the hospital was opened, adding 158 beds plus forty for pediatrics. In 1974, the "Old Main," one of the oldest buildings in the hospital, was demolished and a new modern Mercy Hospital emerged with even better facilities.

The moving force behind this dramatic change was Sister M. Gervase Northrup, who had become administrator in 1969. A native of Iowa, she had joined the Sisters of Mercy in 1945 and held a master's in nursing from the Catholic University of America. Sister Gervase oversaw a massive rebuilding of the hospital during her seven-year tenure; sadly, she died in March 1977, one year before this $37 million project was completed.

Sister Patricia Clare Sullivan, the associate administrator, took over and completed Sister Gervase's work, making Mercy Hospital, Des Moines, one of Iowa's largest and most respected hospitals. Future changes involved a steady improvement in the school of nursing, creating Mercy College of Health Sciences.[3]

Mercy Hospital in Council Bluffs also continued to make progress. In 1920, it became the first Iowa hospital to be certified by the American College of Surgeons, and in 1927 it added eighty beds to its facilities. St. Bernard's Hospital, now exclusively for mental patients, added a wing

Sister Mary Gervase Northrup, RSM.
Credit: Diocese of Des Moines Archives.

in the 1950s. Mercy too, taking advantage of Hill-Burton funds and other revenue sources, also added a 12,000-square-foot addition. These hospitals would expand again in 1968, when a new hospital would be built and the older buildings torn down. Subsequent mergers and reorganization brought the Sisters of Mercy into alliance with other health-care systems in the 1980s and 1990s.[4]

In Corning, an interesting hospital project also unfolded. The need for medical facilities in rural Adams County had long been a concern of local officials and physicians like Dr. C. L. Bain of Corning. The problem of financing a new hospital was partially solved by two bachelor brothers James (who died in 1941) and Thomas Roach (who died in 1942). Both prosperous farmers, they left a sizable bequest of over $250,000 "for charitable purposes" to the discretion of the pastor of St. Patrick's Church in Corning. Fundraising had also been conducted by a local committee, and by 1949 the group had come up with an additional $175,000.

Corning pastor, Father Maurice Powers, administrator of the Roach endowment, approached Mother M. Jolanta Pawlak, provincial superior of the Sisters of St. Felix of Cantalice (Felicians) in Chicago, and requested qualified sisters to staff and operate the hospital, to which she agreed. Powers purchased a forty-two-acre site

Holy Rosary Hospital in Corning.
Credit: Felician Sisters Archives, Chicago, Illinois.

on the outskirts of Corning and assumed direction of the hospital construction. A battle of wills ensued between the pastor who had unrealistic dreams (and no experience) in building the new hospital and the more experienced Mother Jolanta. Powers plunged ahead without architectural plans and good contractors.

Work ground to a halt at one point with excavation done and piles of material stockpiled on the grounds. At one point, the Felicians threatened to pull out of the whole enterprise until a Corning business committee approached them and agreed to contract a professional architect (Des Moines–based Wethrell and Harrison) and engaged the Kuchero Construction Company.[5] In August 1950, the new forty-bed hospital was ready for occupancy, and the first sisters arrived on October 6. The building was finally completed in April 1951 and blessed and dedicated to the Queen of the Most Holy Rosary.[6] Various therapies for polio victims were provided by this hospital. In November 1959, the hospital was awarded a certificate of accreditation.[7] Ultimately, this became part of the Mercy Hospital system.

A New Roman Voice—Bishop Edward Daly

The end of the war brought a leadership change for Des Moines Catholics as, once again, an unknown easterner would be plucked to serve as diocesan bishop.[8] Edward Daly was born October 24, 1894, in Cambridge, Massachusetts, the son of James and Elizabeth Cairns Daly. He attended Boston College High School and studied at Jesuit-run Boston College between 1912 and 1914. In 1914, he entered the Dominican Order's novitiate in Somerset, Ohio. He professed his first vows on September 16, 1915, taking the name Celestine as his religious name. He often signed his letters to his confreres by his nickname: "Cel." Daly finished his theological studies at the Dominican Studium in Washington, DC, and his Dominican confrere, John Timothy McNicholas, archbishop of Cincinnati, ordained him on June 12, 1921.

From 1921 to 1924 his superiors sent him to study theology and canon law at the Catholic University of America, where he attained the lectorate in theology, an important rank in the Dominican Order. In 1923, he was appointed to the staff of the Apostolic Delegation by Archbishop (later Cardinal) Pietro Fumasoni-Biondi and at the same time taught canon law to the Dominican seminarians. Between 1936 and 1948, he served as the personal secretary of the apostolic delegate, Amleto Cicognani. Not until the appointment of Bishop Richard Pates in 2008 would a staffer at Rome's outpost in America (the Apostolic Delegation, today the Apostolic Nunciature) be appointed to the Des Moines See. Daly was first and foremost a canonist and a capable, if sometimes colorless, church bureaucrat.[9]

As all members of the Dominican Order, he was deeply steeped in the theological traditions and devotions of his order. But he was neither a theologian nor a scholar like many of his confreres. He knew how to make the machinery of church life work. He valued secrecy in some things. He appeared to have few, but deeply devoted, friends. His Dominican identity came out primarily in his devotions to Dominican saints, for example, St. Thomas Aquinas and St. Albert the Great. He was especially devoted to the Blessed Virgin Mary. Daly's introverted and staid personality was a contrast with the gregarious Bergan.

On March 13, 1948, the fifty-three-year-old Daly received notification of his appointment to Des Moines. No doubt this was a reward for his long years of service but perhaps also the result of Cicognani's desire for some new blood in the Apostolic Delegation. His appointment transpired with apparently little consultation with the other bishops of Iowa—who likely proposed other candidates from the ranks of Iowa-born clergy. Even Metropolitan Archbishop Henry Rohlman of Dubuque quipped to future Des Moines bishop George Biskup: "Bishop-elect Daly's consecration will take place [in Des Moines] on May 13. We know little about him. From the pictures we have seen in the papers we would come to the conclusion that he would never win in a beauty contest."[10] Daly flew first to Chicago, where some fellow Dominicans greeted him. Bad weather canceled his flight to Des Moines, and, like his predecessors, he arrived in the Iowa capital on rail car.[11]

On May 13, 1948, Cicognani traveled to Des Moines to personally consecrate his long-time secretary, assisted by Archbishop Henry Rohlman of Dubuque and Archbishop John Timothy McNicholas, OP, of Cincinnati, who had ordained Daly to the priesthood. Twenty-two bishops attended this celebration along with hundreds of priests, civic officials, and interested laity. Cicognani noted: "For

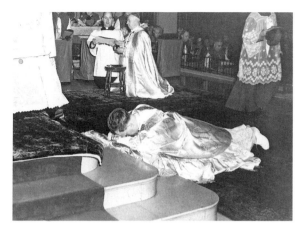

The episcopal ordination of Bishop Daly.
Credit: Diocese of Des Moines Archives.

almost twenty-five years—to be precise from September 27, 1923, Bishop Daly has given his daily work to the Apostolic Delegation. Twenty-five years—nearly half of his life and almost the entire period of his priesthood—fifteen of those years passed with me. Together we have shared labors and preoccupations— together beyond the routine work of every day, we have studied ways of executing faithfully the order and instructions of the Holy See. His assistance has been active, intelligent, assiduous, and devoted."[12]

Daly was feted at the Fort Des Moines Hotel after his consecration. On May 16, 1948, more than three thousand persons turned out for a civic reception at the KRNT Radio Theater, and when it was his turn to speak, Daly offered thanks as one who was "a stranger within your gates."[13] Anxious to be at home in Iowa, he referred to the service of Iowa's sons and daughters in America's wars and invoked the state motto, "Our Liberties we prize and our rights we will maintain." But as had previous bishops, he admitted: "I come to Iowa and its capital city, Des Moines, a stranger," he told the crowd. "I too am a stranger in a strange land. But to the accomplishments, to the aims to the spirit of the people of Iowa and Des Moines I am not a stranger. And with knowledge of how the promise envisioned by our fathers has flowered and matured here, I can truly say, 'It is good to have a home in Iowa; it is good to be in Des Moines.'"[14]

Administrative Restructuring

It was a new era in the Diocese of Des Moines as local Catholics adjusted to their new leader. Daly was a different kind of bishop. As Monsignor Raymond Conley noted in a memoir: "The contrast between Bishop Bergan and his successor . . . became quickly apparent. . . . Scholarly and retiring, he [Daly] shunned personal publicity. And having worked as secretary and archivist for 25 years in the Apostolic Delegation . . . he was used to working for many hours alone."[15] Bishop Daly did much of his work at his house, spending minimal office hours at the chancery, then located in the basement of the St. Ambrose rectory. His domestic needs were faithfully attended by two Adrian Dominican sisters.

His dutiful chancery staff accommodated Daly's quirks. The chancery was only to be opened until noon, but the staff continued to work during the second part of the day. Daly mandated that no one was to answer the phone in the afternoon, unless it was from Daly, and his phone calls were noted by a code of phone rings and hang-ups that staffers were to heed. He also worked on clerical assignments with a level of secrecy that almost seemed comical, delivering the individual letters to priests who were being transferred via taxi service rather than the US mail.[16]

Raymond Conley remembered that Daly's matter-of-fact approach to his coworkers seemed to indicate an indifference to their personal needs. Yet, he was not averse to the pastoral work of his office. Conley recalled: "He visited the sick; offered home Masses for shut-ins; attended wakes, commiserating with those who mourned. . . . He tried to send congratulations to the parent of every child baptized in the diocese, to converts, to felicitate newly-weds."[17]

He shook up the chancery staff, and sent the recently ordained Father Joseph Sondag to higher studies. Sondag was a native of Portsmouth, Iowa, and a product of St. Benedict's College in Atchison, Kansas, and Conception Seminary in Missouri. Ordained by Daly in 1948, he was quickly sent off to school in Ottawa to study canon law and received his degree in 1950. For many years, Sondag would be Daly's master of ceremonies as well as the diocesan corporation's secretary, the officialis of the marriage tribunal, the di-

Bishop Daly receiving a program of Marian devotions.
Credit: Diocese of Des Moines Archives.

ocesan director of both the Propagation of the Faith and the Holy
Childhood Association.[18] When long-serving Monsignor Patrick
McDermott died in May 1963, Sondag was appointed pastor of Ss.
Peter and Paul in Atlantic and later made a monsignor.

Bishop Daly came with a broad knowledge of the inner workings
of the church and the scope of canon law but with very little pastoral
experience. His years in Des Moines reflected both the strengths
and weaknesses of his background. Indeed, the episcopal residence,
once ringing with laughter and dinner parties, went as silent as a
Dominican friary. Daly managed the mundane details of church administration—he accommodated growth, oversaw property acquisitions, and appointed the clergy to their respective posts. But unlike
his predecessors, he took little delight in public events and often
farmed out confirmations to visiting bishops. Daly was a good man
and a dutiful churchman. But in some ways he pulled back from the
engagement with Des Moines and the wider community.

Denominational Walls: Ecumenical Chill

One area where Bishop Daly's conservative ways partially un-
raveled a key accomplishment of his predecessor was in the areas

of ecumenism and interfaith relations. Daly did not carry on his predecessor's outreach to local Protestant and Jewish leaders. He also distanced himself from the National Conference of Christians and Jews (NCCJ), which Bergan had embraced. In 1949, when a local NCCJ conference in Des Moines was to focus on racial issues in the Iowa capital, local African American minister Isaac Metcalf approached Daly, who did agree to cosponsor the event as Bergan had done. But he forbade Dowling boys to participate in panel discussions—worrying that their faith might be jeopardized in these mixed-religion events. Daly himself, unlike Bergan, never attended any of their functions—relegating his "support" to monetary donations.

Daly wrote to his old boss, Amleto Cicognani, who inquired about Catholic participation in these events, "While the Conference enjoyed some recognition, in the last two years or so the good man who heads it here, the Reverend Isaac Metcalf, has felt hurt at the lack of enthusiasm in this office."[19] The next year, Mrs. Elizabeth Wood, a local participant in NCCJ activities, requested permission for Father Robert Welch of the School of Religion at the University of Iowa to come to speak. Daly sidestepped the matter, bluntly stating through a staffer: "The Bishop never gives permissions or approval to the NCCJ and does not now. . . . He wants no part of the NCCJ."[20]

Daly and Ligutti: Tensions

No one seemed to pique Daly more than Monsignor Luigi Ligutti, who had also waded deep in ecumenical waters and into wider policy spheres. Ligutti's work as the executive secretary of the National Catholic Rural Life Conference kept him on the road most of the year (in one year he spent only fifty days in Des Moines).[21] He had been able to secure other priests to manage the office and do other tasks—especially Father Michael Dineen of Milwaukee with whom he worked well at first. Ligutti's interest in land and resources led him to wider local and even international audiences. In 1949 he was named Official Permanent Observer for the Holy See to the Rome-based United Nations Food and Agricultural Organization (FAO).

Already in the 1950s, Ligutti had opened up channels with Protestant pastors and institutions that were interested in land and food issues and international resources. He may have been one of the first Catholic priests to speak at Drake University (for which he received a princely $100 stipend) and address other congregations and non-Catholic associations. He also maintained contact with his friends in the developing Liturgical Movement in Collegeville, Minnesota. His old friend Virgil Michel had died in the late 1930s, but liturgical pioneer Monsignor Joseph Morrison of Chicago was also a friend and promoter of reforms such as the vernacular liturgy.

Ligutti bewailed the refusal of Cardinal Stritch of Chicago to permit Catholic participation in the Second Assembly of the World Council of Churches held at Northwestern University in 1954 at Evanston, Illinois. Ligutti's rather free (for the time) associations with Protestants had been encouraged by Archbishop Schlarmann of Peoria, who dissuaded him from asking for permission to address Protestants. His activities, however, raised the ire of Bishop Daly, who did not approve of such interactions by his clergy.

Daly's antipathy to Ligutti was not subtle, and he began hectoring him about minor matters that in Daly's mind were very important. For example, the prelate became incensed when he discovered that Ligutti had named the upstairs chapel of the Rural Life Conference offices the Shrine of St. Isidore. Lecturing Ligutti as though the priest were ten years old, he curtly demanded to know where Ligutti obtained the "authority" to have a chapel in the first place and the temerity to call it a "shrine." Ligutti had to meekly bow to Daly's occasional bursts of anger.

On one occasion, Daly took grave offense at something Ligutti had written in a Rural Life newsletter and then demanded that the bishop's name be removed from the letterhead of the organization, which listed him as "Moderator." Daly later demanded the removal of Father Dineen, Ligutti's assistant, from the diocese—echoing the demand of Archbishop Meyer of Milwaukee, who did not want the priest to become the executive secretary. In 1960, Ligutti moved to Rome, where he spent the rest of his days—returning to Des Moines from time-to-time.

The treatment of Ligutti was likely visited on other priests who upset or annoyed Daly, who had many virtues, but empathy was not one of them—at least not one he showed to some of his priests. Others, like Catholic Charities head Father Paul Connolly, appeared to have a good and even jovial relationship with the bishop. Connolly recalled in a sprightly memoir that when he was in graduate school at the Catholic University of America, "Bishop Daly would visit when he was in Washington for Bishops' meetings and other events. He invited the Dominicans and me to go out to dinner several times in Baltimore and at the La Salle du Bois in Washington. He taught me how to eat and enjoy oysters in the half-shell. I found out that he also enjoyed his scotch on the rocks."[22]

Indeed, Bishop Daly at first appeared to have few concerns outside of church matters, and there was enough to do to keep Des Moines moving forward in the busy years after World War II. He also had a very serious gallbladder operation in 1952 in Chicago. This surgery, today accomplished with relative ease, kept him in the hospital and convalescing for weeks and forced him to wear an uncomfortable undergarment for the rest of his life. The operation weakened him and caused him to lose stamina.

Managing Robust Growth and Expanding the Catholic Footprint

Daly was content to mind the affairs of the church, and he had a lot to do as he rode the crest of Catholic growth and demographic transition after World War II. As noted earlier, Des Moines and its metropolitan area grew substantially in the era after World War II—in part aided by a 1957 annexation that pushed out the boundaries of the city.

One of the most significant changes that altered life in Des Moines and Council Bluffs, and indeed all of Iowa, was the construction of the interstate highway system. Already in 1957, Des Moines began to plot a route for the new multilane superhighway that would cut through the city and connect with the rest of the interstate system in the west. As it was planned and announced in May 1958, the new route was projected to create a 13.5-mile freeway, I-235, which plunged through the heart of downtown, swooping from east to west, with twenty-one exits, cutting through five hundred acres of land and removing 1,100 dwelling units.[23] Freeway planners tried to avoid taking out large apartment buildings, parks, neighborhood shopping centers, and churches. In the end, only two churches were removed: First Presbyterian on E. Twelfth and Maple and a Mormon church on the same street.[24] But other churches and businesses built near the noisy and smoky freeway would also have to move. The building of I-235 in 1961, which cut through the heart of the downtown, destroyed housing and businesses and transferred many to new communities.

The impact of freeway building and the increase of automobile usage had a deleterious impact on older parish communities, and Catholic institutions struggled for existence. The creation of one of the first of Des Moines's shopping malls led to the purchase of the formerly remote Passionist monastery on Merle Hay Road. Already in the 1950s, the encroaching hustle and bustle of expansion drove the Passionists out of their "retreat," and they sold their property to a developer who created a shopping mall where once black-robed seminarians and priests had raised chickens and sung the psalms. Clearly more traffic would have disrupted the contemplative atmosphere they desired for students and retreatants at their monastery.

The construction of a right-of-way highway and access routes had a disastrous impact on Queen of Apostles Parish in Council Bluffs, causing the parish to shed eighty to ninety parishioners. Added to this was the location of an industrial park, railroad expansion by Union Pacific, and a new shipping port on the Missouri River that also reconfigured the area, causing not only the parish numbers to shrink but also a decline in school enrollments.[25]

Demographic changes in Des Moines also altered parish membership, including the cathedral and St. John's Parish, which began to decline in membership.[26] The Des Moines Golf and Country Club would be bisected by the new freeway. Later, part of this property would be purchased by the Diocese of Des Moines and become the site of a new Dowling High School. This major transformation changed the face of Des Moines and created a corridor to the rapidly expanding western communities of Windsor Heights, West Des Moines, Urbandale, Clive, Bondurant, and Ankeny.

Des Moines soon began to empty into its perimeters, filling up spaces to the north, west, and east of the city. Meanwhile, in Mills County near Council Bluffs, the city of Glenwood grew.

The process of suburbanization accelerated as Des Moines expanded shifting population, resources, and commerce to areas that were once the fringes of the city. Council Bluffs became more closely united with its neighbor, Omaha.

Brick and Mortar: Meeting the Demands of Growth

Existing Catholic churches expanded and new ones were created to play their part in the new suburban culture. During this period of maximum Catholic mobilization, existing parishes built on to their churches or erected new ones to keep pace with the rising tide of Catholic expansion. Schoolroom additions took place at St. Augustin's and Holy Trinity Parishes. St. John's Church now moved forward with renovations to its church and the installation of more of its magnificent stained glass. In 1959, St. Peter's in Des Moines contracted for a new $195,000 church and rectory.[27] Other building projects included Holy Trinity, which built a new church that was dedicated in 1957; two years later they added an annex to its existing schoolbuilding, adding room for what Father Ostdiek called "700 frisky colts." St. Augustin's added four new classrooms and an auditorium to give more room to the 415 pupils attending. St. Michael's in Harlan opened a new $150,000 school in the fall of 1954, where the School Sisters of St. Francis would welcome 170 pupils. Three new classrooms, costing $70,000, were added to All Saints School in Highland Park. A new $100,000 school was erected at St. Mary's in Panama. Father John Aldera built a ten-room addition to Christ the King School, and Monsignor Raymond Conley planned a new school for Visitation Parish in 1960. St. Joseph's Church in Des Moines would break the mold in new church construction. Built originally to accommodate just two hundred, the church was torn down in 1954 to construct a new "functional" structure that was rectangular, not cruciform, in design and would not have excessive ornamentation—a harbinger of the kind of liturgical simplification to come.[28] New churches were erected in Avoca, Walnut, and Griswold in 1956 and 1957.[29] Each of these enhanced the value of the property, created jobs, and provided additional venues for the church to influence people and local communities.

Suburban Expansion:
Adapting to a New Urban Geography

Perhaps the clearest sign of a vigorous Catholic culture was the erection of seven new parishes in the growing suburbs of Des Moines, Council Bluffs, and two other areas. Each of these parish sites adjusted to the new contours of suburban expansion. They often nestled in undeveloped areas that were once farms or stands of trees. As the suburban culture of Des Moines became its destiny and the city's population shifted north and west, Catholic parishes provided anchors for the rapid development of homes, shopping centers, and new schools. The use of automobiles required a different kind of parish "footprint"—one that had ample parking space for parishioners and school parents.

It began already in 1950, when a new parish was founded in Windsor Heights (Des Moines) after Daly received a petition from seventy families living in the area. This new parish—St. Therese of the Child Jesus—was located on eight acres of diocesan property Bergan had purchased in 1939 on the north side of University Avenue between Merle Hay Road and Sixtieth Street, with Father Charles Phelan as founding pastor.[30] A new church/school combination was built in 1951, and in 1952 the school, under the direction of the Sisters of Humility, opened. They received a new convent in 1955, and a new church was built in 1958, while the original church was transformed into classrooms.

Urbandale, no longer a distant suburb, was now in the path of growth. Here, Daly established a parish in 1955 named for the recently canonized St. Pius X at Sixty-Sixth and Oliver Smith Drive. Father Arthur Ring was appointed the founding pastor.[31] Ring, born in 1911, hailed from Neola and was ordained by Bishop Bergan in 1937. He assisted at St. Joseph in Earling and Visitation in Des Moines and served as a professor at Dowling High School from 1943 until 1955. Services were first held on March 1, 1955, in an Urbandale roller-skating rink until building started on a five-acre tract. The first Mass in these new quarters took place July 24, 1955.[32] This first building was a long 60-by-120-foot brick structure, which served as a temporary church. A school was erected in August 1956, staffed by the Sisters of Humility. By 1968, St. Pius X had a new church.

In 1960, Daly founded Our Lady's Immaculate Heart in Ankeny, which had its origins in the 1930s as a mission to the miners of the Carney Mining Company, a coal mining firm. The mine closed, but many miners remained. In 1933, Father Joseph M. Hanson of Visitation Parish in Des Moines had purchased three acres on Highway 69 and built St. Michael's Church; he took care of the spiritual needs of those at the mission. The Carney chapel remained well into the 1980s until it was closed by Bishop Dingman. The World War II ordnance plant supplied another body of population, making Ankeny a viable spot for a new parish.

Ankeny had grown from 1,229 in 1950 to 2,694 by 1960. The additional population made this site too cramped and ten acres were purchased on the northeast edge of town in 1959.[33] In January 1960, former military chaplain Father Woodrow Elias was appointed pastor of the newly created Our Lady's Immaculate Heart Parish.[34] Elias, born in 1916, had become a priest in 1943. Soon after ordination, Elias enlisted as a military chaplain, serving in the Pacific theater in World War II. After his return, he was an assistant in Panama until he was recalled for active duty in the chaplain corps in Korea in 1950. He remained in the military in a variety of posts until called home to start the new parish. In 1961, ground was broken for the new church, and on Easter Sunday, April 29, 1962, parishioners celebrated the Lord's resurrection in these quarters. Catholics from nearby Bondurant also came to the new church.

Daly founded his last parish, St. Mary of Nazareth in Des Moines, in early 1964 when he was home from Vatican II.[35] The new parish was located on eleven acres of the old Edwin Thomas Meredith Estate at Beaver Road and Meredith Drive. The sprawling twenty-six-room mansion is still in use on the parish grounds. Edwin T. Meredith held a number of government jobs under President Woodrow Wilson (1913–1920), including a short stint as his last secretary of agriculture. Meredith was the founder of the Meredith Publishing Company (1902), which printed the popular *Successful Farming* and later *Better Homes and Gardens.* He died in 1928. His widow, Edna Meredith, lived until 1961. When the home was given to the diocese, they did not know what to do with it at first. Chancellor Edward Pfeffer recalled going out there from time to time to check on the condition of the building and at times discovered vandalism.[36]

Edwin Meredith and family.
Credit: Library of Congress Photographs and
Prints Collection.

Eventually, however, the property found good use as the nucleus of
the new parish.

The founding pastor of St. Mary of Nazareth was Father Patrick
Walsh, a native of Ireland, schooled in Listowel and Wexford, and
ordained for Des Moines in 1935. After an assistantship at St. Anthony's in Des Moines and pastorate in Mondamin, he enlisted in
the military in 1942, serving in Hawaii and the South Pacific. He
was decorated for meritorious service in the Korean War, serving two
years in the combat area as assistant Ninth Corps chaplain. He was
later made head chaplain of the Seventh Division and came back to
the United States for service at Fort Meade and later in Germany.
He retired as a colonel. He managed to launch the new parish and
made good use of the old Meredith Home.[37]

Continued Growth in the Metropolitan Areas

Although the number of Catholics in certain parts of the Des
Moines diocese had begun to shrink slightly and some regions
planned for consolidation, other parts of the diocese experienced
growth.[38] In Polk County, two communities, Altoona and Carlisle,

both began to grow, and groups of Catholics began to press for an independent parish. Indeed, Altoona had more than doubled since 1950, growing from 763 to 4,151 in 1974. Carlisle had tripled in size, growing from 2,768 to 9,023. When Altoona butted up against the boundaries of St. Joseph Parish, Monsignor Maurice Aspinwall convinced Bishop Daly to purchase a plot of ten acres in 1959. In 1967, the local people began their own religious education program and a year later created a fund for future development. In 1971, a weekly Mass was offered in Altoona in a Legion Club building and later was moved to a United Methodist Church.

In Carlisle, religious education programs began in 1969, and after a survey of area Catholics, a first Mass was held in a local Lions Club. In 1971, this community was called the St. Elizabeth Community and moved forward with plans to elevate their status from a recognized community to a mission and then a parish. The community purchased a 5.6-acre tract one mile south of Carlisle and continued to raise money for a building program.

Suburban growth went beyond the 1960s. By the late 1970s, the growth of Altoona led to the formation of a new parish under Bishop Dingman. The Altoona group, known as the Southeast Polk Community, had also used a Methodist Church to hold a Saturday evening Mass.[39] By 1983, Altoona was ready for a new parish—the first new parish established in twenty years. Dingman appointed Father Daniel Clarke to be the founding pastor of a church named to commemorate the visit of the pope to Iowa: Ss. John and Paul Parish. Clarke planned to start slow, continuing to build the local faith community while worshiping in a Masonic temple. In the plans was a multipurpose facility that supported worship, education, and social activities.[40] The new church was not ready until August 1985.[41]

Council Bluffs

Existing parishes in Council Bluffs managed to handle the growth of the Catholic population, and Catholics could also avail themselves of churches in nearby Omaha. On October 18, 1956, Our Lady Queen of the Apostles was founded in Council Bluffs, drawing three hundred families from Holy Family Parish on the west side of the city.[42] Its first pastor was Father John F. Hart, who was born in Des Moines in 1917 and ordained by Bergan in September 1943. After assistantships at Portsmouth and Panama and a stint as chancellor in 1948, Hart returned to parish work, first at Irish Settlement in 1952 and then at Council Bluffs in 1956. Here he remained for sixteen years. The first church was an abandoned supermarket, which Hart refurbished and where he celebrated Mass for a year and a half. In the summer of 1957, work began on a $300,000 school/social hall/ church combination.[43] This was ready by June 1958. The parish school opened in the fall and gradually added grades. A new church, built in 1961, grew rapidly and then they added a mission church at Carter Lake.

Figure 1: Catholic Space in Council Bluffs, Iowa, 1964

Council Bluffs, IA 1964

1. St. Francis Xavier
2. St. Peter
3. Holy Family
4. St. Patrick
5. Our Lady Queen of Apostles
6. St. Albert's High School
7. Mercy Hospital

Map by Aaron Hyams

Outlying Counties: Mills and Warren

Two other outlying counties received new churches. In Mills County, the home of a mental institution and a large packinghouse saw the formal establishment of Our Lady of the Holy Rosary in Glenwood, which opened with Father Othmar Kauffman as first pastor.

On September 8, 1957, Bishop Daly canonically established St. Thomas Aquinas Parish in the Warren County community of Indi-anola.[44] This was a brave foray into a part of Iowa that was heavily Methodist and the home of Simpson College, a stronghold of the Methodist Church. Daly appointed Father Hilary Gaul as its first pastor and employed the Hemmers and Meehan architectural firm of Des Moines to design a structure on the heavily wooded 9.2-acre site, calculated to seat between 350 and 400 people who could park in an adjacent surfaced parking area.[45]

Figure 2: Catholic Space in Des Moines, Iowa, 1964

Des Moines, IA 1964
1. St. Ambrose Cathedral
2. Visitation
3. St. Mary's
4. St. John's
5. St. Anthony's
6. St. Peter's
7. Holy Trinity
8. All Saints
9. St. Augustin
10. St. Joseph
11. Christ the King
12. St. Theresa
13. St. Mary of Nazareth
14. St. Pius X

Map by Aaron Hyams

More Catholic Vigor: Catholic Schools

The postwar baby boom gave birth to a school building boom in Des Moines and Council Bluffs. Catholic schools grew in size and number between 1948 and 1964, expanding from forty-one to forty-six.[46] In September 1960, the Catholic newspaper reported that at 10,821, the diocesan school enrollment had hit its existing capacity. Holy Trinity Parish alone had more than seven hundred pupils.[47]

In all, there were fourteen high schools, enrolling 2,066 students by 1959. Both Catholic high schools in Des Moines were doing well and in need of space. The number of girls in Catholic high schools increased from 695 to 1,442—with St. Joseph Academy, Des Moines, alone exploding from 630 to 938 students. In Council Bluffs, additional facilities for high school students opened in 1955, when Mount Loreto, the former novitiate of the Sisters of Mercy, moved their formation program to Omaha and turned the building into a boarding and day school for Catholic girls.

The number of Catholic high school boys went from 740 to 1,275, with the bulk enrolling at Dowling, which leapt from 630 to 920. This began a debate over how best to accommodate the large influx of high school students, a debate that was not resolved until the 1970s.[48] To meet the growing needs of the students Dowling High School also announced the erection of a new two-story chapel and classroom building to replace the 1884 structure known as Flavin Hall.[49] St. Joseph's Academy announced ambitious plans to expand its facilities in early 1961, including twenty-eight new classrooms, science labs, a library, and a cafeteria.[50] What remained was the need for a central Catholic high school for Council Bluffs and the consolidation of smaller Catholic high schools sponsored by parishes.

A Central High School for Council Bluffs

Bishop Bergan had wanted to form a new central high school that included boys in Council Bluffs, but the Depression and the war stymied many of his plans. In addition, he was reluctant to lay the burden of financing the school on the individual parishes who were already struggling to keep up with the growth in their own communities. Existing Catholic high schools were for girls and had been run by either the BVM or Mercy sisters.

Bergan may have been afraid of starting a new Catholic high school and assessing parishes for its support, but Daly was of another mind. As soon as Father Albert Davidsaver arrived in Council Bluffs in 1961, Daly ordered him to begin planning for a new high school. Obedient and loyal, Davidsaver went to work identifying property and helped organize an area fund drive for the new school. By the end of 1962, the fund had acquired more than $1.4 million in pledges.[51]

When the time was right, Daly simply mandated the creation of St. Albert High School and assigned financial quotas to the parishes for the support of the institution.[52] The new school was to be co-institutional. Boys and girls would be in the same building but would have separate classes. Architect James E. Loftus drew up plans for the school. Three Omaha firms were awarded the contracts, and it was hoped construction would be substantially completed by August 1964 and that occupancy by ninth graders could begin that September.[53] In late May, Davidsaver and Father Joseph Ryan of Neola turned over the first ceremonial spades of earth. In June 1963, Bishop Daly appointed Father Daniel Delahant as superintendent of the new St. Albert High School. Born in Beatrice, Nebraska, in September 1924, Delahant had joined the Army Air Force during

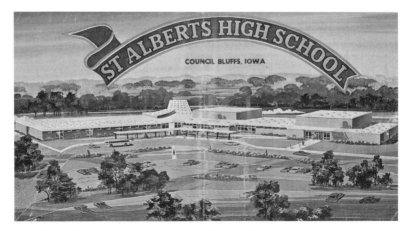

St. Albert High School, 1960s. Credit: St. Albert Archives.

World War II and then entered the seminary. He was ordained in June 1953, had spent eight years at Dowling, and held a master's degree from Creighton University.[54] On July 28, 1963, Daly laid the cornerstone for the new building. He was joined by Delahant and Father Joseph Ryan, as well as Dr. J. Philip Cogley, chairman of the fund-raising campaign, grandiloquently named "Education for Two Worlds."[55] The new $1.5 million school was formally blessed by Daly in June 1964.

St. Albert was built on a "sweeping hillside" and was on a single level in the shape of a "Y," which held the two sections. The new structure had thirty classrooms, an auditorium, a chapel, a cafeteria, a gymnasium, and library facilities. The school phased in its classes, welcoming a freshman class of 175 and gradually shutting down the existing high schools in the area: St. Francis and Mount Loreto in Council Bluffs and St. Patrick's in Neola. The staffing of the school drew on existing religious communities in the Des Moines diocese: the Sisters of Charity (BVM), the Sisters of Mercy, and the Sisters of Humility, along with two diocesan priests, Father Paul Monahan and Father James Watts Kiernan, and lay staff.[56]

The dedication of the new high school gave *Messenger* editor Father Daniel Clarke an opportunity to highlight the often-neglected Council Bluffs Catholic community. Indeed, over the years, Clarke had received many complaints from Council Bluffs residents about the lack of coverage of Catholic life in the city. One letter, from a "Council Bluffs Pioneer" appeared in the September 20, 1963, edition of the paper. The correspondent complained that the paper was not reflective of the diocese but only of the city of Des Moines: "I get a little tired," she harrumphed, "of finding every other article coming from Des Moines." Clarke replied sympathetically that, indeed, he had received many such letters from Council Bluffs but urged the Pioneer to mobilize correspondents in the city and in the parishes to submit information for possible publication. "Communication is a two way street."[57] When the facility was dedicated, the paper put out a glossy, color insert celebrating the dedication of St. Albert. The piece not only carried Daly's speech on the occasion but also sported pictures of the new high school and vignettes of the local parishes.

The decision to build St. Albert brought an end to St. Francis Academy in 1965. This school had been operated by the BVM sisters since 1872 as a day and boarding school. In 1908, the boarding school was closed, and it became a parish elementary and high school. Closed as well was the girls' school opened by the Mercy sisters. St. Albert would play an important role in the evolution of Catholic education and identity in Council Bluffs. In 1973, it would add junior high classes to its program, and, subsequently, the entire spectrum of Catholic education from day-care through high school was under its roof. From 1964 to 2016, 4,167 students would graduate from St. Albert. Two important state politicians, Brent Siegrist (speaker of the Iowa House of Representatives) and Michael Gronstal (majority leader in the state senate), as well as Council Bluffs mayor Matthew Walsh were graduates of the high school. Six priests and two sisters graduated from this school as well.

Daly also hoped to consolidate the handful of small Catholic high schools in Shelby County. In late May 1963, a thirty-acre site off of Highway 191 (the Frank Heese farm, with a view of St. Joseph Church's steeple in Earling) was selected for the new enterprise. Monsignor Michael Schiltz of Panama announced that the new school would open in September 1965. Expecting a first enrollment of about 350, students were supposed to come from Earling, Panama, Portsmouth, Westphalia, and Defiance. It was also hoped that some would come from Dunlap, Harlan, and Woodbine. Architectural plans were sketchy, but the prototype for the new school was Aquinas High School in David City, Nebraska—also a small, rural community.[58] These plans were stymied by the death of Bishop Daly and the general unrest in Catholic education after Vatican II.

Expanding Fundraising

By early 1956, the diocesan paper reported that Des Moines Catholics had spent more than $2 million on school and convent construction.[59] When faced with this expansion—and the need for funds for increasing numbers of seminarians, parish and mission foundations, and schools, especially Dowling—and the increasing demands of diocesan programs, Bishop Daly launched the first diocesan fund appeal since Dowling's fund-raising efforts for the high school in 1917 and 1918. Named the "My Fair Share" Campaign, it was organized in a coordinated fashion. Acting under the advice of professional fund-raisers, Daly hosted an opening event of five hundred volunteers at St. Ambrose Cathedral.[60] The first drive had the ambitious goal of reaching out to eight thousand families for donations. The bishop recruited chairs, divided the ninety-three parishes and missions into regions, and gave them quotas to attain. He also kept up a steady barrage of public events and press coverage to reach out to as many potential donors as possible. The goal, set at a minimum of $1.25 million, was exceeded, as more than $3 million in pledges was reached.[61]

A Shrinking Footprint: The Church in the City

But even as the church flexed its demographic muscles into the expanding suburbs, its historical footprint in the city shrank. This was in part due to the resculpting of the city by federal and state urban renewal and the creation of the expressway system. Although churches were often handled with care with both of these programs, one Catholic Church, venerable St. Mary's on Second and Crocker, was taken out by urban renewal. As noted earlier, this church was first established for German immigrants in 1862. A gem-like Gothic church, it had the river at its back and had lived through many transitions in its ethnic composition. Its pastor, the saintly Father Dominic Weber, OSB, had first been appointed to St. Mary's in 1915. St. Mary's had once had a thriving school and convent, but as time went on people moved away from the old neighborhood to the suburbs, and old ethnic ties—German and Italian—that had also anchored the church evaporated as well. When he first arrived in the summer of 1915, Weber had read the epistle and gospel in German and preached in that tongue. He had stopped using German in services around the time of World War I, however, reflecting both popular antagonism to Germany and the passing of German ethnic identity. As he admitted, "There really was no reason to use it. Everyone understood English by then, and we wanted to lessen a cause for tension in the community."[62] Indeed, strong ethnic differences in Des Moines would fade for a time as the city's population became more homogeneous.

A school at St. Mary's, run by the Benedictine sisters of Atchison, had risen and then fallen, closing its doors for good in 1952. Even though Daly and Weber's Benedictine superiors had pressured the old pastor to give it up and return to the monastery, Weber hung on well into his eighties. He was aided by a few loyal families and a faithful parish trustee, Carl Masker, and his wife who was the church organist. As a parish profile in 1960 noted: "Despite the potentialities of its scenic location, the neighborhood around St. Mary's has progressively decayed in recent years. The school has been closed. Former parish families have joined the flight to the suburbs, few families remain. Two world conflicts and the passage of time have lessened the attraction of links to the fatherland. The future of St. Mary's is in doubt, the past is not. The contributions of the parish to Catholic life of the city and diocese can be attested not only by the families remaining in the congregation but by those who have left to leaven the parishes all over the metropolitan area."[63]

The City Redevelopment Agency promoted the River Hills project, which was anxious to remake the dilapidated section around St. Mary's, and, after negotiation, managed to procure the property from the diocese. The parish's end was announced in January 1961, as the elderly and ailing Weber finally decamped to his Atchison monastery. The elderly pastor planned to slip out of town quietly but was feted by a large turnout of parishioners, clergy, and old friends who showered him with gratitude and praise for his years of service.[64] Within a few months the venerable old structure at Second and Crocker was torn down. One wonders what happened to the small graveyard attached to the church. Father Dominic died in 1964, three years after the closure and destruction of the parish he served so faithfully.

Father Dominic Weber, OSB.
Credit: Photo courtesy of
St. Benedict's Abbey,
Atchison, Kansas, Kansasmonks.org.

Other parish schools in the heart of the city also began to experience decline. St. Ambrose and Visitation schools managed to maintain enough students to remain open but slowly began to go down in numbers. Even with this, there was a concern about racial justice.

Dealing with the City Interracial Issues

One urban issue area where Daly would show some leadership was in public advocacy for African Americans. In 1950, there were nearly nine thousand African Americans living in Des Moines, most of them huddled near the river in a handful of census tracts. The largest concentration was on the east side of Des Moines.[65] African American incomes were low and housing in these areas was not good. A series of articles by Robert Spiegel in the Des Moines *Tribune* examined "Negro Housing" and insisted "Segregation nearly 100% Effective."[66]

Catholic priests had been caring for blacks for many years. One of the first was Father Thomas Murphy. He was a devoted pastor of St. Peter's Church in Des Moines, who took it upon himself to care for the small number of Catholic African Americans in the city and occasionally bringing up African American priests like Divine Word Father Francis G. Wade, who delivered missions to black Catholics and spoke to students at Dowling. When Murphy died in 1951, his obituary noted as well "his persistent convert work among the Negros of Des Moines; in many instances he gave the complete course of instructions to little groups gathered in the home of a prospective Catholic."[67] For a time it was rumored that the Viatorians would begin a parish for African American Catholics, but this never materialized.

In his address at the civic reception welcoming him to Des Moines, Bishop Daly had lauded the "diverse" racial and ethnic peoples who forged a "United People" and praised the fact that the "bigotry, the intolerance, the religious and racial prejudice which have stained many a page of our country's history . . . have not darkened the history of this state."[68] In late 1949, after Rome gave permission, Daly officiated at a pontifical Mass in honor of Blessed Martin De

Porres, a Dominican saint to whom he had personal devotion and who was becoming a patron of African American Catholics.[69]

The African American population of Iowa grew slowly in the 1950s and 1960s, centered primarily in the city of Des Moines. The Civil Rights revolution of the 1950s and 1960s was slow to come to Iowa, but by the early 1960s the demands being made for equal opportunity—housing, jobs, and racial sensitivity—had reached the Hawkeye State. Federal intervention in racial issues percolated all through the 1950s, and during the Kennedy years (1961–1963) racial tensions escalated as African Americans undertook nonviolent crusades to end legal segregation in the south.

The American bishops had taken notice of the shifting currents on racial issues, with some prelates publicly demanding the racial integration of Catholic schools (Washington, DC; St. Louis, Missouri; and Raleigh, North Carolina). Other Catholic activist groups, such as the Catholic Interracial Councils (founded in the 1930s), called out instances of racial discrimination in Catholic parishes, schools, and hospitals, especially in big cities like New York and Chicago. In 1958, the administrative board of the National Catholic Welfare Conference (the policy body of the US bishops) issued a strong letter titled "Discrimination and the Christian Conscience," which strongly condemned racial injustice. The National Conference for Interracial Justice was formed in 1960 and held workshops and conferences highlighting Catholic teaching on racial equality and speaking out firmly against racist practices in the church. In the spirit of these times, sympathetic articles appeared in *The Messenger* chronicling these events, and a small interracial ministry had long been in place at St. Peter's in Des Moines.

Father Clarke's editorship directed *The Messenger* to become even more outspoken in defense of racial justice. In a powerful editorial, "Negroes Need Not Apply," Clarke told the story of a bright African American youth who confided to him the need for a decent job. When Clarke suggested work at a local restaurant, the young man balked: "Oh no father, they would never hire ME at THAT restaurant." Clarke observed woefully that the young man was right. The owner of the restaurant "would not be so brazen as to put a 'Negroes need not apply' sign on his establishment, but the net result would amount to the same."

Clarke urged the passage of a bill before the Iowa legislature that would prevent such hiring discrimination based on "color, religion, or national identity." Invoking the 1958 condemnation of racism by the American bishops, Clarke noted the moral dimensions to the race question and also called out those who used racist techniques in buying and selling homes. "Catholics in Iowa," he insisted, "should unite with their fellow citizens endorsing and supporting an anti-discrimination bill so badly needed in 20th century Iowa."[70]

In the spring of 1963, Newman chaplains of the Midwest gathered at the Savery Hotel in Des Moines to hear talks about interracial issues led by Matthew Ahmann, executive director of the National Catholic Conference of Interracial Justice. The highlight of the gathering, titled "Who Is My Neighbor?," included one of the first ecumenical enterprises since the days of Bishop Bergan: a panel that included Ahmann; Father James Rasmussen, Newman chaplain at Drake University; Dean John W. McCaw of Drake, a member of the United Church of Christ; Rev. Francis Hallenger, pastor of the Lutheran Church of the Good Shepherd in Des Moines; and Father Thomas Pucelik, STD, associate Newman chaplain at the University of Nebraska at Lincoln.[71] Bishop Daly placed Father Paul Connolly, director of Catholic Charities, in charge of interracial efforts.

Just before Bishop Daly left for the second session of Vatican II, he broke again with his reluctance to engage in ecumenical events and joined Reverend Judson Fiebiger of the United Church of Christ and Rabbi Irving Weingart, president of the Iowa Board of Rabbis, and became a co-chairman of the Iowa Conference on Race and Religion, which met September 11–12, 1963. Daly himself offered an address in which he urged action more than words or good feelings: "It is not enough for us to be sympathetic, feel kindly and pray and hope that the Negroes get what they want. . . . Our duty as brothers is to lend active help to them. . . . They have been patient a long time."[72]

In October local Catholics met to consider the formation of a branch of the Catholic Interracial Council in Des Moines. Father Patrick Best of St. Augustin's had taken a lead in pressing for equal rights for blacks in housing. He and attorney Philip Riley also tried to organize the council, which would urge greater Catholic interest in interracial affairs and also monitor racist behavior on the part of Catholic institutions.[73] Already in September a fair-housing ordinance had been introduced to the Des Moines city council and some city Catholics had marched in sympathy demonstrations to make sure it passed.[74]

When the Diocesan Council of Catholic Women had their annual congress that fall, Daly sent them a note from Rome urging them to cooperate "with our colored fellow citizens." He noted:

> In these days our Colored fellow citizens deserve our coopera-
> tion. I say "cooperation" because we should work with them.
> There should be no materialism in your apostolate of charity
> among them. You should aid their cause, as more fortunate
> sisters go to the help of their Father's children. Your good will
> toward them may take you into civic affairs. And in you should
> go without apology and without fear. Every citizen should try
> to advance the common good.[75]

Bishop Daly: Cold War-Era Marian Devotee

Tending to expansion likely occupied a considerable portion of Daly's time, but he also attempted as best he could to provide critical spiritual guidance for the Iowa flock. His tenure of office coincided with the Cold War era in US history—a reality that was deeply felt by Catholics. Cold War fears visited Iowa in the postwar period, as deepening tensions with the Soviet Union and Communist China created a period of great fear and mistrust. The expansion of nuclear arms added to this terror, and the Cold War sporadically erupted into hot war in Korea and later Vietnam.

The outbreak of the Korean War renewed the call for chaplains to serve. Father Stephen Kane, now a major, volunteered and once again plunged himself into the combat zone. He accompanied General Douglas MacArthur's army in their offensive against North Korea in late 1950. But a massive counterattack by North Korean forces, aided by thousands of Chinese troops, forced the army into a bloody retreat on the icy Korean peninsula. Kane wrote to Bishop Daly of the retreat:

> On the march north we were shocked by the vicious atrocities
> that marked our route. . . . One felt glad that military circum-

stances left little pause in a rapid advance, and the sight and stench of mass murders become more or less of passing note. Now we are confronted with an even more heart-rending site, a tragedy without equal—it is the picture of an entire people fleeing the approach of Red Terror. . . . The lanes and mountains are filled with a shivering and famished populace still looking to the New World for the right to live as human beings. It would be a common wish to send our Red and Pinkish citizens to Korea for a wordless sermon most convincing in visual aids.[76]

Other Des Moines priests were summoned back to chaplain duties. Father Francis Sampson had also gone back into the service and in Korea repeated his parachuting heroics, jumping with a rescue team far behind enemy lines to attempt the rescue of a number of American prisoners.[77] By 1951, seven Des Moines priests were serving in the military: Fathers Stephen Kane, Patrick Walsh, Francis Sampson, Joseph Schulte, Woodrow Elias, Ward Bowler, and A. J. Devlin.[78] Walsh received a Bronze Star for his service in Korea.[79] Once again the Catholic press reported the depressing details of casualties from the diocese. The first was Roman Stole, who had attended St. Joseph High School in Earling. Stole had sustained injuries from flying shrapnel.[80]

Cold War tensions gripped the country and had a special dimension for Catholics since Soviet and Chinese assaults on churches and persecution of religion hit home in a powerful way. One way Catholics everywhere reacted to these tensions was through an embrace of a certain kind of Marian devotion—drawing on her prayers to ward off nuclear war and domination by atheistic communism. This had been warmly endorsed by the strongly anticommunist papacy of Pope Pius XII. The pontiff had placed great emphasis on devotion to Mary, sending an emissary to crown her statue at Fatima in Portugal, where she is believed to have appeared in 1917. In 1942, he consecrated the world to Mary and, in November 1950, took the unusual and rare step of pronouncing infallibly that Mary had been taken body and soul to heaven (the doctrine of the assumption). Bishop Daly also demonstrated his deep devotion to Our Lady of Fatima by consecrating the entire diocese to the Immaculate Heart of Mary.[81] On June 13, 1948, he led this consecration in St. Ambrose Cathedral and directed that every parish in the diocese do the same.[82]

Daly's devotion to Our Lady of Fatima was also on display when a new parish church in Portsmouth (the third in its sixty-year history) was renamed in her honor.[83] In a development that no doubt pleased the bishop, Visitation Parish implemented the Fatima-related devotion called the "block rosary" in response to Mary's call for more prayer. Once a week, Visitation parishioners were urged to gather in one of the block's homes to pray the rosary for world peace.[84] Daly would repeat calls for dedication to the Immaculate Heart in late August 1950, and St. Peter's Parish would also commence the block rosary. In October 1950, the famous Pilgrim Virgin Statue of Our Lady of Fatima came to the diocese. On its arrival, it went first to St. Ambrose, where Daly symbolically crowned the statue, and then it proceeded to an array of diocesan parishes, everywhere attracting large crowds.[85] When the statue was transported from Harlan to Portsmouth, a caravan of five hundred automobiles accompanied it.[86] In 1954, Pope Pius XII proclaimed a Marian Year, which was marked in the diocese by large public devotions. In September 1956, Daly issued a pastoral letter dedicating the diocese to the Queenship of Mary and declared St. Pius X as a secondary patron.[87]

Marian devotion was an important Catholic "marker" in southwest Iowa. One important contributor to the cult of Mary was a Council Bluffs physician Dr. Philip Cogley. Cogley, born in 1899 in Council Bluffs, had served in the Army Medical Corps in New Guinea during World War II. He made a war-time promise to build a shrine on his family property, grandiloquently called "Cogleywood." Many people came to see the grotto shrine, and the pious physician formed an Outdoors Shrine Guild and had the Boys Town ceramics shop produce statues of Mary. He built Marian shrines at St. Joseph Cemetery, Mercy Hospital, St. Patrick's Church, St. Mary's Church, and St. Patrick's Cemetery in Neola.[88]

In March 1958, the Catholic newspaper noted the economic impact of Daly's decade of service to the diocese, ticking off his accomplishments, observing the growth of the Catholic population of southwest Iowa from forty-five thousand to more than sixty-two thousand and enrollment in Catholic schools from five thousand to more than 9,600. He had by this time established five new parishes and provided for six more parochial schools. The paper calculated that the capital improvements in new churches, schools, and other parochial buildings alone totaled around $5 million while the expansion of the hospitals of the diocese alone expended more than $7 million in expanded facilities.[89]

Marriage and Family and Care for the Elderly: The Cana Movement

Increasing numbers of Catholic marriages in the postwar era brought more sustained attention from the diocese. In February 1949, Father John Gorman of Assumption Parish in Granger and Father Ward Bowler of Dowling High School invited Jesuit Edward Dowling to speak on the Cana Conference.[90] Father Edward Dowling, SJ, had created this program in St. Louis, and it became quite popular throughout Catholic America. Cana Conferences brought together married couples for day-long seminars to discuss and deepen the understanding of Catholic marriage and examine issues that made married life challenging.

A similar type of experience was created for engaged couples, called Pre-Cana, which included talks by married couples about the demands of Christian marriage and by priests who instructed the couples in the theology of marriage. The Cana experience sought to widen and deepen the understanding of marriage, moving beyond what moral theologians of the day taught as a "legitimate remedy for concupiscence" into a more life-affirming bond that stressed its covenantal aspects. At this first Cana Conference in Granger, 119 attended, including sixty-eight young people from Des Moines Catholic Action. Half of the crowd was single, but twenty-five couples renewed their vows.[91]

The Peak of Catholic Mobilization: An Inter-Diocesan Training Center for Priests

The United States experienced a significant religious revival in the postwar period. Although the reasons for this are complex, the numbers of Americans affiliating with denominations spiked during the 1950s and 1960s. In the Catholic Church in the United States, these postwar years witnessed a huge increase in the numbers of men and women pursuing a church vocation. Monasteries and convents were filled, and dioceses began to build or expand existing seminaries to meet the growth. Formation programs for religious often had to build to accommodate the new numbers and adapt their postulant, novitiate, and juniorate programs (all stages of training to shape the life of a young person entering religious life) to train new recruits to serve with professionalism and zeal in the apostolates. Much of this was encouraged by the women religious who taught in Catholic schools and also by parish priests who encouraged altar servers to consider a priestly career. Many young men who entered the seminary in these days often credited a particular priest or religious sister for encouraging their vocation. Most Catholic families considered it an honor to have a son in the seminary or a daughter in the convent. A smattering of religious movies, for example, *Going My Way* and *The Bells of St. Mary's*, which premiered in 1945, portrayed priests and sisters in a very positive light and were also a source of inspiration.

The process of priestly formation in this era was broken into two parts. The first was the "minor seminary," a six-year program that began after eighth grade for the typical Catholic boy. Four years of high school and two of junior college were taken at a special school. After graduation, the candidates went on to the "major seminary," where they completed philosophical training and then four years of theological study. At the end, for those who persevered, there was the great joy of ordination, first Mass, and then assignment to a parish or diocesan job. The Diocese of Des Moines did not have a minor seminary. The burden of educating these young men on the theological level was split among three seminaries: Kenrick Seminary in St. Louis, Missouri; Conception Seminary in Conception, Missouri; and Saint Paul Seminary in St. Paul, Minnesota.[92]

Southwest Iowa enjoyed its share of this vocation boom. Already Dowling High School had begun to pay its dividends in terms of an increasing number of young men who chose to enter the seminary after high school. By 1949, the diocese boasted a whopping thirty-nine seminarians. In 1950, thirty-eight diocesan seminarians were recorded as studying in various seminaries.[93] Between 1948 and 1964 the number of diocesan priests in the Des Moines diocese surged from 115 to 135.

Providing a native-born clergy for Des Moines was one of the fruits of this era of Catholic growth. For many years, it had been hoped that local men who knew the diocese, whose parents worked in the community, and whose ties to neighborhoods, and especially to Dowling High School, would be able to provide a cadre of leadership for church and community. Not only did the growth of the Catholic population require it, but the traditional source of foreign vocations from Ireland seemed to wither as the largest number of the newly ordained men opted for the sunbelt areas of the United States—Florida, Texas, Arizona, and California. Because of the vocation boom and the presence of a strong Catholic high school that encouraged vocations, Bishop Daly managed to alter definitively the character of the presbyterate—filling it with men native to Iowa. After Daly's death, a priest eulogized him by noting, "During the 16 years with us, he ordained approximately as many young men native of the Diocese as had been ordained during the 36 years before him."[94] A seminary for Iowa lads had opened in Dubuque during the time of Bishop Loras but had closed in 1878. Resources and numbers were good enough to attempt (for a second time) the creation of a major seminary in Iowa. The efforts to do this were well-intentioned and appeared to work but had flaws that just could not be overcome.

In 1949, Bishop Leo Binz of Winona, Minnesota, was sent to Dubuque as coadjutor to Archbishop Henry Rohlman, and he tackled the issue of an Iowa seminary. Binz, from Rockford, Illinois, had himself studied for the priesthood in Baltimore, Washington, DC, and Rome. During his tenure as bishop of Winona, he had opened a minor seminary (which included four years of high school and two of college) for the growing number of high school youth who wanted to be priests in the diocese. Within a year of becoming coadjutor in Dubuque, he wrote the prefect of the Congregation of Seminaries and Universities, Cardinal Giuseppe Pizzardo, "I am . . . deeply concerned because the Archdiocese of Dubuque has not been able to provide a Theological Seminary in accordance with the legislation of the Church, particularly as set forth in Canon 1354." Certain that Dubuque could not shoulder the responsibility of opening its own seminary, he informed Pizzardo, "I have had the opportunity to discuss the situation with His Excellency Archbishop Rohlman and with their excellencies, the bishops of the suffragan dioceses; and while it is not possible for any diocese in the Province, there is a well-grounded hope that a Provincial Seminary may be acceptable to all of us."[95]

In 1951, Binz met with Dominicans Edward Carlson and Edward Hughes, together with Chancellor Monsignor Loras Lane to broach the idea of a provincial seminary (which would include two years of philosophy and four of theology) sponsored by all the dioceses of Iowa.[96]

The Dominicans had already branched out into Iowa and purchased a former convent of the Sisters of the Good Shepherd in the western part of Dubuque and renamed it St. Rose of Lima Priory. They moved into the building in the fall of 1950 and agreed to be the faculty for a new seminary that would be called Mount St. Bernard's. In August 1951, the bishops had purchased Mount St. Agnes, a former Mercy Convent in Dubuque, for $842,000. Costs were pro-rated among the Iowa dioceses with Dubuque paying 42 percent, Davenport 21 percent, Sioux City 23 percent, and Des Moines 14

Mount St. Bernard Seminary, Dubuque.
Credit: Diocese of Des Moines Archives.

percent. Bishop Daly collected the $140,000 needed to pay the Diocese of Des Moines portion by urging Des Moines Catholics to use it as their primary Lenten charity in 1952.[97]

The building sat on ninety-seven acres, adjacent to the new Dominican Priory, and was large enough to house fifty students. Sixteen seminarians would live in the recently purchased structure. Four of them were from Des Moines: Thomas Ryan, Gerald Ryan, Richard Bergman, and Patrick Bacon.[98] The bishops expanded the facility between March and July 1952, adding a new residential wing that could accommodate 142 students plus an expanded chapel and refectory. The project also include a renovation of all the mechanical systems of the old building.[99] By the fall of 1952, there were 102 students. The Franciscan Sisters of the Holy Family, whose motherhouse was in Dubuque, did domestic work at the seminary. To help fund these improvements, Daly launched a $350,000 capital campaign in the diocese, targeting even school-children who eventually raised $3,680 for a new statue of St. Bernard of Clairvaux for the seminary.[100]

Mount St. Bernard Seminary, Dubuque.
Credit: Diocese of Des Moines Archives.

A Clashing of Intentions

From the outset, however, difficulties beset the seminary. The key issue was the curriculum. The Dominican seminarians, who attended class with the diocesan men, had already studied Greek and Latin for two years before beginning their final seminary studies and were able to use the complex *Summa Theologica* of St. Thomas Aquinas and grasp the Latin lectures of their professors. But the complex Latin lectures bewildered the diocesan seminarians from the very start. Few—even those who had majored in Latin at Loras in Dubuque or St. Ambrose in Davenport—were able to understand the spoken Latin used by their professors, nor were they able to grasp the multifaceted thought of St. Thomas Aquinas as their Dominican schoolmates did.

On the evening of October 16, 1951, barely four weeks into the existence of the new seminary, a tense meeting was held between the officials of the seminary and the Dominicans.[101] The diocesan priests conveyed the complaints of the diocesan seminarians who did not understand enough Latin to keep up with the lectures and were not acquainted with the philosophical terms, idioms, and abbreviations used by their professors (known to the Dominican students). Dominican faculty members explained that they had extensive material to cover and could not take the time to explain everything to the struggling diocesan seminarians. Suggestions included taking more time to explain Thomistic method and working with the Latin of the diocesan students.

But what really emerged was a difference in what was necessary for the priesthood in Iowa. Dominican seminarians were preparing, for the most part, for lives in academe—either as college or university professors or even as high school teachers. Moreover, their tradition of preaching required a thorough grasp of the teachings of Aquinas and his chief commentators. Diocesan priests were bound for parish work, where the need for highly sophisticated theological formation was not as necessary.

Parish priests needed to give basic instructions to converts and others, teach children catechism, and of course preach from an authentic body of knowledge about the theology of the church. While seminary consolidation and the use of the Dominicans seemed good on paper, the joining of two different types of seminarians was not always helpful for either group. What was proposed and later adopted was a separation of Dominican and diocesan students—making the seminarians feel less self-conscious and creating a more relaxed academic environment where they could feel free to ask questions and were less fearful of answering.

Eventually, two separate tracks developed at Mount St. Bernard: a *Cursus Academicus* and a *Cursus Seminaristicus*, which offered two different ways of teaching dogma and moral theology. The *Cursus Academicus* followed the text of the *Summa Theologica* and was conducted in Latin with a moral theology component undergirded by Dominic Prummer's *Manuale Theologiae Moralis* and another text by Dominican Benedict Henry Merklebach. In the *Cursus Seminaristicus*, the professors used the *Summa* and proposed lecture outlines in Latin, but then amplified them in English. Those in this course attended all classes at Mount St. Bernard's.[102] The *Cursus Academicus* was discontinued at Mount St. Bernard's in 1960, and Mount St. Bernard students no longer attended classes at the Dominican Priory.

Seminarian learning the rubrics of Mass at Mount St. Bernard Seminary. Credit: Diocese of Des Moines Archives.

By 1955, Mount St. Bernard's welcomed 150 seminarians, most of them from Iowa but others from nearby dioceses and elsewhere.[103] The numbers of ordinations picked up. In 1955, six men, four of them graduates from Mount St. Bernard, were ordained at St. Ambrose.[104] In 1960, five men for Des Moines were ordained on Pentecost afternoon: Lawrence A. Beeson, Leonard Kenkel, James Kleffman, Paul Monahan, and Thomas Pfeffer.[105] Des Moines priests served on the staff of the seminary, including former chaplain Father Albert Davidsaver who arrived in 1955 and served as the seminary business manager.[106] In 1961 Father Benedict Kenkel, who became dean of studies and registrar, replaced Davidsaver.[107] The seminary lasted until 1969. Although never popular with Des Moines priests, it did attempt to provide a training ground for local clergy.

In retrospect, these appeared to be halcyon days for the Diocese of Des Moines and the springboard for additional growth. A season of change was about to begin as Daly commenced his second decade of leadership.

In October 1958, the death of Pope Pius XII brought a wave of official mourning throughout the diocese as each parish offered Requiem Masses for the deceased pontiff. Daly, who came to favor evening Masses, offered one at five o'clock at St. Ambrose on October 13. Before the end of that month, the cardinals in conclave had elected the patriarch of Venice, Angelo Roncalli, to the Throne of Peter. At a dedicatory address for a new St. Patrick's Church in Walnut, Daly urged parishioners to pray for the new pontiff, "that the Lord will preserve him, and give him health, and not deliver him to his enemies."[108] At the end of January 1959, as Pope John XXIII was taking possession of St. Paul Outside-the-Walls, he announced the convocation of an ecumenical council. This won headlines in the Catholic press but no immediate comment from Bishop Daly.[109]

In October 1959, Daly met the new pontiff during his first *ad limina* visit and had the customary photograph—both men attired in white. Daly came back with papal honors for five priests (including a Protonotary Apostolic for the aging Monsignor Vitus Stoll) and three laity.[110] In 1961, the diocese held celebrations to commemorate the fiftieth jubilee of its foundation. Daly issued a pastoral letter urging Catholics to make the year a Eucharistic Year, and the newspaper noted that only three of the sixty-eight priests in the diocese at its founding were still alive: Monsignor Patrick McDermott, pastor of Ss. Peter and Paul in Atlantic; Monsignor James Danahey and Father James McDonald were both retired.[111]

An Outreach to Latin America

Pope John XXIII had asked priest-rich areas of the world to contribute missionaries to the church in Latin America. In Boston, Cardinal Richard Cushing had already formed the Society of St. James to respond to this need, placing volunteer diocesan priests in needy Latin American parishes and missions.

Two Des Moines priests went to Bolivia. Father James Stessman and Father Paul Koch. Koch, ordained in 1961, was a native of Shelby County's St. Mary of the Assumption Parish in Panama (and had a brother who was also a Des Moines priest). Attracted to missionary life and the Society of St. James in Boston (a clearinghouse for diocesan priests willing to work in Latin America),

Father Paul Koch, diocesan missionary to Bolivia.
Credit: Diocese of Des Moines Archives.

already in 1958 he explored the possibility of becoming a missionary. Urged by a Dominican professor to wait until after ordination, he taught for two years at Dowling after receiving holy orders and received permission from Daly in 1963 to join the Society of St. James. Daly sent him to Mexico City to learn Spanish, and he was then sent to Bolivia, where he served in a variety of parishes—from the heights of Bolivia's 13,000-foot Altiplano (Collao, Andean, Bolivian plateau, the widest expanse in the Andes Mountains) to the semitropical area around Santa Cruz in east Central Bolivia. Eventually Stessman joined him and later another priest, Father Robert Weis, was dispatched to Brazil. Koch remained in Bolivia until his retirement in 2009. Koch challenged the assumption of some US politicians that Bolivian activists and farmers were all communists and shared this with Bishop Dingman and later with Republican Senator Chuck Grassley.[112] Koch, like another son of the diocese, Archbishop Leo Arkfeld, SVD (from Panama, Iowa), of Papua, New Guinea, occasionally came home and shared his experiences in the mission field.

A Tragic End

Daly was in place when Vatican II was held and its significance for the diocese of Des Moines will be covered in the next chapter. His term ended quite abruptly and in tragedy. In November 1964, his confidant, Monsignor Joseph Sondag, had flown to Rome earlier to meet Daly for a pilgrimage trip to the Holy Land. The huge TWA airliner (TWA 800) had already stopped at several spots and was fueled up and ready to go. Both the bishop and Sondag were to stop first in Athens and then fly to Israel, where they planned to stay ten days and afterward spend some time in Cairo before returning to Des Moines and the introduction of the new Mass.[113] As the plane departed from Rome's Leonardo Da Vinci airport, it developed trouble and skidded off the runway and blew up. Daly and Sondag were among those who died.

Father Lawrence Beeson, a student in Rome at the time first heard of the crash from a fellow seminarian from Rockville Center who handed him a news account of the incident. He knew right away that Daly and Sondag were on the flight and rushed to call Father Benedict Joseph, OP, the procurator general of Daly's Dominican Order at Santa Sabina, for information and help. The Dominican had not heard of the crash but called the hospitals of San Camillo and San Eugenio, where the crash survivors were being treated. Neither Bishop Daly nor Monsignor Sondag were listed as patients. The next day an agent from the KLM Royal Dutch Airlines picked up Beeson and, with a telegram from the Italian secretary of state, was able to drive him right out on the tarmac where the bodies were left overnight. The airport chaplain had removed the ring from Bishop Daly's finger to keep it from being stolen. Beeson remembered being warned not to touch anything because it was all contaminated. Daly and Sondag were carrying formal documents of two marriage cases (likely dispensations or annulments), and the Italian authorities were searching the wreckage to find them, which they did and returned them to Beeson.

The next day the bodies were transported to the Rome morgue at Campo Verano. Beeson went there with a cassock for Monsignor Sondag's body. Father Benedict Joseph, OP, and Father Alexius Driscoll, OP, had provided a Dominican habit and rosary for Bishop Daly's body as well as vestments. Beeson recalled that the bodies were not terribly disfigured but looked like department store mannequins with no bodily features. The FBI assisted in the identification of the bodies. Daly's body was recognized because he still wore a corset after his gallbladder surgery of many years ago. Sondag had a glass eye, which they were able to test.

Each body was then placed with great reverence by the morgue staff into a metal shipping coffin, which was then soldered shut. Beeson recalled the workman had his young son sit on top of the coffins to

Headline of Daly's death. Credit: Diocese of Des Moines Archives.

make a good seal as he soldered. The metal coffins were then placed in wooden shipping coffins. Daly and Sondag were given a Requiem Mass at Santa Sabina in Rome. In attendance were three cardinals, Dominican Michael Browne, Paolo Marella, and Daly's old boss, Amleto Cicognani, now the Vatican secretary of state.[114] The bodies were returned to America, landing first in New York, where Cardinal Spellman was on hand to offer his respects. Then Beeson went on alone to Chicago, where he was met by Fathers James Rasmussen and Daniel Delahant who had a hearse ready to take the bodies to Des Moines. Sondag's body was returned to Atlantic where funeral rites were held for him at Ss. Peter and Paul Parish.[115]

Daly's funeral took place in early December 1964, with the prelate's remains lying in state in St. Ambrose Cathedral (the coffin was closed). Scores of Catholics filed by his coffin, and Catholic schoolchildren prayed the rosary. Apostolic Delegate Egidio Vagnozzi offered the solemn pontifical Requiem on the high altar of St. Ambrose Cathedral. Archbishop James Byrne of Dubuque offered the eulogy for Daly, whom he lauded. "His life was a lesson in purposeful living. It was a rich life, not to be summed up in one easy epithet."[116]

Funeral procession for Bishop Edward Daly. Credit: Diocese of Des Moines Archives.

Byrne then presided at the graveside rites for the deceased prelate at Glendale Cemetery.

Father James Huston wrote eloquently of Daly, noting that even though the late prelate had not studied in Rome, he loved the city and was a loyal son of the church. He noted as well that Daly had been caught up in the dynamism of the council and the example of Pope John XXIII and that he was grateful "he died with a friend at his side, Monsignor Sondag. 'Joe' had been his right hand man for eleven years. Their years of serving the diocese together had ripened between them a warm and deep affection."[117]

The diocesan consultors elected Monsignor Lester V. Lyons of St. Ambrose as the administrator and initiated the new liturgy of Vatican II on the First Sunday of Advent. Despite its shock, the diocese now prepared to move on to a new age. Pope Paul VI was visiting Bombay, India, and a new era was about to dawn for the Des Moines diocese as both the promise and the challenge of Vatican II began to unfold.

Archbishop James Byrne of Dubuque presiding at the graveside service for Daly. Credit: Diocese of Des Moines Archives.

7

Transnational Changes and a New Iowa Catholicism

From its inception, the Catholic Church in Iowa was a transnational organization, deeply bound to a common set of beliefs and practices that united them with their co-religionists around the world. For a long period these were rather clear sets of theological and administrative principles—many of which dated back to the Middle Ages and even earlier. The main body of Catholic theology was rationalistic—relying heavily on the intellectual legacy of the fathers of the church and the great medieval theologian St. Thomas Aquinas and his interpreters. Since the nineteenth century, Catholicism was very clearly defined by personal and intellectual loyalty to the bishop of Rome, the pope. At Vatican Council I (1869–1871), papal jurisdiction over bishops, priests, religious, and laity was significantly expanded. The definition of papal infallibility, although technically a doctrine with a great number of qualifications, elevated papal authority to new heights. The pope was the church, and the central offices of the church provided clear lines of church authority—a reality reinforced by the codification of a vast array of church regulations and customs in the Code of Canon Law (1918). Official theology and centralized administration created even greater clarity as well as a strongly etched sense of Catholic identity. Catholics knew the truth. They had clear and unambiguous central leadership emanating from the pope, his close advisors, the

Roman curia, and down to local bishops and pastors. This created a very distinct Catholic ethos of confidence, obedience to church teaching, and made the clergy the reference point for any unclear issue. Catholics maintained a close-knit culture: they discouraged intermarriage with people of other faith traditions; they participated in group rituals that reinforced their common identity, for example, the Mass and Friday abstinence. The sphere of Catholic life was, as one historian described it, "so certain and so set apart."

But even in this centralized uniformity, church experiences varied from culture to culture. In the United States, traditions of the separation of church and state, the minority status of Catholics, and the demands of getting along with non-Catholic neighbors gave a certain twist to the Catholic experience. Added to this were the filters used in transmitting church teaching from the pope himself or the various offices of his bureaucracy to the faithful. Even in the midst of what appeared to be external uniformity, there were varieties of opinions and interpretations of official decrees or directives that varied with the person or persons applying them. So even if Catholics in the United States were quite obedient to church laws, they may have interpreted them differently and even dissented from them if they felt it was necessary. For example, Catholics did not heed strong prohibitions on "mixed marriage"—with many marrying "outside" the fold. Not all attended Mass weekly or went to confession with regularity, despite the strong injunctions and threats of eternal damnation that accompanied church directives in these matters.

In the twentieth century, certain Catholic teachings were beginning to come into question—particularly related to reproductive issues. The official prohibition of artificial forms of birth control put some Catholic couples in a dilemma as they struggled to keep the number of their children within the bounds of their financial resources. America entered a period of sustained prosperity after World War II, which lifted many American Catholics into the middle class. More access to higher education created a better educated Catholic laity, capable of more independent thinking and critical questioning of ideas handed down by elders. Advanced education often equipped them for better jobs with higher income and greater social mobility. With more money in their pockets, Catholics became a part of the fast-paced postwar consumer culture of American life. The advance

Bishop Daly with council fathers.
Credit: Diocese of Des Moines Archives.

of liberation movements around the world—including the civil rights movement in the United States—created a willingness to challenge authority. Social tumult created by civil rights activists and those who opposed American policies abroad (particularly the war in Vietnam) created a different atmosphere for Catholics in the United States in the latter part of the twentieth century.

The Second Vatican Council

All of these changes would be refracted through one of the most important developments in international Catholicism in modern times: the Second Vatican Council, which met from 1962 to 1965. An ecumenical council is a momentous event in the life of the church—producing authoritative decrees that are binding on church members. Vatican II was the twenty-first such general council in the history of the Catholic Church and summoned over two thousand of the world's Roman Catholic bishops to Rome. It opened on October 11, 1962, with a stirring gathering of bishops at St. Peter's Basilica, where they heard an address by Pope St. John XXIII that called the council members (bishops, religious superiors, and experts [*periti*]) to deliberate in good faith to make the message of Christ more accessible to the modern world. Pope John rejected the laments of "the prophets of doom" (some of his own bureaucrats) and called for a fresh look not at doctrines themselves, but at how they were to be presented to the world. With Pope John's words ringing in their ears, council fathers, who were advocates of reform, pressed an agenda that gradually picked up steam and changed certain church practices that were in serious need of updating (*aggiornamento*). It also attempted to redefine the sometimes tense relationship between the church and the modern world—stressing more what was good and positive in culture and seeking to build bridges to it. Dialogue, historical awareness, ecumenism, and openness to the "signs of the times" were hallmarks of the new spirit generated by the council. For the bishops who attended, especially those from the landlocked areas of the central United States, Catholicism's international identity came home in a way for which few of them were prepared.[1] The changes that the council mandated directly and powerfully affected the Catholic community of southwest Iowa. These included liturgical reform, especially the translation of Catholic rites from Latin into English, new understandings of the relationships between bishops and priests, and laypersons, subsumed under the shorthand "collegiality"; a fresh look at relations with other faith traditions—not only other Christians but Jews and Muslims as well—ecumenism; and urged a much more irenic relationship between the church and the modern world, embracing especially the principle of freedom of conscience.

The Council Comes to Des Moines

Des Moines Catholics followed the events of the council in the public press and likely through explanations from parish priests and others. Talks given by outsiders such as Dominican Father Richard T. A. Murphy, a professor of Scripture at Mount St. Bernard, noted to a Holy Name gathering in March 1962 that the upcoming event was "one of the great moments in the history of salvation" and predicted that among the fruits of the council would be its endorsement of the lay apostolate.[2]

Of particular interest for the local audience were a series of articles authored for the Catholic newspaper by Father James Huston, a Des Moines priest studying canon law in Rome. His interesting and (for the time) rather blunt reports of the preparations for the council acquainted readers with the feisty debates going on in Rome even before the council began.

In one account, he spoke of the needs of the world that the council might address: "The world needs a spectacle of truth. The half-truth of Communism controls much of the world and threatens any day to take over more of South America, Africa, and Asia." But Huston also saw the need for a great manifestation of Christian Unity: "The Council must also manifest charity. The love that unites the Church must reach out to attract the whole world. We have too often been smug in looking at the fragmentation of Christendom. We must no longer be smug, for we are partly to blame for their division. We can no longer be smug for smugness destroys love. We must no longer be smug for smugness will drive the world away as it has driven it away in the past."[3] Huston also advanced an important line of argument that would have seemed foreign to most Catholics at the time—that

Des Moines priests at Vatican II
(left to right: Huston, Weiland, Daly, Beeson).
Credit: Diocese of Des Moines Archives.

is, the difference between non-essentials and essentials in Catholic belief. In a time when many people practically equated holy water with Holy Eucharist, Huston noted: "Perhaps the Council will state clearly what part of Catholic teaching is essential and comes from Christ and what part is human and non-essential."[4]

Huston seemed aware of the global needs that precipitated the convocation of the council. He noted again the deadening grasp of communism but also pointed to the sputtering gasps of colonialism, which were sparking revolution around the world, the decline of urban living, and rampant consumerism. "Change is the watchword of our age; revolution its battery." He noted: "The Church has a part in all this change and revolution." He lauded the quickening of sacramental life over the past generations that empowered the laity to "take up their God-given tasks as Christ-bearers." Yet he also observed: "The Church has not wholly kept up. . . . We are slow to correct some mistakes, slow to recognize some of our failures, slow to grow where a revolutionary age demands growth."[5] When the council began, Huston and Father Lawrence Beeson were appointed pages for the event and spent many hours observing conciliar events.

Bishop Edward Daly—A Father of Vatican II

Daly, like many of his fellow bishops, was not sure what the calling of Vatican II meant. His years of experience with canonical issues and the decade-plus experience of administering a small diocese had given him some insights. Most of his suggestions for the agenda, however, dealt with the minutiae of liturgical rules and episcopal duties. There was little to indicate that he was truly prepared for the larger issues that the council would engage or the new stance of the church vis-à-vis the modern world.[6] Daly conducted as much business as he could before he left for Rome and directed that Des Moines Catholics should pray a novena for the success of the council.[7] The council's first session closed in early December, and Bishop Daly flew back to Des Moines, celebrating his first Mass in the humble Guadalupe Chapel on December 15.

In his Christmas message to the faithful, he spoke about the council, reflecting the awe and pleasure of many American bishops who for the first time experienced the universality of the church, especially through the sacred liturgy. "There was special inspiration in assisting day by day at Mass in the different rites of East and West, in sonorous Latin and in the melodious tongues which are now classical in their own countries." Of the deliberations he noted approvingly: "In all else, aside from defined truth, there was untrammeled debate. The youngest bishop in the council could take issue with a cardinal; the humblest missionary among us could challenge the erudite dean of a world renowned school of divinity. We heard the soft cadences of Latin from the lips of an Irish classical scholar; the Gallic-flavored Latin of a colored bishop from Africa; the traffic-breaking speech of Spaniards; Latin sometimes as it seemed, of an Italian opera; and once in a while plain Latin as flat as our Western plains." He noted how moved he was with the daily enthronement of the Book of the Gospels followed by the chanting of the Nicene Creed that began every session.[8]

In the intersession, Daly set aside his traditional reluctance to mingle with non-Catholics and made a presentation to the faculty of the Drake University Divinity School on April 22, 1963, in an address titled "A Day in the Vatican Council."[9] (Unfortunately, a copy of this does not exist.) Pope John XXIII died in June 1963, and the diocese joined in worldwide grief for the beloved pontiff. When his successor, Cardinal Giovanni Battista Montini, was elected as Pope Paul VI, the new pontiff announced his decision to continue the council and endorsed the discussions of collegiality and the reform of the liturgy. On his return to Des Moines after the second session, Daly sat for an interview with the Catholic newspaper and rattled off succinct answers to questions posed about the council and the future of the Catholic Church. He lauded the kindliness and spirit of the late Pope John and applauded the passage of the Constitution on the Liturgy (*Sacrosanctum Concilium*, 1963), noting that many bishops (perhaps himself) had been initially skeptical of the changes proposed but had changed their minds between the first and second sessions. He noted that the implementation of the liturgical changes would take time. Some could be done fairly soon; others would take more time.[10]

Most interesting, he noted the initial debates on documents related to anti-Semitism and religious freedom. Of the latter, he believed that this principle had already been clarified in Pope John's encyclical *Pacem in Terris* (1963). On collegiality (the concept that the pope must consult the body of bishops as part of his teaching authority), he took aim at what he considered poor reporting on the subject: "There has been a lot of nonsense uttered about collegiality." He rejected any idea that this concept diminished the sovereign and final power of the pope—all bishops were subject to him. He did suggest, however, that the pope himself could use the College of Bishops like a senate. In the end, the pope still commanded ultimate power.[11]

Daly himself struggled with the fast pace of change. The irrepressible Father Ostdiek, who had recently built a new church, lamented over the proposed liturgical changes in the placement of the altar. He groused: "Your Council, gentleman [*sic*], have been wrecking my brain trying to figure a way to turn that three ton granite altar table around and have the priest face the congregation. The Council is creating more havoc than the firemen over the country did after the Chicago school fire."[12] Daly replied good-naturedly: "Your comments on the Council amused me because I share some of your wonderment. But 'the world still moves' and that goes for our knowledge of doctrine and the needs of pastoral theology. In another few years we shall see seminary courses quite different from what we went through."[13]

But Daly was moved by the restoration of earlier forms of worship, particularly by the renewed rite of concelebration, in those days celebrated only on the occasion of priestly ordination. "Cardinal Doepfner's Mass concelebrated this morning finally converted me to the idea [of concelebration]. It is really the way the priest ordination Mass should be done: all concelebrants at the altar. . . . God willing we shall do it and in the

Father Lawrence Beeson at Vatican II. Credit: Diocese of Des Moines Archives.

vernacular." He asked Ostdiek's patience, "Do have your people pray for the Bishops in Council. These are grave and complicated matters . . . more complicated than those on the outside suspect."[14]

Indeed, as many bishops, Daly experienced a transformation at Vatican II. Exposure to the diversity of the Universal Church, an introduction to new methods of interpreting Scripture, and a better historical understanding of the history of the liturgy all seemed to have an impact on the very conservative and reserved prelate. No one knew this better than Father Lawrence Beeson, who had served Daly in the chancery and in Rome and knew full-well the prelate's somewhat frosty ways. Beeson recalled that Daly carefully studied the council documents every night. "During the council, I saw him as a changing man. At the beginning he was a strict canonist. As the council proceeded he became much more human. He could see things had to change. . . . We ate supper every night with a Benedictine priest, Fr. Placid Jordan, who told the bishop of the various struggles that were going on during the Council. This had a profound effect on the bishop."[15] In his last public act as bishop of Des Moines, Daly did what most of his episcopal colleagues did around the nation: approved the vernacular Mass and directed it to begin on November 29, 1964.[16] It would be Daly's last official public act as bishop of Des Moines.

The Biskup Interlude

On February 3, 1965, the Apostolic Delegation announced the appointment of fifty-three-year-old George J. Biskup, auxiliary bishop of Dubuque, as Daly's successor and the fifth bishop of Des Moines.[17] Biskup was the first native-born Iowan to become the bishop of Des Moines. He was born in Cedar Rapids, the very same year and month that the diocese was born, August 23, 1911, one of three children of Frank and Julia Kida Biskup. The press noted correctly that he was the second prelate given to Des Moines from Cedar Rapids—the other being Bishop Drumm. The Biskups attended St. Wenceslaus Church in Cedar Rapids, a national parish founded in 1874 and set aside for Bohemian or Czech Catholics. The parish sponsored a grade school staffed by the Sisters of Mercy.

Frank Biskup died when the children were young, and Julia worked to keep the family solvent. George's older brother got a job, and Julia scrimped and saved to keep the family clothed and fed.

After high school graduation, George attended Loras College, where he prepared for priestly studies for the Archdiocese of Dubuque. He graduated from Loras in 1933 and was selected by Archbishop Francis J. L. Beckman for studies in Rome, where he met his one-day successor, Maurice Dingman of Davenport. Here he was ordained a priest on March 19, 1937. He became a curate at Dubuque's St. Raphael Cathedral until 1939. Beckman was a collector of fine art, and Loras College had a very significant museum of paintings, artifacts, and other valuables; Beckman apparently wanted to train Biskup to help care for his collection.[18] The museum came to be known at the Columbia Museum and Institute of Art and the sponsor of the Catholic Artists Guild of America. In 1939, he sent young Biskup for graduate studies in fine arts at the University of Iowa and also appointed him the administrator of Holy Trinity Church in Walford, Iowa. From 1940 to 1948 Biskup was on the faculty of Loras College where he founded the art department and was appointed the artist-in-residence.

Bishop George Biskup. Credit: Diocese of Des Moines Archives.

In 1948, Biskup was appointed to the Sacred Congregation of the Oriental Church in Rome, working under prefects (bureau heads) Cardinals Valerio Valeri and Eugene Tisserant. His service to the Curia merited him promotion to the rank of monsignor. During his brief Roman stint, he helped to form the United Service Organization (USO) branch of the National Catholic Community Service—a drop-in center for Americans in Rome not far from St. Peter's. Cardinal Tisserant wanted him to remain longer, but already Biskup had become a workaholic and had developed ulcers. When he returned to Dubuque in 1951, he heeded the advice of physicians and friends and took up golf as a way to relax. Biskup apparently had a delicate stomach and ate only the blandest of foods. He was a chainsmoker, having a cigarette in hand when not acting liturgically or officially. His smoking addiction was the likely cause of his demise at the age of sixty-eight.

In Dubuque, Biskup became chancellor and pastor of St. Joseph's Church in Key West, Iowa. Archbishop Rohlman appointed him vicar general in 1952 and on April 24, 1957, in a rare double ordination ceremony, he and James V. Casey, later bishop of Lincoln and archbishop of Denver, were consecrated bishops by Archbishop Amleto Cicognani in St. Raphael's Cathedral. As auxiliary, he served also as pastor of Nativity Parish in Dubuque.

Over two thousand clerics and laity were present when Biskup was installed in Des Moines on March 19, 1965, the twenty-eighth anniversary of his priestly ordination. A civic reception was held for the new bishop at the KRNT Theater on March 21.[19] A public gathering at Dowling High School brought together students from the school itself and also young women bussed in from St. Joseph's Academy. The students presented Biskup with an image of Mary and an entertainment center consisting of a color television set, radio, and phonograph.[20]

Biskup's reception was warm enough, but some took a negative view of the new prelate: Monsignor Paul Connelly recalled of Biskup, "The word that I had gotten in advance of our new bishop, George Biskup, from Dubuque, was not encouraging. My friends had labeled him a conservative, middle-of-the-road at best, person. As one of the auxiliary bishops in Dubuque, he wanted to have his own diocese for a long while."[21] Connelly did not have long to harden or change his opinions of Biskup, because in a short-time, the bishop was gone.

Biskup attended the last session of the council, returned to Des Moines in early December, and declared: "As we face the future in unity of spirit and endeavor, we cannot fail in fulfilling the fondest hopes of the Second Vatican Council."[22] Father Clarke of the local Catholic press waxed prophetic about the recently closed ecumenical council: "History will record Vatican II as the turning point in the life of the church in the twentieth century. During the past few years changes have been made that would have been thought impossible a decade ago. Some Catholics are still reeling from the changes in the Mass and the exalted place restored to the Bible. The age of excommunication has passed into oblivion and a new era of dialogue has begun."[23]

In July 1967, just as Biskup was feeling at home, it was announced that he was being transferred to Indianapolis to become the coadjutor to Archbishop Paul Schulte. Likely, his most enduring accomplishment was the purchase of the fifty-five acres of the old golf club and the plans to erect a new Dowling High School on the site.[24] Of him, Father Clarke wrote: "The dominant characteristic for which Archbishop [coadjutor] Biskup will be remembered was his approachability. He was a good listener and . . . always had time to listen to suggestions and complaints." Clarke was especially grateful for Biskup's approval of his plans to keep the financially struggling diocesan newspaper alive.[25] Biskup had begun the process of introducing the diocese to the changes of Vatican II. His successor, Maurice Dingman (1968–1986), would take even more dramatic steps to implement the council.

Enter Maurice Dingman

Dingman oversaw a significant change in the direction and presence of the Catholic Church in Southwest Iowa. His appointment was announced in April 1968.

He was born January 20, 1914, in St. Paul, Iowa, one of five children of Theodore and Angela Witte Dingman. He grew up in Lee County, where his parents were farmers, and young Maurice and his brothers contributed to the economic well-being of the family by hard manual labor. His brother Adrian recalled: "He did chores. He milked and drove the team—we cultivated corn with horses. We had a small threshing machine and we threshed for ourselves and our neighbors, and his specialty was making straw piles."[26]

His family's ties to Lee County went back to the origins of St. James Church in St. Paul, Iowa. St. James Church had been around since 1838, a parish for German-speaking Catholics who were pioneers in that area. The small community was eventually able to build a beautiful Gothic structure in 1893 and sponsored a school, which was run by the School Sisters of St. Francis, a teaching order from Milwaukee. Dingman's sister Mary became a member of that community. Dingman's sister Louise continued to live in St. Paul, and it was there that he attempted to recover from the debilitating stroke that ended his career.

The Catholic Church in St. Paul was a significant force in the community. Dingman's pastor was Father Joseph Anthony Rangger, a native of Innsbruck, Austria, who had come to the United States, studied at Milwaukee's St. Francis Seminary, and was ordained for Davenport in October 1891. He arrived in St. Paul in November 1908 and remained there until his death in July 1932.[27] Rangger and the sisters at the school encouraged Dingman's priestly vocation. Years later, Dingman remembered Father Rangger with fondness: "It was he who baptized me, heard my first confession, gave me my first communion and sent me to the seminary." He remembered peering into the rectory window to see the grey bearded old padre with his long stem pipe. In 1928, when Dingman became a boarding student at St. Ambrose Academy, he would visit Rangger on his trips home, and the elderly priest would measure his height—recording his growth on the door frame of one of the rectory doors. Rangger died when Dingman graduated from high school.[28]

After his 1932 graduation, he entered the seminary division of St. Ambrose College, where he studied philosophy and Latin. He graduated in 1936 receiving an AB degree and the college's Culeman Award in philosophy.[29] Dingman came to revere a number of the St. Ambrose faculty. One was Father William Lawrence Adrian, an Iowa-born priest who had studied and been ordained in Rome in 1911. For twenty-four years he taught Latin and coached baseball and football at St. Ambrose. He was also vice president of the college from 1932 to 1935 until his transfer to a parish in Victor, Iowa. In 1936, Adrian was appointed the bishop of Nashville, Tennessee, and was consecrated at Davenport's Sacred Heart Cathedral. Adrian impressed young Dingman deeply and encouraged his priestly vocation.

Dingman was also taken by Father Aloysius Ulrich Hauber, a native of Iowa City who was newly ordained when Dingman met him at St. Ambrose in 1933. Hauber, born in 1885 in Bavaria, came to the United States and attended St. Ambrose College, graduating in 1905. He studied for the priesthood at St. Francis Seminary in

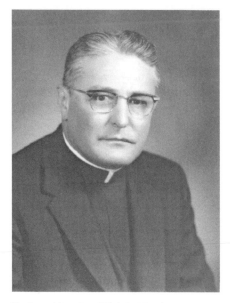

Father Aloysius Ulrich Hauber.
Credit: Used with permission of
the Diocese of Davenport Archives,
Davenport, Iowa.

Milwaukee and was ordained to the priesthood for Davenport in 1908. After some parish experience, he was sent to the University of Iowa where, in 1924, he completed a dissertation in genetics. He returned to St. Ambrose and set up the agricultural department of the college and enhanced its reputation in natural sciences.

In 1926, Hauber became president of St. Ambrose, serving until 1930, when he returned to the classroom.[30] Hauber was one of the more progressive minds on the St. Ambrose faculty and perhaps even in the Roman Catholic clergy at the time. In the midst of the national furor stirred by the Scopes Trial (1925) in Tennessee that pitted evolutionary thought against biblical fundamentalism, Hauber wrote a pamphlet titled "Creation and Evolution: A Catholic Opinion of Evolution Theory" wherein he argued that belief in evolution was not incompatible with religion and especially Catholic thought. He decried those who denied the scientific evidence for evolution, insisting that the Bible was not a science book and that those who opposed "sound scientific theories" were doing harm to the cause of truth.[31] Dingman was deeply impressed with Hauber, who treated him as a colleague and hoped that he would return to St. Ambrose to assist him in teaching biology.

He had also come to know Edward Rohlman, nephew of Bishop Henry P. Rohlman, the bishop of Davenport (and future archbishop of Dubuque). With young Rohlman, Dingman visited the bishop at his home on Brady Street and even spent a Thanksgiving Day with the prelate. On these occasions, Rohlman had the chance to size up the farm boy from Lee County. Dingman was smart, articulate, and tall. The latter feature was important since seminarians destined for advanced study in Rome were often evaluated on their physical appearance—*bella figura* as the Italians described these things. Rohlman sent him to the North American College in Rome where he attended classes at the Gregorian University. On hearing of his appointment to Rome, Dingman wrote, "I am unable to express my gratitude to your Excellency for the honor you have seen fit to give me. I feel unequal to the grave responsibilities now incumbent upon me. . . . I always prayed that I would be sent to a place where I could best fit myself for future obligations. I feel proud that you have seen fit to entrust me with a serious task. . . . I hope Rome shall make me a priest like Bishop Adrian."[32]

Bishop Henry Rohlman of Davenport. Credit: Used with permission of the Diocese of Davenport Archives, Davenport, Iowa.

After getting to Rome in 1936, he wrote to Rohlman frequently. These carefully written letters convey the extent to which young Maurice was filled with *Romanità*—a love of things Roman: "Everything is so very new and thrilling that I seem to be living in an earthly paradise. . . . The ceremonies of Solemn High Mass and Benediction give me the greatest thrill. The seminary finds me more contented and happier than ever before."[33] By early the next year, he wrote Rohlman: "The wonderful 'spirit of Rome' is beginning to exercise its influence on me if a love of its shrines and sacred memories is part of its effect. . . . We have seen many churches since coming to Rome, but the one we love the best and the one which we never tire of visiting is St. Peter's. . . . I myself particularly enjoy the Vatican Crypt where pious people can always be seen kneeling before the tombs of Pope Pius X and Cardinal Merry Del Val."[34]

Rohlman was exceptionally generous to Dingman, underwriting trips all over Europe for him. This young farm boy from rural Iowa got the chance to visit Assisi, Loretto, Venice, Milan, Pisa, and Florence—experiences his contemporaries could only do by reading library picture books or the *National Geographic*. One of the North American alumni in Davenport wrote to Dingman: "Father Madsen [a Davenport priest who had studied in Rome] wrote a few weeks ago stressing the value of our stay here in Rome. He said we should drink in every drop of what the Catholicism of the Eternal City has to offer, this where he must store up the inspiration to carry on after we get back."[35] He indeed lived through the historic transition of the papacy from Pius XI to Pius XII. Rome left its mark on young Dingman—who would later be accused of being disloyal to the pope. He had witnessed the coronation of Pius XII, and, years later (1974), while attending a theological consultation in Rome and celebrating Mass with Pope Paul VI in the Sistine Chapel, he remembered the solemnity of the event and regaled in the singing of the Sistine Choir: "For a brief moment I was transported back to another occasion—the coronation of Pope Pius XII—in 1939 when I heard the same Sistine Choir sing in the Basilica of St. Peter's."[36]

Dingman was ordained a priest in the chapel of Our Lady of Humility in the North American College in Rome, on December 8, 1939, by the rector, Bishop Ralph Hayes, who would be his future bishop. "The great day I dreamed of has come and gone," he wrote to Rohlman. "The day itself is but a memory, but the spirit of the day lives on. The Mass is the real center of my life. Everything seems to take place within its shadow and I pray that it may remain so for all the rest of my life."[37] Dingman enclosed the princely sum of $50—probably ordination gifts—as a contribution to Rohlman's campaign for St. Ambrose College.

War had already erupted in Europe the previous September at the time of Dingman's ordination. He returned to Iowa in June 1940 and hoped to be assigned to Monsignor Hauber at St. Ambrose College to teach science, but he got a mix of classes for high schoolers: algebra, general science, biology, and accounting. In December 1942, the middle of the school year, he was appointed vice chancellor and assistant at St. Mary's Church in Muscatine. He also was appointed secretary to Rohlman and took up residence with him for the next six years. He often accompanied the prelate as master of ceremonies to confirmations, dedications, vow ceremonies, and other pontifical celebrations around the diocese. He spent the summer of 1943 in Ottumwa as a chaplain at a naval air station and resided with the Sisters of the Congregation of the Humility of Mary, for whom he also performed chaplain's duties. At the end of the summer he was sent to the Catholic University of America to study canon law. He remained there until 1946, coming back with a licentiate in canon law. He completed his course work for a doctorate but never finished the dissertation for the degree.

While he was in Washington, in 1944, the Holy See promoted Bishop Rohlman to the Archdiocese of Dubuque and replaced him with Bishop Ralph Hayes. Hayes, a native of Pittsburgh, was also a Roman alumnus, ordained in 1909. Hayes did pastoral work in his home diocese until 1935, when he was made bishop of Helena, Montana.

In 1935, Hayes was called to Rome to serve as the head of the Pontifical North American College. Hayes was a contrast with the affable Rohlman. Much more reserved and less the "people person" than his predecessor, Hayes drew on the expertise of Dingman and the other Davenport young men he had known in Rome to help him govern the diocese.

Dingman finished his studies in Washington, meeting other leading Catholic intellectuals on the Catholic University faculty and other young priests like himself destined for episcopal orders. Probably

Monsignor Dingman as superintendent of schools. Credit: Used with permission of the Diocese of Davenport Archives, Davenport, Iowa.

because he never finished his doctoral degree, his canonical expertise was minimally used. (He served as the Defender of the Bond for the matrimonial tribunal.) To his surprise, Bishop Hayes appointed him diocesan superintendent of schools with residence at the bishop's home and later chaplain at a Carmelite Monastery in Bettendorf, Iowa. Dingman balked at this appointment, claiming he had no training for this work, but he discovered that the tasks of a diocesan superintendent in a relatively small diocese were not overwhelming. He was able to establish contacts with his counterparts around the state, including Des Moines's Lester V. Lyons, who was still rector of St. Ambrose Cathedral when Dingman arrived as bishop.

Dingman and the other superintendents tried to secure public bus transportation for Catholic school pupils but were unable to do so. He also oversaw the consolidation of two separate Catholic high schools in Muscatine and others elsewhere. In a style he would refine during his years in Des Moines, Dingman listened patiently to both sides that still cherished strong parochial loyalties to their school. He managed to help nudge them toward a consolidation and, to his surprise, was appointed principal of the newly created Muscatine Catholic. He taught four classes of religion each week, instituted a class on woodworking and industrial arts (which he studied in a summer course), and kept his finger in chancery work. Hayes loaded him with a lot of work, which the dutiful Dingman accepted even though at times it must have been physically exhausting. Dingman occasionally fell asleep on the job and sometimes behind the wheel of his car. Medical science had not yet discovered much on sleep disorders, but this habit of falling asleep, even when people were talking to him, dogged him all his life. In 1953, he was appointed chancellor of the diocese and in 1956 became a domestic prelate. He also took over duties as the chaplain at Davenport's Mercy Hospital and served as chaplain to the hospital's nursing school.

By the late 1950s, some of Dingman's *Romanità* and what he himself described as his Germanic reserve began to fade away. He later observed that pastoral activity and immersion in groups like the Cana Conferences, where he helped young couples prepare for marriage and family, and the Cursillo, an intense retreat that required personal sharing, began to soften him a bit. Perhaps remembering Ulrich Hauber's embrace of evolutionary theory, he began to push back against his earlier formation of his Roman seminary days that truth was perennial and unchanging. Things changed in life—and sometimes dramatically. By the time he became a bishop, Dingman had changed his thinking quite a bit in some critical areas.

Although Dingman left no particular writings about his inner life, his enthusiastic embrace of Vatican II was typical of many priests of his era. Many of his old teachers and even classmates were now active in the unfolding drama of the council. The documents of the council began to sketch out new directions in liturgy, ecclesiology, relations with other religious traditions, and religious liberty. They injected the word "collegiality" into the Roman Catholic lexicon—reflecting a new ecclesiological understanding that the Spirit resided not only in the pope and bishops but also in the people of God. Baptized Catholics, the people of God as they were now known, were capable of offering important wisdom and support in arriving at critical decisions. He had seen this in action when he brought the two schools together in Muscatine. Listening and helping to find common ground emerged as one of his strengths—even though at times it protracted decisions that had to be made. He had also met men and women of

Bishop Ralph Hayes of Davenport. Credit: Used with permission of the Diocese of Davenport Archives, Davenport, Iowa.

deep faith and spiritual maturity in his work with the Cursillo and Cana. He had a feel for the diversity of a local church, serving as chaplain for such groups as the Knights of Columbus and the Holy Childhood Association. His reputation for fairness and hard work as well as his familiarity with diocesan issues and church bureaucracy were important points in his favor. Dingman also began to look outside the Catholic world to the wider issues of society. Influenced by the strong social justice tradition at St. Ambrose College and his informal relationships with local politicians and policy makers, he became more attuned to the church's role in secular affairs.

Bishop Hayes retired in 1966 and was succeeded by Bishop Gerald O'Keefe. O'Keefe, an auxiliary of St. Paul, had attended all four sessions of Vatican II and came to Davenport committed to implementing the spirit and letter of the council in his new diocese. He established consultative bodies, expanded ministries of social justice, and reoriented the service of the central headquarters of the church to serve the diverse needs of the people of the diocese. He retained Dingman in the chancery, who observed all this change at close range. Indeed, much of what Dingman did in Des Moines, with some adaptations for local conditions, appeared to be in direct imitation of what he had seen O'Keefe doing in Davenport.

By late 1967, Dingman had now aquired the needed experience, credibility, and organizational skills that made him ready to take a parish. In fact, a new man was being trained to take his place in the chancery but left the priesthood. Dingman would never become a parish pastor. Events were set in motion when George Biskup was unexpectedly whisked away to become coadjutor to the See of Indianapolis. The discussions among the Iowa bishops likely surfaced Dingman's name as one of the three submitted to the Apostolic Delegation for transmission to Rome.

On April 2, 1968, his appointment was made in Rome, and it was announced in the United States on April 10, 1968, by Apostolic Delegate Luigi Raimondi.[38] In his statement to the press, Dingman acknowledged his debt of gratitude to his superiors—Rohlman, Hayes, and O'Keefe—but took pains to accentuate his love for Iowa: "As I look forward to my work in Des Moines I am reassured by the fact that I am a native son of Iowa with a deep and abiding love for its soil and the souls of its people. That I will remain to travel its hills and its valleys, to admire its crops and its beauty, is a source of inestimable gratitude."[39] In the next edition of *The Catholic Mirror*, Dingman submitted to a no-holds-barred interview by the editor, Father Clarke. Dingman noted his familiarity with many Des Moines priests and sisters (classmates at St. Ambrose or in Rome, CHM sisters from the Ottumwa motherhouse, and Monsignor Lyons as a fellow superintendent). He paid special tribute to the role of the Cursillo movement in the diocese, which had been a great boon in his spiritual life, and expressed great interest in ecumenical relations. He noted as well the larger group of Catholic children who now attended CCD and pledged to expand the program. He paid tribute to the recently assassinated Martin Luther King Jr. and showed his support for the Catholic press.[40]

His words were humble, collaborative, and hopeful. It was a new era for Des Moines. He was also unafraid to weigh in on sensitive subjects such as birth control. In an interview with the *Davenport Catholic Messenger*, he noted (before the issuance of the papal encyclical on the use of artificial contraception *Humanae Vitae*): "It strikes me that people forget the morality of the act depends in part on its circumstances. . . . As far as birth control is concerned we follow the wishes of Our Holy Father. But in many cases, critical decisions will have to be made. What the future will bring, I don't know."[41]

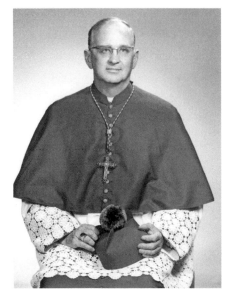

Newly ordained Bishop Maurice Dingman. Credit: Used with permission of the Diocese of Davenport Archives, Davenport, Iowa.

But even at the outset, Dingman showed a propensity to take his sweet time in making decisions. The diocese had been without a bishop for nearly a year. Rather than moving with all deliberate speed, Dingman took from April to July to get himself to Des Moines and down to work. Indeed his first episcopal conundrum was over where to be consecrated a bishop. As he would do many times, he would indulge in a process of "on the one hand . . . but on the other hand." On the one hand, his love for his home diocese was strong and his hero, Bishop William Adrian, had been ordained in Davenport, but, on the other hand, he wondered if he should show respect for the new diocese by being ordained in Des Moines. After some desultory fussing and consulting, he decided to be ordained in Sacred Heart Cathedral in Davenport. Archbishop Luigi Raimondi, the apostolic delegate, presided at the June 19, 1968, ceremony, assisted by the aging Bishop Hayes and Bishop O'Keefe. It was one of the first episcopal ordinations conducted in the vernacular. His formal installation in Des Moines took place at St. Ambrose Cathedral on July 7, 1968, followed by a pontifical low Mass at the Veterans Memorial Auditorium. Nearly two thousand people turned out to greet the prelate. In his homily, he called on the fathers of families to assist him and, using imagery devised by St. Augustine, referred to the assembled crowd as "my dear fellow bishops." At the end of the ceremony, participants sang "America the Beautiful."[42] This began eighteen years of service to the people of southwest Iowa—until he was felled by a stroke in 1986.

$$\sim$$

The changes of Vatican II in practice and especially in attitude were met by a spectrum of reactions. For some Catholics, especially priests and women religious, these changes were for the most part embraced warmly and implemented as quickly as possible. Many lay Catholics also welcomed the changes of the council, particularly the changes in the liturgy (Latin to English) and also the ecumenical and interfaith ventures that seemed to encourage better relations with Protestant and Jewish neighbors. Some priests and Catholics, however, found the changes disconcerting and were disturbed by the sometimes rapid changes that upended years of uniform Catholic practice. Whatever the response, the agenda of the council, in letter and in spirit, provided the context for the history of Catholic life in southwest Iowa, particularly under the episcopal leadership of Maurice Dingman.

Liturgical Reform

On December 4, 1963, the council approved the Constitution on the Sacred Liturgy. The document called for a general renewal of the sacred liturgy, hailed as "the source and summit" of Christian life. The changes would strike many Des Moines Catholics as dramatic, but in many ways they were the culmination of changes that had been going on since the pontificate of Pope Pius X (1903–1914) and certainly accelerated by the international Liturgical Movement, which had its American outreach through Saint John's Abbey in Collegeville, Minnesota. For many years, ideas such as vernacular in the liturgy, encouraging lay participation through the so-called dialogue Mass (one where the people rather than just the server responded to all the Mass parts in Latin), reforms of ceremonials and sacramentals (some in English), and the "restoration" of earlier, more ancient forms of celebrating the Sacred Triduum (Holy Thursday, Good Friday, and Holy Saturday) had prepared the way. In December 1963, the council fathers approved some early adjustments to the liturgy, mandating parts—not all—of the Mass be proclaimed in the vernacular. The bishops' conference in America took on the task of translating portions of the Mass in early 1964. Basically the parts of the Mass up to the Canon (eucharistic prayer) were to be in the vernacular—including, of course, the epistle and the gospel as well as the Nicene Creed. Priests had the option to recite the Breviary in Latin or in English.

In July 1964, the translation for the Mass appeared on the front page of *The Messenger*.[43] It was also announced that the absolution given by the priest for confession could now be in English, and the formula was also printed in the paper.[44] In preparation for the actual beginning of the new liturgy on the First Sunday of Advent in November 1964, study days were planned for the priests of the diocese where the new Mass was demonstrated. On November 3, 1964, at St. John's Parish in Des Moines, Monsignor Edward Pfeffer, the diocesan chancellor, offered the first vernacular Mass in Des Moines. At St. Francis Church in Council Bluffs, Father Joseph Halloran of Montrose, Colorado, did the same.[45]

Shortly after Biskup's installation, the Vatican released modifications in the celebration of Holy Week—allowing concelebration on

Holy Thursday and revising some of the prayers for the Good Friday liturgical service—especially those that were negative to the Jews. Words like "heretics," "schismatics," "infidels," and "pagans" were purged from the lengthy petitions of Good Friday, taking away a barrier that hindered interfaith advance. On his first Holy Thursday in 1965, Biskup concelebrated with twelve diocesan priests—ten monsignori and two "ordinary" clerics.[46]

Liturgical changes continued during the Dingman years. His first use of the all-English rite of ordination was held for the seven members of the class of 1969. This shortened ceremony was also the first held outside St. Ambrose Cathedral in the Veteran's Auditorium.[47] As Rome approved more and more revisions to the rite of the Mass and the administration of the sacraments, the bishops' conference speedily provided acceptable (and transitional) temporary translations. New rites for the Mass, penance, matrimony, and the anointing of the sick began to replace older formulae. On Laetare Sunday in Lent 1970, the diocese received permission to celebrate Mass on Saturday evening as the vigil of Sunday.[48] The priest council petitioned Dingman to ask for permission to have lay eucharistic ministers. In July 1970, Dingman formally designated ninety-seven laymen and religious as extraordinary ministers of the Eucharist.[49]

In a renewal of the rite of admission to the church, emphasis was placed on doing these things publicly rather than in rectory offices or privately. In November 1973, the Catholic newspaper covered the reception of Martha Cabelka into the Catholic Church in a ceremony at St. Joseph Church in Jamaica.[50] In Urbandale, Father Arthur Ring of St. Pius X Parish held a First Communion Mass on December 9, 1973, inviting the children to stand around the altar and to receive Communion under the forms of bread and wine.[51] Liturgical change accelerated as younger priests brought their seminary instruction into the flow of parish practice.

As challenging and unsettling as some of these changes were, the decision to mitigate the traditional Friday abstinence was perhaps even more significant to the average Catholic. "Fish on Friday" was an important cultural marker of local Catholicism. Iowa Catholics and parishes sponsored fish fries to draw them into church halls for fund-raising. Pope Paul VI asked local bishops' conferences to adjust local penitential practices in accordance with local custom and announced plans to mitigate the traditional fast and Friday abstinence rules that had been a defining characteristic of Catholic life for centuries. The US bishops did this in 1966.[52] Indeed, the change in these rules in many ways affected ordinary Catholics more directly than many of the papers and positions taken by the bishops over the years.

Altering Sacred Space: Church Renovations

Area Catholics began to make changes in the liturgical furnishings. At St. Joseph's Church in Earling, a new altar facing the people was constructed by a local craftsman working under the direction of Monsignor Peter Bissen. St. Patrick's in Massena also produced a new altar facing the people and an offertory gift table for the restored offertory procession. Parishes were uneven in their implementation of the directives of the council. St. Mary's in Elkhart moved along under the leadership of Monsignor John McIlhon. They reported that, since October 1964, "there has been congregational singing, . . . there is a new altar facing the people, . . . there is an offertory procession, . . . and communion is received in a standing fashion."[53]

Father Nelo Leto, a skilled handyman, helped parishes build new altars and other furnishings and assisted in modifying sanctuary arrangements for the new liturgy. Some churches, like St. Michael's in Harlan, were built to incorporate the new liturgical forms, but more often, existing churches had to be adapted to serve the new liturgy. In some communities, such as St. Patrick's in Lenox, elaborate altars, statuary, and stained glass were replaced with more simple sanctuary furnishings. The difference between the two sanctuaries was stunning as it was given the before-and-after treatment in *The Catholic Mirror*.[54] Older church sanctuaries were sometimes altered radically, removing elaborate reredos, statuary, and altars. These changes met with mixed feelings by the clergy, laity, and religious.

Church renovations continued, including some drastic renovations carried out in some of the venerable parishes of the diocese. In 1971, St. Boniface in Westphalia, a neo-Gothic gem with elaborate interior décor (reredos, statues, and wall stenciling), was radically changed to a very simple and modern sanctuary, which removed all the old décor, most of the statues, set the Blessed Sacrament on a side altar, and was painted in lighter colors. The Catholic newspaper showed before-and-after shots of the church, describing the new décor as "an artistic masterpiece" and suggesting that it was "worth a visit if you are in the vicinity."[55] A new Vatican II–style church was erected in Greenfield in 1973.

Refurbishing St. Ambrose

Eventually even the mother church of the diocese would come in for a facelift. By 1971, there was an experiment in putting two priests in charge of a parish—co-pastors. These were first used at Christ the King Parish in Des Moines and later at the cathedral. Fathers John Lorenz and James Laurenzo, co-pastors of the cathedral, undertook some long-delayed repairs of St. Ambrose Cathedral.[56] The immediate stimulus for attention to the cathedral came after one steamy evening when a Mass was celebrated to honor the Catholic Rural Life Conference. The cathedral was not air conditioned at the time and one Mass attendant, dressed in a white suit, came into the sacristy after Mass to complain that the shellac on the pews had become moist and stained his pants. At this point both Lorenz and Laurenzo began talking about what they needed to do with the aging building, which had not had much by way of attention since the 1940s.

Indeed, even when Vatican II mandated liturgical changes in 1964, the structure had not changed much, with the exception of a square box altar *versus populi* (turned toward the people) that Monsignor Lyons had installed. Beginning with a discussion of the state of the pews, the conversation soon recognized the need for a more dramatic interior renovation to comply with the liturgical changes of Vatican II and the shifts in ecclesiology mandated by the council and emphasized by Bishop Dingman. In addition to the sorry state of the pews, the place had dim lighting and needed new environmental systems (heating and cooling). It also had a leaky roof, which dropped literally buckets of water in various places. The two men contacted representatives of the New York–based Rambusch Company, experts in church décor, who took the measure of the elegant cathedral and expressed interest in the job. Father Maur Burbach, OSB, of St. Pius X Monastery in Pevely, Missouri, was invited to be a consultant on the project.

Lorenz and Laurenzo insisted that before any interior renovation could be done, the leaky roof had to be fixed. A new slate roof topped the old cathedral with money raised from parishioners through an adopt-a-slate gimmick, which allowed donors to write their names on a tile to be placed in the roof. After the roof, the two priests and Rambusch officials got down to business. Since Dingman did not make this renovation a diocesan affair (although he did later permit a voluntary collection in the parishes) the priests and their lay advisors had to be creative. One of their more controversial fund-raisers was a cathedral "garage sale" held at the Hotel Savery. Realizing that ad hoc and volunteer fund-raising would not be sufficient, St. Ambrose contracted a professional fund-raising operation, co-chaired by Katie and Ted Meredith, owners of a large Des Moines printing company, the Meredith Corporation. The Meredith Corporation was one of the most prestigious businesses in Des Moines. Begun in 1902 by Edwin Thomas Meredith (the same gentleman whose family donated their home to the diocese for St. Mary of Nazareth Parish), the company

Post–Vatican II renovation of St. Ambrose Cathedral.
Credit: Diocese of Des Moines Archives.

first produced a popular farming magazine. Later they produced *Better Homes and Gardens* and also a popular cookbook. The firm grew rapidly and found great success with the adult female market. It also expanded into television. Another major help in the fund-raising were R. W. "Bud" and Mary Nelson of Kemin Industries, a producer of food additives. Dubbed the Second-Century Fund, and coordinated by Zachary Associates, a fund-raising firm, the financing was discussed at the regional meetings held around the diocese in June 1976.[57]

The new plans included a relocation of the new altar beyond the existing sanctuary into the nave and, at Dingman's request, the repositioning of the episcopal chair from the side wall to a place directly behind the altar, with six chairs on either side of the *cathedra* to represent the twelve regions of the diocese. When the old altar was being disassembled, a reliquary containing the relics of St. Ambrose was discovered and later placed under the new altar.[58] Observing that the cathedral had been renovated four times before, Dingman wanted the cathedral to "reflect the best thinking of the Church in liturgical progress."[59]

As with many liturgical remodels, the project hit its share of problems. Donations for the project were slow in coming and rumors floated that the seating in the cathedral would be radically diminished. Rumors flew (all false) that the stations of the cross and the stained-glass windows installed by Bishop Bergan would be removed. Lorenz and Laurenzo stressed how the renovations were in keeping with the demands of Vatican II–era worship.[60] Dingman was able to celebrate Mass at the new altar at Midnight Mass on Christmas 1977. By May 1978, the first phases of the renovation were done, and on May 14, Dingman rededicated the refurbished building and celebrated his ten-year anniversary in Des Moines. The altar had been moved forward and the Blessed Sacrament reserved in the archway between the cathedral and its side chapel. Flexible seating was installed on either side of the altar while pews were retained for the nave. Confessionals in the church were redone into shrine areas and reconciliation rooms created off the sacristy. A new sound system and modern bathrooms finished off the extensive renovation.[61] Most people liked the new décor, especially the better light and sound.

Spiritual Life

The liturgy was the main source of Catholic spiritual life. But the post–Vatican II period also saw an explosion of new religious movements and a renewed emphasis on silent prayer, retreats, and other forms of spiritual life. Women religious, laypersons, and priests were intent on carving out spaces of time for quiet prayer and spiritual direction. With the closing of St. Gabriel of Sorrows Passionist monastery in Des Moines, only a relative handful of religious order priests—mostly Benedictines in Council Bluffs and Creston—still served in the diocese.

At the urging of Father Frank Bognanno, director of renewal, Dingman was urged to seek a deeper spiritual renewal for the diocese. Dingman agreed and declared 1973 to be a Year of Spiritual Renewal; programs were fashioned for all the parishes. Since Des Moines did not have a monastery or motherhouse, Bognanno suggested the diocese sponsor a House of Prayer, as had other dioceses around the country. Dingman concurred and just before going to Rome for his 1974 *ad limina* visit, the bishop concluded negotiations with the Jesuits of the Wisconsin Province to send a team of two priests to open a center for spiritual life and counseling in the city of Des Moines. Jesuits Eugene Merz and Gary Brophy were sent to offer spiritual direction, retreats, and counseling to priests, sisters, and laypersons.[62] The center was called Emmaus House, and the Jesuits made themselves available for service.[63] Sister Mary Dingman, OSF, a sister of the bishop, also joined the staff. Sister Dingman was born in 1919 and entered the School Sisters of St. Francis in 1946. She was a respected mentor to novices and later served as a high school teacher and then provincial of the western province of her order. She joined the staff at Emmaus in 1978 and remained there for over thirty years, providing an anchor of stability as Jesuits came and went.[64]

Later, another center for prayer and retreat opened at Wakonda, on a site near Our Lady of Grace Parish in Griswold. Father LaVern Wingert and a group of Catholics formed a corporation and purchased an old Boy Scout camp, converting a lodge on the 210-acre site into a retreat center with a chapel, kitchen, conference rooms, gift store, and rooms that would welcome twenty-four people. In 1984, ground was broken for more cottages on the site.[65] A further expansion of prayer and contemplative space occurred when the Benedictine sisters of Atchison opened Covenant Monastery in Harlan in 1984.[66]

The Charismatic Renewal

New methods and formats of prayer found a ready reception among local Catholics. Among the most interesting was the emergence of the Catholic Charismatic movement, which blended Catholic prayer and devotional life with the practices of Pentecostalism. The putative origins of this popular and fast-growing form of religious expression were to be found at a meeting of Catholic men and women at Duquesne University in 1967. There, as a group of Catholic laity prayed for the outpouring of the Spirit, they experienced a powerful movement of God in their lives and the immediacy of the Holy Spirit. They began to pray spontaneously, with hands upheld and some even expressed their prayer in a form of "prayer language," called "glossolalia." The power of the experience (later identified as baptism in the Spirit) and the interest it spurred in Sacred Scripture, intercessory prayer, healings, and other manifestations of the gifts of the Spirit described in the New Testament soon attracted thousands of followers. Parishes began prayer groups, some of which grew quite large. Large national rallies at the University of Notre Dame, Life in the Spirit seminars, prayers, enthusiastic singing, hand-clapping—all gave witness to a vibrant new form of religiosity. Des Moines diocesan Catholics were soon caught up in the enthusiasm.

In early 1970, Catholics from the four dioceses in Iowa met at St. Joseph's Church in Des Moines at a gathering of the Catholic Charismatic Renewal. Diocesan liaison Father Frank Bognanno was on hand to greet them on behalf of the diocese. These energetic and spirit-filled Catholics heard talks from a variety of devotees of this free-flowing and expressive prayer—more familiar to Pentecostals and other evangelical groups than to Catholics. In his welcome, Dingman urged the group to stay close to the church and close to the bishops.[67] The core Charismatic group, the Life in the Spirit Community, began with a simple prayer gathering in 1972 at Dingman's residence, attracting ten to twelve people. Although originally not a Charismatic group, it evolved into one and swelled to over four hundred people and transferred its meetings to the chapel at St. Ambrose Cathedral. Twice a year they would offer the popular "Life in the Spirit" seminar, which culminated in a special prayer for the release of the Holy Spirit in the life of the believer (baptism in the Spirit). Prophecy, speaking in tongues, and even healings took place at these enthusiastic meetings.[68] In 1982, the newspaper carried the stories of many people in the diocese who had been touched and transformed by the renewal—some lifelong Catholics, others who had been alienated from the faith but who had returned, and even one person who claimed to be an atheist before she met the Charismatic community.[69] The renewal stirred a great deal of enthusiasm among some Des Moines Catholics as they began to sample some of the religious practices seen only in Pentecostal churches.

Ecumenism

The Charismatic Renewal brought many Catholics into contact with Pentecostals and other evangelical groups they would have shunned in previous times. Vatican II created a new way of viewing non-Catholics. In a series of documents on revelation (*Dei Verbum*, 1965), religious freedom (*Dignitatis Humanae*, 1965), and relations with non-Christians, especially Jews (*Nostra Aetate*, 1965), and ecumenism (*Unitatis Redintegratio*, 1964), the council laid the foundation for a new era of amity with fellow Christians, Jews, Muslims, and even nonbelievers. It involved stressing their common doctrinal heritage and, for Catholics, placing a new emphasis on the Scriptures at Mass and also in personal study. For non-Christians, especially Jews, it required stressing the common heritage in the Hebrew Scriptures and greater Catholic sensitivity to the ways in which Catholic liturgy and ethics were entwined with Judaic principles. For nonbelievers and also those who believed in religious pluralism (religious freedom), it upheld the rights of conscience and recognized the good in those who did not share trinitarian or even theistic beliefs. Bishop Dingman was far more active in ecumenical activity than his predecessor, and even more than Bishop Bergan. Within a couple of months of his installation, Dingman stepped forward to cooperate with other church bodies in prayer, in dialogue, and especially "in promoting social projects," what he called "civic ecumenism. . . . We can work together in such fields as race relations, the war on poverty, international peace, etc."[70]

Dingman would make good on his 1968 pledge. In a rare gesture of amity that would not have been possible under either Bergan or Daly, Dingman graciously offered the use of St. Ambrose Cathedral for the ordination of Episcopal Bishop Walter C. Righter in early 1972.[71] Dingman met often with other faith leaders, and in early 1973, a group of them issued a call for peace in Vietnam.[72] The diocese had always stood aloof from the Iowa Council of Churches that had been formed in 1952. In 1976, however, Dingman linked the diocese with the Iowa Inter-Church Forum, a body of Christian churches that offered the opportunity for discussion of issues of common interest. Although it restricted its public statements to those that were unanimously agreed on and mandated that joint work done by denominations be conducted independently of the forum, it represented an important milestone in ecumenical affairs for Des Moines.[73] Twelve churches joined the new organization and solemnized it by a covenant ceremony at Des Moines's St. Augustin's Church. Dingman served as the Catholic representative to the board.[74] He formed warm personal bonds with many non-Catholic leaders and clergy and appeared regularly at city and state ecumenical events. On one occasion, he and Rabbi Jay Goldburg of Tifereth Israel Synagogue in Des Moines spent a night in the Des Moines city jail to dramatize the poor conditions there.

Dingman made much of the annual Week of Christian Unity (formerly called the Chair of Unity Octave) that took place at the end of January. From a week of prayers "for the return of separated brethren," post–Vatican II bishops transformed the event into a moment to celebrate the beliefs and practices Christian groups had in common. One gathering, recalled by Sister Mira Mosle, BVM, took place at Red Oak. The gathering emphasized the common sacrament of baptism, and the celebration filled the local Catholic church. Afterward, a festive dinner was highlighted by remarks by Dingman and Lutheran Bishop David Brown.

Changes in Priestly Formation

Vatican II would effect important changes in formation of priests and religious. It affected the kind of church they would serve and in the ways they were prepared to work in the church. A new sense of the role of all baptized Christians, changes in liturgy and public prayer, and a more historical understanding of the role and function of priests reshaped clerical education.

The seminaries were among the first to feel the winds of change. A rethinking of seminary education came from a consideration of the major documents of Vatican II on Scripture, liturgy, and ecclesiology. *Optatam Totius* (the Decree on Priestly Formation, 1965) provided guidance to adapt seminary formation to suit national needs.

The most palpable change was in seminary discipline, which shifted more responsibility to the individual candidate to monitor his spiritual and personal life than ever before. Rector Frederick Heles helped prepare a new rulebook that dramatically altered the earlier edition of 1961. This earlier text had 108 prohibitions, exhortations, and admonitions under nineteen different headings. In its stead, the seminarians received four mimeographed pages that delineated seminary rules in general terms. Seminary prayer schedules included the introduction of Lauds and Vespers as the official morning and evening prayers of the seminarians. The daily schedule was less regimented, with many spiritual exercises left to the discretion of the seminarian rather than done in common. They were given more free time on Wednesday and Saturday afternoons and were allowed to set up a student government. The new regulations placed responsibility on the shoulders of seminarians to keep good order, cleanliness, periods of quiet, and responsibility for study. Young men in the seminary were glad to have these new "freedoms," and most, but not all, understood the level of adult maturity they required.

There was also significant change in the seminary curriculum. Pope Pius XII, in his apostolic exhortation *Menti Nostri* (1950), had urged an upgrading of seminary studies insisting the seminarian's secular studies should be "in no way inferior" to the studies of their non-seminarian peers. Across the nation, efforts to have the seminaries officially accredited revealed that the students were carrying far too many credit hours per semester. Also, a gradual reorientation of the seminary curriculum had been taking place since the early 1960s, moving away from the neo-Thomism that had been the hallmark of seminary training. Instead, professors stressed the historical roots of Catholic belief, introduced students to the most recent scholarship on the Bible, and offered instruction in ecumenism and liturgical history and practice, and, to the relief of all, instruction was delivered exclusively in English.

Likewise, the council's insistence, primarily through *Gaudium et Spes* (Pastoral Constitution on the Church in the Modern World, 1965) and *Dignitatis Humanae* (Declaration on Religious Liberty, 1965) called for an even more intense engagement with the "world." Seminaries, which were often closed off from the world around them by walls and strict rules governing the movement of seminarians off campus, insulated young men from secular influences. The post-conciliar seminary did an about-face and expected future priests to engage the world they once shunned. Mount St. Bernard's attempted to adjust. Likewise, new pastoral programs allowed seminarians to experience some of the realities of ministry through the introduction of field education, which moved them into actual conditions of pastoral ministry. Helping in parishes through teaching catechism or working with parish youth, taking census, or assisting with special liturgical service also became a feature of priestly training. Pastoral internships were begun in the diaconate year (the last year before becoming a priest). This program sent seminarians back to the diocese to do diaconal work: administering Communion, proclaiming the gospel at Mass, baptizing, and teaching catechism. Monsignor John McIlhon of Holy Trinity praised diaconal internships: "When I was in the seminary, we had absolutely nothing like this. I was a deacon for eleven months and was able to administer Holy Communion four times. . . . I did manage to baptize one of my brother's children but it was a federal case. . . . I really envy Wayne [Gubbels] and Ken [Gross] for the opportunity that they are getting now to share intensely in the priesthood."[75]

The seminary curriculum also exposed future priests to the new intellectual and social challenges facing the church in the present moment (the signs of the times), such as atheism and secularism, and the work of Protestant and Jewish theologians such as Martin Buber,

Paul Tillich, and Karl Barth. The writings of men active at Vatican II (and the documents of the council) were on every seminarian's shelf. These included the works of Fathers Karl Rahner, SJ, Hans Küng, Joseph Ratzinger, and Godfrey Diekmann, OSB, and newer American commentaries on conciliar change penned by Fathers Eugene Kennedy, MM, Charles Curran, and Monsignor John Tracy Ellis. New administrative structures for the academic and formation programs were designed to more directly integrate the intellectual and pastoral aspects of the seminary years.[76]

The changes in discipline and curriculum were welcomed, but as most rapid change inaugurated after a period of strictness, they created some chaos and unrest. Seminarians found ways to rebel. Some grew their hair longer, sported beards and mustaches (formerly forbidden), and spoke up more defiantly to seminary faculty and future pastors. Others tested the limits of celibacy by dating. Since prayer times were made optional, some began skipping Mass, regular confession, and common prayer. These and other developments earned the suspicion and later the ire of the supporting bishops, particularly Archbishop James Byrne of Dubuque, in whose archdiocese Mount St. Bernard's Seminary was located. Ultimately, complaints from the bishops about the faculty, seminary discipline, and poor pastoral preparation brought about the demise of the seminary.[77]

Mount St. Bernard's never had a popular following among many of the Des Moines clergy who found it far too confining and educationally underwhelming. When the seminary closed in 1969, Des Moines seminarians were once again sent to other seminaries.

Clergy Generational Issues

Parish clergy were the visible face of the Des Moines church. Many Catholics related to their church community through the mediation of their priest who presided weekly at Mass and celebrated the sacraments that Catholics needed. The priest could be a good friend in time of need, a counselor, and a source of wisdom, or sometimes he could be cranky, authoritarian, and eccentric. The role and status of clergy was a matter of importance to the average Catholic in the pew, as were the sisters who ran the schools and hospitals (and in the postconciliar period were religious education directors, liturgists, and administrators). Much changed in their lifestyle and approach to people during this period.

Because his episcopate coincided with the changes of Vatican II and other shifts in American social and cultural life, Dingman's years in Des Moines saw the end of the period of expansion that had marked all American dioceses after World War II. Shrinking numbers of clergy grew increasingly worrisome. He began with 134 diocesan priests in 1968. By 1986, Dingman's last year, this number fell, by death and priestly resignation, to 122. The number of priests from religious orders also declined from eight to four.

The mood of some of these older priests was summarized in the funeral homily delivered for Monsignor Lester V. Lyons in November 1973 by Father James Holden, co-pastor of Sacred Heart Church in West Des Moines. Praising the recently deceased Lyons, he paid tribute to his generation of priests, "some of the greatest men alive today." With a veiled swipe at younger clergy, he noted: "These are the men who were educated in the most rigid discipline the seminary system could devise. They gave their youth to God, gladly, freely, not counting the cost. . . . They were trained not to challenge or question authority, never to show disrespect. A colloquialism could express it, i.e., they were trained not to 'cop out.' They entered the priesthood for life and no matter what the cost, they were determined to finish the race." Holden spoke of the tough assignments, "days of personal trial, loneliness, and misunderstanding beyond belief." Yet he insisted, "They weathered the storm. . . . They were molded to love the church and obey the church."[78] Some older priests were also put off by the emphasis on social justice that was embraced by Dingman and some of the younger priests, sometimes in quite radical ways. But tensions between older and younger clergy were sometimes hard to bridge as younger priests opted for different styles of celebrating liturgy and personal attire and held different attitudes toward authority. Some older priests looked askance at the younger men and were scandalized by the resignations from the priesthood.

In a departure from previous procedure, Dingman urged the retirement of some of the older men. A first attempt at a clergy tenure policy was floated in 1973 but was not approved by the bishop because it did not "grandfather" (allow those to remain who were appointed before the policy) priests over sixty-five. In 1977, another more flexible clergy tenure policy was introduced and approved. Associates were to have terms no longer than three years. Pastors could stay for seven. Most important, a pastor's term was not unending. Although policies were flexible enough to permit extensions and alterations, a priest was expected to move on a regular basis and once he turned seventy-five had to consider other options rather than parochial administration. This policy was approved by a vote of eighty-four to ten by the priests.[79]

The new policies began to move out some of the venerable and often outspoken priests in the Des Moines diocese. Among them was Father Francis Ostdiek, the first priest ordained by Dowling for the diocese and the founder of Holy Trinity Parish. When he formally retired from ministry in 1969, the *Mirror* reported: "Father Ostdiek is a man of strong convictions. The article continued, "One may disagree with him, but at least there is no doubt about where he stands on a given issue." Ostdiek would live to greet the pope who came to Iowa in 1979.[80]

Monsignor Michael Schiltz, pastor of St. Mary's of the Assumption in Panama, also decided to call it quits after forty-five years of service. Serving in Shelby County much of his priesthood, Schiltz was a beloved figure, ministering to his flock and also growing apples on a twenty-five-acre tract. Schiltz contributed to the Shelby County reputation of fostering vocations and encouraged over thirteen people to join the priesthood and religious life.[81] In July 1973, an ailing Monsignor Lester V. Lyons retired. A fixture at the cathedral since 1935, he had been ordained by Bishop Drumm. Lyons served for many years as vicar general and was the administrator of the diocese three times. He had also served as superintendent of schools for many years.[82] Lyons died of cancer in October 1973.[83] As noted earlier, he was replaced by a team-ministry of Father John Lorenz of the Leon Team Ministry and Father James Laurenzo of the Social Action Division of the Catholic Council for Social Concern.[84]

The Permanent Diaconate

Some bishops at Vatican II had wanted to open the question of mandatory celibacy for diocesan priests, but the question was withdrawn by Pope Paul VI who insisted on the maintenance of the discipline. Married clergy were embraced by the restoration of the permanent diaconate in 1967 by Pope Paul VI through the motu proprio *Sacrum Diaconatus Ordinem.* This document not only restored an ancient order of the church but also opened it to married laymen. It took time to develop policies and programs of formation and to screen candidates, but various dioceses around the United States embraced this change. At their meeting of December 17, 1968, the Des Moines priest council expressed an interest in having the program in the Des Moines diocese. Monsignor John McIlhon, the diocesan CCD director, chaired a special subcommittee consisting of Fathers Edward Kelly and James Rasmussen to discuss the possibility of introducing the order in Des Moines. McIlhon sent a questionnaire to twenty priests in the diocese to inquire about local interest and what deacons would actually do. McIlhon noted, "I was amazed at the quick response. . . . 16 of the 20 responded in four days." Breaking down the ministries into Service of Word, Service of Worship, and Service of Charity, he laid out a series of suggestions that included preaching, presiding at some services, managing religious education, sick and hospital calls, and youth work.[85] The priest council debated the beginning of the program in Des Moines and barely approved it on May 6, 1969, by a forty-four-to-thirty vote. Dingman, concerned about the opposition, went slowly.

In August 1969, Dingman appointed Father Duane Weiland, diocesan director of religious education, to gradually initiate the program. Weiland held a general meeting for those interested in November 1969, to which a number of men applied. The program took shape through the early months of 1970. Candidates mostly came from the Des Moines or Council Bluffs areas. Eventually ten men were part of the first class and a formal program was drawn up and submitted to the national office of the permanent diaconate in Washington, DC. Weiland moved the candidates through their paces, including study weeks at Saint John's Abbey in Collegeville, Minnesota. Specific areas of instruction were provided along the way: Scripture, presiding, sacramental theology, etc. These themes provided grist for regular meetings of the candidates in the Des Moines and Council Bluffs locations. The entire group would be brought together at different times for periodic workshops held at the Colfax Interfaith Center or other venues that would cap the term's instruction.[86] On June 4, 1972, eight men were ordained the first permanent deacons in the Diocese of Des Moines.[87] In 1974, a second class of eight men was ordained, hailing from Earling, Altoona, Des Moines, Council Bluffs, Afton, and Dunlap.[88] Many of these deacons provided important pastoral and administrative service to the parishes of their assignment.

Monsignor Stephen Orr recalled that the early classes of deacons concentrated on social justice ministries rather than liturgical and administrative duties. They were involved in jail and prison ministry, work with the homeless and food programs, and social justice ministries for peace. It was rare to see them vested on the altar or giving homilies. This gradually changed with deacons moving into a more visible liturgical ministry, preaching and administering parishes.

Collegiality

Bishop Daly had groused about the council's discussion on collegiality, insisting that the pope always had the last word. The council itself, however, modeled the value of collegiality and sought the active participation of bishops working together with each other to advise and direct the future of the church. Inspired by the dynamics of Vatican II, priests, sisters, and laypersons sought more active collaboration and input on diocesan affairs. Bishop Dingman would encourage this on a variety of fronts.

In the small diocese of Fargo, North Dakota, a priest association modeled on the Chicago group had developed and was blessed by Bishop Leo Dworshak. This group drew up a formal structure of an organization with rules to govern meetings. In March 1967, nineteen priests of Des Moines gathered at St. Columbanus rectory in Weston to ponder whether it was time for such a movement in the Des Moines diocese. This group issued a call to all 125 diocesan priests and to Bishop Biskup to attend a meeting at St. Mary's Hall in Elkhart to discuss the Fargo plan. Only thirty-six attended, but they created an ad hoc association of priests that would be voluntary (stressing that they were not forming a "union"). These priests were anxious to have some say in the direction of diocesan affairs and better knowledge of decisions being made.[89] After the transfer of Bishop Biskup in 1967, this group petitioned the head of the National Conference of Catholic Bishops, Cardinal John Dearden, to have some say in who would be appointed the next bishop of Des Moines.

In September 1968, Dingman met with this group and assured them that he wanted to work with the priests to meet the challenges of the times and the mandates of Vatican II. "I think a bishop should listen to the consensus of opinions. Then when he knows where he wants to go, what goals to achieve, he should be a leader." To the priests he declared: "I think the greatest thing is for you to have ideas and give them to me."[90] In a departure from existing custom, in October 1968, Dingman convened a three-day priest gathering at a Holiday Inn rather than a retreat house. The agenda was not just spiritual topics but sessions on *Humanae Vitae*, the magisterium of the church and authority, celibacy, communications between bishops and priests, the ministerial and common priesthood, dogma, the laity, racism, infallibility, and freedom of conscience. Dingman attended the sessions and concelebrated Mass with the priests.[91] At that meeting Auxiliary Bishop James Shannon of St. Paul–Minneapolis urged the priests to study the behavioral sciences and adopt an "inductive" approach to priestly ministry. Instead of telling parishioners what they must think and say, the priests were encouraged to study them and learn from their lives how best to proclaim the Gospel.[92] The association formally dissolved at the end of a three-day clergy retreat and formed a new body called the Council of Priests, modeled after similar organizations in Rockford, Illinois, and St. Paul–Minneapolis, Minnesota. It drew up a constitution, which Dingman approved just before Christmas. Its distinctive feature was that there were no elected representatives. It was a "committee of the whole": any of the 130 priests in the diocese at the time could participate and be a member.[93]

This dynamic body, which met quarterly, would be the impetus behind many of the changes in the early years of Dingman's episcopate. In discussing the scope of this body's influence, Dingman noted that it was to be an "advisory, not decision making" entity.

But he noted, "In most instances, I don't think this distinction is of much consequence. A bishop has great respect for the zeal and knowledge of his priests. It would be foolhardy for him to ignore the advice of his presbytery. . . . I can foresee very few instances in which the bishop would disagree totally with a near unanimous opinion of his priests."[94] Dingman would make good on his commitment to collegiality and patient dialogue. Dingman later described a sometimes tense but respectful relationship with one of his priests: "Nothing will jeopardize our trust. . . . Our dialogue exemplified the best meaning of that term. I call it ecclesial dialogue. It is a dialogue in a setting of Church. It is a dialogue in which we look at the 'signs of the times'. As you and I remember the short phrase in the Document of Evangelization which states very simply: 'The gentle action of the Spirit.'"[95]

Rethinking the Center and the Periphery: Regional Communities

Dingman also sought to hear many voices as he decided the fate of Iowa's rural areas. Rural areas were shrinking in numbers, as was the number of active priests in the diocese. Rural counties were undergoing significant economic and demographic change in the 1980s as corporate agriculture and generational attitudes toward rural life changed. Small farming of any kind began to disappear. Likewise, younger people who often went away to college did not wish to return and live in their small towns after graduation. New roads were built, including major highways that connected to the interstate system, that did away with the once-thriving railroads (and the jobs they brought). Old county seats now began to retool themselves with boutique shops, bed and breakfasts, and hosted small art and music festivals that brought in tourism. Those who remained had to figure out how to do more with less and ponder questions like "how do we market our community?" Covered bridges, birthplaces of famous Americans like John Wayne and Glenn Miller, government institutions like mental facilities and prisons became the economic mainstays of these regions. Catholic churches, often the most attractive buildings in the area, were compelled to adjust. Schools closed, old buildings were torn down, and many parishes built large halls and social centers with breakout rooms for parish meetings and religious education. Rural Catholic life was never robust in much of southwest Iowa, but the survival of the church in these areas required creative thinking and planning.

Dingman was anxious to broaden the scope of consultation and "ownership" of diocesan life, a response to the constant complaint of diocesan "peripheries" that no one listened to them or took their needs seriously. In 1969, the solution was proposed by the new Council of Priests that advanced the idea of regional communities to replace the four deaneries of the diocese. These regional communities were intended to build ties among their respective participants and represent their needs and concerns to a wider diocesan-wide community. In imitation of the twelve apostles, Dingman approved the creation of twelve regional communities, clustering areas around the diocese into subunits, accountable to wider diocesan control. "Central to our thinking must be the concept of 'community.' We face the threat of individuals and groups within the Church cutting themselves off from each other and no longer trying to communicate with each other." Dingman emphasized that the new structure existed to promote dialogue and mutual understanding.[96] In 1975, regional councils were created to further tighten the bonds of unity among people of a particular area.

Other Consultative Bodies

Most congregations of women religious underwent significant administrative change in the late 1960s. Chapters of renewal reworked the administrative structures of the congregations, introducing more team leadership and wider participation of all members in decisions affecting the community. Rules regarding prayer life, communal living, the use of the religious habit, and the structure of the day were reworked to implement the directives coming from Vatican II and the "signs of the times." In late 1969 as well, women religious of the diocese organized a Sisters' Council with representatives from every congregation with an apostolate in the Des Moines diocese. In February 1970, they organized an executive council and began to devise an agenda for the fuller participation of women religious in the life of the diocese. Dingman, who had worked closely with such a council in Davenport, urged the sisters to go forward with this project.[97] He showed his support by arranging and underwriting an annual weekend for sisters with a speaker and formal program. Although this body did not have the same standing or influence as the Council of Priests, Dingman found it a helpful tool in keeping up with the needs of the sisters and encouraging their work for the diocese. Dingman had as one of his priorities bringing women religious into positions of leadership in the diocese.

In July 1969, Dingman formed an ad hoc committee headed by layman Richard Aller to draw up preliminary guidelines for the creation of parish councils. This committee sent out the guidelines to the regional communities in April 1970. Here he was assisted by Father Frank Bognnano.[98] Bognanno was born in Des Moines, a son of Holy Trinity Parish, and lived for a time in Bakersfield, California. He began studies for the priesthood after his graduation from Dowling. Part of the first class ordained by Bishop Biskup in 1965, he was first assigned as an assistant to Monsignor Albert Davidsaver at Council Bluffs. Bognanno had a sharp mind and exceptional organizational skills, and Dingman tapped him to coordinate renewal efforts around the diocese. He was very instrumental in helping found the Council of Priests, the regional divisions of the diocese, and later the regional councils, the Sisters' Council, and the Diocesan Pastoral Council.[99]

Father (Later Monsignor) Frank Bognanno Director of Renewal. Credit: Diocese of Des Moines Archives.

Dingman also created a diocesan board of education in 1969, an idea floating since the days of Bishop Drumm. Meeting with parents at Dowling High School in October 1968, he proposed a board consisting of twelve people: the bishop, three priests, two sisters, and six laypersons. The new board would be able to better understand the complexities of Catholic school governance (individual parish direction) and above all the problems of financing. Dingman noted: "We are witnesses of profound changes in our Catholic educational system. Out of this crisis will come quality schools that will fulfill our highest hopes. And the credit will be in the hands of lay people. They are the voice of the community. They speak with the voice of the Church."[100]

A final consultative body emerged in early 1978, the Diocesan Pastoral Council (DPC). Long in the works, Dingman linked its origins with the Council of Priests, the creation of the twelve regions, the formation of parish councils in 1970, and the establishment of functioning regional councils in 1975. In 1976, he formed an Ad Hoc Diocesan Pastoral Council Study Committee, which worked for eighteen months to prepare a series of recommendations. This committee included representatives of all the regions, a representative from the deacons, and Father Frank Bognanno.

After this committee submitted its report, Dingman set up a trial Diocesan Pastoral Commission. This body laid out the rationale and priorities of the Diocesan Pastoral Commission—to advise the bishop on the needs of the people of God, to raise money, and to set the priorities for future ministries. The DPC was also to host an assembly every three years that brought the representatives of the regions together for celebration, deliberation, and prayer. The proposed DPC would consist of three laypersons, one priest, and one sister from every region and would meet quarterly.[101]

The first meeting of the new DPC took place on March 17, 1978, at the Country Squire Motel in Atlantic. At the first meeting, an array of voices offered views on subjects related to the structure of the DPC. Dingman was insistent that its ministerial vision be grounded in the inclusive ecclesiology of Vatican II. Much of the first meeting was spent building good relationships among the diverse membership and creating an atmosphere of trust and openness critical to the effective functioning of the group. Bognanno helped direct the meeting and committees were established to work on issues coming before the body.[102] Some expressed concern that this was just another church body that created meetings to attend. Citing these fears, the editor of *The Catholic Mirror* replied that the preparation for this body "was long and broad-based, and the model was more practical."[103]

In November 1971, Dingman issued the first complete report of diocesan finances in the history of the local church. "This is an effort of your diocesan leadership to be accountable to those whom we serve."[104] In late 1972, an extensive report was issued laying out the priorities of the diocesan budget overseen by chancellor Monsignor Edward Pfeffer. Funded programs included the Office of Religious Education, which included schools, CCD, campus ministry, and ministry to the hearing impaired. Pastoral priorities were the offices of Christian Worship, Ecumenism, Marriage Tribunal, Renewal, and Communication. Dingman also created an Arbitration and Conciliation Board to solve internal disputes that arose in the diocese.

Collegiality on Steroids: Multiple Voices in Local Church Decisions

Listening to the people became a leitmotiv of Dingman's episcopate. His belief in the participatory action of all members of the church governed his efforts to respond to the shifting demography of diocesan life and the shortage of priests. It began in Council Bluffs.

Council Bluffs was always a challenge to Des Moines's bishops. This city had a sizeable Catholic population consisting of five parishes with schools. It was a thriving and active Catholic community with its own distinctive religious culture. As with most cities at a distance from the diocesan headquarters, there was a tendency to feel neglected by the local bishop. The 130-mile trip from Des Moines to Council Bluffs was not easy, especially in the winter months. Hence, at times, Council Bluffs Catholics valued their relative autonomy and resisted plans from "outside." The city also had its own east side–west side sensibilities that added a further layer of complexity to dealing with common issues. Daly had pressed forward with the plans for a Catholic high school by simply mandating that the parishes pay for it, and this created a burden of debt (and some resentment) among parishioners. After Vatican II, religious communities of women began to shrink their commitment to Council Bluffs schools, and the schools themselves began to become a bigger drain on parish finances. It was left to Dingman to step up to consolidate and coordinate schools in the community.

By 1970, the city had a merged Catholic school board that began debating the future of Catholic education in the city and the difficult finances of the central high school. In a letter to a fellow monk, Father Maurus Kennedy, OSB, pastor of St. Peter's, reflected on a meeting of the school board in March 1970 and highlighted the financial problem faced by the parishes: "My teachers [at St. Peter's] cost me $25,800 next year and St. Albert's High School [the central high school of Council Bluffs] will cost the parish about $14,000. . . . The total income of the parish last year was only $58,098.58."[105] The next year financial conditions grew worse. Kennedy spoke often with neighboring pastor, Father John Hart of Queen of Apostles Parish, informing him that he had to borrow $5,000 from the diocese (on top of other loans) to get through May and June. "Last year our Merged School teachers and assessment from St. Albert's H.S. amounted to over $40,000 and that's a lot of hay for this parish."[106] In late September 1971, a meeting of all the parish councils and some members of the new Diocesan School Board met with Bishop Dingman at St. Albert High School to deal with the finance issue. It was decided to get an outside committee "to evaluate our parishes and schools and come up with some suggestions and present it to the Diocesan Board and the Bishop."[107]

A Davenport priest, Father Robert Walters, was brought in to begin the process. When time ran out on his contract, Dingman tapped Father Lawrence Beeson to complete the work. In 1972, an ad hoc committee was formed and debated the issues and advanced a major reorganization of the Council Bluffs schools, which took into account the strong east side–west side loyalties of the community. The decision was not easy. After a four-and-a-half-hour meeting and

Father (later Monsignor) Lawrence Beeson. Credit: Diocese of Des Moines Archives.

six ballots, the school board of Council Bluffs voted to retain three of the five school buildings. Kindergarten to grade three would be located at Holy Family, grades four through six would be at Queen of Apostles School. The Junior and Senior high would be located at the St. Albert's building. The grade schools at Neola and Missouri Valley would remain open but St. Francis's, St. Peter's, and St. Patrick's buildings would close[108] Beeson, commenting on the plan, observed, "A youngster that goes to our schools from first grade to high school will spend the first six years on the west side and the second six years on the east side . . . so it evens out." Beeson later reported halfway into the first year of the program that despite the loss of 169 students, the program was strong in many ways.[109]

But the parishes were still burdened with heavy debt from the St. Albert building project, and paying it off created friction among the parishes. School buildings, like those of St. Francis and St. Patrick parishes, could be sold and some of the proceeds, it was hoped, would go to retire the debt of St. Albert. Parishes that did not have disposable property to sell, however, felt disadvantaged. The St. Albert debt was only one problem. A more pressing issue was the fate of Council Bluffs' first Catholic Church: St. Francis Xavier. The church building's crumbling foundation and declining population were a source of concern.

In August 1973, the Council Bluffs region met under the direction of Bishop Dingman to study the alignment of parishes in Council Bluffs. Dingman asked Monsignor Edward Pfeffer, the chancellor, to be his liaison with the group. The region elected a deacon, Dennis Kirlin, to direct the process. The Center for Applied Research in the Apostolate (CARA), under the direction of Father Canice Connors, OFM Conv., and Frank Sheets, was brought in to conduct the process. On the docket was the fate of St. Francis Xavier's property, the status of St. Peter's Parish (would it continue its national parish identity?), and the possibility of consolidating St. Francis and St. Peter. In the hopper as well was the Catholic reaction to a local urban renewal program that would alter neighborhoods around St. Peter's.[110]

By December, after lengthy discussions on every level, the steering committee issued a report outlining objectives and strategies to address the issues of the community: parish properties, schools, sacramental preparation programs, and coordination of ministerial

The interior of St. Francis Xavier Church,
Council Bluffs, before its demolition.
Credit: Diocese of Des Moines Archives.

activities. The role of health-care institutions (Mercy Hospital) was also brought under the purview of this new plan. The primary finding of the report was to have a functioning regional board that would strategize, define, and submit to the bishop recommendations in the various areas of mutual concern in Council Bluffs. This report was reprinted in *The Catholic Mirror*.[111]

The regional board called for disposing of the building of St. Francis Church and selling the property except for the rectory, which was to be a residence for priests and a worship site. St. Peter's was made a diocesan parish, ending its status of as the last national parish in the diocese. Dingman traveled to Council Bluffs on the weekend of December 13–14, 1974, to preach at each of the parishes, noting his general acceptance of the plans and his pleasure with the committee.[112] In July 1975, St. Francis Xavier Parish, the oldest church in Council Bluffs, Father McMenomy's pride, was canonically suppressed and the next month the old church was demolished. Although the parish had been declining for some years, some noted the historical significance of the building and its importance to Catholics in Council Bluffs. St. Francis and the schools attached to it had served the people of Council Bluffs for many generations.

The plan was not uniformly admired by the people of Council Bluffs and there was still some resistance among people and clergy. Typical of some clergy reaction was the cantankerous Benedictine Father Maurus Kennedy, pastor of St. Peter's, who had been part of the deliberations. He disliked the process and the result so much that he chose to be transferred after the plan was in place, writing bluntly to a member of his community: "This self-study farce that has taken up so much of our time in those endless and useless meetings the past two years. I personally think that this was the most farcical adventure that was ever devised and conducted by a group of intelligent men. . . . They just don't have enough money to run the Catholic education program they have here."[113]

Kennedy's retirement and departure came of his own volition (and the nudging of his superiors in Atchison). To "clear the way" for the new Council Bluffs configuration, Dingman transferred a number of area clergy to other assignments. Father John Hart was moved to Winterset already in August 1972; Monsignor Michael Schwarte and his assistant at St. Patrick's also moved. New pastors for St. Peter's and St. Patrick's were appointed. Beeson and Dingman had tried to listen to as many voices as they could in the community and involve a spectrum of people—clergy, lay, and religious—in the planning. Whatever the bumps in the road, Dingman felt that Council Bluffs

Priest Regional Meeting.
Credit: Diocese of Des Moines Archives.

was on the road to a smooth and well-coordinated ecclesial existence and that it had a vision.

Regions Develop

These regional communities acknowledged two stark realities: the numbers of Catholics living in these rural areas were declining; the number of priests available to be full-time pastors in these parishes was also going down. Groups of priests now agreed to work in teams to manage several parishes in a region. One of the first, the Leon Regional Community, was formed by Monsignor Paul Connelly, Father John Lorenz, and Father James McIlhon after the retirement of Father Maurice Culhane, the pastor of Immaculate Conception Parish in Maloy and St. Joseph Church, Mount Ayr. The new arrangement designated the three priests to be co-pastors of the churches in Ringgold, Clarke, Decatur, and Wayne Counties. Two would live at the rectory of St. Brendan Parish in Leon, and a third at St. Bernard in Osceola. Connelly was appointed the coordinator of the group, but the leadership rotated each year.[114] This idea worked well on paper, but the two parishes that lost their resident pastors were angry.[115]

The Leon arrangement won a bit of national prominence as it became a chapter in *New Directions for the Rural Church*, coauthored by Glenmary priest Father Bernard Quinn and research staffer David Byers. Glenmary's special expertise in rural ministry brought a wealth of context to this and other efforts to preserve the vitality of the rural church. The authors outlined the complex financial and decision-making processes the Leon community had developed to preserve autonomy and unity in the region. Meeting pastoral needs was the priority—celebrating Mass, confession, and various sacraments as well as visiting the sick in the county hospitals in the area.[116] The original team of Lorenz, McIlhon, and Connelly were eventually replaced by three young priests: Larry Hoffman, Jerry O'Connor, and Joe McDonnell. The demanding schedule of these team ministers required around thirty thousand miles of travel a year and shifting responsibilities for various duties.

In late 1981, five parishes in the Shenandoah Regional Community—Sacred Heart, Bedford; St. Clare's, Clarinda; St. Mary's,

Red Oak; St. Mary's, Shenandoah; and St. Joseph's Vilisca—formed Southwest Iowa Parishes United and agreed to coordinate their services, create an interparish council, and coordinate staff meetings.[117] In 1983, regional planning took shape in Catholic-rich Shelby County, which had lots of churches and institutions, producing a new plan in 1985 that adjusted to the decline in priest personnel.[118] A team ministry in Harrison County brought together several parishes. Of these team efforts, an enthused Father Frank Cordaro wrote: "What is happening here in Harrison County with the concept of Team Ministry is on the cutting edge of Church these days, and I'm grateful to become part of the effort."[119]

Adapting Parish Consolidation Diocese Wide

The use of the self-study method in Council Bluffs seemed to work well, and Dingman urged that it be adapted for other regional groupings of the diocese. In 1975, the last Benedictines in the diocese, Father Maurus Kennedy of St. Peter's in Council Bluffs and Father Otho Sullivan of St. Malachy's in Creston, returned to their Atchison monastery, terminating a relationship that dated back to the previous century. Creston had two parishes and two schools and now declining clergy. After a study, Creston's two parishes became one and relocated to the Immaculate Conception site. Although St. Malachy's had a very good sense of history, perhaps nobody remembered that the original decision early in the century to have two parishes had caused a ruckus.

In Harrison County, three parishes in Modale, Mondamin, and Pisgah were "canonically dissolved" and formed a new entity, Holy Family in Mondamin. In September 1975, Father James Freeman took on the task of consolidating three parishes in Southeast Warren County: St. Mary's in Lacona, St. Augustine's in Milo, and St. Mary of Perpetual Help in Rosemount. Milo and Rosemount had separate pastors for a long period. Lacona, where Freeman was assigned, had eighty families, Milo had forty-nine, and Rosemount had thirty-three. Freeman, soon the only priest for this area, formed a joint council of the three churches and planned for the future. None of them were far from each other, and most of the kids attended public schools.[120] In 1978, these three parishes were canonically suppressed and a new consolidated parish named Holy Trinity of Southeast Warren County was created by Bishop Dingman.[121]

In early 1976, Dingman called on the Shelby County parishes in Defiance, Earling, Harlan, Panama, Portsmouth, and Westphalia to undertake a self-study, asking them to focus on their Catholic schools and religious education programs. Dingman once again urged a broader vision for the cause of Catholic education in Shelby County, which he noted had "a glorious history."[122] Shelby completed their information gathering by the fall of 1976. Sixteen hundred questionnaires were sent with over 1,400 returned. Outside consultants from Creighton University helped compile and formulate a series of alternative plans for the schools and religious education programs. With declining school enrollments (total all schools: 918 in 1970, and 582 in 1976), plus the issue of distances between schools, the plan faced some serious challenges.[123] The meeting process went on until October 20, 1977, and in the end the Shelby County schools agreed to merge, closing the schools at Defiance, Westphalia, and Portsmouth and urging parents to send their children to schools in Earling, Harlan, and Panama. The plan was formally submitted to Dingman in November, and he approved it in a letter to the Catholics of Shelby County, noting only that his instruction to include adult education had not been heeded.[124]

At a clergy convocation in November 1970, Dingman gave a state of the diocese address and outlined his views of the future of the diocese. He began by praising the collegiality and open discussion of the various councils he had encouraged: the Council of Priests, the Sisters' Council, the regional communities and parish councils. He looked forward to the creation of the Diocesan Pastoral Council. He lauded the beginnings of the permanent diaconate program. "I look forward to the time they will be ordained and become an integral part of the ministry of service to our people." He praised the diaconal internship programs being developed by the seminaries attended by diocesan seminarians and he encouraged a further development of team ministry. He also suggested a reorganization of the chancery, allowing the chancellor Edward Pfeffer to handle more day-to-day affairs and proposed hiring a full-time financial administrator to free him to do more administrative work. He tackled the ticklish issue of the tenure of diocesan priests, noting that he had earlier rejected a vote in favor of it by the Council of Priests because he felt it did not represent a consensus among the priests. He encouraged diversity in prayer and flexibility in meeting pastoral needs.

Most important, the address provided him the opportunity to crystallize the philosophical underpinnings of his episcopate. He affirmed the value of collaborative decision making and the practice of subsidiarity, letting decisions be made on the lowest levels. He believed in consolidation of efforts and resources to make the work of the church more effective. He identified his role as a point of unity for the people of the diocese—to keep things moving together and going forward on a path of renewal. In view of these philosophical goals, he set practical goalposts: urging more study and thoughtful reflection on the Word of God, active involvement of the people in church life, and establishing a pastoral council in the next five years. He promised more resources and attention to social needs, chaplaincies, and fostering agencies of consultation and collaboration among priests, sisters, and laity.[125]

Administrative Changes

The changing nature and volume of work in the post–Vatican II era required more space than the tiny cathedral basement. One of Biskup's first moves was to transfer the operations of the chancery from the small basement of the cathedral rectory to the old Christ Child Home, which no longer functioned as an orphanage.[126] By November 1966, the buildings had been refurbished. The new chancery provided space for a more efficient and professional administrative operation of the diocese. Into the new quarters would be relocated the chancery, the tribunal, the office of the school superintendent, the Confraternity of Christian Doctrine, Propagation of the Faith, and the vocations office.[127]

Dingman breathed life into the relocation and dramatically expanded the staff working for the diocesan central offices. Having been a chancery hand much of his priestly life, he was well acquainted with the requirements of central leadership. He retained the services of Daly's chancellor, Monsignor Edward Pfeffer. Pfeffer, a native of

Father (later Monsignor) Edward Pfeffer.
Credit: Diocese of Des Moines Archives.

Des Moines and one of two priest brothers ordained for the diocese, was one of the first to be invited by Daly to the recently opened St. Bernard's Seminary in 1948. Ordained in 1956, he was sent immediately to the Angelicum in Rome to complete a licentiate in canon law in 1958. After a brief stint at Holy Trinity (his home parish) and teaching at Dowling, he was appointed by Daly to the chancery in 1963. His work involved helping the bishop with whatever tasks were at hand—a sort of administrative assistant. But in addition to other administrative duties, Pfeffer was also largely responsible for oversight of diocesan finances, a job he kept until the appointment of a lay finance director.

A Role for Women

Perhaps the most important of Dingman's personnel changes were his efforts to include more women in positions of authority in diocesan life. He had always worked closely with sisters' congregations during his time in Davenport and had shed some of his celibate-culture unease around women during his years in Cursillo. Dingman's acknowledgment of the role of women stemmed from his deeper understanding of the theology of baptism. He also seemed to imbibe and understand some of the dynamism of the Second Wave Feminism that had made significant progress in American society in the 1960s. Civil Rights laws passed in 1964 had stigmatized overt discrimination against women. A growing visibility of women in heretofore mostly male professions, for example, law and medicine, and also in politics began to change cultural patterns of thinking about the role of women in society. Advocacy organizations like the National Organization of Women (1967) pushed hard against stereotypes in public media and the glass ceiling in hiring as well as wage discrimination. Within the Catholic Church, concerns about male patriarchy and dominance were also being voiced. The movement to ordain women to the priesthood began in the Episcopal Church (1976) and caught the attention of Roman Catholics. Dingman seemed to be at least peripherally in touch with these shifting cultural currents and was quite public about his "conversion" to support of the Equal Rights Amendment (ERA) to the Constitution, which picked up considerable steam in the 1960s and 1970s. He was quite sure that Catholic support was necessary for this potentially revolutionary recognition of the rights of gender in American life.

Even more, he lamented the fact that often the church had resisted aspects of modernity. Supporting gender equality and the ERA was a chance for the Catholic Church to "get on board" with an important social issue. Among his fellow bishops, Dingman stood out for his support for the role of women in ministry. His friend, Bishop Thomas Gumbleton, auxiliary of Detroit, recalled that he had participated in an ecumenical service that highlighted a woman minister. The presence of a vested female was unusual at the time, and even Gumbleton was a bit taken aback. But not so Dingman. He spoke up for women religious at meetings of the bishops and at one point referred to feminism as "a movement of the spirit." He was comfortable with women in ministry and, although he never publicly departed from the official ban on women's ordination, he expressed from time to time his willingness to consider and discuss it. Of course this was not possible under the pontificate of Pope John Paul II.

Practicing what he preached, he named a number of women to his staff and his inner circle. He retained Sister Elizabeth Clare Schindler, OP, an Adrian Dominican, who began as an elementary school consultant under Biskup, who had hired her as superintendent of schools to replace Father James Holden. Schindler created a curriculum library and carved out a space in the diocesan bureaucracy for the care of the schools. She would be on hand for some interesting times with her new bishop, himself a former superintendent. When she was elected provincial of her congregation in 1978, her replacement was BVM Sister Dolores Marie McHugh.[128] As the diocese changed to conform to Vatican II–era demands, new offices were created for special needs.[129] This involved changes in the Department of Education, the Department of Religious Education, and the Renewal Office, which had been created under Biskup. New standards and criteria for church annulments meant new personnel for the matrimonial tribunal.[130]

Sister Elizabeth Clare Schindler, OP. Credit: Dominican Archives in Adrian, Michigan.

Diocesan Reorganization Goes Deeper

Dingman significantly reorganized Catholic Charities in 1970 and created an umbrella agency called the Catholic Council of Social Concern. It had three entities: (1) a Catholic Social Service Division, which continued the original mission of the charities offices

Sister Dolores Marie McHugh, BVM. Credit: Archives of the Sisters of Charity of the Blessed Virgin Mary.

(child care, counseling, care for the elderly, foster home placements). (2) A Division of Social Action was an effort to bring the Des Moines diocese behind the cause of social justice. It dealt with justice issues and assistance to minorities, the poor, homeless, and the hungry. It also worked with community affairs, hunger, the correction system, the elderly, and legislation. (3) A Division of Family Services oversaw family life education, family planning, formation for the engaged, marriage counseling and enrichment. Branches of this outreach were to be found in Des Moines and Council Bluffs, and this agency also handled local participation in national programs: Respect for Life, Human Development, and Overseas Collections.[131] Later, Family Services sought independence from the Social Concern's Council and affiliated with the chancery.[132]

The Division of Social Action studied many local problems and brought them to Dingman's attention. For example, a 1975 study commissioned by the Catholic Council for Social Concerns discovered serious malnutrition among the elderly, complicated by an unwillingness on the part of these stubborn folks to use federal programs to help. Another report of the National Council of Churches studied hunger in the United States and discovered that Decatur County, in the Des Moines diocese, was one of the fifteen poorest in the United States.[133]

A Ten-Year Retrospective

By 1978, ten years into Dingman's administration, the structures and reality of diocesan life had changed considerably. The numbers of Catholics overall had shrunk, and church demographics were altered. Catholics were increasingly concentrated around metropolitan Des Moines while rural parishes had begun to empty out. The number of priests declined as well. The diocesan bureaucracy and the efforts funded by the diocese had grown, with a budget of $417,000 for fiscal year 1978–1979—up 7 percent from the previous year. Some of the funding went to new offices created by the changed priorities of the diocese. Questions were raised by members of the finance committee of the Diocesan Pastoral Council wondering if a small southwest Iowa diocese could truly afford all these offices and expansion.[134]

Diocesan funding came from a number of sources, but the chief form of revenue was from the annual assessment on the parishes. In 1978, at the recommendation of the Diocesan Pastoral Council, Dingman announced that he was inaugurating a diocesan-wide fund appeal, one of the first since the one launched by Bishop Daly. The first drive, headed up by Christ the King Pastor Lawrence Burns, sought to raise $750,000 to help with the budgeted expenses of the diocese.[135]

In June 1979, Monsignor Edward Pfeffer left the post of chancellor to become a pastor. His replacement was Father Stephen Orr. Orr, like his predecessor, was a native of Des Moines, an alumnus of St. Augustin School, Dowling, and Loras College, Dubuque. He was sent by Dingman to the North American College in Rome and was ordained to the priesthood in July 1974. His first assignment was to the faculty of St. Albert High School, and he performed pastoral duties in Council Bluffs. In July 1978, Dingman sent him to the Catholic University of America for graduate work in church administration. When he returned in July 1979, he was appointed chancellor and assisted Dingman with research and other canonical duties.[136]

Orr's appointment coincided with a redefinition of the chancellor's duties. Acting on recommendations of the finance council of the diocese and the Diocesan Pastoral Council, financial management of the diocese was now placed in the hands of a new lay finance director, Michael Walsh. The well-organized and competent Orr met weekly with Dingman and the communications director, Sister Mira Mosle, BVM, to lay out the agenda and survey the activities for the week. Rosemary Mosman, long-time secretary to bishops, kept the office running smoothly.

Orr took over Dingman's correspondence, often drafting letters for the busy bishop's signature and organizing the somewhat disordered clutter of Dingman's office. He recalled that he kept Dingman's schedule folder in his own office so that the bishop would have to come into to his office at least once a day. Orr also served as master of ceremonies for Dingman and often chauffeured him around the diocese, as did many staff members. On the long trips from place to place for liturgical or other purposes, Dingman often slept in the rear of the car while Orr or others drove. The arrangement was difficult at first for the bishop who did not wish to have people doing things for him that he could do for himself. Orr helped clear away time, however, and swept away bureaucratic clutter so that Dingman could focus on the things that were necessary and important to him.[137]

Ministry to Youth

Ministry to the several college campuses in the Des Moines diocese resulted in the creation of a Newman Community non-territorial parish at Drake University in 1969.[138] Ministry to Catholic youth also took place through parish activities and diocesan-wide programs. Father Thomas "Tank" De Carlo, a native of Des Moines, was a son of Holy Trinity Parish and became a leader in this field for many years. In the early 1960s he worked at the Catholic Youth Camp in Boone, Iowa, directed by Father Nelo Leto. After his 1969 ordination, De Carlo became director of the camp, which ran for the last two weeks of summer. He worked in parishes and then in 1974 managed to convince Dingman to allow him to work full time in youth ministry together with Father Terry Lindsley. He carved a niche for youth ministry, having an office at the St. Joseph Educational

Father Thomas "Tank" DeCarlo.
Credit: Diocese of Des Moines Archives.

Center on the Dowling campus. De Carlo helped organize TEC (Teens Encounter Christ) retreats. In 1972, Fathers De Carlo and Lindsley helped launch a specialized youth program held in an old warehouse, donated by a Cursillista named Gary Dalby, which they renamed "Where House" ("Where It's At"). The site would move three times but was open three days a week and provided a venue for Catholic youth from a number of parishes to hang out, play pool or pinball, have dances, and speak informally with the priests. Mass was celebrated there on Sunday afternoons and one year offered an Easter Vigil that drew hundreds to the site. De Carlo summed up the ministry's goals: "Rap (talk), rec, and religion."[139] Lindsley left the priesthood in 1975, but the youth center went on until 1981. De Carlo continued his work with the Catholic Youth Camp, which gradually expanded the number of weeks it was in session.

The old 4H Camp at Boone was soon inadequate, and in 1983, under the auspices of the St. Thomas More Catholic Youth Camp, ten acres were purchased on Lake Panorama near Panora. De Carlo had been haggling for the location since 1979 but finally was able to secure the deal with the help of a loan from the Knights of Columbus. The plans were for a multiuse facility: a summer camp but also a place for parish groups and others.[140] Teens Encounter Christ, a popular high school youth program, also had a popular following in the Des Moines diocese. The center made extensive expansions to the original building but began to hit serious financial difficulties in 1984.[141]

The Abortion Issue

The January 1973 *Roe v. Wade* decision, legalizing abortion up to the first trimester, hit the Catholic community like a thunderbolt. Opposition to the ruling was instant and Catholic health-care institutions such as Des Moines's Mercy Hospital declared their unwillingness to have abortions in their facilities. Within days of the ruling, Dingman noted: "It is the teaching of the Church that human life is sacred, that abortion is wrong."[142] That year, when Dingman issued his Lenten guidelines, he included an appeal for more money for the Catholic Council for Social Concern "as they strive to serve the needs of those who may be tempted to seek an abortion."[143] In late April, Dingman affixed his name to a strong pro-life statement issued by all the bishops of Iowa. "We shall, by all lawful and proper means, seek redress of the injustice resulting from this unfortunate decision."[144]

Conclusion

In 1974, Dingman made a trip to Rome to report on the state of the diocese to Pope Paul VI. Dingman provided the statistics of diocesan life: eighty thousand Catholics out of a population of 625,185 persons, served by eighty-nine parishes. He noted the high incidence of poverty in many of the diocese's rural areas and the gradual collapse of parishes in these rural counties. He pointed to the presence of 114 active priests, only six of whom were religious. He observed that in the five year period, eight priests had left the active ministry, nine had died, nineteen had retired, and sixteen had been ordained. There were 211 sisters, of whom 122 were teachers in twenty-two elementary and two high schools. Over 260 laypersons were now teaching in the schools. The two major hospitals in the diocese had undergone substantial renovations. Four new churches, six parish centers, three rectories, and one educational center were built.

Four years later, in June 1978, Dingman made another required visit to Rome to report on the state of his diocese. This time he resided with an ailing Monsignor Luigi Ligutti, who shared his home and had one of his relatives transport Dingman to wherever he wished to go in Rome. On the day of his visit with Pope Paul VI, Dingman was dropped off at the huge Cortile of San Damaso. Here he remembered once again his student years, when he and many other seminarians were greeted by the newly elected Pope Pius XII who urged them: *Orate, et iterum dico Orate!* (Pray! I say it again Pray!). Coming into the Apostolic Palace he was warmly greeted by the pontiff who spoke of the Eucharist. "The Holy Father seemed reluctant to let us go . . . and asked us to return to see him again."[145] That would be the last time he saw Paul VI in the flesh. The pope would die less than two months later.

A Force for Justice

Vatican II's Constitution on the Church in the Modern World (*Gaudium et Spes*, 1965) created the intellectual and spiritual space for Iowa Catholics, especially their leaders, to meet new social and cultural realities with a new stance and a new voice. Urged to "read the signs of the times" and to apply the timeless truths of Christianity to the needs and hopes of the modern world ignited the spirit and vision of Catholics to a significant extent in the period of the 1960s through the 1980s.

Catholics in southwest Iowa stepped up to the challenges of their era and tried to make a difference. Assessing the impact of the church takes us into a different sphere. In previous chapters we have seen how urban space, education, health care, and economic impact reflected the Catholic presence. Here, we consider Catholic agency in terms of moral suasion—a less tangible and harder to read aspect of religious presence. Iowa Catholics took note of issues of urban affairs, racism, and economic injustice, especially as these affected farmers. Catholic leaders spoke out on American foreign policy in Latin American countries as well as nuclear defense policy. These issues—based on Catholic social teaching and supported by other American bishops—and formerly off limits to religious leaders, were now considered worthy of comment and action. Whether these stands affected or changed the thinking of people is hard to gauge. Nonetheless, Iowa Catholics and their leaders would speak their minds and let the chips fall where they may. These challenges all piled up in a singular way during the episcopate of Maurice Dingman. One of them was a new urban demography.

Urban Affairs

Cities were becoming the primary locus of Catholic life in southwest Iowa. The changes created by the expansion of suburbs, the destruction of neighborhoods because of freeway construction or urban redevelopment, the shifting of population, the aging of buildings, and the upward mobility of many Catholics created a set of realities that required response. As we have seen, a new burst of suburban expansion, especially to the north and west of Des Moines, gave birth to new parishes in heretofore undeveloped areas. St. Pius X in Urbandale and St. Mary of Nazareth in Des Moines, as well as Our Lady's Immaculate Heart in Ankeny were among the new parishes that benefited from increased or relocated population growth. Much of this, as we have seen, was made possible by the development of the federally funded interstate system, which had a significant impact on the demographics of metropolitan life in both Des Moines and Council Bluffs.

The church had always had a big footprint in the cities and Catholic institutions had contributed to social stability and economic life. Rising concerns about the future of American cities and growing sensitivity to the conditions of minorities who lived in these cities became a concern of state and local governments. It also became a concern of the Catholic Church.

Dowling High School:
Catholic Education and Urban Presence

One of the most momentous urban decisions made by the Catholic Church in the Diocese of Des Moines was the decision to relocate Dowling High School to the burgeoning suburb of West Des Moines. This issue intersected with larger concerns about urban stability, race relations, and class issues. Discussions about the future of the high school had been on the agenda of local Catholic authorities since the time of Bishop Daly. Benefiting from the sharp increase in Catholic school-children after the war, Daly had not only founded the new St. Albert High School in Council Bluffs (and wanted a new one in Shelby County) but also contemplated renovating the now-aging buildings on the Dowling campus.

Dowling had been a fixture on Des Moines's landscape since the World War I era. It had grown in size and enrollment over the years, still catering exclusively to boys. The old buildings were showing their age and even the newer structures, like the gym, were wearing out. The neighborhood around Dowling had also been in transition through the 1950s and 1960s. Gradually inhabited by lower-income people, some felt it began to look shabby, and concerns grew among parents about the safety of their sons, especially for night activities.

At the same time, there were declines in the number of children attending Catholic schools. Between 1968 and 1987 (Bishop Dingman's term) the attendance at Catholic elementary schools in the Diocese of Des Moines fell from 9,832 to 5,866. Numbers in Catholic high schools also remained somewhat stagnant—with 1,304 boys and 1,250 girls in schools and dipping to 916 and 907, respectively. Religious education for public school-children meanwhile also dipped from 13,430 to 10,080.[1] At the same time, the number of Catholics grew from eighty-one thousand in 1968 to eighty-six thousand by 1986, more and more of them concentrating in Des Moines and its environs.

Catholic Space in Des Moines, IA, 1987

Map by Aaron Hyams

Des Moines Golf and Country Club.
Credit: State Historical Society of Iowa.

Daly's ideas for a new Dowling on the original site died with him on the Roman runway. Nonetheless, his successor, George Biskup, seized an opportunity created when freeway expansion divided up the Des Moines Golf and Country Club on the growing west side of the city. With the advice and consent of a newly formed administrative council of Dowling High School, Biskup negotiated the purchase of fifty-five acres of this old golf course through a special corporation set up for Dowling High School. The price for this parcel was $322,000, paid from a fund that had been set up by Bishop Dowling himself.[2] The new property created a different context for the future discussion of the popular boys' high school. Although no immediate plans for the relocation of Dowling were made, it was clear, at least to some, that the school would transition to new facilities at the site.[3]

Locating Dowling: A Practical and Moral Issue

The first act of the multiyear drama took place at an October 1966 meeting of the Dowling administrative council. This nineteen-member body formally decided to build a new Dowling High School for boys on the fifty-five-acre site in West Des Moines. To this end, they engaged Lawrence E. Twigg and Associations of

Belleville, Illinois, to plan a fund-raising program and looked for architects in Des Moines to draw plans for the new school.

Right from the start, however, a tug of war began about the potential relocation of the school. Some worried that the potential West Des Moines location would disadvantage students in some parts of the city. Others noted that the current property footprint of the school was less than the forty-four-square-acre minimum demanded by the North Central Accreditation agency. Monsignor Lester Lyons, chairman of the ad hoc New Dowling Committee, checked with state agencies about requirements for a new high school and also consulted with President/Principal Father Frank Nugent who informed him that most of the 1,045 students enrolled by the school would have easy access to the new site. There would be problems, however, for students from the parishes on the south side (St. Anthony, Christ the King, St. John, Cumming), but they might be better served by another location.

An offer was made for forty acres in nearby Warren County, but the board voted to build a new Dowling on the West Des Moines site and to hire the Smith, Vorhees, and Jensen Architects of Des Moines to begin work on preliminary drawings. Occupancy of the new site could not take place until September 1967, so there was time to plan, raise funds, and prepare for a transition.[4] But Biskup's short tenure and an apparent lack of consensus on the wisdom of moving slowed the process down. Two sides soon formed: those who favored the move and those who did not.

As noted earlier, Daly had planned to rebuild a new Dowling on its present site. When Biskup purchased the land in West Des Moines and floated the idea of erecting a new high school there, advocates for the "Daly plan" appealed for reconsideration on the basis of urban concern and social justice. Even though the Dowling area was in decline in many ways—a disincentive for the school to stay—the federal government had formulated plans to stabilize changing urban communities.

For a time, rumors floated that the area around Dowling was under consideration for a grant from one of the urban initiatives of the Johnson era, the Model Cities program. In this scenario, keeping Dowling at its current location would make it an anchor for efforts to upgrade and improve the surrounding neighborhood. Dowling itself might be eligible for certain federal funds to upgrade and improve their aging facilities and increase their outreach to urban minorities.

They also argued that to move Dowling at this time would make it seem as though the church was fleeing impoverished areas and minority populations, in effect practicing another form of white flight. Put somewhat on the defensive by these arguments, proponents of moving the school argued pragmatically that the old buildings were not worth preserving and that the neighborhood was on a path of decline that might jeopardize student safety and the future economic viability of the school. Many of the parents of the students echoed these concerns.

Drawing in the New Bishop

This discussion generated so much passion that within a few days of hearing of Dingman's nomination to the See of Des Moines, advocates of both sides motored to Davenport to lobby him to their side. Two lay faculty members, George Cordaro and Robert Nizzi, wrote to Dingman in Davenport, arguing for a new site and buildings, insisting "in the light of vast changes in education today new facilities are imperative." Dowling, they noted, "is the only major Catholic secondary school in Iowa which has not constructed the majority of its educational facilities in the last fifteen years. . . . Can we look forward to the future with hope to practice our profession in a Catholic high school with first class facilities?"[5]

Robert Wadle, who served on the Dowling board, disagreed with a potential move, writing to Dingman that "we cannot afford the required four and one half to six million dollars for the project." He cited other problems. The nineteen parishes supporting the school were falling behind in their assessments, Biskup had purchased the land without consulting the board, and a quarter of the students now enrolled would not attend a relocated school. He also noted, "Our present site is now in the area of Model Cities. . . . It is possible that we can obtain help through this Model Cities program." Wadle also challenged those who noted that the present location did not have the forty-four acres of land demanded by the North Central Accreditation agency, arguing that more land could be had and that a workaround of this requirement was possible. He concluded, "May I suggest that you take a sincere look at this problem and I pray that your decisions will be wise ones."[6]

When Dingman finally arrived in Des Moines, he addressed the issue within a month of being installed. In August, he announced to the press that he was not ready to make a decision until he had tended to other priorities, for example, setting the wider goals and getting a handle on the personnel and financial resources of the diocese.[7] The Dowling issue was then subjected to a painstaking process of discussion. These efforts to arrive at a consensus put off the final decision to relocate and build for at least two years. Dingman first placed the question before each of the nineteen school boards of the parishes affected. When these bodies reported to the diocesan school board on June 30, 1969, many acknowledged the problems with the old site (buildings, neighborhood, etc.), but there was no clear consensus of what to do—stay or leave.

Dingman temporized. Although he probably was personally convinced of the benefits of moving the site, he took special pains to listen to the arguments on the other side. He appointed a committee of ten people who favored keeping the old site and asked again for their reasons.[8] Five meetings were held during the month of July 1969 with the "1964 Group" (because that was the year Daly had offered his plans to keep the old site).

This group presented a medley of reasons for retaining the old site (money, possibility of getting more land, etc.) but came down heavily on the imperatives of the social doctrine of the church, quoting especially Pope Paul VI's encyclical *Populorum Progressio* (On the Development of Peoples, 1967) stressing economic justice for the poor. They even cited the findings of the National Advisory Commission on Civil Disorders (also known as the Kerner Report, 1968) on the urban riots of 1967, which suggested that one of the reasons for urban violence was the flight of stabilizing institutions in American cities. They reworked the 1964 plan and believed they had dealt with the financial issues and the assessment burden on the parishes. Dowling was a part of Des Moines and should remain in its current location as a visible sign of the church's commitment to the inner city.[9]

But other voices had to be heard as well. Dingman called in an external consultant, Christian Brother Anthony Wallace, FSC, from the National Catholic Education Association. Wallace examined Dowling's physical plant and its programs and spoke with its faculty and students. In the summer of 1969, at a meeting held in the Dowling library, he issued a report calling the present buildings "a fire trap" and condemned everything from the library (where the meeting sharing this report was held) to the science labs. He urged those attending the meeting to think ahead twenty-five years, urging that a new Dowling be not just a high school but a center for CCD and also for ecumenical affairs. He even suggested that a new multipurpose Dowling building could garner some federal education grants and foundation funds.[10] In early September, Dingman wrote an open letter to people in the diocese recapping the contentious process and promising a decision by the end of September.[11]

Finally, in October 1969, after a fifteen-hour meeting, the diocesan board of education voted (10–2) to build a new Dowling High School on the West Des Moines site. The significance of this to the wider community was noted by the bold headline on the *Des Moines Register*: "Dowling to Move to W.D.M." announced the news to the community.[12] What convinced the group and Dingman was the decrepitude of the old buildings and the concern of parents who were skeptical of sending their sons to this location.

Prospects for federal aid were nil as the Nixon administration had begun to phase out the Model Cities program with the first cuts coming on July 1, 1969. Potential funding for Des Moines was scheduled to disappear on October 15.[13] With no prospect of help for the aging neighborhood, the locale of the school was no longer feasible for many students. Indeed, 63 percent of Dowling students lived in West Des Moines.

But more positively, consultations with people like Brother Wallace had opened up some new possibilities that would make the new high school conform more to the changes in religious instruction that had come out of Vatican II. One critical change was the decision to make the new Dowling coeducational. This, as we shall see, created some distress with the BVM sisters who ran St. Joseph Academy.

The new school also provided an opportunity to create a catechetical center and implement a new "total approach" to religious education. The buildings could be used for high school purposes during the day but in the evenings would be available for CCD and—what was then a new and refreshing change—adult education sessions. In fact, Dingman had already earlier announced that there would be a new direction in transmitting the Catholic faith to the young: urging less memorization and encouraging more personalistic ways of communicating Catholic teachings and identity. Dingman wrote a letter to the people that was read at Masses throughout the diocese, reflecting on the controversial decision and insisting it was a correct "prudential decision" that it had the support of the Greater Des Moines Catholic community. Praising the process by which the decision was reached, he rejoiced that the mission of the new Dowling would be a new chapter in the history of Catholic education. "It will be a center where lights will burn brightly every day and far into the evening proclaiming to our community that we are a people intent on knowing more about our faith."[14]

The opponents of the move did not remain silent, even after the decision was made. In November 1969, Father Jacob Weiss, the Catholic representative to the Des Moines Area Council of Churches reported to Monsignor Luigi Ligutti: "The Dowling move still divides Des Moines—not just Catholic Des Moines, but all of the community. I arranged a meeting between Bishop Dingman and 20 of his young priests who were deeply disturbed by the decision to move Dowling. We met one evening in the bishop's living room from 9–12:30 AM. . . . The talk was honest and probing and nothing was left unsaid about ANYTHING! I had never experienced anything like this before. No one else had either." Weiss then scheduled a meeting between Dingman and progressive Protestant clergymen "which lasted just as long."[15] Sensitive to the needs of the poor who would be "abandoned" by the move, discussions were begun to turn the old facility into a Social Concern Center.[16]

The "Old" Dowling

Clearly, Dingman felt some guilt over departing the city. A handout sheet distributed to the press and interested parties tried to explain the rationale for the move. One of the hypothetical questions asked: "What can be done with the present site?" The response was tentative—it depended on the location of a new freeway, the desire of local residents to use the site as a neighborhood park and community center, or the dimming prospect of Model City planning.[17]

But Dingman was pretty sure that the old buildings had to be put to some good social use as a signal that the church was not abandoning the neighborhood. Indeed, one report to Dingman noted, "It's a prime area from which to offer various types of service to the community, while at the same time contributing to the upgrading and rehabilitation of the total community."[18] In June 1972, the nonprofit Community Concerns Corporation, which was leasing three of the four buildings on the campus for $2,000, desired to buy the old Dowling site. The diocese put a price tag of $475,000 on the property. Natalie Reese, the director of the Social Action Division of the Catholic Council for Social Concerns and also the main agent for Community Concerns Corporation, was a key player in this proposal. The diocese made a formal announcement of the deal.[19] Efforts to win funds from United Way and to entice Polk County Social Services to lease space fell flat. The United Way would support programs but not buildings.[20] Ultimately, an evangelical church, the

St. Joseph Academy. Credit: Used with permission of
Mount Carmel Archives of the Sisters of Charity
of the Blessed Virgin Mary, Dubuque, Iowa.

Kingsway Ministries, purchased the buildings for $300,000.[21] Later, they sold the complex to the City of Des Moines.

The fate of the old Dowling campus reflected a transition in the urban presence of the Catholic Church in the city of Des Moines. Declining school enrollments brought about mergers. St. Ambrose, the oldest Catholic school in the city, merged its schools with others. In 1980, urban schools began to feel the crunch as the older Des Moines parishes of Visitation, St. John's, and St. Peter's were compelled to merge their struggling schools. Primary and upper grades would be taught at St. John's and St. Peter's while older children would attend school at Visitation (a newer building).[22] The newly consolidated entity was renamed Holy Family School.[23] In 1970, the Catholic press noted that Catholic elementary schools had more lay teachers than religious (158 to 112).[24] Catholics were transiting to the suburbs as they did in other urban locations around the nation.

The New Dowling: The Coeducation Question, the BVM Sisters, and the Fate of St. Joseph's Academy

While many supported the move of Dowling to West Des Moines, the BVM sisters, who had begun secondary education in the city, reacted with hesitation and even some anger. In particular, the sisters were concerned over the threat that a new coeducational school would pose to their enrollment and precarious finances. Although located in an upscale neighborhood, the academy would need new buildings and additional land to accommodate potential enrollment and athletics.

Yet another piece of the St. Joseph story involved the number of sisters who were available to work at the school. The sisters' communities were changing significantly. In 1968 the BVMs held a "chapter of renewal" that reworked their governmental structures and opened up new options for the placement of sisters. Sisters were now given greater leeway to select their individual ministries, and some moved out of education altogether.[25] Added to this, there was a decline in the numbers of applicants to the religious life and a flow of departures of professed sisters. The shrinking and aging membership of the community led to a reevaluation of the ministries they could afford to staff and support.

In the fall of 1969, they had commissioned a study by the Center for Urban Development in Education (CURE) to assess the viability of continuing their eight BVM-owned high school apostolates, including St. Joseph's Academy. (This same firm had studied the viability of their grade and diocesan high schools.) The firm reported back in late January 1970 that the sisters were receptive to the new diocesan education program in Des Moines and that they had plans down the line to sell the academy.

As the sisters were pondering the future of their apostolates, the future of the new Dowling took a step forward. Some parents wanted to continue single-gender education at the new Dowling, but a growing consensus urged the merger of Dowling and St. Joseph Academy into a new coeducational endeavor. But the question was timing. Some of the sisters did not favor a new coeducational Dowling just at that moment. Some wanted to keep the academy; it already had a new building and could have been adapted to new needs. Some wished to have a larger subsidy from the Diocese of Des Moines to keep it going. In January 1970, however, when the diocesan school board voted to make the new Dowling a coeducational institution, some of the sisters felt miffed. Community leadership, under Sister Roberta Kuhn, BVM, had to negotiate these difficult waters. Might the diocese delay the coeducation plans? Could a subsidy shore up the future of the academy?

After all the time the deliberations took, neither Dingman nor the board would countenance any changes in the plans. Nor could they advance money to the sisters. Recognizing the work of the sisters and their integral role in building the Des Moines Catholic community, a plan was developed to give the BVM sisters a hand in the new

Sister Roberta Kuhn, BVM. Credit: Used with permission of Mount Carmel Archives of the Sisters of Charity of the Blessed Virgin Mary, Dubuque, Iowa.

school. Dingman insisted that the new catechetical center could be called the St. Joseph Educational Center (a note of continuity with the academy). This broader-based institution would include sister administrators and faculty and not only emphasize traditional high school education but also be a center for CCD, campus ministry, and adult education opportunities. "We envision the new Dowling as contributing to all facets of religious education." Included as well were "training sessions for CCD teachers, and a facility for high school religious education."

A questionnaire was sent to the sponsoring parishes of the high school to see if they could get behind this new concept.[26] The survey eventually polled one hundred religious and lay leaders and reached out to twelve thousand Catholic families. The results strongly supported the idea of a new school, believed in the new concept of a central religious education center, and promised to support a fund-drive for the new enterprise. In the summer of 1970, plans went forward to construct a new $4.5 million Catholic educational center on the West Des Moines site.[27]

Even though he had $3 million in pledges, Dingman needed more, and fund-raising went ahead as ground was broken for the new school. He wrote to the people: "We are embarking on a new program that is far wider than just a high school for our Community. It will be an educational center that will encompass all our educational needs—high school, C.C.D. and adult education."[28] In August 1970, Dingman designated Father Frank Nugent as president of Dowling and coordinator of the Dowling/St. Joseph Educational Center.

Dingman appointed an old friend, Monsignor Alver W. Behrens of the Diocese of Sioux City, to be the principal of Dowling—the first non–Des Moines priest to hold the post. A former diocesan superintendent of schools in Sioux City, he had been ordained in 1945 and held a master's in education from Creighton University. As part of the alliance with the BVM sisters, Sister Mary Judith Sheahan, BVM, was appointed the new vice principal of Dowling.[29] In his opening meeting, Behrens described himself as a "farm boy from Templeton [Iowa], a good listener, and a fair but tough disciplinarian." He promised to lead the high school effectively and get it through an important rendezvous with the North Central Accreditation organization.[30]

In October, architectural drawings were released to the public depicting the new facility, which would welcome as many as 1,800 new students "regardless of race, color, or creed." A $3.8-million fundraising drive was launched, spearheaded by Dr. Daniel F. Crowley, a local physician, and Mrs. Neil McGarvey of Des Moines.[31] Behrens was replaced by Father John Acrea, who became interim principal, and Father Richard Wagner assumed the role of president. In September 1971, layman William R. Baas of Des Moines was selected as the first lay principal of Dowling.[32]

When the school opened in the fall of 1972, its logistical problems included traffic, providing enough bus transportation, and lunchroom congestion. The school also fell short of the 1,700 hoped-for students. But Principal Baas gave an optimistic report on the problems and secured the purchase of three new busses to help transport students.[33] In 1976, the school undertook another $300,000 campaign to replace the used furniture they had brought from the old site, upgrade and expand classroom facilities (creating a television studio), and set aside money for a student scholarship fund.[34] Baas remained principal until 1980.

Dowling's New Existence

Careful attention was given to the other aspect of the new post–elementary education program. In early 1972, Father Gene Stephany was recruited to oversee all of the components of the new school's wide-reaching education program.[35] Stephany and his staff inaugurated the St. Joseph's Educational Center on the Dowling Campus, offering by the fall of 1972 a rich array of adult education classes covering Scripture, liturgical studies, formation in Catholic doctrine, and morality. "My heart is filled with gratitude," Dingman wrote, "to those who have brought us to this plateau of progress and success."[36]

The concept of the educational center was a new one for Des Moines Catholics, who thought in terms of either Catholic schooling or after-hours CCD. Dingman encountered complaints from both sides, who felt he favored one over the other. Instead, he urged people to stop thinking in such polarizing terms, urging instead a concept of "total religious education," which encompassed all

New Dowling. Credit: Dowling High School Archives.

existing options and above all urged a continual growth in faith throughout the life of a typical Catholic.[37] Father Gregory Baum, OSA, a noted Canadian theologian active at Vatican II, inaugurated the Christian Culture Lecture for the new institute.[38]

On May 14, 1972, Archbishop Luigi Raimondi, apostolic delegate to the United States, flew to Des Moines to dedicate the new education center.[39] As the celebrations were taking place, graduates of St. Joseph's Academy were bidding a fond farewell to their beloved school: "We leave this place soon," noted Sister Mary Roberta Kuhn, president of the BVM sisters, "closing a chapter in the history of the BVM community and the Des Moines community as well. But everything important we gained here we will take with us. It will live as long as we do."[40] The last class graduated 210 young women. In all, St. Joseph's Academy had given diplomas to 5,198 women over the eighty-seven years of its existence. Its impact on the community was incalculable. Even today, its former site—inhabited by an osteopathic medical school—is still beautiful.

Relocation

Dowling's move out of the city was not without its critics, and other transfers were also subjected to similar scrutiny. This included the Bishop Drumm Home, which had been founded in 1939 by Bishop

Bergan and the Sisters of Mercy. By the late 1970s, the area around the home was declining and the sisters announced a plan to relocate the home in Johnston, a thriving suburb near St. Mary of Nazareth Parish. As with the Dowling move, strong opposition was voiced by clergy and local residents. From the pulpit at St. Joseph Church, Father David Polich expressed admiration for the Sisters of Mercy and liked the idea of having the home near a working parish, but he underscored his opposition to the move: "I realize the Home is not located in the best neighborhood in the city, but is it the Christian response to run? I see it as a negative witness." Father John Zeitler expressed his displeasure with the process in the Holy Trinity Parish bulletin, noting that many of the members of the Drumm board resided in west-side or northwest-side city parishes. "None of the less affluent parishes are represented. Any other questions?"[41] Nonetheless, the move was made. A new ten-acre site in Johnston was secured and a new facility prepared. In late September 1980, the move took place.[42]

Engaging a Wider World: Social Justice

The moral and spiritual implications of urban affairs were just the beginning of public engagement in social issues. In many states the task of monitoring the acts of the legislature fell to the local bishop of the diocese, who may have had a priest who could keep tabs. Bishops of Des Moines may have performed this task, but the job of lobbying the state on behalf of the church was substantially upgraded when, in 1966, the bishops of Iowa gathered to form the Iowa Catholic Conference—the official lobbying arm of the Catholic churches of the Hawkeye State. This body tracked governmental activity on welfare, health, education, and other relevant issues on behalf of the church. In 1969, Timothy McCarthy, a lawyer and a member of St. Augustin's Parish, was named its first executive director, and Vern Feldman, a youth probation officer from Linn County, became the head of the Social Welfare Department of the council.[43] McCarthy and Feldman kept a close eye on legislative activity in the Iowa statehouse.

Rome continued to process conciliar changes and send them to the newly invigorated national bishops' conferences for consideration, adaptation, and implementation. In the late 1960s, the US bishops reconfigured the National Catholic Welfare Conference, creating two new organizations: a United States Catholic Conference (USCC), which would draw on the expertise of priests, religious, and laity to address social and theological issues, and a United States Conference of Catholic Bishops (USCCB) to function as a collegial body for the American bishops. The two parts of the conference were to work in tandem—the USCC providing ideas, position papers, and critical study; the bishops suggesting or receiving these issues and then pondering them in their own respective committees and annual plenary sessions. There were many issues to consider as the United States underwent some serious internal political and social upheavals in the 1960s and 1970s. The conferences played a big role in American Catholic life until 1998, when its powers were limited by the motu proprio of Pope St. John Paul II, *Apostolos Suos*. Dingman played an active role in the USCCB, representing the concerns of his state and region to the wider body of bishops.

Catholics, Contraception, and Public Policy

The invention and safe use of hormonal oral contraceptives provided a window into changing Catholic priorities and produced some interesting engagement with public policy.

Artificial contraception had been banned and considered seriously sinful by the Catholic Church since the 1930s and even before. When the Pill was invented in the 1950s and approved for general distribution in the 1960s, a lively debate broke out among Catholic moral theologians, population control experts, and physicians over the validity of its use for Catholic couples.[44] Even though the "ordinary teaching" was formally upheld, more and more Catholic women began to use the Pill—and did not always feel as though they were committing mortal sin. By the time of Vatican II, the fathers of the council wanted to debate the issue, but it was removed from conciliar deliberation and handed over to a ten-person committee by Pope John XXIII. Pope Paul VI expanded the commission to sixty and Catholics lined up on both sides of the issue.

In the United States in 1965, in *Griswold v. Connecticut*, the Supreme Court knocked down anti-contraception laws in Connecticut and elsewhere. At the same time, local communities began developing family planning policies in conjunction with government-sponsored urban aid and anti-poverty programs. Planned Parenthood, a reproductive rights group founded in 1916, also began distributing information about the use of contraceptives. Contraceptive use became more common—even among Catholic women. Catholic families, which had traditionally been large, became smaller.

The local Des Moines Catholic leadership naturally adhered closely to the church's prohibitions on artificial contraception. This became problematic when the local Planned Parenthood organization submitted a plan to the Washington Office of Economic Opportunity (OEO)—a War on Poverty program of the Johnson administration—calling for a family planning service for low-income areas in Des Moines. This proposal was submitted through the local Community Action Organization—also set up by the federal War on Poverty to elicit grassroots support for effective anti-poverty measures. Overpopulation or having more babies than a family could support was tagged as one of the reasons for persistent poverty. Catholics often supported anti-poverty programs (such as Head Start, Job Corps, or Model Cities) but hesitated when federal money was attached to things they felt were immoral or contrary to the teaching of the church.

Des Moines Catholic authorities reacted negatively, decrying the application's approval and filing a sharp minority report about the violation of conscience entailed in the proposal. Making various types of contraceptive information and devices available was unacceptable. Father Daniel Clarke at *The Messenger* issued a strong condemnation of the proposal, laying out Catholic objections to artificial contraception and in particular its availability to unmarried women. He urged the OEO to reject the petition because it did not have wider community support. When Planned Parenthood insisted that preventing unplanned pregnancies was saving taxpayers money through less spending on health and education programs, Clarke insisted that limiting births was not the best way and lamented that the local "power brokers" could have gotten behind early education programs like Head Start instead of this one.[45]

Reactions to Clarke's anti–birth control articles and editorials reflected the new spectrum of opinion that was emerging among Catholics on issues that were thought to be fixed and unchangeable.

Some correspondents praised the editor for holding up Catholic teachings. One correspondent, however, Jeanie Shuck of Des Moines, wrote: "Your paper prints news against birth control to the exclusion of any liberal attitudes that may exist in the Catholic Church." Shuck insisted, quoting the comments of a University of Notre Dame paper that urged a change in church teaching: "There is evidence that contraception is not intrinsically evil and in fact in some circumstances it could be permitted and even recommended." She took on the argument for what would be called "natural family planning": "I have known families faced with trying to control their family numbers by the rhythm method. The psychological damage caused by the least effective method of limiting human births can truly be dehumanizing."

Father Clarke replied sharply, batting away Shuck's complaints about his coverage of the "radically liberal viewpoints concerning birth control" and deriding them as mere "opinions" and those who advanced them as "pseudo authorities." To those who suffered "psychological damage" from the ineffective use of rhythm methods, he lectured, "The Church cannot be blamed for the failure of medical science to perfect better methods." Moreover, the paper was small, he argued, and he could not possibly include everything.[46]

In July 1968, Pope Paul VI came out with the long-awaited encyclical *Humanae Vitae*, in which he upheld the traditional ban on all forms of artificial contraception. Dingman loyally, but probably with qualms, supported the Holy Father. "At this moment, I call on the people of the diocese of Des Moines to give loyal obedience to this teaching of the Church. This document contains the authentic teaching of the Church, and is binding on the consciences of all Catholics." He did, however, urge the flock not to consider this decision as a matter of victory or defeat and counseled "compassion for those who will experience great difficulty in their efforts to achieve the lofty ideal held up for us by Pope Paul."[47] Catholics in Des Moines would be polarized on this issue.

Catholic Workers and Des Moines: Frank Cordaro

Birth control and later abortion would become the paramount social issues on the agenda of the Catholic Church in Iowa and

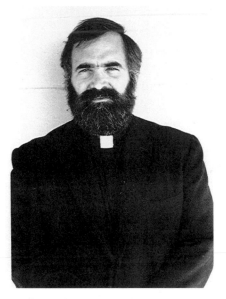

Frank Cordaro as young priest.
Credit: Diocese of Des Moines
Archives.

elsewhere. Other Iowa Catholics, however, assigned higher priority to urban poverty and systemic injustice. Under Dingman, these issues received considerable attention. Deeply committed activists opened up two Catholic Worker Houses in Des Moines that radically challenged attitudes toward the poor and embraced a philosophy of nonviolence. Based on the work of Dorothy Day and Peter Maurin, the houses were sites of hospitality for the poor. One of the cofounders of the Catholic Worker houses in Des Moines was Frank Cordaro.

Cordaro was from an Italian-Catholic family in Des Moines.[48] Born in 1951, he attended Catholic grade school and then went on to Dowling High, where his father was a popular coach. A popular athlete and president of his class and of the student body, Cordaro's goal was to be like his father, who died tragically on Easter Sunday of his senior year (1969).

After pursuing an undergraduate degree in physical education, Cordaro decided to study for the priesthood, and Dingman accepted him as a student for the diocese. He was sent to Aquinas Institute in Dubuque, and it was during his years of theological study that he experienced a deep conversion to social justice activism. He spent one summer at an African American and Puerto Rican parish in South Bronx, an experience that opened him up to the gritty realities of urban poverty and violence.

A second summer was spent at a Catholic Worker House in Davenport, where he came under the influence of one Margaret Quigley who explained the philosophy of the Worker. He devoured William Miller's classic biography of Day, *A Harsh and Dreadful Love*, and was encouraged by the positive response he received from Bishop Dingman about Day and her works. As he noted in many venues, the experience with the Catholic Worker Movement reshaped his ideas about ministry and provided an ideological and spiritual home for his activist spirit. He returned to Aquinas to finish his studies but dropped out of the seminary when he fell in love with a woman who shared his ideas. Cordaro and Joseph DaVia opened the first Catholic Worker House (now called the Philip Berrigan House) in September 1976 at 713 Indiana Street. They were later joined by Edward Polich. The residence could hold between eight and twelve people. Cordaro, DaVia, and Polich were the staff who welcomed the guests and helped support the project by begging and outside jobs.

Although the diocese had no formal affiliation with the house, Dingman supported it financially and otherwise, appearing on March 19, 1977, to bless the residence (the feast of St. Joseph). The house was soon overwhelmed with guests and when opportunities to expand presented themselves, Cordaro and others took them.

In 1977, a second Catholic Worker House opened next door named the Monsignor Luigi Ligutti House of Hospitality at 1301 Eighth Street (today named the Rachel Corrie House). Among its staff was Father John Zeitler, a priest of the Erie diocese who had come to Des Moines and served for a time at Holy Trinity Parish. Zeitler had met Dorothy Day in the 1950s before entering the seminary. He also made contacts with Mother Teresa of Calcutta and Jean Vanier, the founder of L'Arche, a ministry to the severely disabled. Committed to inner-city work after his ordination, he toiled in the central city and suburbs and managed to secure a master's degree in social work at the University of Pittsburgh. He came to Des Moines in 1974 and dedicated himself to social justice ministry.[49]

In 1989, a third house, called Bishop Dingman House, was opened at 1310 Seventh Street. Although not connected to the Des Moines houses, a Strangers and Guests Catholic Worker Farm was opened in Maloy by Brian Terrell and Betsy Keenan. Rehabilitating these houses brought lots of volunteer efforts from students at Dowling High (where Cordaro would later be inducted into the athletic hall of fame) to the Knights of Columbus. Other helpful guests and volunteers helped to fix the houses (some of which were on the verge of condemnation) and to supply the needs of the feeding program, which eventually located itself at the Bishop Dingman House. The Catholic Workers put out a simple mimeographed newsletter called *Via Pacis* (the way of peace).[50]

Viewed from an external perspective, although these houses were not officially affiliated with the local Catholic Church, they used Catholic ideas and inspiration and local priests, deacons, religious, and laity to help them along. They helped, with other private agencies (e.g., Salvation Army and Rescue missions), to shore up the safety net in the city of Des Moines.

Cordaro continued his journey as a peace activist. In 1979, he dramatically dumped fire-lace ashes and issued a statement denouncing nuclear weaponry in the presence of President Jimmy Carter at a conference held at the White House to discuss the SALT II Treaty.[51] In December 1980, he and others changed the wording on a sign at Offutt Air Force Base outside of Omaha from "Peace is our Profession" to "War is Our Profession." Arrested and charged with damaging federal property, he was given probation. When he missed a court appearance while protesting the trial of Gary Eklund, who was the first Iowan to resist mandatory draft registration, he was sent to jail.[52] Cordaro would spend many months in jail or local lock-ups for various acts of civil disobedience.

In 1983, Cordaro went back to his seminary studies and weathered the difficult reintroduction to seminary life at Saint John's Seminary in Collegeville, Minnesota. After a brief diaconal stint in

Bishop Dingman celebrating Mass at DMCW, December 1981. Credit: Courtesy of the Department of Special Collections and University Archives, Marquette University Libraries.

Corning, he was ordained to the priesthood in 1985 by Dingman; he was first assigned to rural Harrison County, where he served on a pastoral team and tried to immerse himself in the issues of his rural parishioners and the farm crisis.

Not all priests were willing to engage in civil disobedience like Cordaro, but they did embrace Vatican II's call for greater engagement in the world. Already in 1975, the Council of Priests had begun forming a Peace and Justice Committee that would coordinate with the Catholic Council for Social Concerns. Newly ordained Father David Polich, who had been mentored in social justice issues by his parents and also during his seminary formation at Moreau Seminary of the University of Notre Dame, eagerly joined the group, and the committee became a clearinghouse for social justice issues. Polich recalled that the committee took stands on conditions in Central America and the arms race, but also on local issues, like the decision to relocate the Drumm Home from its urban site to Johnston.[53]

One of the initiatives of social action–minded priests and Des Moines Catholics was the formation of a consciousness-raising organization known as the Catholic Peace Ministry. The origins of this were with the Peace and Justice Committee of the Council of Priests. As Father David Polich recalled, this body had created a Disarmament Task Force, which focused on the revived nuclear Arms race of the Reagan era. Polich and others (Frank Cordaro and Bob Brammer) decided to pursue the hiring of a staffperson for the task force.[54]

The result was the hiring of Franciscan Sister Gwen Hennessey, OSF, who was invited to head the new enterprise. Hennessey had entered the Franciscans of Dubuque in 1951 at the age of seventeen. She spent many years teaching grade school and catechism but took summers to work with the poor—spending one period alongside farmworkers who were organizing in California under the leadership of Cesar Chavez. Her brother, a Maryknoll priest stationed in Guatemala, wrote letters home decrying the tyranny of landholders and the rich. In 1979 Hennessey stepped down from teaching and became involved with Clergy and Laity Concerned, a social action group located in Chicago. She took classes with the Jesuits, who then had a school of theology in Hyde Park, studying with famed liberation theologian Roger Haight, SJ. Her sister, also a religious, was a peace activist.

Dingman approved of her hiring and the diocese made a $500 contribution of seed money for the ministry. When she came to Des Moines in 1981, Hennessey faithfully served the mission of the task force, educating and mobilizing people around the issue of nuclear disarmament. She also threw her energies into raising the consciousness about American foreign policy in Central America. Even though the organization had the name "Catholic," it was truly an ecumenical endeavor and was first housed in the American Friends Service Committee at Forty-Second and Grand in Des Moines.

Later, in July 1985, Dingman moved the work into the chancery and provided it a small budget and resources. (Sister Gwen had a car and apartment rent.) Hennessey and her coworkers helped raise awareness about international issues of peace and justice. She invited speakers to the diocese such as Fathers Bryan Hehir and Robert Drinan, who were articulate exponents of Catholic social teaching. Other speakers included antiwar activist Philip Berrigan and columnist Colman McCarthy. Her advocacy of Central American refugees caused her to offer shelter to people fleeing for their lives, and she also helped them navigate the legal system. Dingman strongly supported the ministry and encouraged Sister Gwen's work with Central American refugees. She held her post until 1992, when she departed to study at Maryknoll.[55]

As head of the diocese, Dingman's stands on controversial issues naturally drew the most attention and the support of many Catholics in southwest Iowa. Unlike any other bishop in the history of the diocese, Dingman spoke out on a number of public issues in sometimes very forceful ways. He always tried to ground his public positions on the writings of Vatican II and his collegial interactions with his fellow bishops. He listened to people of a variety of viewpoints (although he was never favorably inclined toward the views of conservatives) and absorbed an immense amount of criticism without wanting to retaliate.

Although not a scholar, he did understand basic issues, read and consulted widely, and felt keenly the need to lead his community, even at the risk of being unpopular. His strongly held positions on certain topics such as defense policy, international relations, and the penal system may not have enjoyed the support of many in the diocese—priests, religious, or laity—and hence cannot provide a totally accurate picture of the influence of the Catholic Church. Des Moines had never had a bishop, however, as forthright in his advocacy of economic justice, prison reform, capital punishment, the role of women, foreign policy, especially in South and Central America, and the arms buildup of the Reagan years. In the end, many, though not all, of the positions he espoused were quite prophetic.

Taking a Stand on the Farm Crisis

Dingman had grown up on an Iowa farm. He knew rural Iowa, talked with its people, understood their problems, and believed, as did many Catholic rural life activists, that the country life and the hard work of the farm was spiritually uplifting and purifying. He also seemed to have a bit of the Iowa populist in him—suspicious of big concentrations of wealth and power—and was often uncomfortable with the wealthy.

Until felled by a stroke in 1986, Dingman would be a strong voice for the needs of rural America. Family farms, like that of his father's, began to disappear, and rural communities (and parishes) lost members. Elected president of the chief Catholic lobbying arm of the American hierarchy for rural issues, the National Catholic Rural Life Conference in 1977, he studied the complex issues surrounding this transition. He also learned from the rural parishes of the Des Moines diocese.

Young people did not want to stay on the farms. A parish profile of St. Mary's in Panama in heavily Catholic Shelby County noted in May 1980: "Relatively few of the young people are able to stay here and farm or live and even fewer will be able to farm into the future. There are a sizeable group of unmarried guys. . . . We do not have a man with a college degree in the parish, and only several women. Many of those over fifty never had a high school education. . . . The small farmer that is most of our people, are in a struggle for survival."[56] Dingman pondered this and other reports from his farming counties. From pastors, Dingman heard of other dysfunctions in rural parishes: alcoholism, premarital pregnancy, spousal abuse, and chronic debt.

In an address picked up by the National Catholic News Service at Thanksgiving time, Dingman lamented the abuses of the land:

farming methods that caused high soil losses; the conversion of millions of acres to feed urban sprawl; highway development and dams that scarred the natural landscape; strip mining, which devastated rural communities and altered the nature of land. He noted: "Who will control the land? We see productive land shifting from small landowners into the lands of large farmers, developers, speculators, and other outside interests."[57] These issues would consume his time and interest in the 1980s.

Already in 1978, Dingman took the lead in producing a major document in defense of humane farm policies titled *Strangers and Guests*, crafted by a committee of nine Midwestern bishops and twelve diocesan representatives and endorsed by forty-four Midwestern dioceses. Dingman helped shepherd the document through several drafts and offered substantial input. In March 1980, Dingman hosted a meeting of the committee in Des Moines.[58] It was officially issued on May 1, 1980. In late March 1981, he marched at the head of a crowd of six hundred people and labor leaders at a Rally for Jobs and Human Dignity sponsored by several farm, labor, and church organizations.[59]

In February 1982, he welcomed nine hundred protestors to St. Ambrose Cathedral marching to the state capitol to demonstrate against President Ronald Reagan, who had been invited to address the legislators. A "Heartland Declaration to President Reagan" decried the president's economic program and was signed by various Catholic leaders. Dingman himself spoke to the crowd and urged, "Let us do whatever we have to do humbly."[60]

At an ecumenical forum at St. Peter's Church, Des Moines, in September 1982, Dingman and Bishop L. David Brown of the American Lutheran church shared their concerns for rural life. Brown stressed the value of the land and the family farm, decrying the lack of resources in rural America. Dingman spoke of Shelby County as the farming center of southwest Iowa and asked, "Did you ever think in your wildest dreams that corn would drop below $2.00 a bushel? . . . You are not getting a fair price. . . . I think you should bargain collectively."[61]

Dingman's advocacy of the family farm continued into the remainder of the decade as long as he was bishop. In 1984, he and the other bishops of Iowa issued another pastoral on the farm crisis.

Dingman's advocacy for the beleaguered farmers was steady. His highest moment of visibility came in February 1985, when he made a dramatic appearance at a National Crisis Action Rally held in the Hilton Coliseum of Iowa State University at Ames organized by the National Farmers Organization.

Nearly fifteen thousand people crammed into the auditorium from twenty states to hear speeches condemning the farm policies of the Reagan administration. Dingman's speech, noted the *New York Times*, "gave an emotional warning of a threat he saw to farm life." In a way reminiscent of the great Populist orator William Jennings Bryan, Dingman dramatically held up a white cross before the thousands of people in the stadium. This cross, on which Jesus died, was also representative of the crucifixion many farmers were feeling as they faced the loss of their homes and farms. He warned: "I come before you today to tell you, if we do nothing, the bells will have tolled for the American dream. . . . We have forgotten our roots as a people of the land, roots as a people of faith and roots to stretch to the dream of our ancestors. And now we are in grave danger of losing the land."

His speech brought the crowd in the Hilton Coliseum to their feet to pledge resistance to policies that killed the family farm.[62] Farm foreclosures were a sad part of rural life in Iowa. In Harrison County,

Bishop Maurice Dingman holding cross at National Crisis Action Rally. Credit: Diocese of Des Moines Archives.

Father Frank Cordaro noted the tragic sales and tried to offer support and even resistance to these auctions. In 1985, he described the sale of the property of Bob and Theresa Sullivan, "a deacon in our Church and a lifelong farmer from Earling, Iowa." Sitting with the Sullivans as the "debtors were there to pick over the carcass to make sure nothing was missing," he noted, "It was all done in a cold and calculating manner. Little human warmth at this wake. . . . It was not easy to sit next to Theresa as tears came to her eyes while she dug in her purse for a Kleenex."[63] The activist Cordaro dramatized the sales, at one point planting seventy-four crosses to symbolize the seventy-four sheriff sales in Harrison County from 1980 to 1985. Other priests, deacons, and laypersons offered support and sympathy to the farmers who lost their land.

In March 1986, the daily *USA Today* interviewed a host of religious leaders about their Good Friday and Easter messages. Dingman repeated the theme of his speech: "We in Iowa are in a farm crisis. This week is very meaningful to farmers in my diocese. . . . Historically, a farmer carried the cross behind our Lord (Simon of Cyrene). . . . In our own times, these farmers are carrying . . . the cross of unjust prices, a cross of being ignored by their government by other parts of our economy. . . . Present days farmers are carrying the beam of their own bankruptcies."[64]

Prison Ministry

No other bishop took note of civic affairs as did Dingman. His misgivings about the Dowling move and the accusations that the church was abandoning the city struck a nerve. He believed he had to be an active participant in the life of the city. In 1977 he was asked by the Polk County board of supervisors to chair a committee that would study conditions at Polk County correctional institutions. He accepted the task, as he later noted, "to dispel the widespread myth that Catholic bishops interest themselves in only two issues: Catholic schools and abortion." He and the twelve other commission members visited the Polk County jail. To draw attention to the poor conditions at the jail, he agreed to spend a night in a jail cell together with fellow commission member Rabbi Jay Goldberg of Tifereth Israel Synagogue in Des Moines. The experience was token but unnerving. This jail and the others were dilapidated, with harsh lighting and poor conditions for prisoners. Lying in the cell, he was constantly awakened. Pictures of him in prison attire made the local newspapers.

To bring about change in these jails required public awareness and agreement to fund a new facility. He enlisted the help of Bernard Vogelsang, the director of court services for Iowa's fifth judicial district. Vogelsang had many years of experience with the penal system and had long argued for a more humane system that provided better sanitary conditions, decent quarters for the imprisoned, and a justice system that placed an emphasis on reconciliation rather than punishment. Dingman publicly urged Polk County residents to pass a new bond issue to build a new correctional facility.[65] The bond issue lost by 1 percent, but the next year it passed resoundingly.[66]

Justice in the Wider World

Dingman's social conscience was not restricted to southwest Iowa. When assassins gunned down Archbishop Oscar Romero of El Salvador in March 1980 while he celebrated Mass, Dingman joined a march in downtown Des Moines in company with Maryknoll Father Roy Bourgeois to protest the slaying.[67] Deeply influenced by journalist Penny Lernoux's *The Cry of the People*, and its account of fourteen families who controlled El Salvador, he drew analogies with the twelve companies that controlled US agriculture.

Sister Gwen Hennessey's work raising awareness of conditions in Latin America and the perils of American policy also had an influence on the bishop. In 1985, when he traveled with diocesan missionary Father Paul Koch to Bolivia, Guatemala, El Salvador, and Nicaragua, he prayed at Romero's tomb. With Hennessey's and Koch's tutelage and his own study, Dingman became a sharp critic of Reagan-era policy in Central America.

When he arrived in the Nicaraguan capital he heard the news that the United States was providing $27 million to aid the contras in their battle with the leftist Sandinista government of Nicaragua. "The very day we visit Nicaragua would be the very day that I would suffer the humiliation of my country financing the contras whose torture, rape, kidnapping, murder and other acts of terrorism against the population of Nicaragua are well known."

On this trip he sought out and visited Maryknoll Father Miguel d'Escoto, the foreign minister of the country who was fasting, and spent an uncomfortable fifteen minutes with him where the Nicaraguan spoke only intermittently. Dingman tried to explain to the American press the reasons behind d'Escoto's service to Nicaragua despite his suspension as a priest by the Vatican. On his return, he stood with Bishops Walter Sullivan of Richmond and auxiliary Thomas Gumbleton of Detroit to denounce the Reagan administration's actions in the region, noting a prayer petition he heard: "That President Reagan would leave us alone."

Speaking Out on American Defense Policy: The Nuclear Option

His dissatisfaction with Reagan-era politics extended as well to the arms build-up of the era. Dingman took aim at what he considered the dangerous nuclear policies of the government and the ratcheting up of tensions with the Soviet Union. In 1980, the diocese began sending small donations to the Disarmament Task Force of the Council of Priests, dedicated to challenging the acceleration of the nuclear arms race under Reagan.

Dingman and social action priests of the diocese closely followed the deliberations of the American bishops who undertook a serious examination of nuclear weaponry and the morality of the first strike. Increased emphasis on nuclear weapons as a deterrent to Soviet aggression was one of the thrusts of the defense policy of the Reagan years. Reagan had also proposed a fanciful idea (derisively nicknamed Star Wars) to identify and destroy incoming enemy missiles out of the sky—thereby enhancing the prospect of America "winning" a potential nuclear exchange with the Soviets.

Dingman enthusiastically endorsed the efforts of his brother bishops in the National Conference of Catholic Bishops, strongly rejecting the idea of a nuclear first strike and asserting the right of the bishops to speak out on this matter, even if it incurred the ire of some Catholics. "Arms control may well be a political issue," he noted, "but . . . it is a political issue with moral implications." Dingman insisted: "We must embark on a process that will eventually eliminate all nuclear weapons."[68]

In late February 1983, Dingman scheduled ten listening sessions around the diocese to hear the views of Iowans on the subject of the proposed pastoral.[69] In May 1983, the bishops issued "The Challenge of Peace: God's Promise and Our Response," which posed a serious challenge to the arms policies of the Reagan administration. Dingman was an enthusiastic supporter: "I want to see that letter implemented in every detail."[70]

When confronted by the further build-up of nuclear weapons by the United States, Dingman and others grew more militant. In February 1985, Dingman and the Social Justice Committee of the Council of Priests sponsored a conference/retreat called Faith and Resistance at Holy Rosary Church in Glenwood. Over six hundred people attended the sessions led by Jim Wallis of *Sojourners* and Father Daniel Berrigan, SJ, with several others. One of the key speakers was Thomas Cordaro, a brother of Frank and already well known for his embrace of nonviolent passive resistance.[71]

The Glenwood gathering offered opportunities to pray and study about nonviolent resistance but also encouraged them to act.[72] The group, with Dingman, went to the gates of the Strategic Air Command at Offutt Air Force Base outside of Omaha, where several of them crossed a forbidden line and were arrested. One of them, Mrs. Angela Cordaro, explained how her sons Thomas and Frank taught her about poverty and social justice. This helped her, she said, to see the connections between poverty and the arms build-up. At the Faith and Resistance conference/retreat she gathered the courage, along with 226 others, including priests and sisters, to cross the line.[73]

Dingman seriously pondered walking with them and submitting to arrest. But he stood back, explaining that he and a group of like-minded bishops were going into a retreat near Omaha and planned to go to Offutt again on November 27 and there decide whether to just pray or "engage in a non-violence act of civil disobedience."[74] He was still pondering this when a stroke took him down in 1986.

After the rally, Dingman flew to Washington to stand at the side of Congressmen Byron Dorgan of North Dakota and Thomas Daschle of South Dakota to deplore Reagan's veto of $4.5 billion for farm credit while at the same time pressing for the building of the MX missile for the same amount. Dingman condemned the MX as "immoral" and his comments were picked up by the National Catholic Press Service. He linked the money withdrawn from the farm economy and spent on weapons of mass destruction as two sides of the same crisis.[75] Dingman returned with demonstrators to Offutt in August 1985 and broached his plans to walk across the line and submit to arrest for nonviolent protest.[76] In the end, he held back.

How much did this influence the people of southwest Iowa? How much did it anger them? Likely, Dingman received letters from both groups. Nevertheless, he put Des Moines on the map by his actions. By 1985, more and more people took note of the "moral activism" of Bishop Maurice Dingman, including syndicated columnist Colman McCarthy, who noted the opposition the bishop had been receiving. "In the opinion of many, Dingman deserves to be locked up." But McCarthy also recognized the introspection and tentativeness with which Dingman approached his decisions: "Where do you go and how far do you get ahead of your people? Where do you place yourself?"[77]

Dingman must have worried about the impact of his statements and actions, and although he appeared to be quite sure of himself, and not troubled too much by doubts about his beliefs, the opposition he received for his positions from fellow bishops and some of his own priests and fellow Catholics troubled him. In a letter to one of his seminarians, who was also a social activist, he wrote: "You are suffering a great deal for your beliefs and you are suffering within the institutional church. This is true of Bishop [Thomas] Gumbleton [of Detroit], Father [Marvin] Mottet [of Davenport], Father [Roy] Bourgeois [Maryknoll]. . . . I would like to be classed in that same group. I am asking you to suffer that same misunderstanding."[78]

Dingman and the Equal Rights Amendment

He also stood out by being one of the few US Catholic bishops to endorse the Equal Rights Amendment to the Constitution. His reason: he did not want to be on the wrong side of history. "It is an interesting historical note that the bishops of the United Sates opposed women's suffrage when this was debated. Could we be in a similar position when the history of our time is written that the subject is the Equal Rights Amendment?"[79] In 1982, the amendment failed to gain the necessary states for ratification. Dingman's concern for the welfare and rights of women was genuine. He brought many women into positions of authority in the diocese and expressed guarded sympathy for the ordination of women.

Continued Ethnic Accommodation: Mexicans and Southeast Asian Refugee Resettlement

The Catholic Church in Des Moines had never taken a respite from its care of immigrants and provided significant spiritual and material assistance to the next waves of newcomers. In the late 1960s, the cause of Latino people also merged with issues of racism, societal injustice to farm workers, and Catholic Church advocacy for their right to organize and bargain collectively. Further, ethnic pride and self-consciousness also attached itself to church work with Latinos. Catholic images and icons—particularly, for Mexicans, the image of Our Lady of Guadalupe—served as sources of faith and collective identity.

Southwest Iowa Catholics had been ministering to Mexicans since the 1940s. Railroad workers in Valley Junction were among the first to receive care. For years, the priest assigned to "Mexican Work" was Father Henry C. Pouget, a native of France. Enticed to the southwest by the stories of French missionaries to the Indians and the Mexicans, Pouget came to America and was ordained by Archbishop Jean Baptiste Salpointe of Santa Fe. In addition to being a skilled musician (organist and chant leader), Pouget was also multilingual (his native French, Spanish, Latin, and English) and did missionary work by horseback, at one point meeting Billy the Kid, but he ran into problems in Santa Fe.[80] He taught for a while in Maryland but eventually ended up as a missionary in the Canal Zone, remaining until the canal was built and earning praise from George W. Goethals, the chief engineer of the Panama Canal.[81]

He incardinated into the Diocese of Des Moines in 1914 and there, while chaplain of Mercy Hospital, he took care of a mission of St. John's Parish in Highland Park. This eventually became All Saints

Parish. He served at pastorates in Maloy and Lenox. After forty-three years of priesthood and no shortage of problems at Lenox as well as a near fatal car accident, Bishop Bergan urged him to move to Dowling College in 1935. "I shall give you $40 a month and you could take care of the Mexicans at Valley Junction and Des Moines. . . . We could start a little Mexican Mission at Valley Junction." Pouget took charge of ministry to the Spanish-speaking people "in and near Des Moines" until his health broke down. He died in March 1948.

Pouget had never been able to provide Mexican Catholics their own space. East-side Visitation Parish was the sponsor of the first permanent spiritual home for the city's Latinos. At the direction of Monsignor Hanson at Visitation Parish a small mission was begun in the 1940s in a five-room bungalow at SE Fifth and Scott Streets. The significance, culturally and spiritually, of providing an independent space to a community was an important benchmark for the city's Latino community. Rapid growth of the Mexican community led to the construction of a bigger chapel in honor of Our Lady of Guadalupe at SE Eighth and Scott.[82] Aided by a $10,000 grant from Visitation, and work from parish men, the new chapel, built under the direction of Father Othmar Kauffman, used lumber from an old store Visitation had purchased and a donation of a house by the John Brophy family. The 30-by-64-foot church had a concrete basement and stucco exterior. Kauffman made the pews, a local artist provided the painting of the Lady of Guadalupe, and altars and statuary donated from other churches and institutions finished off the interior. Bishop Daly presided at the occasion of the first Mass there as Mexican families and children sang hymns in a procession from the old home to the newly constructed chapel.[83] Overseen by Visitation and a host of assistant pastors over the years, the Spanish-speaking ministry flourished.

During the 1960s, the plight of farm workers in California and elsewhere had been focused by the work of Cesar Chavez, a Catholic layman who dramatized the difficult plight of farm workers (Mexicans and Filipinos) by organizing the United Farm Workers (UFW). The UFW attempted to organize workers and called for boycotts of grapes and lettuce harvested by workers afraid to join the union. In Iowa, Latino activism began to pick up steam and local churches and priests were invited to participate. In 1972, Dingman invited the nation's first Mexican American bishop, Patricio Flores of San Antonio, to celebrate a festive Mass at St. Ambrose. Recognition of Hispanic needs by the Catholic Church was a pivotal part of integrating this growing community into the wider ambit of Des Moines life.

Ministry to the Spanish-speaking population now expanded. Des Moines priests with bilingual gifts, such as Father David Polich, had worked with the growing numbers of Mexicans, many of whom worshiped at Visitation Parish's Our Lady of Guadalupe mission. In 1972, Colombian-born Father Luis Lesmes began service to the diocese, the first native-born Spanish speaker to serve in the diocese. Lesmes, ordained in 1962, had come to the United States in 1967 and worked in radio in Chicago. He came to Des Moines, attracted by the work of Bishop Dingman, and worked with Polich and Spanish-speaking coordinator, Eddie Zamora.[84] Lesmes wrote occasionally for *The Catholic Mirror* and kept alive the activity of the Guadalupe Chapel attached to Visitation Parish.[85] Several diocesan priests, including Father James Polich, studied Spanish and were able to minister to the growing numbers of Hispanics in the diocese. Later, the Hispanic community would find one of several spiritual homes in Des Moines at the old Visitation Church, renamed it Our Lady of the Americas.

As Hispanic needs were being recognized and tended to by the Catholic community, the aftermath of the Vietnam War brought hundreds of thousands of Southeast Asian refugees to the United States. With active leadership of Dingman, a number of Vietnamese (including many "Boat People") refugees came to Des Moines, where they created their own cultural enclave. Many of them were Catholics and found a worship home at St. Peter's Parish in Des Moines. At the October 4 papal Mass, Vietnamese Catholics in native attire were among those who presented the gifts to the pontiff. Shortly after Pope John Paul's visit, Kenneth M. Quinn (the civilian coordinator for security at the October 4 Mass and later the US ambassador to Cambodia) joined Iowa Governor Robert Ray and four other American governors in visiting refugee camps in Thailand and the Cambodian border, where, as Quinn recalled, "we confronted a scene of human suffering right out of Dante's *Inferno*.[86]" Quinn and Ray were horror-stricken by the site of more than thirty thousand emaciated Cambodian refugees, survivors of the genocidal Khmer Rouge, but devastated by illness and starvation and dying at the rate of fifty to one hundred per day. Ray snapped pictures of the sad scenes that were later published in the *Des Moines Register*. Recalling the injunction of the pope to farmers to use their harvests to feed the hungry of the world, Dingman, Rabbi Jay Goldburg, and Bishop Frederick Strickland of Corinthian Baptist Church, who had been with the Holy Father on October 4, stepped forward to urge Governor Ray's leadership in addressing this human catastrophe. This led to Ray's founding of Iowa SHARES (Iowa Send Help to Aid Refugees and End Starvation), which raised more than $600,000 to ship food and medicine and to recruit Iowa volunteer medical workers to the refugee camps. Special sermons and collections occurred at many churches in the diocese as part of this effort. Catholic Relief Services was chosen to deliver the first shipment of food and medicine, most of which appropriately arrived on Christmas Day 1979. With Dingman's support, Ray also welcomed hundreds of Hmong and Laotian peoples who came to Des Moines. Many of them were rural people who required help adjusting to living in the United States.

Catholic Social Services was in charge of making accommodations and assigned diocesan resettlement director, Lawrence Breheny, who worked with Icthus Community Sister Patricia Scherer to help them find sponsors and homes.[87] Scherer, a former Dominican of Springfield, Illinois, formed a diocesan group of sisters who were rec-

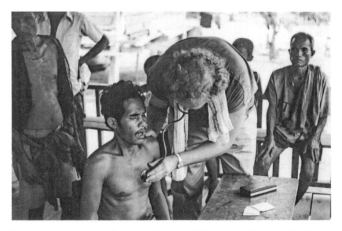

Doctor treating refugees. Credit: Governor Robert D. Ray.

ognized by Dingman. Later Sister Scherer directed the ministry until her retirement in 2014, assisted by Ly Pao Yang (later a permanent deacon) who helped as a staff catechist. Father Joseph McDonnell, who became pastor at St. Ambrose, helped provide a welcoming atmosphere for the mostly Southeast Asian community.[88] McDonnell's warm embrace continues to this day at the mother church of the diocese.

Dingman helped sustain the refugee program financially in any way he could. In 1984, he submitted to a "roast" by friends and colleagues that raised over $25,000 for this work in a rollicking event at the Des Moines Marriott.[89] One writer marveled at Dingman's willingness to be skewered by fellow bishops, a sitting governor and two of his predecessors, a rabbi, nuns, priests, judges, and journalists. "It was worth the money ($35 per plate) to hear his Excellency called 'Ding-Ding' and 'Mo.'" Dingman took it all in good humor, thanking the diners for helping him usher in "the winter of my life" and noting that a good cause is always preceded by suffering. "So I pray: 'send the suffering, Lord' because the sooner we get the suffering over, the sooner we'll get to victory."[90] Little did he know that his prayer would be answered two years later when he suffered a debilitating stroke.

The fairly liberal path laid out by Dingman was pursued in the belief that he was implementing the letter and the spirit of Vatican II. His engagement with local and national public affairs, his desire for collegiality, and his concerns for the fate of the church in the city drew him and the church more deeply into the life of southwest Iowa than ever before. These Catholic initiatives were perhaps the most overt and open evidence of how the Catholic Church played a role in the shaping of local culture and society. When the international leader of the Roman Catholic Church decided to pay a visit to the Des Moines area in 1979, however, the profile of the church was raised higher than it had ever been—or could have been—imagined by Catholics of the previous eras.

9

"Oh What a Splendid Day It Was"

The Papal Visit

Dingman was in Erlanger, Kentucky, on October 16, 1978, attending a consultation of Catholic Rural Life directors, when he heard the news of Cardinal Karol Wojtyla's election to the papacy. "I am pleased we have a pope from Poland. He has suffered greatly in his life along with his people, and we need that example of one who has lived that paschal mystery intensely."[1] Less than one year after hailing the new pontiff's election, Dingman would be standing at his side at the Living History Farms in Urbandale, welcoming him to Iowa and introducing him to people from Iowa and all over the Midwest.

Pope John Paul II Comes to the Heartland: A Historical First

The papal trip of October 1979 was a highlight not only in the history of the Diocese of Des Moines but for all Iowa and the Midwest. Even today it is hard to describe the enthusiasm and energy the trip generated, especially among those who were doing the planning. A permanent memento, the specially crafted quilt/banner that was the logo for the event, hangs in the lower level of the pastoral center of the diocese. The image also adorns diocesan stationery.

But as important as it was to Catholics, it was also a significant event in the religious history of Iowa itself. The papal visit put Iowa, especially metropolitan Des Moines, in the international eye for a day. Indeed, one newspaper account suggested that John Paul had drawn the biggest crowd ever gathered in Iowa.[2] Presidents, statesmen of various types, and prominent businesspeople had all traveled to the Hawkeye State, but few had the stature and public presence of the Bishop of Rome. No one in his or her wildest dreams could have imagined that the pope would travel to Iowa. Iowa Catholicism got a shower of positive attention it had never known—and that it happened in the traditionally Protestant southwest corner of the state was nothing short of remarkable.

Pope John Paul II was the most travelled pontiff in the history of the Catholic Church. He made 129 trips outside of Italy and seven alone to the United States. The first of these to the United States included the major cities of Boston, New York, Chicago, Washington, DC, and Des Moines.[3]

The idea of inviting the pope to visit Des Moines originated with Joseph Hayes, a Truro-area farmer. Hayes had attended several meetings discussing the pastoral *Strangers and Guests* and was moved by the reflections on the land and rural America. Monsignor Paul Con-

Joseph Hayes and Sister Mira Mosle with editors of
Catholic Voice in Omaha.
Credit: Sister Mosle Personal Collection.

nelly, pastor of Immaculate Conception Church in St. Mary's, Iowa, had gotten to know Hayes, who was a part-time farmer and full-time factory worker at a John Deere plant. After John Paul's plans to visit the United States were made public in 1979, Hayes suggested to Connelly that the pontiff should be invited to visit Iowa and that he planned to write a letter to the pope inviting him to Iowa. Connelly recommended that Hayes give it to the local bishop if he had any chance of it being taken seriously.

Hayes took him at his word and composed a letter. When Bishop Dingman appeared at a farewell luncheon Connelly threw for Dominican Sister Janet Michael, a diocesan director of communications, Hayes, who attended the gathering, asked for the attention of all at the table and read the contents of the letter. He then asked Bishop Dingman to do what he could to bring the pope to Iowa.[4] Perhaps at a gathering hosted by Ben and Peggy Haller, Dingman heard the suggestion of the Living History Farms at Urbandale. This lovely spot, set on rolling hills, would be perfect to highlight the rural beauty of Iowa's farmland. Dingman then touched base with his staff, who also supported the idea. He then sent a letter to Bishop Thomas Kelly, OP, the general secretary of the United States Catholic Conference, requesting the pope to come to Des Moines. Hayes's letter to the pontiff was enclosed.

Coordinating the Papal Extravaganza—
Church, Private Industry, and Local Government

To Dingman's shock, Monsignor Robert Lynch, the executive secretary of the US Conference of Catholic Bishops and the coordinator of papal travel in the United States, phoned the Des Moines bishop and asked him to draw up a proposal that would allow for a four-hour papal visit. A startled Dingman shared this at first with his chancellor Stephen Orr, who took the original phone call from Lynch.

Dingman then turned to his go-to man on many fronts, Father Frank Bognanno. Bognanno, who had recently attended one of John Paul's enthusiastic audiences in Rome, thought a visit might be possible and got to work right away. Bognanno's practical mind turned immediately to logistics: a large site, helicopters, motorcade, security, etc. A popular priest, he was also one of the diocese's bridges to the wider business community and facilitated their participation in the project. With a team of eleven others, he drafted the outlines of preparations and events for a papal visit. Inserting the hastily assembled plan in a leather-bound gold-ring-binder, Bognanno had it hand delivered to Kelly in Washington by a personal courier. He managed to coordinate all of the complex parts of the papal trip in six short weeks. Other dioceses required two years.

A week after the proposal was delivered, Dingman, Bognanno, and key staff were summoned to a meeting with Bishop Paul Marcinkus, a Chicago priest who worked in the Vatican and who was the point man for the American trip. He planned to come to Des Moines to scout out the possibilities. Marcinkus and Lynch noted the need to highlight rural America, but in a way that would not take too much time away from a visit to Chicago. Des Moines seemed perfect—just a short plane ride from Chicago. Bognanno scurried to put flesh on the bones of the proposals in the binder. He contacted a friend, Robert Galligan, CEO for the Gibbs Cook Implement Company in Des Moines, who promised six helicopters for the papal trip. Later, President Jimmy Carter offered the presidential helicopter, the "White Top," for the papal visit. Marcinkus came with Monsignor Lynch and the group, including Sister Mira Mosle, BVM, Chancellor Father Stephen Orr, local law enforcement, and of course Bishop Dingman, drove him to the proposed site.

When Marcinkus arrived, he asked if there was a small rural church the pope might visit. Bishop Dingman then took Marcinkus to the small St. Patrick's Church in Irish Settlement, which was opened for inspection. Next, they went to the Living History Farms, the Urbandale tourist site. When the group inspected the site, Marcinkus found a hill and said "Mass here." In a meeting later with Dingman, Marcinkus said he would recommend the pope visit Des Moines, which would include a visit to the Irish Settlement parish and an outdoor Mass at the Living History Farms. The date was eventually fixed for October 4, the liturgical feast of St. Francis of Assisi. After consulting Marcinkus, Dingman contacted Governor Ray about the possibility of a papal trip. Father Orr, with the help of Father Bognanno, was able to track down the governor on a river boat on the Mississippi. The governor gave his assurances that the state would be of assistance.[5]

In later discussions of why the pope chose this relatively remote area for a visit, some invoked the work of Monsignor Luigi Ligutti, whose advocacy of rural life was now legendary. But in an interview Marcinkus noted "the Joe Hayes connection. . . . John Paul is the kind of man who would be impressed by an invitation from a farmer and a factory worker from Truro who sat down and wrote a letter of invitation to the pope."[6] Perhaps, Marcinkus had also opined, the rolling Iowa hills would remind him of the countryside in his beloved Poland.

The final approval came by the last week of August, and on August 29, 1979, the news was shared with the general public. A smiling Hayes appeared on the front page of the *Des Moines Register* flanked by Dingman and William Murray, a professor of agricultural economics and chair of the board of the Living History Farms. A banner headline in the *Des Moines Register* proclaimed: "Proud Iowa Awaits the Pope."[7]

From that point forward Bognanno and his team planned and coordinated every major detail of this extraordinary event. The team included Sister Mira Mosle, BVM, communications director; Michael Walsh, diocesan finance director; Alvin Barcheski, a former official of local television station WHO; William Schaefer, head of the National Catholic Rural Life organization and a staff person from that organization, Sister Helen Vinton; Mary Ann Simcoe of the diocesan liturgy office; and Father Orr of the Chancery. Kenneth Quinn was the liaison with the governor's office.

Colonel Harold Thompson of the Iowa National Guard headed up all the logistics: highway patrol, other law enforcement, transportation, parking, and other emergency services. Thompson's professionalism and diligence were critical to the success of the gathering. He and others worked nonstop to coordinate the liturgical, spiritual, security, transportation, and logistical measures.[8]

Even before the formal announcement was made, Dingman and Bognanno used the basement level of the episcopal mansion as their general headquarters. Thirty phone lines were installed and cubicles were set up to deal with public relations, media, medical needs, and diocesan preparations for the event. When the trip was formally an-

Papal visit team. From left to right: Michael Walsh, diocesan finance director; Bob Galligan, president of Gibbs Cook Co., chair of the planning committee; Father (later Monsignor) Steve Orr; Sister Mira Mosle, communications director; Father (later Monsignor) Frank Bognanno; Bishop Dingman; Sister Helen Vinton from National Catholic Rural Life Conference; Nancy Stefani, Catholic Charities Development Office (her name then was Nancy Perazelli); and Al Barcheski, public relations consultant who had worked many years for WHO-TV. Credit: Diocese of Des Moines Archives.

nounced, Bognanno and Dingman spread the news that there would be room for everyone who wanted to come to see the Holy Father, and about 350,000 did so—the largest single religious gathering in the history of the state.

For fund-raising Dingman chose Richard Hunter, the director of development for the St. Joseph Educational Center, to lead the efforts and recruited R. W. "Bud" Kemin, head of Kemin Industries, to seek donors for the $1 million to $1.3 million needed to host the event.[9] The Meredith Printing Company provided significant support, producing a handsome coffee-table volume for sale to commemorate the event. Other memorial items were generated: lapel pins, cassette tapes, and a watercolor of Pope John Paul done by local artist Bill Fultz of Des Moines.

Plans for housing visitors were coordinated in part by the Chamber of Commerce. As the day of the visit drew near, local gas dealers were anxious about their supplies of fuel; road access to Urbandale and other related sites were blocked off, and commuters were told to seek alternate routes. The Polk County Board even decided on September 7 to give a paid holiday to employees, which was immediately contested by the Iowa Civil Liberties Union (ICLU)—suspended and then reinstated by a federal judge.[10]

The media were given daily doses of information as it became available through daily press conferences on the lawn of the episcopal residence. Various details emerged. One article noted the prohibition against women distributing Communion at the papal Mass. It was denounced as a "direct slap in the face" to women by the spokesperson for the Des Moines task force on justice for women in the church.[11] Local Poles were also unhappy that they did not have a more active role in planning and welcoming the pontiff—one of their own.[12] Since St. Patrick's Church in Irish Settlement had been without a pastor, almost as an afterthought Dingman appointed twenty-eight-year-old Father John Richter, who had only been ordained in June 1978, to head the community.[13]

Smoothing the ruffled feathers of those who felt they had a right to be closer to the pontiff required a lot of patience. The team took a calculated risk that the weather would be good and did not provide a shelter for the pope in case of inclement weather. Seeking the help of the Most High, the bishop's chapel became a daily prayer chapel with each Des Moines parish being assigned a specific day to pray for good weather.

The Papal Visit: An Iowa Event

As they unfolded over the years, Pope John Paul's visits often favored local preparations that highlighted the unique features of the place he stopped. He sought venues that accentuated the Catholic contribution to an area and also symbolic artifacts that drew on local art and employed local artisans, craft materials that emphasized what artistic director John Buscemi characterized as the "vernacular." Localities were challenged to make sanctuary furniture (altar, pulpit, presider's chairs) as well as chalices, altar cloths, and communion vessels from local materials. Native fabrics and motifs were expected for the vestments the pope would wear. This may have begun with his trip to Iowa.

Since the pastoral on agriculture, *Strangers and Guests*, Dingman's love and concern for the land and the beauty of the Iowa terrain became the focal point for the preparations for the event. There was also a political agenda. As the *Des Moines Register* noted on the day of the papal trip: "For Catholics, the papal trip will draw attention to "Project Heartland." This was an attempt by bishops in 12 Midwestern states to stimulate a broad discussion of the moral questions raised by mechanized farming, extensive use of chemicals on the land, the decline of the family farm and the rise of corporate agriculture."[14]

Iowa's rich agricultural heritage was to be on display: the plowed land, the sown seed, the fruitful earth—simple yet powerful messages that could easily become vessels of Catholic sacramentality, the land broken and blessed by God. Mass in an outside field in the rising beauty of autumn filled the bill. Bognanno, by chance, had met John Buscemi, a Madison, Wisconsin, priest-artist, when the diocese adopted his Emmaus Program. Buscemi had redone the artwork for the Emmaus literature in Madison and Bognanno liked his work.[15]

Ordained in 1974, Buscemi had long been active in liturgical design and décor. As his first assignment at St. Francis Xavier Church in Cross Plains, he had become acquainted with the use of quilts for liturgical décor and worked with parishioners to produce a series of these attractive banners for various liturgical seasons and even for

Artwork for papal visit.
Credit: Diocese of Des Moines Archives.

the episcopal ordination of a Madison auxiliary bishop. Buscemi's work had come to the attention of the National Pastoral Musicians, a large association of church musicians, and he had served as artistic director for the group's convention in Chicago's McCormick Place.

Bognanno invited Buscemi to be one of the main artistic directors of the upcoming papal visit, and he joined Deacon David Malena, an official the Meredith Printing Company, a major sponsor of the event. Meredith offered office space for him to do his work for the event. Buscemi also worked with others at Dingman's residence, bonding with a score of others who were working nonstop over the relatively short time they had to prepare for the event. When Malena tragically died before the papal visit, many of the decisions fell to Buscemi.

Focusing on the papal liturgy, Buscemi planned to position the altar at an optimal location for the position of the sun. Drawing on the theme of the land that is opened to receive the seed, he wove into the artistic design of the altar, the ambo, and the décor a thoughtful and rich meditation that linked the "vernacular" of the Iowa soil with the timeless beauty of the Catholic Mass. Artificial hills were created to elevate the site—the highest of these hills being the place of the ambo (pulpit) where the Word of God would be proclaimed, noting that all, even the pope, were under the Word of God. Working together with four women, he helped create the most memorable creation of the event: a quilt that would depict the four seasons that Iowa experienced as a rural state. He noted: "the cross will be brown and the four 'petals' of the cloverleaf patters will represent the seasons: blues and grays for winter, light greens and yellow for spring, greens and browns for summer, and rust and orange for fall."[16] This logo became the emblem of the Catholic Church in southwest Iowa.

The emphasis on the vernacular found expression in the liturgical furnishings. The altar and ambo for the papal Mass were constructed of hundred-year-old white oak timbers salvaged from an Iowa corn crib donated by Pioneer Hi-Bred International and constructed by Des Moines Millwork Manufacturing in Clive, Iowa.[17] Other Iowa products were also to be used: earthenware altar vessels, locally made altar cloths, and fruits of the field to be brought at offertory time (pigs and lambs were considered and vetoed).

A week out from the papal visit, Dingman held an ecumenical vespers service at the Living Farms site. Ministers of other faith traditions and over five hundred participants attended the event to pray for the success of John Paul's journey to America.[18] As the pontiff winged his way to America, an aging and ailing Luigi Ligutti, who spent his life putting rural issues before the public, wrote: "I will be thinking of you and all my friends there." Even though he could not be there, the pope's journey was for him the crowning point of a lifetime—a visit to the land he loved and to the people he loved.[19] The night before the papal visit, Buscemi and the workers and craftspeople who contributed to the event had a picnic on the grounds, which were by that time closed off, for security reasons, to all others.

As the time of his arrival drew near, the *Des Moines Register* wrote a cranky editorial, wondering what Pope John Paul stood for "other than fidelity to orthodox Catholic teachings" and listed a number of topics they wished the pope would raise, among them economic justice and consumerism. "If he is bold enough to voice disappointment with American society, or brash enough to suggest repentance, many Americans may wish that he had stayed in Rome."[20] But even the churlishness of this editorial could not dampen the enthusiasm of those who now converged on Des Moines for the event of a lifetime.

"Oh What a Splendid Day It Was"

The big day, October 4, 1979, arrived and the papal plane landed at Des Moines; the pontiff was welcomed by Governor Robert Ray. Lined up were people in wheelchairs, including now retired Father Frank Ostdiek. It had been a long journey from his ordination by Dowling to this moment—one he could scarcely have imagined. For the first time since they were built, the section of Interstate 80/35 was closed around Des Moines. The National Guard and State Troopers (ninety-five at one site) were out in force. Schools and businesses closed, power crews were on hand for any emergency, and Northwestern Bell installed nearly four hundred phones for the event.

The entourage helicoptered to Cumming, near the farm of John and Marilyn O'Connor, where two hundred parishioners of St. Patrick's Church, Irish Settlement, were waiting for a prayer service. The small, rural church, one of the oldest in the diocese, was surrounded by farm fields and a nearby cemetery; the visuals of the event captured the strong faith of Iowa's rural frontiers. Here the pontiff reflected on a passage from the Acts of the Apostles that spoke of the gathering for the breaking of bread and prayers. John Paul II extolled the small community and urged its unity with the wider diocese and the church.

The pope was transferred by helicopter to the Living History Farms. Various informants recalled that Dingman had looked forward to the helicopter trip as a time to bend the pope's ear on some subjects. He carefully rehearsed them, but when the time came, the pontiff nodded off in the helicopter and the moment was lost.[21]

The prayers in the episcopal chapel had "worked." Although the day had started off chilly, by the time the Mass began it was a beautiful autumn day in Iowa. Various estimates pegged the crowd at nearly 340,000. Dingman formally welcomed him and the bishops from rural dioceses who joined in the celebration. Among the visitors were farmers from various parts of the United States: "The providence of God is very evident in this knoll and in all of rural America," a proud Dingman declared.[22]

In his address, Pope John Paul II once again singled out the importance and value of farming, linking those who work with the land to the literal sustenance of the people of America. The pontiff declared: "Here in the heartland of America, in the middle of the bountiful fields, I come to celebrate the Eucharist. . . . Every day the farmer is reminded of how much he depends on God. . . . Conserve the land well, so that your children's children and generations after them will inherit an even richer land than was entrusted to you (papal homily, Des Moines, Oct. 4, 1979)."

After the Mass, the pope made his way back to the Des Moines airport, thanking everyone for the kind

Pope John Paul II and Bishop Dingman at papal visit. Credit: Diocese of Des Moines Archives.

hospitality, and then jetted off to Chicago and Washington, DC. "Oh what a splendid day it was!" opined the now buoyant editorial page of the *Des Moines Register*. Of its wide-ranging significance, the *Register* noted: "We can recall no event so ecumenical in character encompassing not only the entire Christian community but embracing those of other beliefs and a good many of no belief."[23] Dingman, in a thank-you note to his fellow bishops, summed it up best: "It was a Catholic, a Civic, an Ecumenical, a Rural event that will live long in our memories."[24]

When the pope lifted off, he left a treasure trove of memories and good will. His visit cost over $875,000, only $300,000 of which had been raised in the diocese. Dingman faced a huge $500,000 debt. An appeal to fellow bishops in the Midwest, however, reduced the deficit and eliminated the debt.[25] Funds were also raised by selling the commemorative books produced by the Meredith Printing Company.

The Papal Visit and Historical Memory

The papal visit was the most important development in the history of the Diocese of Des Moines and perhaps the most significant religious event in the history of the State of Iowa. The enthusiasm felt by the planners and the participants can scarcely be described. Pope John Paul II returned to the United States several other times, and Des Moines would be contacted for its experience—one of the quickest preparations for any of the trips. (The Diocese of Phoenix had nearly two years to plan.)

The Meredith Printing book was one of the many memorabilia that came out of the event and that cemented the visit in the memory of many. At the Irish Settlement church, a group picture of those who attended the pope's visit was taken, and memorial plaques were set up in the small church. One year after the trip, Dingman led a pilgrimage of 110 diocesan people to Rome to commemorate the papal visit.[26] The highlight came at the general papal audience when the pope welcomed the members of the pilgrimage: "My greetings to everyone back home in Iowa." Sister Mira Mosle carried back a four-pound stone from the original foundation of St. Peter's to be inserted in the ecumenical church being erected on the site of the papal Mass at the Living History Farms.[27]

Subsequent papal visits always awakened memories of the event which came to be a kind of unofficial regular celebration in the diocese. Many reminisced about the day. Jane Olsasky of Panama remembered that the day was cold and damp, but all that changed: "As we saw the helicopter above us, rays of sunlight came with it as the Pope stepped on to the land. . . . Pope John Paul II was a gentle speaker and spoke in several languages for the mass. He spoke of how we should take care of the land." Kathleen Schmitz, who had traveled with her parents from Sioux City, slept in a van overnight to be close to the Living History Farms. She remembered that when the papal helicopter landed, "Tears were in our eyes. What a moment in history we were getting to witness." Later, when the diocese celebrated its centenary in 2011, now-Monsignor Bognanno cajoled a local composer to insert a song about the visit in the musical he was preparing. Tom Quiner used the papal homily as his inspiration and wrote: "O, Iowa, God's precious gift! The land He kissed in the morning mist. O, Iowa, This precious heartland! Heed God's command, Subdue the earth with gentle hands."[28]

Planning for the Future

The papal visit was truly a watershed moment and an impetus for further renewal in the diocese. From the time of his accession to the Des Moines See in 1968 to the election of John Paul II, Dingman had significantly transformed the administration of the diocese—introducing the principle of collegiality at virtually every level of church life and attempting to mobilize Catholic participation in the life of the church. The reconfiguration of the church's ministry followed the changing demographics of church life in Iowa. The Catholic population was shifting from its traditional urban and rural settings to the growing suburbs and exurbs of the city. The numbers of Catholics grew, but where they lived changed.

New concepts of religious education that stressed life-long learning were impacting the way parishes structured their annual programs and budgets. Growing priest shortages required consolidation and merging of parishes, especially in rural areas. The existing Catholic school system—never robust to begin with—shrank even further as schools lost pupils in many places as well as religious sisters to teach. The shrinkage was also reflected in where and how the bishop lived.

The Episcopal Residence in a Changing Des Moines: Shrinking the Diocesan Footprint

Even though Catholic population as a percentage of the twenty-three counties of the diocese would peak at 14 percent by 1990, the growth was uneven, favoring cities more than rural areas. Adjusting to this required some downsizing and readjusting to new realities. Adding to this were the growing shortages of priests and religious. Fewer and fewer were ordained each year. Priestly resignations and deaths further reduced the available people for ministries. At this same time, there was also a chosen strategy of simplifying church externals in line with Vatican II and Dingman's own personal modesty.

One emblem of this was the bishop's enormous home which had been purchased by Bishop Bergan. Dingman had opened it as a general meeting site for the diocese. Priests were welcomed to host ordination receptions on the property and prayer groups were also invited to meet there. The papal trip was coordinated from this building. Dingman himself had always felt a bit uncomfortable in the old home, and his fellow bishops around the country were downsizing their residences to strike a less imperial and remote pose with the priests and people. Dingman would do the same.

In early 1980 he had allowed the mansion to be redecorated for a fund-raiser for the Des Moines Symphony Guild. He was compelled to leave the house with his staff of sisters while the decoration went on, and for the three weeks of the show, Dingman temporarily relocated to St. Augustin's Convent. This move came in conjunction with the action of Diocesan Pastoral Council to assess the general space needs of the diocese. Vicar General Frank Nugent led a special Space Needs Taskforce to study, plan, and report on the urban footprint of the local church apart from its places of worship.

In addition to the episcopal mansion, ideas on the table involved renovating the old Bishop Drumm Home—now moved to Johnston—for diocesan offices and housing for the elderly. The taskforce's report urged the sale of the residence (as per Dingman's wish), rejected rehabbing the old Drumm Home, and sought out new office space. The episcopal mansion was listed for sale in April 1980.[29] In late August 1980, it was quietly announced that it had been sold to Dr. Ismael Naanep, a gynecologist, and his wife Dr. Belen Fernandez, a psychiatrist.[30]

The final day of his residence was October 4, 1980—one year to the day that Pope John Paul II had celebrated Mass at the Living History Farms.[31] As he prepared to move, Dingman took time to acknowledge the generous love and service of his two Adrian Dominican housekeepers, Sisters Marie Kevin Scanlon and Ghislaine Dumont. Scanlon had been at the residence for the terms of Bishops Daly and Biskup. Dumont had stayed thirteen years, for a time driving Dingman to appointments.[32]

Dingman at first moved to a small apartment on Arlington Avenue in Des Moines. His final residence was at Mercy Park Apartments next to Des Moines Mercy Hospital. He had a simple residence with two bedrooms and a single bath. It was here he would be felled by the stroke that began the end of his episcopate and life. Dingman felt more comfortable in his new modest surroundings, but the visible diocesan footprint in Des Moines continued to shrink.

The diocese received nearly $350,000 for the old mansion, and this was set aside for the purchase of a new central headquarters for the diocese. In late December 1982, it was announced that the diocese had purchased a building at 818 Fifth Street. The building, a two-story concrete and glass office building owned by the Raccoon Valley Investment Company, was near the Veteran's Memorial Auditorium and cost the diocese $789,000. In exchange, the diocese sold two buildings that had belonged to the chancery at 2910 Grand. The new building brought together the chancery, *The Catholic Mirror*, and the Catholic Council for Social Concern. The *Mirror* had been located at 914 Grand Avenue and the CCSC building at 700 Third Street.[33]

Other Downsizing and Readjusting: Planning for a Priestless Future

The vocation boom of the postwar era ended once Vatican II was over. Fewer and fewer men presented themselves for ordination, and a number of the ordained dropped out of the active ministry, many to marry. In 1985, the Harlan Region planned for the reduction of the number of priests available for weekly services. Following on this, the Diocesan Pastoral Council undertook a study of available priests and projected retirements. The number crunchers at the DPC estimated in 1985 that there was one priest for every 1,119 Catholics—an average at best—since it was much higher in urban parishes. The demographic shifts of the diocese were clear: Des Moines had the largest priest-to-parishioner ratio, while smaller regions had a smaller ratio (Leon had 433 to 1; Indianola, 615 to 1; Atlantic, 659.5 to 1; Guthrie Center, 722 to 1; Shenandoah, 762 to 1; Harlan, 822 to 1; Creston, 870 to 1; inner city Des Moines, 915 to 1). The number of Catholics had grown from 70,434 in 1960 to 89,317 in 1985. The number of priests declined in that period from 113 to ninety-seven. There were sixty seminarians in 1965 and only seventeen in 1985. No priests were ordained for Des Moines in 1979. The median age of priests in 1974 was forty-six. By 1985, it was fifty.[34] In 1985, a plan for parish administrators was prepared by the DPC and approved by Bishop Dingman.[35]

As any major organization facing a shortage of critical personnel, the Diocese of Des Moines was compelled to rethink its priorities and the administrative structures that kept the enterprise going forward. In July 1985, yet another major restructuring of diocesan administration was inaugurated. Following an evaluation of diocesan administrative structures by the New York–based National Pastoral Life Center, a new structure placed the chancellor, Father Stephen Orr, as the moderator of the staff. Under him were newly reconfigured offices: Parish Services, Social Concerns, Ministry Formation, and Administrative Services. Additional changes refocused the decision-making bodies of the diocese to better coordinate their activities with the central offices.[36]

This new configuration took a hard look at the diocesan priorities of serving the poor and maintaining pastoral services. Confronting the new administrative set-up was the specter of a $300,000 deficit in the three-year budget. Painful discussions ensued, and downsizing, cuts, and various economies were laid out. Most significant, it was determined that the diocese would suspend publication of *The Catholic Mirror*, which would result in a savings of $192,000 to the diocese. The paper had become a financial drain. Advertising and subscription revenues were not enough to keep it going without a hefty diocesan subsidy. Dingman sadly announced in March 1986 that he was terminating the staff (with severance pay) and suspending the publication of the newspaper for fourteen months.[37]

The council also decided to defer the creation of a lay ministry position and a social action position and eliminate two positions on the Catholic Council for Social Concern. The laid-off officials were informed of their departure after the DPC meeting in Atlantic.[38] All of this took place as the diocese decided to commemorate its seventy-fifth anniversary by raising $5 million for priest pensions and retirement. This brought a small outburst of protest.

One caustic letter from the wife of one of *The Catholic Mirror* staff decried the poor treatment of laypeople—a meager pension program and poor wages. "No, Bishop Dingman," an angry Mary Anne Dorsett Dubec wrote in one of the final editions of *The Catholic Mirror*, "lame apologies will not suffice." In a pointed hit on the prelate's international travels, she concluded bitterly that Catholic social justice was not being served as certain of the staff laid off were going to find it difficult: "Clergy who think otherwise should stay out of the pulpit. . . . They might also consider less worldwide travel in the name of justice, and seek it instead in their own back yards."[39]

Dingman's Last Years

The eighties would bring additional work and engagement for Dingman but also the onset of bad health for the Des Moines bishop. Dingman's struggle with a sleep disorder continued during his years in Des Moines and probably got worse. He often took brief catnaps to restore his flagging energy during the day. On occasion he embarrassingly fell asleep talking to someone (as he did with some poor priest who came to discuss his woes with him; the priest just took it as an act of God and tiptoed out of the room).

But even more ominously, he fell asleep at the wheel while driving any distance. Chancellor Monsignor Edward Pfeffer at first marveled at Dingman's ability to snap back to life after a small nap. "My marveling began to taper off, however, toward the end [of his years of service] when I began to realize that the catnaps were occurring with greater frequently, not only while seated at his desk, but also while seated at the wheel of his car. More than a few times I was with him on the road and had to grab the wheel to keep us from going into the ditch." He recalled one particular trip back from a confirmation in Creston where Dingman nodded off at the wheel only ten minutes after leaving the celebration.[40]

Through the middle part of 1981, Dingman also experienced shortness of breath and chest pains. An angiogram in August revealed the need for coronary artery bypass surgery. On August 13 he went in for the delicate surgery, which included seven bypasses—a cardiac surgery quite unusual at the time. He cancelled appointments for two months to recuperate.[41] For peace and quiet he went to the home of his sister Louise in his hometown of St. Paul, Iowa.

By 1983, he was sufficiently recovered to make what would be his last *ad limina* to Rome. This trip was a nightmare of missed flights, lost luggage, and a befuddled bus driver in Rome who started taking the visiting bishops to Assisi rather than the papal summer residence at Castel Gandolfo. Despite being late for a meeting with the pope, he managed to visit briefly with Pope John Paul II. The subject at issue for these visits was the status of women religious. During Dingman's short time with the pontiff he brought up the issue of habits for women religious—a subject being considered by the bishop's conference. To a skeptical John Paul, Dingman was sure that some *modus vivendi* could be worked out with patient dialogue. The pontiff gave him no indication of approval.

Dingman fit in a final visit with an ailing Monsignor Luigi Ligutti.[42] Ligutti, who had officially retired in 1971, passed on in early 1984 and was buried in Iowa.[43] Ligutti's storied career had taken him to every corner of the globe, but he still cherished his identity as an Iowan and received the Iowa Medal, the highest honor bestowed by the state. He was buried in Granger among "the People I love."

No sooner did he return from Rome than the bishop had one of the most frightening experiences of his life. On Saturday, October 8, 1983, Dingman was returning home from a very tiring day. He had ordained five new permanent deacons that evening and attended a reception for them, and then did some work at his office. He was

Bishop tells of kidnap ordeal

Headline of Dingman's kidnapping. Credit: Des Moines Public Library.

planning to drive to Davenport the next day to pick up Bishop Gerald O'Keefe and then motor to Rockford for the seventy-fifth anniversary of the diocese. At eleven o'clock at night he stopped at a convenience store to gas up his car. After paying the bill, he got back into his car and a robber who had hidden in the back popped up and told Dingman to be still while he summoned an accomplice. The two men drove off and demanded money from Dingman or a bank card—neither of which Dingman had.

They then set off to Waterloo, Iowa, about 130 miles northeast of Des Moines, driving erratically and smoking marijuana and referring to Dingman as "Preacher Dude." They arrived at Waterloo and were met by a third man. They went into a house and ordered Dingman to sit still in the car. The frightened bishop contemplated running for his life, but, having recently had seven bypasses, he worried that he would not have the stamina to escape. Finally, about four o'clock in the morning, one of the men came out and ordered him to drive back to Des Moines. He had Dingman drop him off after giving the bishop back the watch he had taken from him. Dingman arrived home—shaken, but grateful he had not panicked.[44]

Pondering the ordeal, Dingman responded as one might expect: compassionately. He wanted to have the men apprehended, "so we can help them."[45] Interviewed by the press, Dingman noted that he now knew firsthand what it meant to be a victim of crime and came away more deeply convinced that a just penal system would look at the causes rather than the symptoms of criminal behavior: "Did these fellows [his abductors] have a job? What does the lack of employment mean to someone? If I were in their position, what would I do?"[46]

When they were captured, Dingman did what he could to help the men, only one of whom responded positively to his acts of forgiveness and kindness. After the ordeal was over, Dingman received a generous note from Dr. Jerry Schmalenberger of St. John's Lutheran in Des Moines, reminding him that Martin Luther had also been abducted "in a similar fashion" and taken to the Wartburg Castle. While commending Dingman for "speaking so kindly about your abductors to the press and media," he also humorously noted that Luther had produced a vernacular version of the Scriptures during his captivity. "I'm waiting for you to announce your new translation of the Bible that was accomplished while you were abducted recently!"[47]

The Stroke

On April 17, 1986, just after he had delivered the bad news about the closure of the diocesan paper the *Mirror*, Dingman collapsed in his kitchen about five thirty in the morning. He was discovered a half hour later by Sister Julaine Schaefer, FSPA, his housekeeper and was rushed to Mercy Hospital, where it was discovered he had suffered a massive stroke. Father Michael O'Meara, his new chancellor (Father Orr had been appointed to the faculty of the Pontifical North American College), kept people informed about his status and informed pastors that they had to carry on the confirmations that the bishop had scheduled.

The stroke was the effective end of his ministry. He clung to life and managed to recover enough to sit in a wheelchair, but he was not the same person. To the shock of staffers and family, the stroke left him with a propensity to break out in bursts of sustained profanity. Only a few were spared this unusual blue streak.[48] O'Meara and staff helped keep the diocesan machinery running.[49]

After his condition was stabilized, he was permitted to recuperate at his family home in St. Paul, Iowa, cared for by his sister Louise. The long-term prospects for his recovery were bad, however, and the damage to his brain was extensive. It was a miracle he had survived this massive trauma.[50] His alma mater, St. Ambrose in Davenport, conferred their prestigious *Pacem in Terris* award on him also in 1986. Previous recipients of this prestigious award included Cardinal Joseph Bernardin, St. Teresa of Calcutta, Dorothy Day, and Saul D. Alinsky.

He joined the celebrations of the diocese's seventy-fifth anniversary in the summer of 1986. There he welcomed other bishops, friends, and coworkers in a festive Mass. Historical writing that accentuated the "felt religion" of Des Moines Catholics was accentu-ated. In January 1987 he traveled to Chariton and preached from his wheelchair at Iowa's fifth annual Celebration of Christian Unity organized by the Iowa Inter-Church forum. Dingman began his homily, but could not go on. He handed the rest of his sermon to the chancellor, Father Michael O'Meara, to read: "I beg your indul-gence; I don't quite measure up."[51]

As time went on and his situation deteriorated, it was apparent to those around him that Dingman's days as bishop were numbered. In fact, even before the stroke, as early as 1984, Dingman had started to come to grips with retirement. This occurred when a select com-mittee of priests (five in all, chosen by the Council of Priests) unani-mously urged him to resign. While they expressed support for his efforts, they pointed to the low morale of the diocesan clergy. The men were not happy and felt it was time for Dingman to step aside. This news jarred him. Certainly he was aware of a level of discontent with his decisions and, even more, of the great amount of time it took him to make any decision of import. Priests also felt shut out by his "attention" to the laity. As Dingman himself admitted in a lengthy memorandum, "I am popularly known as a 'People Bishop.' . . . The result has been the impression that Bishop Dingman is not a priest bishop. The logic is that you cannot be both."[52]

After this meeting, Dingman ran the question of his retirement past fellow bishops in a Jesus Caritas group (a support group for clerics) he had been attending for many years. Discerning the "signs of the times," he noted, "Health is not a major concern." He had survived the bypass surgery well and only suffered from a bit of bursitis. (He had not yet had the stroke.) But he was worried about the declining support of the priests. Nonetheless, the bishops urged him to stay, trying to reassure him that problems between bishops and priests were a reality they all faced and that he was an impor-tant voice on some critical issues, especially the conditions of rural America. They urged him to request an auxiliary bishop if he thought he needed help.

Dingman rejected the idea of an auxiliary but found the criticism of the priests "difficult to accept."[53] Here he alluded to criticism of a decision to build the St. Thomas More Center "and incur a debt not of my making. . . . Should this mistake be placed in my lap?

Is it a mistake? . . . Should I have left the Center to go bankrupt?" He plaintively asked in a lengthy memorandum directed to no one in particular: "Why not take the blame, depart and permit a new Bishop to pick up the process!"[54] Dingman spent some time talking to trusted friends and conferring with Father Eugene Merz, SJ, his spiritual director. In the end he decided he would turn in his resignation in August 1986.[55]

The vote of no-confidence from the priests rattled him. Perhaps he wondered if he had done any good at all—especially if those closest to him felt he was a drag on their morale. After the stroke in 1986, matters only got worse as Dingman also sank into a deep and almost impenetrable depression, especially when various therapies did not help him improve his mobility or energy. All this wore heavily on his sister Louise, who cared for him in her home with the assistance of Sister Maria Friedman, FSPA.

Names had already been floated among the Iowa hierarchy as possible bishops as early as 1979, including Frank Nugent, the vicar general of diocese, and Edward Pfeffer, then the chancellor. After the stroke, the question now was whether the original plan to retire in 1986 would be followed. Dingman at first may have believed that he could recover enough to manage affairs, but the need for nearly

Bishop Maurice Dingman with his people.
Credit: Courtesy of the Department of Special Collections and University Archives, Marquette University Libraries.

continual care made some—including his sisters—wonder if this were possible. By June 1986 he had let it be known to a journalist: "I am doing a lot of thinking about it [retirement]. I am seeking advice. . . . I believe in the redemptive power of suffering. What will result from all of this is in the hands of God."[56]

On August 11, 1986, he was able to follow through with his original plan and with the support of his friends and family, including a long-time friend and former superintendent of schools, now bishop, William E. McManus of South Bend, Dingman submitted his letter of resignation to Pope John Paul II. This was accepted on October 14, 1986, and Dingman was appointed apostolic administrator. On February 8, 1987, the pope appointed William Bullock, an auxiliary of the Archdiocese of St. Paul and Minneapolis, to the See of Des Moines—beginning what would be a dynasty of succession of St. Paul auxiliaries to the Iowa diocese.

Dingman lived four more years in his broken body, staying for a time with his sister at her home, until he was transferred to the Bishop Drumm Home in Johnston, and finally to Mercy Hospital, where he died peacefully on February 1, 1992, in the presence of his family members and friends. Father Stephen Orr celebrated Mass with him at his bedside while he clung to life and again after he expired. Bullock was summoned to say the prayers of the dying and the diocese said farewell to its longest-serving shepherd.

A gentle editorial in the *Des Moines Register* noted of Dingman at the time of his retirement, quoting religion editor William Simbro: "He fits the blueprint of a bishop as drawn in the 1960s by Vatican II: a chief pastor moving among his people, sharing responsibility, gently guiding, listening as well as speaking, facilitating rather than ordering." The editorial went on: "This slight man with wisps of snow-white hair would not seem an imposing figure, but in his quiet, graceful manner Dingman is a powerful, spiritual presence."[57] Perhaps someone read this to the ailing bishop before he died. It certainly would have pleased him.

Epilogue

Catholic leadership after Dingman drew from a pool of priests from the Archdiocese of St. Paul and Minneapolis: William Bullock, Joseph Charron, CSsP, and Richard Pates. Each of these bishops brought his own particular spiritualities and administrative strengths to the administration of the Diocese of Des Moines. Future historians will have plenty to say about them when the passage of time offers the required perspective. A new cultural and social era had dawned by the end of the 1980s, and American society (and the Catholic Church) became polarized on a series of issues, including abortion, homosexuality, gay marriage—an array of issues termed "culture wars." Iowa, with its strong evangelical Protestant majority, became one of the major centers of these battles, especially during the Iowa caucuses that prepare the way for the presidential primaries.

Catholic militancy on some of these issues was encouraged by certain aspects of the pontificates of John Paul II (1978–2005) and Benedict XVI (2005–2013). The loving pontiff who visited Des Moines in 1979 at the dawn of his papal reign insisted on a "return" to an older form of church orthodoxy and pulled back from certain Vatican II–inspired initiatives that were believed to have gone too far.

Pope Francis, elected in 2013 after the resignation of Pope Benedict, appears to be altering some of the initiatives of the previous two pontificates, departing at least in style, though rarely in substance, from his predecessors. Pope Francis has focused attention on one of the key themes of the visit of Pope John Paul II to Des Moines: the emphasis on caring for the land. The pontiff's 2015 apostolic exhortation *Laudato Sí*, with its call for care of the earth and concern for climate change, certainly resonates with the heritage of Monsignor Luigi Ligutti and Bishop Maurice Dingman.

Catholics in southwest Iowa are still a minority faith community. Their rivals are the now diminished forces of Protestantism but also an increasing number of people—many of them young—who are called "Nones," people who claim no denominational affiliation. As in the rest of the nation, more and more people are dropping out from organized religion and denominational membership. The older Catholic culture, formed by a central leadership, a common theological discourse, and various distinctive cultural and spiritual "markings" has faded. Likewise, the energies and optimism of the immediate post–Vatican II era are also things of the past.

Catholics occupy positions of leadership in state and national politics and reflect different political strains. The first Catholic governor of the state was Terry Branstad (1983–1999, 2011–2017), who converted from Lutheranism. After setting the record for the longest-serving governor in the United States, he went on to serve as the US ambassador to the People's Republic of China. His successor, Democrat Tom Vilsack (1999–2007), is also a Catholic and later served eight years as secretary of agriculture in the Obama administration. Firebrand conservative congressman Steve King is a convert from Methodism. Liberal former senator Tom Harkin is a graduate of Dowling High School.

Remaining a viable spiritual, social, and cultural force requires a different set of strategies than earlier generations. Some elements remain. Catholicism is still a brick-and-mortar reality in this part of Iowa. Two new parishes—St. Francis of Assisi in West Des Moines and St. Luke's in Ankeny, and the designation of St. Peter's for the Vietnamese Catholic Community—have created sacred space in important residential areas. In 1992, the diocese reaffirmed its presence in downtown Des Moines when it received the gift of the modernistic Home Federal Savings and Loan building located directly across the street from St. Ambrose Cathedral. This masterpiece was designed by the famed architect Ludwig Mies van der Rohe in 1962. After the collapse of the Savings and Loan Industry, the property was purchased by local philanthropist Edward Ochylski and donated to the Diocese of Des Moines, which transformed it into a pastoral center. In 2016, an $8.5 million renovation of the building began, preserving the space for the beautification of Des Moines.

As always, Catholics do what they can to enhance the urban landscape. The juxtaposition of the classic St. Ambrose and the modernistic old bank building reflects the old and the new. Next to the cathedral, the old rectory, still emblazoned on its distinctive turret with the coat of arms of Bishop Thomas Drumm, was also refurbished by Bishop Richard Pates. The church has decided to stay in the city.

But the ever-shifting demographics of Catholic life will require new strategies. Joining the growth of the Greater Des Moines area, the Diocese of Des Moines has experienced new members, exceeding 10 percent in the last ten years. Catholics in the 1990s and the 2000s continue to adjust to demographic change and the still shrinking numbers of priests and religious. Adapting to a growing Catholic population, St. Patrick's Church in Council Bluffs has built a new hall on its east side. Smaller numbers of priests have required recruitment from abroad. Dowling's faculty, which once had a number of full-time priest instructors, now has only one. The number of women religious working in and for the diocese has dwindled to eight or less (as of 2017). At the same time, local Catholics have taken the lead in helping immigrants, especially Hispanics, Southeast Asians, and Africans, settle and adjust to life in the Midwest. Similar to the rest of the United States, the diocese has seen a dramatic increase in Hispanic population, especially in the last ten years. Weekly Mass in Spanish has grown in eleven locations, doubling in number in the last nine years.

Among the other challenges is the legacy of clerical sex abuse. Those who experienced this at the hands of priests, religious, and laypersons working for the diocese would naturally view the history of the diocese through a very different lens. This abuse was not publically visible during the chronological period covered in this book. But, in fact, Catholic priests in the Diocese of Des Moines abused the authority and trust of Catholic young people entrusted to their care. How earlier bishops received these painful revelations and what they did with them was not available in the archival sources at present. During Bishop Dingman's time, one case surfaced. In

1988, under Bishop William Bullock, some of the first policies were put in place to handle these situations in a more consistent manner. These guidelines were later updated in 2002, when the bishops of the United States developed the Dallas Charter with an added emphasis on responding to the needs of the victims and significant resources and attention to programs intended to educate those who work for the diocese about this problem. It also required background checks of all those who work for or volunteer for service with a diocesan entity. Compliance with the demands of the Charter was assured by the Bishops' Office of Child and Youth Protection, which sent respected external observers to each diocese. Bishop Joseph Charron accepted the recommendations of the first auditors of the Des Moines policies and adjusted diocesan response accordingly. The pain suffered by the victims of this abuse and the early ethic of official silence and disbelief are a blot on the history of Des Moines Catholicism as they are of the universal church today. As of 2004, the Diocese of Des Moines paid out nearly $700,000 in settlements with victims.

So much has changed since the day in 1912 when the erudite and kindly Bishop Dowling appeared in Des Moines and doffed his silk high hat to the crowds who turned out to greet him. It is also running counter to trends in other Midwestern Catholic dioceses in experiencing a growing Catholic population. The eastern urbanite, Austin Dowling, thought that the Holy See had planted him in green pastures. Seventy percent of the Catholic population is now located in the Des Moines metropolitan area. The diocese has weathered significant changes and even summoned the resources to welcome a pope in a homey and memorable way that must still be the envy of many who plan for these now familiar journeys. Although history is never a good road map for the future, this can be one lesson taken from this account of the past one hundred years: the Catholic Church in Des Moines will continue to meet the challenges and joys of the years ahead.

Notes

Introduction—pages xv–xxvi

1. Dorothy Schweider, "Rural Iowa in the 1920s," *Annals of Iowa* 47 (1983): 104–15.

2. The religious history of Iowa has many chroniclers. A sampling of the bibliography includes, John Nye, *Between the Rivers: A History of the United Methodism* (Commission on Archives and History: Iowa Annual Conference of the United Methodist Church, 1986).

3. Sister Mary Helen Carey, "The Irish Element in Iowa to 1833" (MA thesis, The Catholic University of America, 1944).

4. William Cronon, "Storytelling," *American Historical Review* 118 (February 2013): 6–7. I am grateful to Douglas Firth Anderson for this passage.

Chapter 1—pages 1–55

1. Dorothy Schwieder, *Iowa: The Middle Land* (Iowa City: University of Iowa Press, 1996), 3–11.

2. Madeleine M. Schmidt, CHM, *Seasons of Growth: History of the Diocese of Davenport, 1881–1891* (Davenport: Diocese of Davenport, 1981), 46.

3. Silvana R. Siddali, "'Principle, Interest and Patriotism All Combine': The Fight Over Iowa's Capital City," *Annals of Iowa* 64 (Spring 2005): 111–38.

4. The date is sometimes given as August 12, 1911, but the text in the *Acta Apostolica Sedis*, the official record of the actions of the Holy See has August 6. "Erectionis Diocesis Desmoinensis," *Acta Apostolic Sedis* (30 September 1911): 479.

5. The Dominicans (Order of Preachers) were a community of brothers dedicated to preaching and the intellectual life. They were founded by St. Dominic in the thirteenth century and take their popular name from him. Mazzuchelli was a member of this community.

6. The Congregation of the Mission or Vincentians/Lazarists is a religious community dedicated to preaching, seminary education, and work with the poor. They were founded by St. Vincent De Paul, a French priest, in the seventeenth century.

7. Sister Benvenuta Bras, OP, "The Tradition of Father Mazzuchelli as Architect of the Old Capitol in Iowa City," unpublished paper in Archives of the Sisters of St. Dominic of Sinsinawa Mound, 1993. This copy was provided by Sister Lois Hoh, OP, archivist of the Sinsinawa Dominicans.

8. "Historical Churches of East Des Moines, Iowa, MPDF," paper in possession of author given by Mary Neiderbach.

9. "St. Patrick's Irish Settlement," pamphlet, Archives Diocese of Des Moines (hereafter ADM).

10. In 1890, a dispute would arise about the sale of this property, and Bishop Henry Cosgrove of Davenport contacted De Cailly, a pastor in Fort Madison to repeat the history of the purchase. Louis De Cailly to Henry Cosgrove, January 31, 1890, found in Michael Flavin Priest File, ADM.

11. Johnson Brigham, *Des Moines, The Pioneer of Municipal Progress and Reform of the Middle West Together with the History of Polk County, Iowa* (Chicago: S.J. Clarke Publishing, 1911), 453–57.

12. "Where St. Ambrose Once Stood a Towering Building Will Rise," *Des Moines Register* (April 4, 1963): 47 (clipping in St. Ambrose Parish File, ADM).

13. Schmidt, *Seasons of Growth*, 74.

14. John F. Kempker, "History of the Church in Polk County, Iowa," reprint of Kempker's 1912 history done for the centennial of the diocese, copies in ADM.

15. The Society of San Sulpice (Sulpicians), founded in France during the eighteenth century by Fr. Jean Jacques Olier, are a community of Catholic diocesan priests who live in common and dedicate themselves to the education of clergy. They played an important role in the beginnings of Catholic life in the United States and founded some of its more important seminaries.

16. Sara McBride, "Beginnings of Catholicity in Des Moines: A Series of Extracts from Father Kempker's MS Account," *Iowa Catholic Historical Review* 3 (October 1931): 14–24.

17. "Rev. J. F. Brazill," in Lorenzo F. Andrews, *Pioneers of Polk County, Iowa and Reminiscences of Early Days* (Des Moines: Baker-Trisler Co, 1908), 30–33.

18. John Lorenz to George Mills, July 1, 1966, St. Ambrose Parish File, ADM. The Iowa Building and the Des Moines Theater appeared in a piece done by George Mills, "A Swinging Place," *Des Moines Sunday Register*, 30 June 1996, 2C.

19. This anecdote is recorded in Kathleen O'Brien, *Journeys: A Pre-Amalgamation History of the Sisters of Mercy of Omaha Province* (Omaha, NE: Sisters of Mercy, 1987), 438.

20. "Priest and Patriot," *Iowa Messenger*, 5 September 1885, n.p.

21. "The Very Rev. John Brazill," *Iowa Messenger*, 29 August 1885, n.p.

22. "Priest and Patriot," *Iowa Messenger*, 5 September 1885, n.p.

23. "The Will Contested," *Iowa Messenger*, 19 September 1885, n.p.

24. "Priest and Patriot," *Iowa Messenger*, 5 September 1885, n.p.

25. Michael Flavin to Henry Cosgrove, January 15, 1890, Michael Flavin Priest File, ADM.

26. "To the Right Reverend Bishop Henry Cosgrove," undated petition in Michael Flavin Priest File, ADM. This battle with the east Des Moines Catholics—who were also told by Cosgrove not to go into debt—went on until the summer of 1891. Michael Flavin to Henry Cosgrove, July 10, 1891, Michael Flavin Priest File, ADM.

27. See Barbra Mann Wall, *American Catholic Hospitals: A Century of Changing Markets and Mission* (New Brunswick, NJ: Rutgers University Pres, 2010)

28. A description of the expansion of hospitals by the Sisters of Mercy is found in M. Jane Coogan, BVM, "Sowers Spread the Seeds," in *Seed Harvest: A History of the Diocese of Dubuque*, ed. Mary Kevin Gallagher (Archdiocese of Dubuque, 1987), 32–33.

29. "Mercy Hospital Observes 50th Anniversary," *The Messenger*, 8 December 1944, 1 & 2.

30. Data Card, Michael Flavin Priest File, ADM.

31. M. Kenney, Martin Flynn, W. H. Walsh, Chas. O'Donnell, J. B. McGorrisk, P. H. Burns to Henry Cosgrove, February 5, 1890, Michael Flavin Priest File, ADM.

32. Michael Flavin to Henry Cosgrove, January 15, 1890, Michael Flavin Priest File, ADM.

33. James J. Egan to Henry Cosgrove, February 20, 1890; Michael Flavin to Henry Cosgrove, February 24, 1890, Michael Flavin Priest File, ADM.

34. Michael Flavin to Henry Cosgrove, May 28, 1890, Michael Flavin Priest File, ADM.

35. "Dedication of St. Ambrose," *Iowa State Register*, 11 October 1891, 6

36. Ibid.

37. Daniel Mulvihill Priest File, ADM.

38. All Saints Parish History (Stuart), ADM.

39. "Msgr. Martin S. McNamara Passes Away," "Msgr. Hanson Extolls Value of Priesthood at Dear Friend's Funeral," *The Messenger*, 11 February 1949, 6.

40. For a solid history of Council Bluffs, see Lawrence H. Larsen and Karl A. Dalstrom, *Upstream Metropolis: An Urban Biography of Omaha and Council Bluffs* (Bison Books, 2007); see also, "The Council Bluffs Story Through the *Non Pareil's Eyes*," *Palimpset* 42 (September 1961): 415–48.

41. "'Upon This Rock,'" *The Daily Nonpareil*, April 26, 1887, clipping.

42. "St. Francis Xaviers [*sic*]," *The Daily Nonpareil*, April 24, 1889, clipping. See also, "St. Francis and the Catholic Presence," in William E. Ramsey and Betty Dineen Shrier, *Silent Hills Speak: A History of Council Bluffs, Iowa*, Council Bluffs Public Library Foundation (Barnhart Press, 2002), 250–53.

43. The kindly McMenomy told Sister Mary Xavier "not to go to Mass, as we needed so much rest." Quoted in Rachel Daack Riley, "BVM Catholic Schools and Teachers: A Nineteenth Century U.S. School System" (PhD dissertation, University of Iowa, 2009), 94.

44. "Memoria in Aeterna," *The Daily Nonpareil*, n.d.

45. Edward J. Harkin, "A History of the Catholic Church, Decatur County, Iowa" (pamphlet), ADM.

46. Lawrence H. Larsen, et al., *Upstream Metropolis: An Urban Biography of Omaha and Council Bluffs* (Lincoln: University of Nebraska Press, 2007), 189–92.

47. The foregoing is taken largely from O'Brien, *Journeys*, 401–15.

48. Quoted in ibid., 409.

49. Quoted in ibid., 426.

50. James A. Clifton, "Merchant, Soldier, Broker, Chief: A Corrected Obituary of Captain Billy Caldwell," *Journal of the Illinois State Historical Society* (August 1978): 185–204; O. J. Pruitt, "Some Iowa Indian Tales," *Annals of Iowa* 32 (January 1954): 203–16.

51. Larsen, *Upstream Metropolis*, 26. For more on de Smet, see "Father de Smet—His Services to the Society and His Religious Life," *Woodstock Letters* 3 (1874): 59–65; Hiram Martin Chittenden and Alfred T. Richardson, eds., *Life, Letters, and Travels of Father Pierre-Jean De Smet, S.J., 1801–1873*, 4 vols. (New York, 1905).

52. Bart Kane, "An Irish Blessing: Priests for Southwest Iowa," in *Jubilee of Faith* (Diocese of Des Moines, 1986), 70–71.

53. Francis J. O'Connell Priest File, ADM.

54. The powerful impact of Germans on the development of US Catholicism is the object of significant scholarship. Germans insisted on the right to operate parishes and institutions that perpetuated their language and their heritage of organizational structure. Many German Catholic leaders worried about "leakage" of German speakers to other religious communities. Dubuque had a precedent with Holy Trinity Catholic Church, founded in 1850. The classic text on German American Catholics is Colman A. Barry, OSB, *The Catholic Church and the German Americans* (Milwaukee: Bruce Publishing, 1953); see also J. Philip Gleason, *The Conservative Reformers German American Catholics and the Social Order* (Notre Dame, IN: University of Notre Dame Press, 1968).

55. For more on German immigrants to Des Moines, see *Des Moines, Center of Iowa: Survey of Historic Sites* (Des Moines Plan and Zoning Commission, 1983), 88–90.

56. "Parish Profile, No. 92, St. Mary, Des Moines," *The Messenger*, 20 May 1960, 3.

57. Taken from Barbara Bevin Long Henning and Patrice K. Beam, *Des Moines and Polk County: Flag on the Prairie* (Sun Valley, CA: American Historical Press, 2003), 64–65. See also *Des Moines, Center of Iowa, "Italian Newcomer,"* 105–9.

58. J. J. Liter to James Davis, October 18, 1906, St. Anthony File, ADM.

59. Ibid.

60. Victor Romanelli to James Davis, October 19, 1906, St. Anthony File, ADM.

61. Kempker, "History of the Church," 45.

62. When explaining why he would not ring his church bells to commemorate the eighth anniversary of Prohibition, Father O'Connor stated that he foreswore participation in active politics and claimed, "Men are well aware that the Holy Spirit does not promise any more political light to the pulpit than the pew. . . . Likely God does not vouchsafe a special light to the man in the pulpit upon any matter whatsoever since the great expenditure of time and money in the education of clergymen with, the Lord knows, meager enough results at times." Letter to *Chariton Leader*, "Fr. O'Connor Tells Why His Church Bells Were not Rung," undated clipping in O'Connor Priest File, ADM.

63. St. Patrick Parish History (Corning), ADM.

64. St. Patrick Parish History (Missouri Valley), ADM.

65. Hennig and Beam, *Des Moines and Polk County*, 24.

66. Ibid.

67. See Don L. Hofsommer, *Steel Rails of Hawkeye Land: Iowa's Railroad Experience* (Bloomington: Indiana University Press, 2005); for railroad development in Council Bluffs, see Sidney Halma, "Railroad Promotion and Economic Expansion at Council Bluffs, Iowa, 1857–1869," *Annals of Iowa* 42 (Summer 1974): 371–89.

68. "Shelby County Has Produced 200 Religious Vocations," *The Messenger*, 26 July 1946, 6 & 5.

69. Obituaries (Father Edmund Hayes), *The Malvern Leader and the Omaha World Herald.*, n.d., c. 1928.

70. St. Patrick Parish History (Imogene), ADM.

71. "Greenfield Woman, 89, Serves as Sacristan," *The Messenger*, 10 November 1961, 1.

72. Robert R. Denny, *Bicentennial Reflections: The History of the Des Moines Public Schools, 1846–1876* (Des Moines: Des Moines Public Schools, 1976).

73. Helen Marie Burns, "Active Religious Women on the Iowa Frontier: A Study in Continuity and Discontinuity" (PhD dissertation, University of Iowa, 2001), 115–16.

74. Riley, "BVM Catholic Schools and Teachers," 31.

75. Quoted in Burns, "Active Religious Women," 177.

76. Riley, "BVM Catholic Schools and Teachers," 181–82.

77. Ibid., 186.

78. The hazardous ride of these first BVM sisters is recorded in ibid., 68.

79. "Sketch of the Foundation and Growth of St. Joseph Academy," Mount Carmel Archives of the Sisters of Charity of the Blessed Virgin Mary (hereafter BVM Archives).

80. "Sisters in Des Moines Diocese," *The Messenger*, 28 April 1951, 1.

81. "Sisters in the Des Moines Diocese: The Congregation of the Humility of Mary," *The Messenger*, 27 April 1951, 1 & 4.

Chapter 2—pages 57–71

1. Minutes of Bishop's Council, 1886–1891, Archives Diocese of Davenport (hereafter ADD).

2. Minutes of Meeting of Bishop's Council, August 16, 1888, ADD.

3. For details on the creation of Sioux City, see Richard J. Roder, *Frontiers of Faith: A History of the Diocese of Sioux City* (Sioux City: Diocese of Sioux City, 2001), 183–212. Roder notes the aspirations of Father Brazill to have Des Moines created as a diocesan see and the objections offered.

4. James J. Keane to Diomede Falconio, December 18, 1902, IX Davenport.22-Progetto di divisione della diocese e sede in Des Moines (1902–1904), Archivio Vaticano Segreto (hereafter AVS).

5. Press Clippings, Diocese of Davenport, ADD.

6. Henry Cosgrove to Diomede Falconio, October 27, 1903, IX Davenport.22-Progetto di divisione della diocese e sede in Des Moines (1902–1904), AVS.

7. John J. Keane to Diomede Falconio, October 30, 1903, IX Davenport.22-Progetto di divisione della diocese e sede in Des Moines (1902–1904), AVS.

8. John J. Keane to Diomede Falconio, January 5, 1904, IX Davenport.22-Progetto di divisione della diocese e sede in Des Moines (1902–1904), AVS.

9. Henry Cosgrove to Diomede Falconio, January 9, 1904, IX Davenport.22-Progetto di divisione della diocese e sede in Des Moines (1902–1904), AVS.

10. Philip Garrigian to Diomede Falconio, January 12, 1904, IX Davenport.22-Progetto di divisione della diocese e sede in Des Moines (1902–1904), AVS

11. Richard Scannell to Diomede Falconio, January 13, 1904, IX Davenport.22-Progetto di divisione della diocese e sede in Des Moines (1902–1904), AVS.

12. Michael Flavin to Diomede Falconio, January 8, 1904, IX Davenport.22-Progetto di divisione della diocese e sede in Des Moines (1902–1904), AVS.

13. Ibid.

14. Rev. Joseph F. Nugent to Diomede Falconio, June 19, 1904, IX Davenport.22-Progetto di divisione della diocese e sede in Des Moines (1902–1904), AVS.

15. D. Mulvihill, Matthew Gleeson, D. Molyneaux, James McDonald, James Quinn, Thomas Loftus, James Curtin, Henry Malone, M. S. McNamara, James Cleary, J. J. Couday, B. J. Fitzsimmons, Michael Flavin to Diomede Falconio (n.d. but received July 27, 1904). IX Davenport.22-Progetto di divisione della diocese e sede in Des Moines (1902–1904), AVS.

16. "Will Name Coadjutor This Week," *Des Moines Register*, August 29, 1904, 1. (Clipping courtesy of Archie Cook.)

17. "See Question Up Again," *Des Moines Register*, 24 December 1902, 2. (Clipping courtesy of Archie Cook.)

18. James Davis to Diomede Falconio, March 2, 1907, IX Dubuque 25b, Progetto di erezione di un nuova provincia ecclesiastica con sede in Omaha, Neb. (1902–1903/1905/1907), AVS.

19. Petition to Diomede Falconio, February 26, 1907, IX Dubuque 25b, Progetto di erezione di un nuova provincia ecclesiastica con sede in Omaha, Neb. (1902–1903/1905/1907), AVS.

20. Ibid.

21. For a spread of urban statistics, see http://www.iowadatacenter.org/archive/2011/02/citypop.pdf.

22. Lawrence H. Larsen, "Urban Iowa One Hundred Years Ago," *Annals of Iowa* 49, no. 6 (1988): 445–61; Thomas F. Drummong, "Des Moines 70 Years Ago," *Annals of Iowa* 31 (October 1952): 460–66.

23. Some of the activities of the Commercial Club involved restructuring municipal government in Des Moines. See Samuel P. Hays, "The Politics of Reform in Municipal Government in the Progressive Era," *Pacific Northwest Quarterly* 55, no. 4 (1964): 157–69.

24. Letter of the Commercial Club of Des Moines, Iowa to Diomede Falconio, January 12, 1909, IX Davenport.35 Cattolici di Des Moines per divisione della diocesi (1909), AVS.

25. Albert Cummins to Diomede Falconio, February 5, 1909, IX Davenport.35 Cattolici di Des Moines per divisione della diocesi (1909), AVS.

26. James J. Davis to Geis Botsford, Secretary, Commercial Club, January 2 (?), 1909, January 12, 1909, IX Davenport.35 Cattolici di Des Moines per divisione della diocesi (1909), AVS.

27. Richard Scannell to Diomede Falconio, May 23, 1911; Richard Scannell, Philip James Garrigan, James Keane, James Davis to Gaetano De Lai, Secretary of Sacred Consistorial Congregation, May 23, 1911, IX Davenport 38-Proposta di divisione della diocese e erezione della nuova Des Moines (1911), AVS.

28. Diomede Falconio to Richard Scannell, May 28, 1911, IX Davenport 38-Proposta di divisione della diocese e erezione della nuova Des Moines (1911), AVS.

29. "Relazione per la proposta erezione della nuova diocese di DES MOINES nello Stato di Iowa, Stati Uniti d'America e totalmente presa dal presente territorio di Davenport," IX Davenport 38-Proposta di divisione della diocese e erezione della nuova Des Moines (1911), AVS.

30. Gaetano De Lai to Diomede Falconio, August 14, 1911, IX Davenport 38-Proposta di divisione della diocese e erezione della nuova Des Moines (1911), AVS.

31. Diomede Falconio to James Davis, August 31, 1911, IX Davenport 38-Proposta di divisione della diocese e erezione della nuova Des Moines (1911), AVS.

32. Petition of Priests of Clinton County to Diomede Falconio, September 13, 1911; Diomede Falconio to George W. Heer, September 24, 1911, IX Davenport 38-Proposta di divisione della diocese e erezione della nuova Des Moines (1911), AVS.

Chapter 3—pages 73–103

1. "Des Moines' First Bishop Arrived 50 Years Ago," *The Messenger*, 4 May 1962, 1.

2. By "practicing" I mean any Catholic who attended Mass regularly, was moderately informed about the organization and basic tenets of the faith, and valued church membership as spiritually and socially desirable.

3. "Installation of Bishop Dowling," *The Western World*, 12 May 1912, 1.

4. Ibid.

5. Ibid.

6. Mary Frances Teresa Dowling was born June 14, 1866. She remained at home until the death of her parents and then entered the Sisters of Mercy in November 1898. She served many years as a teacher of lower grades in Catholic schools and died January 31, 1951. Archives of the Sisters of Mercy of the Americas. The only other work done about Bishop Dowling was Marvin R. O'Connell, "The Dowling Decade in Saint Paul" (MA thesis, St. Paul Seminary, 1955).

7. Sister M. Antonine Dowling, RSM, "Biographical Sketch of Most Rev. D. A. Dowling, D.D., Archbishop of St. Paul" (hereafter Biographical Sketch), copies in ADM and in the Archives of the Archdiocese of St. Paul and Minneapolis (hereafter ASPM).

8. John E. Sexton and Arthur J. Riley, *History of St. John's Seminary Brighton* (Boston: Roman Catholic Archbishop of Boston, 1945), 55.

9. Joseph M. White, *The Diocesan Seminary in the United States: A History from the 1780s to the Present* (Notre Dame, IN: University of Notre Dame Press, 1989), 168.

10. Austin Dowling, "Father Hogan as a Teacher," Address at Fifth Annual Meeting of the Alumni of St. John's Seminary, Brighton, MA, February 4, 1902, copy in ADM.

11. Ibid.

12. Christopher Kauffman, *Tradition and Transformation in Catholic Culture* (New York: Macmillan, 1988), 168–77.

13. O'Connell, "Dowling Decade," n.p.

14. Of his tenure as a seminary professor it was noted: "It has been said of him that he was first and foremost a priest, in whom it may be added lived a brilliant student and professor. He also was possessed of an attractive personality, and thus added immeasurably to the faculty's reputation with the student body." Sexton and Riley, *History of St. John's Seminary*, 84–85.

15. Kauffman, *Tradition and Transformation*, 189–91.

16. Text of speech, undated but likely in 1918, Dowling Papers, ASPM

17. This book has been photostatically reproduced. William Byrne and William Augustine Leahy, *History of the Catholic Church in the New England States* (Boston: Hurd & Everts Co., 1899).

18. Text of speech, undated but likely in 1918, Dowling Papers, ASPM.

19. "Biographical Sketch," ADM.

20. "Bishop Dowling Evades Questions and Interviews Daily News Reporter," undated clipping, Dowling Papers, ASPM.

21. Austin Dowling Memoir (Dowling Papers, Archives of the Archdiocese of Minneapolis-St. Paul (hereafter Dowling Memoir ASPM).

22. Ibid., n.p.

23. These statistics are derived from "Diocese of Des Moines," *Official Catholic Directory*, 1912–1919 (P. J. Kenedy and Sons).

24. Dowling Memoir, ASPM, n.p.

25. Dowling Memoir, ASPM, n.p.

26. "Msgr. Ligutti Comments on Dowling," *The Catholic Mirror*, 19 November 1970, 1 & 12.

27. Dowling Memoir, ASPM, n.p.

28. Austin Dowling to Thomas W. Drumm, July 15, 1919, Drumm Papers, ADM.

29. "Simonaical" is the "selling" of spiritual gifts/grace, e.g., charging someone for the celebration of Mass. Money is given for Mass, but strictly speaking it must only be a free-will donation. The term itself stems from the example of Simon Magus (the Magician) described in the Acts of the Apostles who offered to perform Christ-like miracles for free. He was struck dead by the apostles for such behavior.

30. Among the "Founders" were Dowling himself, Michael Flavin, Vitus Stoll, James A. Troy, Wilhelmina Coolbaugh, and the Sisters of Mercy. "Donors of $1,000 Become Founders and Share in Masses," undated clipping Dowling High School File, n.d.

31. Dowling was apparently concerned that this promise be kept as he explained to Drumm, "As a stimulus for contributions of $1,000 I established a fund of $2,000 from which I derived income equal to two stipends a week. I kept this in my own hands lest the bonds for any reason might be thrown into the general fund—and the trust not kept." Austin Dowling to Thomas W. Drumm, July 15, 1919, Drumm Papers, ADM.

32. The anecdote of Dowling cleaning the toilets is found in Vincent A. Yzermans, *The People I Love: A Biography of Luigi Ligutti* (Collegeville, MN: Liturgical Press, 1976), 14–15.

33. Austin Dowling to Luigi Ligutti, March 12, 1918, Monsignor Luigi G. Ligutti Papers, LGL, Series 1.1, General Correspondence "D," Archives of Marquette University (hereafter AMU).

34. Joseph Senn, "Coolbaugh Hall," clipping in scrapbook in Dowling High School Collection, ADM.

35. Austin Dowling to Thomas W. Drumm, June 20, 1919, Drumm Papers, ADM.

36. Austin Dowling to Thomas W. Drumm, July 15, 1919, Drumm Papers, ADM.

37. David Roggensack, "Shaw Hall," Dowling Scrap book, ADM.

38. Austin Dowling to Luigi Ligutti, October 30, 1917, Monsignor Luigi G. Ligutti Papers, LGL, Series 1.1, General Correspondence "D," AMU.

39. Austin Dowling to Luigi Ligutti, July 22, 1918, Monsignor Luigi G. Ligutti Papers, LGL, Series 1.1, General Correspondence "D," AMU.

40. "Msgr. Ligutti Comments on Dowling," *The Catholic Mirror*, 19 November 1970, 1 & 12.

41. Boylan was born in New York in 1889 and, like Dowling, moved to Rhode Island where he attended school in Providence and St. Bernard's Seminary in Rochester. He was ordained to the priesthood in 1915 in the city of Providence although he had incardinated into the Des Moines diocese. After a brief curacy in Council Bluffs, he was drawn into the plans for the new Des Moines College. He studied at the Catholic University and was appointed to the faculty of the college in 1918.

42. "College in Des Moines Renamed in Honor of the Late Arbp. Dowling," undated clipping in Dowling Papers, ASPM.

43. "Bishop Dowling's Farewell Talk to Children," n.d. in Des Moines File, Mt. Carmel, BVM Archives.

44. Yzermans, *The People I Love*, 7–8.

45. Austin Dowling to Joseph Nugent, September 27, 1914, Visitation Parish File, ADM.

46. "Monsignor J. M. Hanson Plans Party to Mark 90th Birthday," *The Messenger*, 10 August 1956, 1; "Bishop Officiates in Rites for Msgr. Joseph Hanson," *The Messenger*, 2 January 1959, 1.

47. George Toher Priest File, ADM.

48. Kathleen O'Connor, "A Brief History of the Early Missionary Work in 'Little Mexico,' Council Bluffs, Iowa," ADM. The fate of this little chapel is unknown.

49. Austin Dowling to Thomas W. Drumm, December 13, 1920, Dowling Papers, ASPM.

50. A pious but nearly contemporaneous account of the coming of the Passionists to Des Moines is found in Father Felix Ward, CP, *The Passionists: Sketches Historical and Personal* (New York: Benziger Brothers, 1923), 404–9.

51. Typescript History of St. Gabriel's Monastery," n.d., Passionist Archives, Chicago, Illinois; "City's Growth Closes Picturesque Monastery," clipping book in ADM, August 1, 1958, *Register*.

52. *Passionist Bulletin* 14, November 21, 1945, 47. Passionist Archives, Rome.

53. *Passionist Bulletin* 7, July 9, 1944, 41–42, Passionist Archives Rome.

54. "Land North of Grimes Bought by Passionists for New Monastery," *The Messenger*, 22 November 1957, 1.

55. Lilian McLaughlin, "When Monastery Bells Rang at Merle Hay Mall," in *Jubilee of Faith* (Diocese of Des Moines, 1975), 26–27.

56. Kathleen O'Brien, RSM, *Journeys: A Pre-amalgamation History of the Sister of Mercy, Omaha Province* (Omaha, NE: Sisters of Mercy, 1987), 441.

57. Quoted in O'Brien, *Journeys*, 447.

58. Ibid., 448.

59. John Bonzano to Austin Dowling, December 21, 1916; John Bonzano to Austin Dowling, January 11, 1917, Dowling Papers, ASPM.

60. "Copia Relationis ad S. Sedem Apostolicam Pro Diocesi Des Moinensi in Statu Iowa, U.S.A. Ab anno Domini 1912 usque at annum 1919," Dowling Papers, ASPM.

61. "Father Pat," *The Messenger*, 17 May 1963, 4.

62. Sec Taylor, "Sittin' In," May 14, 1963, clipping in Patrick McDermott Priest File, ADM.

63. "Requiem Mass Offered for Pastor of Atlantic," *The Messenger*, 17 May 1963, 1–2.

64. "Noted Chaplain Who Served in Diocese Dies," *The Messenger*, 26 February 1954, 1.

65. James A. Troy to Austin Dowling, March 20, 1916, James A. Troy Priest File, ADM.

66. James A. Troy to Thomas Drumm, July 13, 1920, James A. Troy Priest File, ADM.

67. *Catholic Bulletin*, March 15, 1919, clipping in Dowling File, ADM.

68. Dowling Memoir, ASPM, n.p.

Chapter 4—pages 105–44

1. Leland L. Sage, "Rural Iowa in the 1920 and 1930s: Roots of Farm Depression," and Dorothy Schweider, "Rural Iowa in 1920s," both in *Annals of Iowa* 47 (1983): 91–103; 104–15.

2. Annual Catalogue of the Officers and Students of St. Joseph's College, Dubuque, Iowa, 1896–1897. Drumm is listed as a student in this catalogue. Loras College Archives, Loras College, Dubuque.

3. Two general histories refer to the "ecclesiastical" department at St. Joseph/Loras College. See Mathias Martin Hoffmann, *The Story of Loras College, 1839–1939* (Dubuque: Loras College Press, 1939). Archbishop Hennessy had hoped to have both a major and minor seminary at the campus but had to abandon his plans for a major seminary. The idea would later be revived in the 1950s with the creation of Mount St. Bernard's Seminary. See also Francis P. Friedl, *The Loras College Story: 150 Years* (Dubuque: Loras College Press, 1990). Friedl notes that a new residence for clerical students was constructed in 1952–1953 (named St. Pius X Seminary), where Des Moines students lived and did their collegiate and philosophy studies in preparation for the major seminary (see p. 67).

4. *General Register of Fellows and Students, 1903–1904*, Archives of the Catholic University of America. Drumm is listed for only one year.

5. Founded in 1885, the parish congregated in a small frame church until 1891 when Father Timothy Sullivan erected a magnificent new church and created a school with the old church structure, staffed by the BVM sisters. Before he died in 1914, Sullivan built a new school. When Drumm arrived in February 1915 he raised money to pay off the debts left by his predecessor. He also built a convent that allowed the sisters to move out of the school. "History of St. Patrick's Church," Archives of the Archdiocese of Dubuque.

6. "New Bishop of Des Moines Started as Iowa Farm Hand," *Des Moines Register*, 30 March 1919, 1. See also "Cedar Rapids Man is Des Moines Bishop," *Des Moines Register*, 29 March 1919, 1.

7. Austin Dowling to Thomas W. Drumm, March 30, 1919, Drumm Papers, ADM.

8. Austin Dowling to Thomas W. Drumm, no date, Drumm Papers, ADM.

9. "Tender Welcome to Bishop Drumm," *Des Moines Register*, 23 May 1919, 14.

10. "Visita Della Diocesi di Des Moines Iowa, February 18, 1931," IX Des Moines 13 Visita Apostolic, 1931, 1933, AVS.

11. James Troy to Pietro Fumasoni-Biondi, May 14, 1926, IX Des Moines, (Diocesi) 8, Rev. James J. A. Troy parochianni di Dunlap contro di lui; suo caso contro l'ordinario di Des Moines (1925–1926, 1928), AVS

12. "Visita Della Diocesi di Des Moines Iowa, February 18, 1931," IX Des Moines 13 Visita Apostolic, 1931, 1933, AVS.

13. Thomas W. Drumm to Francis W. Doyle, June 21, 1928, Francis Doyle Priest File, ADM.

14. George J. Toher to Thomas W. Drumm, April 22, 1933, George Toher Priest File, ADM.

15. William Appleby to Thomas W. Drumm, April 27, 1927, William Appleby Priest File, ADM.

16. William Appleby to Thomas W. Drumm, January 27, 1928, William Appleby Priest File, ADM.

17. Much of the foregoing is taken from Vincent A. Yzermans, *The People I Love: A Biography of Luigi G. Ligutti* (Collegeville, MN: Liturgical Press, 1976), 1–45.

18. At the Baltimore seminary, the young Ligutti became close friends with Father Joseph Morrison of Chicago, later rector of Holy Name Cathedral and a local supporter of the liturgical movement, and Father Louis Arand, SS, who later became president of Theological College in Washington, DC. He also included among his friends Father Thomas Gorman of Los Angeles, who later became a newspaper editor and bishop of Reno and eventually bishop of Dallas. He also came to know the future Chicago Archbishop John Patrick Cody with whom he carried on a lively correspondence.

19. Austin Dowling to Luigi Ligutti, February 19, 1917, Monsignor Luigi Ligutti Papers, LGL, Series 1.1, Box 1, "General Correspondence, Outgoing, 1922–1982," Folder 1920s, AMU.

20. Among his Catholic University colleagues were important future leader of the Catholic Church in America including Father John O'Grady, future head of the National Conference of Catholic Charities, and liturgical movement leader Dom Virgil Michel, OSB, of Saint John's Abbey in Collegeville, Minnesota.

21. Luigi Ligutti to Father Maurice Powers, January 4, 1922, Monsignor Luigi Ligutti Papers, LGL, Series 1.2, "General Correspondence, Incoming 1917–1983" Box "D," AMU.

22. Yzermans, *The People I Love*, 21.

23. The Confraternity of Christian Doctrine (CCD) was in reality a more comprehensive program that organized parish life assigning roles to laity according to six types: teachers, fishers (those who recruited children), helpers, parent-educators, etc. Devised and promoted by the Bishop Edwin Vincent O'Hara of Great Falls, Montana, it was gradually embraced by other American bishops, who often appointed a full-time cleric to oversee the program for the entire diocese.

24. "Father Hubert E. Duren to Offer Solemn Mass for Jubilee on July 9," *The Messenger*, 4 July 1947, 6 & 5.

25. "Priest's Proven Plan Provides Inexpensive Home Ownership," *The Messenger*, 24 October 1958, 10.

26. Hubert Duren Priest File, ADM.

27. Recollections of Barney Zimmerman, "The Great Depression and Drought of the Thirties," in *The Bicentennial History of Shelby County* (Shelby County Historical Society, 1976), 363–64.

28. Sister Romain (Monica) Muskat to Sister M. Theresa, April 15, 1984, St. Boniface Parish Files, 2-011, Box 14, Folder 3, Reunion, 1986, Archives of the School Sisters of St. Francis (hereafter ASSF).

29. No documentation could be found regarding this first synod of Des Moines.

30. *Code of the Diocese of Des Moines Decreed in Diocesan Synod Held June 15th, 1923 In the Chapel of Des Moines Catholic College and Promulgated September 8th, 1923* (Diocese of Des Moines, copy in ADM).

31. "Growth of Area Created Need for Organized Approach to Charity, Social Welfare Problems," *The Messenger* (Special Insert for Golden Jubilee of Diocese of Des Moines), 15 June 1962, 11.

32. Thomas W. Drumm to Francis O'Connell, October 2, 1922, Francis O'Connell Priest File, ADM.

33. Thomas W. Drumm to Francis O'Connell, November 1, 1926, Francis O'Connell Priest File, ADM.

34. "St. Ambrose Cathedral, at Des Moines, Enlarged and Remodeled at Cost of $90,000," undated clipping, St. Ambrose File, ADM.

35. "Cathedral Organ Recital, October 4," *Catholic Messenger,* 3 October 1929, 10.

36. John T. Noonan Priest File, ADM.

37. "Own Your Own Home: Beaver Park," undated flyer by B.C. Hopkins, copy courtesy of Mary Neiderbach.

38. Ostdiek actually convinced clergy friends to help him defy the bishop (whose power in those days was well-nigh absolute) and even appealed to the apostolic delegate. Amazingly, he was successful and remained at the parish until his retirement in 1969. Ostdiek's famous refusal to move at Drumm's demand made him something of a legend—especially as he grew older and more cantankerous. Although many of his contemporaries attained the coveted rank of "monsignor," Ostdiek was always denied—according to legend—because Drumm had blackballed him for his act of disobedience. Ostdiek, however, lived long enough to greet Pope John Paul II who visited Des Moines in 1979.

39. St. Joseph Parish History, St. Joseph File, ADM.

40. Mother Stanislaus Hegner to Joseph Steiger, n.d. "St. Joseph Earling File," ASSF.

41. See Father Carl Vogl, "Be Gone Satan!: A True Account of an Exorcism in Earling, Iowa in 1928," original copy 1935 (Charlotte, NC: Tan Books, 2010).

42. "Exorcist and Energumen," *Time Magazine* 27 (February 17, 1936).

43. Peter Bissen Priest File, ADM.

44. "Father Shaw Dies in Council Bluffs," *The Messenger*, 17 January 1964, 1.

45. For some general works on the Klan, see David Chalmers, *Hooded Americanism: The History of the Ku Klux Klan* (Duke University Press, 1987); William Rawley, *The Second Coming of the Invisible Empire: The Ku Klux Klan of the 1920s* (Mercer University Press, 2016); Thomas R. Pegram, *One Hundred Percent American: The Rebirth and Decline of the Ku Klux Klan in the 1920s* (Ivan R. Dee, 2011).

46. J. C. Maher to Thomas W. Drumm, April 15, 1924, Chapel Car File, ADM.

47. M. J. Culkins to Thomas W. Drumm, April 18, 1924, Chapel Car File, ADM.

48. "Official Report of Mission Held at Corydon, Iowa, May 19 to May 25 Inclusive," n.d., Chapel Car File, ADM.

49. William Appleby to Vitus Stoll, May 26, 1924, Chapel Car File, ADM.

50. William Appleby to Vitus Stoll, n.d., Chapel Car File, ADM.

51. "Official Report of the Mission to Non-Catholics at Humeston, Iowa, Week ending June 1, 1924," Chapel Car File, ADM.

52. William Appleby to Vitus Stoll May 30, 1924, Chapel Car File, ADM.

53. William Appleby to Thomas W. Drumm. June 6, 1924, Chapel Car File, ADM.

54. James J. A. Troy to Vitus Stoll, July 16, 1924, Chapel Car File, ADM.

55. James J. A. Troy to Vitus Stoll, August 6, 1924, Chapel Car File, ADM.

56. "Chapel Car: Through Southern Iowa on the Chapel Car," n.d., copy in IX Des Moines, (Diocesi) 8, Rev. James J. A. Troy parochianni di Dunlap contro di lui; suo caso contro l'ordinario di Des Moines (1925–1926, 1928), AVS. Maria Monk was the "author" of a scurrilous and widely circulated anti-Catholic tract in the 1830s. Monk alleged that she was a nun who had been impregnated by a priest. Her "memoir," *Awful Disclosures of Hotel Dieu*, was a bestseller and still in circulation in the twentieth century.

57. These figures are derived from "Diocese of Des Moines," *Official Catholic Directory* (OCD), 1920–1934 (P. J. Kenedy and Sons). While they may be essentially correct, OCD statistics are prone to inaccuracy.

58. The Diocesan Council of Catholic Women was an umbrella organization of all the various Catholic women's groups that existed in the diocese. Formed in the 1920s by Bishop Drumm, this organization was one of the main vehicles for the activism of Catholic laywomen in the diocese. They worked in a number of capacities: taking the census of Catholics, reaching out to immigrant groups, pressing Catholic issues with local politicians. Each year they held a large diocesan-wide conference where they debated issues and identified tasks that needed to be done.

59. "Reverend Father and Beloved Brethren," June 1, 1931, Circular Letter to Priests, September 27, 1931, Drumm File, ADM.

60. John Boylan to Luigi Ligutti, January 12, 1922, General Correspondence Incoming, 1917–1983, LGL, Series, 1.2, Monsignor Luigi G. Ligutti Papers, AMU.

61. John Boylan to Thomas W. Drumm, June 25, 1922, Boylan Priest File, ADM.

62. Austin Dowling to Thomas W. Drumm, April 17, 1919, Drumm Papers, ADM.

63. Austin Dowling to Thomas W. Drumm, October 19, 1920, Drumm File, ADM.

64. Minutes of a meeting of the executive officers of the Des Moines Catholic College, September 7, 1932, Dowling High School Files, ADM.

65. Report of Father John Boylan to the Board of Trustees, January 16, 1933, Dowling High School Files, ADM.

66. Minutes of meeting of board of trustees of the Des Moines Catholic College, May 1, 1933, Dowling High School Files, ADM.

67. Ibid.

68. J. J. Boylan, E. Leo Ford, L. Gannon, J. P. Shaw, J. J. Aldera, P. J. McStay, P. A. Bissen, L.V. Lyons, Robert A. Walsh, and T. J. Costin to Thomas Drumm, June 5, 1933, Dowling High School Files, ADM.

69. J. Murphy to Amleto Cicognani, June 14, 1933, IX Des Moines, Visita Apostolica, 1931, 1933, AVS.

70. "Dear Father and People of Des Moines," July 17, 1933, Drumm File, ADM.

71. Ibid.

72. Joseph M. Hanson to Amleto Cicognani, September 6, 1933, IX Des Moines (Diocesi), 15 Central High School di Des Moines ricorsi contro il vescovo Thomas W. Drumm (Rev. J. M. Hanson, Rev. F. B. Ostdiek), 1922, AVS.

73. Francis Ostdiek to Amleto Cicognani, September 8, 1933, IX Des Moines (Diocesi), 15 Central High School di Des Moines ricorsi contro il vescovo Thomas W. Drumm (Rev. J. M. Hanson, Rev. F. B. Ostdiek), 1922, AVS.

74. "Resolution of Sympathy," January 6, 1934, minutes of the board of Des Moines Catholic College, Dowling High School File, ADM.

75. Raymond Conley, "Memories of a Many Splendored Life," n.p. Raymond Conley Priest File, ADM.

Chapter 5—pages 145–86

1. Quoted in Lisa Lynn Ossian, "The Home Fronts of Iowa, 1940–1945" (PhD dissertation, Iowa State University, 1998), 5–6.

2. Circular Letter to Priests, September 27, 1931, Drumm File, ADM.

3. Thomas P. Murphy to Thomas W. Drumm, January 1933, Thomas Murphy File, ADM.

4. Clipping in Thomas P. Murphy Priest File, ADM.

5. Rev. J. J. Judge to Mother Stanislaus [Hegner] August 22, 1932, 2-011, Box 13, Folder 7, Rosemount, Iowa, St. Mary School, Archives of the School Sisters of St. Francis.

6. Gerald Bergan to Mother Stanislaus Hegner, March 9, 1935, 2-011, Box 13, Folder 7, Rosemount, Iowa, St. Mary School, Archives of the School Sisters of St. Francis.

7. W. J. Kleffman to Gerald Bergan, March 21, 1941, A. J. Drexler Priest File, ADM.

8. Bishop Bergan Golden Jubilee of Priesthood Booklet, 1965, Box 15, Archives of the Archdiocese of Omaha (hereafter ADOm).

9. Dunne himself was not a model of hard work. A report from the apostolic delegate wrote that Dunne "lost control, exceeding in avarice and freedom with word, he spent the winters in Florida or Cuba, returning just in time to bless the Holy Oils on Holy Thursday, and he spent much of the time in the summer in the country fishing in the lakes." Bergan would not imitate his bishop's indolence. Visita Apostolica Peoria, AVS, n.d.

10. Quoted in Stephen Szmrecsanyi, *History of the Catholic Church in Northeast Nebraska* (Omaha, NE: Catholic Voice Publishing Co., 1983), 271.

11. Ibid.

12. "Monsignor" in the US context is a honor bestowed on "worthy" priests by a bishop. It was usually given to men who served in diocesan administration or stood out for their excellence in some academic or professional role. In Europe "monsignor" is used often to refer to bishops.

13. "Church Honors Bishop Bergan," *Des Moines Register*, 14 June 1934, 1.

14. "The New Bishop Came to Des Moines," *The Western World*, 28 June 1934, 24.

15. "Bishop Bergan Welcomed to Diocese," *Des Moines Register*, 21 June 1934, 1 & 3.

16. "Bishop Bergan's First Sermon," *The Western World*, 28 June 1934, 3.

17. "Bergan Is Again Welcomed," *Des Moines Register*, 23 June 1934, 3.

18. "Grist," *Messenger*, 24 December 1937, n.p.

19. Michael W. Schwarte, "Gerald Bergan, The Joyful Bishop," *Jubilee of Faith* (Diocese of Des Moines, 1986), 28.

20. "Bishop Bergan Ordained Young Men to the Priesthood," *The Western World*, 28 June 1934, 24.

21. Thomas O'Meara, OP, "Forum," *Worship* (January 1994): 55–56.

22. Szmrecsanyi, *History of the Catholic Church in Northeast Nebraska*, 272.

23. Szmrecsanyi, *History of the Catholic Church in Northeast Nebraska*, 272–75.

24. Don Gard, "Granger Marks Homestead Jubilee," *The Catholic Mirror*, 19 September 1985, 1 & 10.

25. For a complete account of the Granger Homesteads and other similar experiments, see David S. Bovee, *The Church and the Land: The National Catholic Rural Life Conference and American Society, 1923–2007* (Washington DC: The Catholic University of America Press, 2010), 111–12.

26. See Bovee, *The Church and the Land*, 152–75 and *passim*.

27. These statistics are taken from "Diocese of Des Moines," *Official Catholic Directory, 1935–1947* (New York: P. J. Kenedy and Sons, 1934–1949).

28. Typical was Father Leo Gannon, who had been ordained in 1931 and served at the school for eleven years. Gannon, a tough disciplinarian, from time to time, decked unruly students. This form of corporal punishment became less and less acceptable, however, and the hard-edged Gannon became known for encouraging Des Moines lads to consider a priestly vocation. At one point he took one of them to an ordination in Atlantic to have him witness this strange and awesome rite. "Father Gannon," *The Catholic Mirror*, 24 January 1974, 6.

29. John Boylan Report to Des Moines College Board of Trustees, January 16, 1933, Minutes of the Board of Trustees, Dowling High School File, ADM.

30. Gerald Bergan to John P. O'Mahoney, CSV, March 6, 1939, Provincial Office Correspondence, Archives of the Clerics of St. Viator (hereafter ACSV), Arlington Hts., IL.

31. John P. O'Mahoney, CSV, to Gerald Bergan, March 21, 1939, Provincial Office Correspondence, ACSV.

32. Gerald Bergan to John P. O'Mahoney, CSV, April 18, 1939, Provincial Office Correspondence, ACSV.

33. Gerald Bergan to Richard J. French, CSV, March 10, 1942, Provincial Office Correspondence, ACSV.

34. Minutes of a Special Meeting of the Board of Trustees of Dowling College, April 15, 1942, Dowling High School File, ADM.

35. Richard J. French, CSV, to Gerald Bergan, April 8, 1942, Provincial Office Correspondence, ACSV.

36. Richard J. French, CSV, to Gerald Bergan, April 15, 1942, Provincial Office Correspondence, ACSV.

37. Gerald Bergan to Richard J. French, CSV, June 1, 1942, Correspondence with Des Moines, ACSV.

38. Lowell Lawson to Gerald Bergan, June 2, 1942, Correspondence with Des Moines, ACSV.

39. Gerald Bergan to Lowell Lawson, June 17, 1942, Terminated Posts, Iowa, ACSV.

40. Richard French, CSV, to Gerald Bergan, June 17, 1942, Correspondence with Des Moines, ACSV.

41. Meeting of the Board of Trustees of Dowling College, January 9, 1951, Dowling High School File, ADM.

42. "26 Are Preparing for Diocesan Priesthood," *The Messenger*, 4 October 1946, 6.

43. Among them was the 1947 announcement of the first Mass of Jesuit Father Virgil C. Blum, a native of Defiance who, after his ordination, sang his first Mass at St. Joseph Church in Earling. Blum, who would become a popular political science instructor at Marquette University, was an important voice in advancing the cause of public financing of Catholic education and a bitter foe of anti-Catholic sentiment in the press and in public life. "Rev. V. C. Blum, S.J., to Sing First Mass in Earling June 24," *The Messenger*, 13 June 1947, 6.

44. "Requiem Mass Offered for Father Molyneaux," *The Messenger*, 30 April 1965, 1.

45. "Official," 29 August 1941, *Des Moines Register*, 1.

46. Ossian, "The Home Fronts of Iowa," 37.

47. Ibid., 84.

48. Ibid.

49. Quoted in ibid., 127.

50. Ibid., 101–2.

51. Ibid., 81.

52. These included John F. O'Connor, Stephen Kane, P. J. Walsh, Francis L. Sampson, Albert Davidsaver, Joseph M, Schulte, J. A. Devlin, T. J. Barrett. and Woodrow Elias for the army. For the navy, Milo Tennessen, Valerian Balthasar Schomer, Edward Harkin, and Maurice Schulte and Thomas Moriarty, who was an auxiliary chaplain to Fort Des Moines. Source, "Diocese of Des Moines" *Official Catholic Directory* (New York: P. J. Kenedy and Sons, 1942–1945).

53. Albert Davidsaver to Gerald Bergan, September 12, 1940, Albert Davidsaver Priest File, ADM.

54. Albert Davidsaver to Gerald Bergan, August 20, 1943, Davidsaver File, ADM. Bergan reproduced some of Davidsaver's letters to him on the pages of the Catholic newspaper. See "Former Osceola Priest Says Catholicity in Australia Is Great," *The Messenger*, 26 November 1943, 6 & 5 (the odd numeration was a trademark of the *Register* chain, which put local news on the last page and if it spilled over located the rest on the previous page).

55. "Des Moines Priests Wounded in Encounter with Japanese Soldier," *The Messenger*, 24 March 1944, 1; "Chaplain Davidsaver Returns to Duty after Wound Heals," *The Messenger*, 16 June 1944, 1; "Chaplain Albert Davidsaver Is Recovering from Jungle Rot," *The Messenger*, 27 October 1944, 1.

56. Joseph Devlin Priest File, ADM.

57. "Chaplain T. J. Barrett Died in Burma Camp," *The Messenger*, 30 June, 1944, 6 & 5.

58. Stephen Kane to Gerald Bergan, n.d. [likely 1943], Stephen Kane Priest File, ADM.

59. Ossian, "The Home Fronts of Iowa," 171–72.

60. Stephen Kane to Gerald Bergan, n.d. [likely 1943], Stephen Kane Priest File, ADM.

61. "Des Moines Priest Reported Missing in Africa," *The Messenger,* 12 March 1943, n.p.

62. Stephen Kane to Gerald Bergan, September, 1943, from Prison Camp POW 1524, Stephen Kane Priest File, ADM.

63. Stephen Kane to Gerald Bergan, n.d. [likely latter 1943], from Prison Camp POW 1524, Stephen Kane Priest File, ADM.

64. "Chaplain Kane, Freed from Nazi Prison, Arrives in U.S.," *The Messenger,* 8 June 1945, 6; "Rev. Stephen W. Kane, Imprisoned for 28 Months Is Promoted to Major," *The Messenger,* 29 June 1945, 1.

65. "Paratroopers Select Fr. Francis Sampson as Hero of Invasion," *The Messenger,* 4 August 1944, 6; "Chaplain Tells of 'Chute Jump' into France," *The Messenger,* 13 October 1944, 1 & 2; "Father Sampson, War Chaplain, Is Listed Missing," *The Messenger,* 26 January 1945, 6; "Unofficial Word Indicates Fr. Sampson Is a Prisoner," *The Messenger,* 16 March 1945, 1; "Chaplain Sampson Is Prisoner of Germans," *The Messenger,* 30 March 1945, 1; "'Tall Corn Land' Viewed with Joy by Liberated Chaplain," *The Messenger,* 22 June 1945, 6.

66. John P. Cody to Gerald Bergan, July 15, 1943, Shenandoah Parish File, ADM.

67. Patrick Cummins, OSB, "The Iowa War Prisons" n.d., ADM.

68. "S. Sgt. Ernest A. Block of Earling Killed in Action," *The Messenger,* 23 February 1945, 1.

69. "Tragedy Strikes Again in Earling Resident's Home," *The Messenger,* 14 July 1944, 1; "Earling Man Missing Three Years Is Prisoner in Burma," *The Messenger,* 9 March 1945, 1.

70. "Memorial Mass Offered for Capt. Clarke of Marine Corps," *The Messenger,* 7 July 1944, 1.

71. "4,203 Men and Women of Diocese in Armed Forces," *The Messenger,* 11 February 1944, 5.

72. "Diocesan Honor Roll Has 166 Gold Stars," *The Messenger,* 18 January 1946, 1.

73. "Dowling Student Life Is Affected by War," *The Messenger,* 27 February 1942, 1; "Defense Classes Being Taught in Parish Halls," *The Messenger,* 6 March 1942, 1.

74. "Novena in Earling Is for Men in Service," *The Messenger,* 13 March 1942, 1.

75. "Many Continue Novena to Sorrowful Mother," *The Messenger,* 14 July 1944, 1.

76. "Fr. Duren of Westphalia Composes Victory Song," *The Messenger*, 2 January 1942, 1.

77. "Former Wiota Postmaster Writes Home about His Visit to Rome," *The Messenger*, 28 July 1944, 6.

78. "Fr. Aspinwall Speaks at Civic Celebration," *The Messenger*, 24 August 1945, 6 & 5.

79. Lester V. P. Lyons to Gerald T. Bergan, August 25, 1970, Bergan Personal File, Box 22, S67, S 1, F22, ADOm.

80. "Grist," *The Catholic Messenger*, 11 March 1938, 3.

81. Clipping, "Rare Stained Glass in Des Moines Cathedral," undated, Bergan Personal File, ADM. Bergan even included a window to honor his patron St. Gerald and also one of St. Paul of the Cross to honor the Passionists whom he highly esteemed.

82. "Cathedral Modeling Is Completed for Christmas," *The Messenger*, 22 December 1944, 1.

83. "Parish Debt Payments Double 1942 Figure," *The Messenger*, 25 February 1944, 1. See also, "Dunlap Parish Plant Freed of Indebtedness," *The Messenger*, 7 July 1944, 6; "Successful Drive Pays Off Malloy Church Indebtedness," *The Messenger*, 6 October 1944, 1; "Mortgage Is Burned by Parish in Audubon," *The Messenger*, 23 February 1945, n.p.

84. "26,000 Slashed from Defiance Parish Debt," *The Messenger*, 5 February 1943, 1; "Improvements are Made on Parish Church, Greenfield," *The Messenger*, 12 February 1943, 1; "St. Joseph's Parish to Celebrate Mortgage Payment," *The Messenger*, 25 June 1943, 1; "All Saints, Stuart Pays Off $21,500 in Debts," *The Messenger*, 27 August 1943, 6.

85. "1944 Was a Banner Year for Debt Reduction," *The Messenger*, 16 March 1945, 1.

86. "Bishop to Consecrate St. Anthony's Church," *The Messenger*, 13 December 1946, 6.

87. "St. Augustin's Church to Be Consecrated," *The Messenger*, 28 August 1947, 6.

88. Edward Daly to Thomas Moriarty, September 2, 1953, Thomas Moriarty File, ADM.

89. John Aldera Priest File, ADM

90. Paul Marasco Priest File, ADM.

91. Paul Marasco to Maurice Dingman, June 19, 1971, Shenandoah File, ADM; "Bishop Established New Parish in Clarinda," *The Messenger*, 26 June 1942, 1.

92. "Bishop Will Dedicate Clarinda Church Sunday," *The Messenger*, 16 June 1944, 1.

93. "Bishop Daly to Dedicate New Villisca Church," *The Messenger*, 9 July 1948, 6 & 5.

94. "Original Painting of Holy Family to Be Blessed in Villisca Church," *The Messenger*, 8 August 1948, 6.

95. Don Gard, "Drumm Home to Move to a New Site," *The Catholic Mirror*, 25 May 1978, 1 & 12.

96. It had twenty-three rooms, one of which became a chapel, a solarium, a paneled library, a sunken outdoor garden, a three-car garage, servants quarters, and was heavily wooded with oak and hickory trees and a frontage of 350 feet on Thirty-Seventh Street. Next to it was a large greenhouse. The house had originally been built for wealthy banker Arthur Reynolds, later chairman of the board of Continental Illinois Bank and Trust in Chicago. The Herrings bought it in 1915 and lived there until the senator died in September 1945. "Home of Late Senator Herring Bought for Bishop's Residence," undated clipping, Priests, vol. 1, ADM.

97. "Bishop Dingman of Des Moines to Sell Traditional Residence," *Witness*, 8 May 1980, clipping in Dingman File, ADM; "D. M. Couple Buys Bishop's Mansion," *Tribune*, 29 August 1980, clipping in Dingman File, ADM.

98. Gerald Bergan to Luigi Ligutti, August 22, 1934, Luigi Ligutti Priest Files, Folder 3, ADM.

99. Luigi Ligutti to Gerald Bergan, August 23, 1934, Luigi Ligutti Priest Files, Folder 3, ADM.

100. Nick Lamberto, "Archbishop Bergan: A Doer, Friend to All," clipping, *Des Moines Sunday Register*, 31 July 1966, Bergan Files, ADM.

101. John McIlhon, "Man for All Seasons," *The Catholic Mirror*, 9 December 1965, 4. McIlhon used the popular shorthand of "ecumenical" to refer not only to contacts among various Christian groups but also with non-Christians. The proper term for Jewish-Christian interaction is "interfaith" as opposed to ecumenical.

102. Maurice Dingman, "Pastoral Letter," July 10, 1969, *Catholic Mirror*.

103. "Cardinal Spellman Guest of Bishop Bergan," *The Messenger*, 16 May 1947, 6 & 5.

104. "Mixed Emotions Greet Notice of Bishop's Elevation," *The Messenger*, 20 February 1948, 6.

105. "Father Edward C. Daly of Apostolic Delegation is Des Moines Bishop," *The Messenger*, 19 March 1948, 1.

106. "Archbishop-Elect Bergan Plans to Leave Des Moines March 30," *The Messenger*, 26 March 1948, 1.

107. I. E. Metcalf to Gerald T. Bergan, February 13, 1948, Farewell Letters, Box 30, ADOm.

108. Martin M. Weitz to Gerald T. Bergan, n.d. Farewell Letters, Box 30, ADOm.

109. J. M. Hanson to Gerald T. Bergan, n.d. Farewell Letters, Box 30, ADOm.

110. Maurice Dingman to Gerald T. Bergan, n.d. Farewell Letters, Box 30, ADOm.

Chapter 6—pages 187–33

1. Lisa Lynn Ossian, "The Home Fronts of Iowa, 1940–1945" (PhD dissertation, Iowa State University, 1998), 242–44.

2. Ibid., 246–47.

3. For a full discussion of the changes at Mercy Hospital from the 1950s through the 1990s, see O'Brien, *Our Journey Together*, 330–35.

4. "Mercy Hospital: Caring for a Community," in William E. Ramsey and Betty Dineen Shrier, *Silent Hills Speak: A History of Council Bluffs, Iowa* (Council Bluffs Public Library Foundation: Barnhart Press, 2002), 210–16.

5. "Construction Moving Rapidly on New Hospital in Corning," *The Messenger*, 3 March 1950, 6.

6. "New Rosary Hospital Is Dedicated in Corning Ceremony," *The Messenger*, 13 April 1951, 1.

7. "Felician Sisters to Run New Hospital in Corning," *The Messenger*, 18 July 1946, 6 & 5; "History of Rosary Hospital," n.d., Parish Files, St. Patrick's Church, Corning, Iowa. In 1989, this hospital came under the administration of the Sisters of Mercy. See O'Brien, *Our Journey Together*, 421–22.

8. "Bishop-Elect to be Consecrated in Early May," *The Messenger*, 26 March 1948, 1.

9. Daly worked well with his religious superiors, including the politically astute Terrence Steven McDermott, OP, who reigned as provincial from 1930 until 1955. McDermott was adept at cultivating influential Roman officials. The archivist of the Dominicans observed: "His [McDermott's] file is full of thank-you notes from Roman officials acknowledging his shipments of cigars, meats, liquors, and so on; Shortly after World War II he gave Cardinal Giuseppe Pizzardo a Cadillac." Daly performed routine tasks for McDermott, offering canonical advice, seeking permissions for travel to Rome, dispensations, etc., and was McDermott's channel to Cicognani and through him to Rome. Letter of Archivist of Dominican Fathers, R.C. Mac Donald, to author, n.d.

10. Henry Rohlman to George Biskup, April 10, 1948, Rohlman Files, Archives of the Archdiocese of Dubuque (hereafter AAD).

11. "Bishop-Elect to Arrive in Des Moines, May 10," *The Messenger*, 30 April 1948, 6; "Bishop-Elect Edward C. Daly, O.P., to Be Raised to Episcopacy in Des Moines, Thursday, May 13," *The Messenger*, 7 May 1948, 1.

12. "Archbishop Cicognani Preaches at Installation," *The Messenger*, 21 May 1948, 1.

13. "Over 3,000 Greet Bishop Daly," *The Messenger*, 21 May 1948, 1.

14. "Sermons and Addresses on the Occasion of the Episcopal Consecration of the Most Reverend Edward C. Daly, O.P., S.T.M., Bishop of Des Moines, May 13, 1948," Copy in Daly Papers, ADM.

15. Raymond Conley, "Memories of a Many Splendored Gift," pamphlet in Raymond Conley Priest File, ADM (hereafter Conley Memoir).

16. This information was provided by Monsignors Lawrence Beeson and Edward Pfeffer, both of whom worked in the chancery under Daly. Interview with Monsignor Lawrence Beeson, December 2013, Des Moines, Iowa (hereafter Beeson Interview).

17. Conley Memoir.

18. "Msgr. Sondag Marks 10th Year as Chancellor," *The Messenger*, 29 June 1962, 1.

19. Edward Daly to Amleto Cicognani, January 10, 1951, Daly Papers, ADM.

20. Diocesan Official to Elizabeth Wood, ADM

21. The foregoing is taken from David S. Bovee, *The Church and the Land: The National Catholic Rural Life Conference and American Society, 1923–2007* (Washington DC: The Catholic University of America Press, 2010), 152–75.

22. In 1950, Daly took *Messenger* editor Raymond Conley on a trip to Rome for the Holy Year. En route, he stopped to pray at the Shrine of Our Lady at Fatima and then arrived in the Eternal City, where he and Conley resided with the Dominicans at the Order's Santa Sabina Church. They both saw some of the sights and were fortunate to have a private audience with Pius XII. Afterward, there were meetings with other prominent figures in Rome associated with the American church: Cardinal Pietro Fumasoni-Biondi, who had been the apostolic delegate before Cicognani; Bishop Martin J. O'Connor, rector of the North American College; and other Americans in the curia or heading up local residences or colleges. Conley recalled with special affection the Mass in St. Peter's Basilica commemorating the eleventh anniversary of Pius XII's coronation where Daly was the only American bishop in attendance. Paul Connelly, "Fences and Gifts," memoir, n.d., p. 32, ADM. "Bishop Confers in Private Audience with Holy Father," *The Messenger*, 24 March 1950, 6 & 5.

23. "Freeway Route!" Special Section, *Des Moines Tribune*, 13 May 1958, Section 5.

24. "2 East D.M. Church Buildings in Path," "Freeway Route!" Special Section, *Des Moines Tribune*, 13 May 1958, Section 5.

25. "Queen of Apostles, Council Bluffs," *The Catholic Mirror*, 9 December 1965, 3.

26. "Work in Deprived Areas," *The Catholic Mirror*, 20 July 1967, 1.

27. "St. Peter Parish to Build $195,000 Church, Rectory," *The Messenger*, 17 April 1959, 1; "New St. Peter Church to Be Dedicated Oct. 23," *The Messenger*, 21 October 1960, 1.

28. Daly was irked that Aspinwall had put in light switches on the altar and ordered them removed. Edward Daly to Maurice Aspinwall, April 28, 1955, Maurice Aspinwall Priest File, ADM; "Bishop to Bless New St. Joseph's Church

April 27," *The Messenger*, 22 April 1955, 1 & 2. This issue also included pictures of the church on page 4, including a Shrine to the Sorrowful Mother.

29. "Contract Let for $50,000 Church in Griswold," *The Messenger*, 27 July 1956, 1.

30. "New Parish Established in Windsor Heights Section," *The Messenger*, 23 June 1950, 3.

31. "Bishop Announces Erection of New St. Pius X Parish," *The Messenger*, 25 February 1955, 1; "Fr. Arthur Ring Named 1st Pastor of St. Pius X," *The Messenger*, 24 June 1955, 1.

32. "First Mass Offered In New St. Pius X Parish," *The Messenger*, 29 July 1955, 1.

33. "Site Is Purchased for New Church to Serve Ankeny," *The Messenger*, 9 October 1959, 2.

34. "Erection of Ankeny Parish to Become Effective January 6," *The Messenger*, 1 January 1960, 1; "Newly Named Ankeny Pastor Is Native of Visitation Parish," ibid.; "Plan Open House at Ankeny," *The Messenger*, 27 April 1962, 1.

35. "St. Mary of Nazareth Parish Is Established," *The Messenger*, 31 January 1964, 1.

36. Interview with Monsignor Edward Pfeffer, Dowling High School, August 2013. The Meredith Corporation was an important benefactor of the Diocese of Des Moines, not only providing this house, but aiding in the renovation of St. Ambrose Cathedral, providing a memorable book to honor the visit of Pope John Paul II in 1979, and helping the publication of this present volume.

37. Walsh's exploits were interesting, witnessing the death of Japanese prisoners tried and executed by the Allies after the war at Subgame Prison and even walking with Japanese leader Hideki Tojo to the gallows as well as General Jennie Dobra, the engineer of the 1931 Mukden incident that led to the Japanese invasion of Manchuria. He also spoke with Colonel Kingro Hashimoto who helped sink the US gunboat *Panay* in 1937 while anchored on the Yangtze River. Walsh served twenty-two years in the military.

38. "Iowa Catholic Population Grows," *The Catholic Mirror*, 12 May 1977, 1. The headline may be deceiving. There was growth in both the Dubuque and Sioux City dioceses, but both Davenport and Des Moines registered slight losses. Des Moines went from 78,813 in 1976 to 78,325 in 1977. Catholics were only 18.9 percent of the state's total population.

39. "Altoona, Carlisle Communities Want Parishes," *The Catholic Mirror*, 8 December 1976, 1–2.

40. Betty Murphy, "Parish Established in Altoona," *The Catholic Mirror*, 3 November 1983, 1 & 16.

41. "Ss. John and Paul Church Dedicated," *The Catholic Mirror*, 3 October 1985, 16.

42. "Fifth Council Bluffs Parish Established," *The Messenger*, 26 October 1956, 1.

43. "Council Bluffs Parish Plans First Building," *The Messenger*, 22 February 1957, 1.

44. "Decree Published for Parish in Indianola," *The Messenger*, 6 September 1957, 1.

45. "Plans Completed for Church in Indianola," *The Messenger*, 31 January 1958, 1. The church was dedicated on December 21, 1958. "Dedication Rite Set for Indianola Church Dec. 21," *The Messenger*, 19 December 1958, 1.

46. "10,426 Students Enrolled in Diocesan School System," *The Messenger*, 18 September 1959, 1. The high schools were as follows: Dowling (Des Moines); St. Joseph Academy (Des Moines); St. Francis, Mount Loreto (Council Bluffs); St. Peter's (Defiance); St. Joseph's (Dunlap); St. Joseph's (Earling); Assumption (Granger); St. Patrick's (Imogene); St. Joseph's (Neola); St. Patrick's (Perry); St. Mary's (Portsmouth); St. Boniface (Westphalia).

47. "See's School Hit Capacity as 10,821 Are Registered," *The Messenger*, 23 September 1960, 1. "St. Joseph's Church Being Razed as New Church Is Planned," *The Messenger*, 26 February 1954, 1; "Contracts Signed for St. Joseph's Church," *The Messenger*, 2 April 1954, 1; "New Holy Trinity Church Blessing, Apr. 28," *The Messenger*, 26 April 1957, 1; "Holy Trinity School Annex Rushed," *The Messenger*, 4 September 1959, 1; "Four Classrooms and Auditorium Will Be Added at St. Augustin's," *The Messenger*, 12 March 1954, 1; "New Harlan School Cost $150,000," *The Messenger*, 27 August 1954, 1; "$70,000 Addition Started at Highland Park School," *The Messenger*, 10 June 1955, 1; "Bishop to Lay Cornerstone of Panama School," *The Messenger*, 22 July 1955, 1; "10-Classroom School Planned by Christ the King Parish," *The Messenger*, 8 November 1957, 1; " Christ, King School, Dream Now Reality," *The Messenger*, 4 September 1959, 1; "Work to Start This Month on New Visitation School," *The Messenger*, 8 July 1960, 1; "$2,750,000 Expansion at Mercy Hospital," *The Messenger*, 13 May 1955, 1; "Souvenir Issue Marking the Dedication of the $3,000,000 Addition to Mercy Hospital, Des Moines," *The Messenger* 10 April 1959, 1; "$555,000 Drumm Home Wing Will Rise," *The Messenger*, 8 March 1957, 1; "New Building Scheduled at Dowling High School," *The Messenger*, 22 July 1955, 1; "Flavin Hall Erected in 1884 to Be Razed for Chapel Site," *The Messenger*, 5 August 1955, 1.

48. These statistics are derived from the *Official Catholic Directory, 1948–1964* (New York: P. J. Kenedy and Sons).

49. "Dowling High Chapel Cornerstone Rite Set," *The Messenger*, 7 September 1956, 1.

50. "St. Joseph's Plans Expansion," *The Messenger*, 10 February 1961, 1 & 7.

51. "Pledge $1,402,000 for St. Albert's," *The Messenger*, 14 December 1962, 1.

52. Beeson interview.

53. "St. Albert's Bids Opened," *The Messenger*, 3 May 1963, 1 & 2.

54. "Father Delahant Appointed Superintendent," *The Messenger*, 7 June 1963, 1.

55. "Bless Cornerstone at St. Albert's," *The Messenger*, 9 August 1963, 1 (with picture).

56. "Bishop Daly to Bless St. Albert's Sunday," *The Messenger*, 5 June 1964, 1; "Great Day of Dedication," *The Messenger*, 12 June 1964, 1.

57. "Faithful Pioneer in Council Bluffs," *The Messenger*, 20 September 1963, 4.

58. "New Central High School For Shelby County," *The Messenger*, 24 May 1963, 1 & 5.

59. "Over $2,000,000 Spent in Decade on School, Convent Construction," *The Messenger*, 17 February 1956, 1.

60. "Bishop Opens Fund Appeal for St. Joseph Academy," *The Messenger*, 12 May 1961, 1.

61. "Diocesan Drive Launched," *The Messenger*, 14 October 1955, 1. This edition with bold, red headlines, also included Daly's own message laying out diocesan needs: "$1,250,000 Minimum Goal Set," *The Messenger*, 21 October 1955, 1; "Pledges Reach $3,000,000," *The Messenger*, 2 December 1955, 1; "Campaign Total Goes over $300,000 Mark," *The Messenger*, 9 December 1955, 1.

62. Quoted in "St. Mary's End of An Era," *The Messenger*, 13 January 1961, 1.

63. "Parish Profile No. 92," *The Messenger*, 20 May 1960, 3.

64. The parish bells, which had been rung by the sexton and then by Weber himself after he had to let the employee go, were sent over to St. Pius X Parish in Urbandale. Other church furnishings were scattered: the stations of the cross to Sacred Heart Church in West Des Moines, the pipe organ to St. John's in Des Moines, rectory furniture to Holy Trinity, the censer to St. Mary of the Assumption in Lacona, the candlesticks to St. Mary of Perpetual Help in Rosemount. The altar and other sanctuary furnishing found their way to the lower church of St. Anthony's Parish. "St. Mary's End of an Era," *The Messenger*, 13 January 1961, 1; "Bells of St. Mary's Will Not Be Silenced," *The Messenger*, 3 March 1961, 1.

65. For more information on African Americans in Des Moines, see *Des Moines Center of Iowa: Survey of Historic Sites* (Des Moines Planning and Zoning Commission, 1983), "Negro Americans," 94–100.

66. Robert H. Speigel, "A Penetrating Look at Negro Housing Here; Segregation Nearly 100% Effective," *Des Moines Tribune*, 26 June 1956, 1 & 4.

67. Clipping in Thomas P. Murphy Priest File, ADM. especially at St. Peter's Parish in Des Moines.

68. "Sermons and Addresses on the Occasion of the Episcopal Consecration of the Most Reverend Edward C. Daly, O.P., S.T.M., Bishop of Des Moines, May 13, 1948," Copy in Daly Papers, ADM.

69. "Mass of Bl. Martin Set Nov. 5th," *The Messenger*, 28 October 1949, 6 & 5.

70. "Negroes Need Not Apply," *The Messenger*, 22 March 1963, 4.

71. "Who Is My Neighbor?," *The Messenger*, 19 April 1962, 1. Other speakers included Canadian biblical scholar Father David Stanley and Earl Coverdale, associate editor of *The Messenger*. See also "Inform Minorities of Innate Dignity," *The Messenger*, 26 April 1963, 1.

72. "Sympathy Is Not Enough," *The Messenger*, 20 September 1963, 1.

73. "Discuss Formation of Interracial Council," *The Messenger*, 11 October 1963, 1.

74. "Fair Housing Ordinance," *The Messenger*, 11 October 1963, 4.

75. Edward Daly, "Cooperation with Our Colored Fellow Citizens," *The Messenger*, 18 October 1963, 1.

76. Stephen Kane to Edward Daly, January 11, 1951, Stephen Kane Priest File, ADM.

77. "Fr. Joseph Schulte Called to Active Army Service," *The Messenger*, 17 November 1950, 1; "Fr. Sampson of D-Day Fame Hero in Korea," ibid.

78. "Father Devlin to Serve as Army Chaplain," *The Messenger*, 29 June 1951, 6.

79. "Chaplain Patrick Walsh Awarded Bronze Star for Heroic Service in Korea," *The Messenger*, 28 September 1951, 1.

80. "Former Earling Student Casualty in Korean War," *The Messenger*, 10 November 1950, 1. Later, Mathias Peter Leinen of Portsmouth died in action. "Portsmouth Man Killed in Korea, Requiem Offered," *The Messenger*, 28 September 1951, 1. Philip Spooner of Mandarin, also died in battle; "Mandarin Service Man Reported Killed in Korea," *The Messenger*, 30 May 1952, 1.

81. Daly called for rededication of parishes and the diocese to Mary, "Bishop Calls for Rededication to Mary's Pure Heart," *The Messenger*, 18 August 1950, 6 & 5.

82. "Diocese to Be Dedicated to Immaculate Heart of Mary," *The Messenger*, 11 June 1948, 1. This press notice also printed the formal directive of the bishop and a copy of the prayer to be used in the dedication.

83. "Cornerstone of Church to Be Laid," *The Messenger*, 7 October 1949, 6.

84. "Block Rosary in Visitation Parish," *The Messenger*, 28 July 1950, 6.

85. "Block Rosary Groups Started at St. Peter's," *The Messenger*, 1 September 1950, 3; "Pilgrim Virgin Statue Will Visit Diocese on Oct. 26," *The Messenger*, 1 September 1950, 3; Pilgrim Virgin Statue to Be in Diocese Two Weeks," *The Messenger*, 20 October 1950, 1. The statue arrived first at St. Ambrose and then was sent to Dowling, next to the following Des Moines parishes: St. John's, St. Peter's, and Visitation. It then was placed in Bayard, Perry, Atlantic, Portsmouth, Neola, Imogene, and Council Bluffs. "Faithful Flock to Join Mary's Peace Plan," *The Messenger*, 3 November 1950, 1.

86. "500 Autos Accompany Pilgrim Virgin Statue," *The Messenger*, 10 November 1950, 1.

87. "Diocese Is Dedicated to Queenship of Mary," *The Messenger*, 28 September 1956, 1.

88. "The Foxhole Promise," in Ramsey and Shrier, *Silent Hills Speak*, 151–53.

89. "Our Congratulations and Prayers, Your Excellency," *The Messenger*, 14 March 1958, 1.

90. "1st Cana Conference in Diocese Set in Granger," *The Messenger*, 28 January 1949, 6.

91. "First Cana Conference Held in Granger," *The Messenger*, 11 February 1949, 6.

92. "Diocese Now Has 39 Seminarians," *The Messenger*, 23 September 1949, 1.

93. "38 Diocesan Young Men Studying in Seminaries," *The Messenger*, 13 October 1950, 1 & 3.

94. "Msgr. Schiltz's Address," *The Messenger*, 26 March 1965, 3

95. Leo Binz to Giuseppe Pizzardo, October 16, 1950, Mount St. Bernard, Box 1, Archives of the Archdiocese of Dubuque. (hereafter AAD.)

96. "Notes in Memorandum," Rector/Faculty File, Mount St. Bernard, Box 1, AAD.

97. "Make Seminary Chief Charity, Bishop Exhorts Faithful," *The Messenger*, 22 February 1952, 1.

98. "Mount St. Agnes Bought by Province Bishops as Seminary Building," *The Messenger*, 26 August 1951, 1; "16 Students are Enrolled at Mount St. Bernard's," *The Messenger*, 7 September 1951, 1.

99. "Iowa's Four Bishops Detail Plans for Area Seminary," *The Messenger*, 15 February 1952, 1. To pay for the additions to the seminary, the Diocese of Des Moines was assessed $350,000. "Campaign Begins for Dubuque Seminary," *The Messenger*, 14 March 1952, 1.

100. "Children in Diocese Donate $3,680," *The Messenger*, 4 June 1952, 1.

101. "Notes in Memorandum," Rector/Faculty File Minutes of Meeting of October 16, 1951, Mount St. Bernard, Box 1, AAD.

102. Interview with Monsignor Lawrence Beeson, May 11, 2012, Des Moines, Iowa.

103. "Mt. St. Bernard Seminary Opens Doors to Largest Class," *The Messenger*, 25 November 1955, 3.

104. "6 to Receive Holy Orders in St. Ambrose on June 9," *The Messenger*, 3 June 1955, 1.

105. "Five Young Men to Be Ordained," *The Messenger*, 3 June 1960, 1.

106. "Rosemount, Milo Pastor Named to St. Bernard Staff," *The Messenger*, 18 February 1954, 1.

107. "Priest of Diocese Given Seminary Post of Dubuque," *The Messenger*, 28 July 1961, 1.

108. "Bishop Delivers Address at Dedication in Walnut," *The Messenger*, 7 November 1958, 1 & 2.

109. "Pontiff Reveals Plans for Ecumenical Council," *The Messenger*, 30 January 1959, 1.

110. "Papal Honors Given to Eight in Diocese," *The Messenger*, 27 November 1959, 1.

111. "Diocese Begins 50th Jubilee Year Aug. 12," *The Messenger*, 11 August 1961, 1.

112. Telephone Interview with Father Paul Koch, August 28, 2017. Fr. Koch noted that in addition to learning Spanish, he was also required to learn the indigenous languages of Bolivians, e.g., Chechua.

113. "Bishop Daly, Msgr. Sondag Die in Airplane Crash," *The Messenger*, 27 November 1964, 1 & 2.

114. Beeson interview. See also Father Lawrence Beeson, "The Last Day of Bishop Daly in Rome, Italy," *The Messenger*, 4 December 1964, 2.

115. Beeson interview.

116. "Pontifical Requiem Mass Celebrated for Bishop Daly," *The Messenger*, 4 December 1964, 1 & 3.

117. "Bishop Daly, O.P.," *The Messenger*, 4 December 1964, 4.

Chapter 7—pages 235–95

1. In the early twenty-first century, serious disagreements erupted among churchmen and scholars about the meaning and intent of conciliar documents. Some dismissed them as "pastoral" and therefore not binding in the same way doctrinal definitions of earlier councils had been. Others argued that interpretations of council documents needed to pursue a "hermeneutic of continuity" that emphasized the ways in which reform was in keeping with the time-honored traditions of the church. This "hermeneutic of continuity" was a polemic against those who saw the council as a radical break with the teachings of previous councils, a "hermeneutic of discontinuity." The best discussion of the dynamics and letter of Vatican II can be found in John W. O'Malley, *What Happened at Vatican II* (Cambridge, MA: Belknap Press of Harvard University Press, 2010). See also James C. Heft and John O'Malley, eds., *After Vatican II* (Grand Rapids, MI: Eerdmans, 2012).

2. "General Council of Church Is Great Moment in History," *The Messenger*, 6 April 1962, 1 & 9. The Holy Name Society was a diocesan-wide organization of Catholic men with local parish units. These men pledged themselves to avoid irreverent use of the name of Jesus. They also dedicated themselves to encouraging devotional life, frequent Communion, and public displays of piety. Most diocesan parishes had a branch of this organization.

3. Father James Huston, "Who Needs a Council," *The Messenger*, 29 June 1962, 1 & 7.

4. Father James Huston, "The Council and Unity," *The Messenger*, 13 July 1962, 1 & 3.

5. Father James Huston, "Your Job in the Council: God's People in Action," *The Messenger*, 20 July 1962, 1 & 2.

6. When the Vatican began what they called the "Antepreparatory" phase of the council, they solicited suggestions for agenda items. Daly had more than a few. Some of them were liturgical. He wanted only one Rite for the Latin Church, the cessation of the practice during High Mass of having the celebrant read things that were being sung by the subdeacon (the epistle) and the deacon (the gospel); he called for revisions in the Breviary and pruning away feasts and lessons "according to historical norms." Most interesting, he urged a partial use of the vernacular in the Mass prayer and Scripture readings—also in the conferral of sacraments and blessings. He proposed modification in the official visitation of religious houses and the end to the advertising of Mass stipends in newspapers. He urged better preparation for CCD teachers, and he was particularly insistent that seminaries give better preparation for preaching and that priests understand "their grave moral obligation to prepare sermons." Perhaps reflecting his experiences with Mount St. Bernard's, he urged an apostolic visitation of seminaries every ten years and that Ordinaries be obliged to send priests and laypersons for suitable training in fields pertinent to church life. Daly was especially interested in some deliberation on the "exemption" of religious communities, which uncoupled them, in some circumstances, from the authority of local ordinaries. *Antepreparatoria Volumen I, pars VI, Acta et Documenta Concilio Oecumenico Vaticano II*, ADM.

7. "Bishop Asks for Novena for Success of the Council," *The Messenger*, 28 September 1962, 1.

8. "Bishop Daly's Greetings," *The Messenger*, 21 December 1962, 1.

9. "Bishop Daly Addresses Drake Faculty," 26 April 1963, 1.

10. Liturgical changes had been unfolding slowly through the late 1940s and throughout the 1950s. In 1947 Pope Pius XII had issued the encyclical *Mediator Dei*, which stressed among other things the need for more active participation by all in the liturgy. In 1955, he issued the decree *Maxima Redemptionis Nostrae*, which restored the ancient liturgies of Holy Week and urged their implementation in parishes. Some Des Moines parishes were quick to put these new rites into effect. Daly was cautious in changing these things.

11. "Bishop Daly Comments on the Council," *The Messenger*, 3 January 1964, 1.

12. Francis Ostdiek to Edward Daly, October 19, 1964, Francis Ostdiek Priest File, ADM. The Chicago school fire that Ostdiek referred to was the tragic Our Lady of the Angels blaze that killed ninety-three school-children and three BVM sisters in December 1958. The poor condition of the school

brought about a major change in school building plans all over the nation. The new regulations insisted, for example, that open stairwells had to be enclosed so as to prevent the upward ascent of a fire.

13. Edward Daly to Francis Ostdiek, October 29, 1964, Francis Ostdiek Priest File, ADM.

14. Ibid.

15. Lawrence Beeson, "Bishop Daly, A Gentle Friend to Seminarians," in *Jubilee of Faith* (Diocese of Des Moines, 1976), 12.

16. "Official," *The Messenger*, 20 October 1964, 1.

17. "Bishop George J. Biskup Appointed to Des Moines," *The Messenger*, 5 February 1965, 1.

18. For Beckmann's love of art and desire for "culture" at his college, see William E. Wilkie, "Seeds Must Die," in *Seed Harvest: A History of the Archdiocese of Dubuque*, ed. Mary Kevin Gallagher, BVM (Archdiocese of Dubuque, 1987), 84–87.

19. "Diocese Welcomes Spiritual Leader," *The Messenger*, 26 March 1965, 1 & 3.

20. "Joint Reception Held for Bishop at Dowling," *The Messenger*, 9 April 1965, 1.

21. Monsignor Paul Connelly, "Fences and Gifts," 34–35, Memoir, Paul Connelly Priest File, ADM.

22. "Bishop Biskup Returns to Des Moines from Rome," *The Catholic Mirror*, 16 December 1965, 1.

23. "A New Era," *The Catholic Mirror*, 16 December 1965, 4.

24. "Bishop George Biskup Named Archbishop of Indianapolis," *The Catholic Mirror*, 27 July 1967, 1 & 8.

25. "Ad Multos Annos," *The Catholic Mirror*, 3 August 1967, 4.

26. The main source for the life of Dingman was his authorized biography by Sisters Shirley Crisler, SFCC, and Mira Mosle, BVM, *In the Midst of His People: The Authorized Biography of Bishop Maurice J. Dingman* (Iowa City: Rudi Publishing, 1995). The quote is taken from "Bishop Never Said 'No" If He Could Find a Yes," clipping, The Hawk Eye, October 9, 1986, Dingman Papers, ADM.

27. Joseph Rangger Priest File, Archives of the Diocese of Davenport (hereafter ADD).

28. "Challenges in Church Ministry," *The Catholic Mirror*, 27 November 1980, Vocation Insert., 1b.

29. A good description of Dingman's years at St. Ambrose College can be found in George McDaniel, *A Great and Lasting Beginning*, 87–115.

30. "Rural Life Award Winner Sees Biology as 'Cat, Corn Course," *The Messenger*, 23 December 1955, 5.

31. McDaniel, *A Great and Lasting Beginning*, 88.

32. Maurice Dingman to Henry P. Rohlman, August 17, 1936, Dingman Files, Archives of the Diocese of Davenport (hereafter ADD).

33. Maurice Dingman to Henry P. Rohlman, November 11, 1936, Dingman Files, ADD.

34. Maurice Dingman to Henry P. Rohlman, February 9, 1937, Dingman Files, ADD.

35. Maurice Dingman to Henry P. Rohlman, April 3, 1938, Dingman Papers, ADD.

36. "A First at the Vatican," *The Catholic Mirror*, 26 September 1974, 17.

37. Maurice Dingman to Henry P. Rohlman, January 11, 1940, Dingman Papers, ADD.

38. "Appoint Msgr. Maurice J. Dingman New Bishop of Des Moines Diocese," *The Catholic Mirror*, 11 April 1968, 1.

39. "Bishop-Elect Dingman's Statement," *The Catholic Mirror*, 11 April 1968, 1.

40. Dingman Interview, *The Catholic Mirror,* 18 April 1968, 1 & 2.

41. Charles Roberts, "Church Dies with Christ to Reach the Promised Land," interview from Davenport *Catholic* Messenger, reprinted in *The Catholic Mirror*, 25 April 1968, 2.

42. "Diocesan Community Welcomes Bishop," *The Catholic Mirror*, 11 July 1968, 1 & 7.

43. "English Text for Ordinary of Mass," *The Messenger*, 24 July 1964, 1

44. "Absolution from Sins Now Given in English," *The Messenger*, 31 July 1964, 1.

45. "Preview of English Mass," *The Messenger*, 23 October 1964, 1.

46. "Bishop Concelebrates Mass," *The Messenger*, 9 April 1965, 1.

47. "Ordain Seven Diocesan Priests," *The Catholic Mirror*, 15 May 1969, 1 & 8. These priests were Gary Bisignano, Terrence Lindsley, Keith Engel, Anthony Aiello, Terry C. Lees, James Laurenzo, and Thomas DeCarlo.

48. "Diocese Received Permission to Offer Saturday Evening Masses," *The Catholic Mirror*, 26 February 1970, 1.

49. "Bishop Dingman to Confer Extraordinary Privilege," *The Catholic Mirror*, 23 July 1970, 1.

50. "Received into Church," *The Catholic Mirror*, 12 December 1973, 1.

51. "Urbandale First Communion," *The Catholic Mirror*, 2 January 1974, 3.

52. "Friday Abstinence, R.I.P.," *The Catholic Mirror*, 24 November 1966, 4.

53. "St. Mary's Elkhart," *The Messenger*, 2 April 1965, 3.

54. For this before and after picture, see "Church, Rectory Renovated at Lenox," *The Catholic Mirror*, 27 October 1966, 5.

55. "Before and After of Westphalia," *The Catholic Mirror*, 17 June 1971, 8.

56. The foregoing is taken from a phone interview with Reverend James Laurenzo, February 28, 2015.

57. "Funds Needed for Cathedral Renovation," *The Catholic Mirror*, 10 June 1976, 3.

58. John F. Lorenz, "Memories of St. Ambrose Cathedral" unpublished ms. in St. Ambrose Parish File, ADM.

59. "Bishop Asks for Community Participation," *The Catholic Mirror*, 11 March 1976, 1 & 10.

60. Mary Jo Schmidt, "Cathedral Renovation Drive Moving Slowly," *The Catholic Mirror,* 3 August 1976, 13; William Simbro, "Historic Windows Stay," *Des Moines Tribune*, 20 March 1976, 3.

61. Don Gard, "Commemorate Bishop, Cathedral," *The Catholic Mirror*, 11 May 1978, 1–2.; "Diocese Dedicates Cathedral," ibid. 16 May 1978, 1, 10,; "Diocese Celebrates a New Pentecost," ibid., 12.

62. "Welcome Jesuits to the Diocese," *The Catholic Mirror*, 12 September 1974, 1.

63. "Emmaus House in Capital City," *The Catholic Mirror*, 10 October 1974, 3.

64. "Sister Mary Dingman" File, Archives of the School Sisters of St. Francis.

65. "Prayer House to Add Cottages," *The Catholic Mirror*, 19 April 1984, 10.

66. Elizabeth Murphy, "Monastery to Open Near Harlan," *The Catholic Mirror*, 1 November 1984, 20.

67. "Charismatic Renewal Meeting," *The Catholic Mirror*, 12 February 1970, 6.

68. Betty Murphy, "Charismatics Praise Life in the Spirit," *The Catholic Mirror* 29 April 1982, 1 & 3.

69. Betty Murphy, "Charismatics Share Faith View," *The Catholic Mirror*, 6 May 1982, 3.

70. "Pledge Cooperation in Ecumenical Activities," *The Catholic Mirror*, 17 October 1968.

71. "Cathedral Ordination," *The Catholic Mirror*, 28 January 1972, 1.

72. "Personal Witnesses," *The Catholic Mirror*, 4 January 1973, 1.

73. Peter Dubec, "Diocese to Join Inter-Church Forum," *The Catholic Mirror*, 14 October 1976, 1& 12.

74. Peter Dubec, "Twelve Denominations Join Inter-Church Forum," *The Catholic Mirror*, 21 October 1976, 1.

75. Quote from Don Gard, "Innovative Diocesan Diaconate Program," *The Catholic Messenger*, 29 October 1970, 1. "Diocesan Diaconate Program," *The Catholic Messenger*, 5 November 1970,1 & 2.

76. Father John F. Boyle, "Significant Changes at Mt. St. Bernard Seminary," *The Catholic Mirror*, 6 October 1966, 8. "Seminary Integrate Theology and Experience," *The Catholic Mirror*, 13 October 1966, 2.

77. Kevin O'Rourke, OP, to Archbishop Leo Byrne, July 10, 1968, Box 3, Mount St. Bernard, AAD.

78. "Homily Extols Cathedral's Pastor," *The Catholic Mirror*, 8 November 1973, 5.

79. Peter Dubec, "Tenure Policy for Priests Approved," *The Catholic Mirror*, 21 July 1977, 1 & 8. The editor of the paper commented on the policy, "The church, the diocese, and the parish are not founded on a personality cult, basing loyalty and cooperation on the power, ideology, and charisma of a particular person" (ibid., 4).

80. "Father Ostdiek Retires," *The Catholic Mirror*, 14 August 1969, 1 & 6; Quote from "Father Ostdiek Marks 60th Year in Priesthood," ibid., 12 May 1973, 1 & 3.

81. Don Gard, "Msgr. Michael G. Schiltz Retiring," *The Catholic Mirror*, 14 August 1969, 7.

82. "Msgr. Lyons Retires as Cathedral Pastor," *The Catholic Mirror*, 12 July 1973, 1–2.

83. "Funeral Mass Wednesday for Msgr. Lester Lyons," *The Catholic Mirror*, 1 November 1973, 1 & 3.

84. "Pastors for Cathedral and Lenox Bedford Named," *The Catholic Mirror*, 20 September 1973, 1 & 3.

85. "Will Married Deacons Serve D.M. Diocese?," *The Catholic Mirror*, 10 April 1969, 1 & 4.

86. Don Gard, "Permanent Diaconate Restored," *The Catholic Mirror*, 4 March 1971, 1 & 3. "Permanent Diaconate Restored," ibid., 11 March 1971, 1 & 3.

87. These men were Richard Aller, Robert Bray, John Jarvis, Donald Joslin, Dennis Kirlin, Larry Knotek, Harry Langdon, Loren Ritz. In November, David Malena, who was only thirty-two at the time his class was ordained, was at first refused a dispensation to be advanced to orders. This was later reversed and he was ordained in a separate ceremony in November 1972 at Sacred Heart Church in West Des Moines. "Will Ordain Deacon Sunday," *The Catholic Mirror*, 23 November 1972, 1.

88. "Reflective Men, Charged by the Lord," *The Catholic Mirror*, 18 April 1974, 10–11.

89. "Plan Priest Association," *The Catholic Mirror*, 2 March 1967, 1.

90. "Bishop Dingman Addresses Local Priest Association," *The Catholic Mirror*, 3 October 1968, 1 & 3.

91. "Diocesan Clergy Form Presbytery," *The Catholic Mirror*, 31 October 1968, 1.

92. "We Must Change Our Style," *The Catholic Mirror*, 31 October 1968, 1 & 7.

93. "Presbytery," *The Catholic Mirror*, 7 November 1968, 4.

94. "Why Have a Priest's Council," *The Catholic Mirror*, 13 March 1969, 4.

95. Bishop Maurice Dingman to Frank Cordaro, December 13, 1983, Frank Cordaro Papers, "Bishop Dingman File" Catholic Worker Collection, Marquette University Archives.

96. "Reorganize Diocese of Des Moines Among 12 Regional Communities," "Coordinating the Work of Renewal in the Diocese," *The Catholic Mirror* 27 March 1969, 1.

97. Don Gard, "Diocesan Council of Sisters," *The Catholic Mirror*, 12 February 1970, 1 & 5.

98. "Parish Council Guidelines Published," *The Catholic Mirror*, 16 April 1970, 1. A copy of the guidelines was included in tabloid form in the newspaper.

99. Bognanno became intrigued with the Catholic Charismatic Renewal and helped bring it to Des Moines. An achievement that would win him national acclaim was the foundation of a spiritual renewal program for priests known as the Emmaus Program. This program was begun in Chicago and Bognanno had worked on it with other leaders in the field of spiritual renewal. In 1974, it was structured and promoted by the National Organization for Continuing Education of the Roman Catholic Clergy. In the fall of 1977, it was begun in three dioceses Burlington, Vermont; Memphis, Tennessee; and Omaha, Nebraska. Consisting of small-group sessions, common prayer, retreats, and reunions of those participating, it was later brought to Bognanno's home diocese in 1980. "Priests Begin Emmaus Program," *The Catholic Mirror*, 18 October 1980, 2.

100. "Bishop Present Blueprint of Board of Education," *The Catholic Mirror*, 24 October 1968, 1 & 3.

101. "Final Report: Interim Diocesan Pastoral Council," *The Catholic Mirror* 19 January 1978, n.p. See also Dingman's letter announcing the new council, "DPC: A New Model for a Renewed Church," ibid.

102. Peter Dubec, "DPC: A Sign of Diocesan Unity," *The Catholic Mirror*, 16 March 1978, 1 & 12; "DPC Offers New Vision of Service," *The Catholic Mirror*, 23 March 1978, 1.

103. "DPC," *The Catholic Mirror*, 30 March 1978, 4.

104. "Annual Report to the people of the Diocese of Des Moines," *The Catholic Mirror*, 11 November 1971, 1–4.

105. Maurus Kennedy to "Dear Family," March 17, 1970, Kennedy File, Archives of the Abbey of St. Benedict, Atchison, Kansas (hereafter AOSBA).

106. Maurus Kennedy, OSB, to "Dear Family," May 26, 1971, Kennedy File, AOSBA.

107. Maurus Kennedy, OSB, to "Dear Family," October 1, 1971, Kennedy File, AOSBA.

108. "Board Votes School Merger for Council Bluffs Area," *The Catholic Mirror*, 17 February 1972, 1. "Sequence in Council Bluffs, September 1971 to June 1975," Letter of Monsignor Lawrence Beeson to author.

109. "School System Stronger Following New Merger," *The Catholic Mirror*, 14 December 1972, 1–2.

110. Monsignor Lawrence Beeson provided the information about this sequence of events and the people involved.

111. "Pastoral Plan: Catholic Community of Council Bluffs," *The Catholic Mirror*, 5 December 1974, 9–12.

112. "Bishop Approves C.B. Pastoral Plan," *The Catholic Mirror*, 19 December 1974, 11–14.

113. Maurus Kennedy, OSB, to Denis Meade, OSB, September 8, 1975, AOSBA.

114. "Form Priest Team Ministry," *The Catholic Mirror*, 20 April 1971, 1 & 8; "Launch Team Ministry," ibid., 28 April 1971, 1 & 3.

115. Paul Connelly describes the Leon Region in his memoir, "Fences and Gifts," 35–37.

116. David Byers and Bernard Quinn, *New Directions for the Rural Church* (New York: Paulist Press, 1978), 81–97. See also Mary Jo Gianville, "Co-Pastors Share Authority, Duty," *The Catholic Mirror*, 28 April 1977, 1 & 12.

117. Peter Dubec, "Five Parishes Form Cooperative Model of Ministry," *The Catholic Mirror*, 8 November 1981, 1 & 12.

118. Don Gard, "Region Plans for Ministry Needs," and Elizabeth Murphy, "Diocese Studying Plan for Parish Administrators," *The Catholic Mirror*, 7 February 1985, 1 & 16.

119. "Letters from a Country Priest," n.d. (c. 1985), Cordaro Papers, AMU.

120. Don Gard, "Parish Problems Analyzed," *The Catholic Mirror*, 6 November 1975, 1.

121. "A New Parish in S.E. Warren County," *The Catholic Mirror*, 16 February 1978, 1.

122. "Bishop Requests Participation in Shelby County Self-Study," *The Catholic Mirror*, 5 February 1976, 1 & 10.

123. Mary Jo Gianville, "Shelby County Self-Study Nears End," *The Catholic Mirror*, 21 October 1976, 1 & 12.

124. Don Gard, "Shelby County Schools to Merge Next Year," *The Catholic Mirror*, 15 December 1977, 1 & 2; "Shelby County Recommendations," ibid., 3.

125. "Bishop Dingman Views Future of Diocese," *The Catholic Mirror*, 19 November 1970, 7.

126. "Christ Child Home Will Close May 1," *The Catholic Mirror*, 10 March 1966, 1.

127. "Chancery Moves to New Location," *The Catholic Mirror*, 24 November 1966, 1.

128. "New School Head Says: 'Publicize Our Program," *The Catholic Mirror*, 1 July 1978, 2.

129. Don Gard, "Sister Leaves School Office, Will Assume Role as Provincial," *The Catholic Mirror*, 1 July 1978, 2.

130. Don Gard, "Chancellor: Flunkie or Flanker to Bishop," *The Catholic Mirror*, 25 June 1970, 1 & 8.

131. "Catholic Council for Social Concern: Fifty Years," *The Catholic Mirror*, 16 September 1976, special section, n.p.

132. Sr. Mira Mosle, "Family Life Seeks New Affiliation," *The Catholic Mirror*, 26 March 1981, 1 & 12.

133. Sherry Ricchiardi, "Role of Church Criticized," *Des Moines Register*, 16 September 1979, 6E.

134. Peter Dubec, "Budget Tops $400,000 for 1978–79," *The Catholic Mirror*, 12 April 1978, 1 & 12.

135. "Diocese Announces Annual Appeal," *The Catholic Mirror*, 16 November 1978, 1 & 10.

136. Don Gard, "Chancellor's Role Is Changing," *The Catholic Mirror*, 17 January 1970, 3.

137. Interview with Monsignor Stephen Orr, April 22, 2015, Des Moines, Iowa.

138. "Establish Drake Newman Community Parish," *The Catholic Mirror*, 15 January 1970, 1. Rev. T. Nicholas Tormey was appointed chaplain of the Drake enterprise.

139. Don Gard, "Rap, Recreation, Religion," *The Catholic Mirror*, 26 April 1972, 1. Phone Interview with Father Thomas DeCarlo, May 26, 2015.

140. Peter Dubec, "Group Buys Retreat Site, Youth Center," *The Catholic Mirror*, 16 June 1983, 1 & 10.

141. Betty Murphy, "Center Faces Financial Problems," *The Catholic Mirror*, 9 February 1984, 16.

142. "Chief Teacher of the Diocese," *The Catholic Mirror*. 25 January 1973, 1.

143. "Friday Penance Encouraged," and "Mercy Hospital Not Open for Abortions," *The Catholic Mirror*, 8 March 1973, 1.

144. "Iowa Bishops Pro-Life Statement," *The Catholic Mirror*, 3 May 1973, 1.

145. "Bishop Tells About Papal Audience," *The Catholic Mirror*, 29 June 1978, 8.

Chapter 8—pages 297–33

1. These numbers are derived from the *Official Catholic Directory*, 1969–1987 (New York: P. J. Kenedy and Sons).

2. "Annual Report to the people of the Diocese of Des Moines," *The Catholic Mirror*, 11 November 1971, 4. This was noted by Monsignor Edward Pfeffer in the report.

3. "Purchased New School Site," *The Catholic Mirror*, 23 June 1966, 1.

4. "Green Light Given for Dowling Plans," *The Catholic Mirror*, 3 November 1966, 1.

5. George Cordaro and Robert Nizzi to Maurice Dingman, April 11, 1968, Dowling H.S. File, ADM.

6. Robert E. Wadle to Maurice Dingman, May 23, 1968, Dowling H.S. File, ADM.

7. Nick Lamberto, "Bishop Dingman Delays Plans for New Dowling High School," 4 August 1968, *Des Moines Sunday Register*, clipping in Dowling H.S. File, ADM.

8. Nick Lamberto, "Bishop Asks Dowling Backers of Present Site to Tell Views," 2 July 1969, *Des Moines Register*, clipping in Dowling File, ADM.

9. Memorandum to Board of Education from Dingman (undated but likely August 1969) "Dowling Site," Dowling H.S. File, ADM. The members of the 1964 committee were Jim Cooney, John Tapscott, Roger Landwehr, Joseph Fusano, Phil Riley, Ralph Guisinger, Peter Tursi, Vern Feldman, Jack Manders, and Edward McCartan.

10. Don Gard, "Report Given on the Condition of Dowling High School," *The Catholic Mirror*, 7 August 1069, 1.

11. Maurice Dingman to "My Dear People," September 5, 1969, Dowling H.S. File, ADM. See also "Dowling Decision This Month," *The Catholic Mirror*, 11 September 1969, 1.

12. Nick Lamberto, "Dowling to Move to W.D.M.," 1 October 1969, *Des Moines Register*; see also Julie Zelenka, "The Dowling Issue 'No Right or Wrong," 1 October 1969, *Des Moines Tribune*, both are clippings in Dowling File, ADM.

13. "Model Cities Fund to be Slashed 42%," undated clipping from *Des Moines Register*.

14. Maurice Dingman to "My Dear People," October 2, 1969, letter to be read at all Masses. Dowling H.S. File, ADM.

15. Jacob Weiss to Luigi Ligutti, November 12, 1969, Monsignor Luigi Ligutti Papers, LGH 1.1, General Correspondence, "W," AMU.

16. "New Dowling Center Will Achieve Total Education," *The Catholic Mirror*, 2 October 1969, 1 & 8.

17. Information Sheet on the New Dowling, p. 2. n.d Dowling H.S. File, ADM.

18. "Proposal for Use of Dowling Site," n.d., 1, Dowling H.S. File, ADM.

19. Richard Hatfield, "Old Dowling Buildings Purchased," *Des Moines Register*, 3 June 1972, clipping in Dowling H.S. File, ADM.

20. Jerald Heth and Janet Bowers, "Seek United Way Aid to Buy Dowling High," *Des Moines Register*, 5 June 1972, 2; Jerald Heth, "Bar Funds to Buy Old Dowling High," 6 June, 1972, 10. (Clippings in Dowling H.S. File, ADM.)

21. "News Release: Sale of Dowling Property," August 8, 1974, Dowling H.S. File, ADM.

22. Don Gard, "School Reorganization Plan Approved by Board," *The Catholic Mirror*, 27 March 1980, 1 & 12.

23. "New D.M. School Named Holy Family," *The Catholic Mirror*, 22 May 1980, 12.

24. Don Gard, "Lay Teachers in Catholic Schools," *The Catholic Mirror*, 14 January 1970, 1.

25. The story of BVM renewal after Vatican II is related in Kathryn Lawlor, BVM, *From There to Here: The Sisters of Charity of the Blessed Virgin Mary From 1942–1972* (Dubuque: Mount Carmel Press, 2010), 127–60.

26. Letter of Bishop Maurice Dingman, "Dowling Educational Center," *The Catholic Mirror*, 4 June 1970, 1.

27. "Will Build New Coeducational Center on West Des Moines Site," *The Catholic Mirror*, 6 August 1970, 1 & 3.

28. Pastoral Letter," and "Vote Immediate Building of New Dowling Ed. Center," *The Catholic Mirror*, 7 January 1970, 1.

29. "Name New Principals for Dowling, St. Joe's," *The Catholic Mirror*, 27 August 1970, 1.

30. "New Era at Dowling," *The Catholic Mirror*, 15 October 1970, 1.

31. "New Education Center Plans Revealed," *The Catholic Mirror*, 8 October 1970, 1 & 8.

32. "Layman Named Principal," *The Catholic Mirror*, 30 September 1971, 1–2.

33. "Dowling Enrollment Rises," *The Catholic Mirror*, 11 October 1973, 4.

34. "Fund-Raising Drive Announced for Dowling High School," *The Catholic Mirror*, 13 May 1976, 2.

35. "Dowling Director Interviewed," *The Catholic Mirror*, 13 January 1972, 1.

36. "St. Joseph's Educational Center, Center of Adult, Teem Religious Education," *The Catholic Mirror*, 31 August 1972, 7.

37. Maurice Dingman, "Total Religious Education," *The Catholic Mirror*, 31 August 1972, 8.

38. "Father Baum to Open Series," *The Catholic Mirror*, 28 September 1972, 7.

39. "D.M. Community Witnesses Dedication of New School," *The Catholic Mirror*, 18 May 1972, 1 & 3. A color supplement to the paper was also issued featuring articles about the new center.

40. "Last Look at St. Joseph Academy," *The Catholic Mirror*, 18 May 1972, 1.

41. Don Gard, "Drumm Home to Move to New Site," *The Catholic Mirror*, 25 May 1978, 1 & 12; "Priests Opposed Drumm Home Move," ibid., 8 June 1978, 1–2.

42. Mary Kiernan Harney, RSM, "Drumm Home Residents Prepare for Big Move," *The Catholic Mirror*, 14 August 1980, 3.

43. "Iowa Catholic Conference," *The Catholic Mirror*, 19 February 1970, 1 & 2.

44. For the most thorough discussion of US Catholics and the contraception issue, See Leslie Tentler, *Catholics and Contraception: An American History* (Ithaca, NY: Cornell University Press, 2009).

45. "Operation No-Start," *The Messenger*, 30 July 1965, 4 & 8.

46. "Letters to the Editor," *The Messenger*, 6 August 1965, 4.

47. "Bishop's Statement," *The Catholic Mirror*, 1 August 1968, 4.

48. Cordaro shared his embrace of social activism in many different venues. One of the most succinct was "Resistance and Priesthood—A Developing Model," *Via Pacis* 12, no. 5 (n.d.) DD-CW, W-21, Box 13, Marquette University Archives. See also Frank Cordaro, "Dear Dad," *Catholic Rural Life* 33, no. 2 (April 1983): 19–21. Cordaro also provided a lengthy oral memoir at the Midwest Catholic Worker Retreat in Sugar Creek, Iowa, August 26, 1989, transcript Cordaro Papers, AMU.

49. "Fr. Zeitler Joins Worker Movement," *The Catholic Mirror*, 4 August 1977, 12.

50. Copies of Catholic Worker materials are to be found in "Des Moines Catholic Worker, Via Pacis Correspondence, November 1976–May 1978," DD-CW, W-21, Box 13, AMU.

51. "Anti-Salt Demonstrator Disrupts Cater Talk," clipping, *Washington Star*, 30 November 1979, Des Moines Catholic Worker Papers, "Church Newsletter Bulletins, DD-CW W-211, Box 2, AMU.

52. Peter Dubec, "Cordaro Protests Draft Registration," *The Catholic Mirror*, 4 November 1982, 16. Cordaro Interview, Cordaro Papers, AMU.

53. David Polich, "In the Midst of His People," *Des Moines Register*, 5 April 2014, 23A.

54. The proposal for this staff person is outlined in a letter of Bob Brammer to Bishop Maurice Dingman, January 29, 1980. A copy of this was provided to the author by Father David Polich.

55. David Polich, "A Brief History of the Catholic Peace Ministry," April 13, 1994, in possession of author. Phone interview with Sister Gwen Hennessey, OFM, September 21, 2016. See also David Polich, "Catholic Peace Ministry's 25th Anniversary," *The Catholic Mirror*, 18 August 2006, 3. Polich and Sister Hennessey noted that Bishop William Bullock eliminated the CFM as a diocesan office in 1991 but that it had continued as an independent entity under other leadership, see William Simbro, "Two Diocesan Ministries Disbanded," clipping, *Des Moines Register*, 30 November 1991.

56. Parish Profile, May 1, 1980, St. Mary's Panama File, ADM.

57. "Land Is a Gift," *The Catholic Mirror*, 2 November 1978, 3.

58. Bart Pollock, "Bishops Plan Land Statement Changes," *The Catholic Mirror*, 20 March 1980, 1 & 12. See also Bovee, *The Church and the Land*, 245.

59. "Unemployment Protest," *The Catholic Mirror*, 2 April 1981, 1.

60. "1,500 Brave Cold to Vent Grievances," *Des Moines Tribune*, 9 February 1982, 1.

61. Peter Dubec, "Meeting Explores Rural Problems," *The Catholic Mirror*, 7 October 1982, 12.

62. William Robbins, "Farmers at Iowa Rally Sound Call for Federal Aid," *New York* Times, 28 February 1985; Peter Dubec, "Farm Rally Cites Crises Afflicting Rural America," *The Catholic Mirror*, 7 March 1985, 1 & 16.

63. "Letter from A Country Priest," August 24, 1985, Cordaro Papers, AMU.

64. "Inquiry Topic: The Holy Season," USA TODAY, 28 March 1986, 9A.

65. "County Jail Is Moral Issue," *The Catholic Mirror*, 2 November 1978, 1 & 20.

66. This episode is described in Crisler and Mosle, *In the Midst*, 152–54.

67. Sister Lois Spear, "Services Commemorate Archbishop Romero," *The Catholic Mirror* 26 March 1981, 1–2.

68. Dingman was interviewed by the Catholic press on his impressions of the developing pastoral on peace. "The Bishops and Nuclear Morality," *The Catholic Mirror*, 2 December 1982, 4.

69. "Meetings Scheduled to Discuss Pastoral," *The Catholic Mirror*, 10 February 1983, 1.

70. "Bishop Reflects on Civil Disobedience," *The Catholic Mirror*, n.d.

71. Tom Cordaro, "Deterrence and the Gospel," in "Faith and Resistance" program of the conference provided by Father Dave Polich, 45–54.

72. Sister Carla Oberzzut, RSM, was a participant and described her reactions to the conference, which gave her the courage to challenge the nuclear build-up of the United States under Reagan. "Faith and Resistance," *The Catholic Mirror*, 7 March 1985, 10.

73. Angela Cordaro, "Faith and Resistance," *The Catholic Mirror*, 7 March 1985, 10. Pictures of the action at Offutt were included in the Catholic newspaper of that day.

74. "Bishop Reflects on Civil Disobedience," *The Catholic Mirror*, n.d.

75. Jerry Filteau, "Bishop Dingman: MX Is Immoral," *The Catholic Mirror*, 21 March 1985, 1.

76. "Four From D.M. Diocese Arrested at SAC Base," *The Catholic Mirror*, 22 August 1985, 11. Those who were detained included Msgr. Paul Connelly and Fr. Thomas Coenen; Fr. David Polich, pastor of St. Michael's, Harlan;

Merle Hansen, president of a farmer's alliance; Charles Wolford of St. Patrick's Parish in Missouri Valley.

77. Colman McCarthy, "Des Moines Activist Bishop," *Des Moines Register*, 3 May 1985, is clipping in Dingman Files, ADM. See also Dan Gillmor, "Moral Activism Is Iowa Bishop's Mainstay," *Kansas City Times*, 18 October 1985, clipping in Dingman Files, ADM.

78. Bishop Maurice Dingman to Frank Cordaro, December 13, 1983, Cordaro Papers, "Bishop Dingman File," AMU.

79. "Bishop Explains Support of Iowa ERA," *The Catholic Mirror*, 30 October 1980, 3. Dingman wasn't totally correct in citing the opposition of the Catholic bishops to women's suffrage. Some were opposed; others, like his predecessor Dowling, were indifferent; many said nothing on the subject. There was no coordinated action by the American bishops against women's suffrage—although many of them likely held common gender biases about the competence of women to make sound political judgments.

80. Edward Dyer, SS, to Austin Dowling, October 12, 1914, Pouget Priest File, ADM.

81. A copy of Goethal's letter dated February 11, 1914, and other documents recommending him to Bishop Dowlng are in Pouget Priest File, ADM.

82. "Four Des Moines Parishes Expand Facilities," *The Messenger*, 2 July 1948, 6.

83. "Our Lady of Guadalupe Chapel to Be Blessed Sunday," *The Messenger*, 8 October 1948, 6.

84. Don Gard, "Serving the Spanish-Speaking," *The Catholic Mirror*, 7 September 1972, 1 & 2.

85. "Guadalupe Celebrates 25 Years," *The Catholic Mirror*, 11 October 1973, 11.

86. "Quinn: Further Reflections: A Papal Visit with Lessons for Debate on Biotechnology," *Des Moines Register*, 4 October 2013; Ambassador Kenneth M. Quinn to author, May 6, 2017. Quinn is currently the president of the World Food Prize located in Des Moines.

87. Bart Pollock, "Diocese Resettles 1,300 Refugees," *The Catholic Mirror*, 27 March 1980, 1 & 12; "Refugee Program Tries New Approach," *The Catholic Mirror*, 3 April 1980, 12.

88. Elizabeth Murphy, "Refugees Enrich Parish Life, Faith," *The Catholic Mirror*, 27 December 1984, 13.

89. Betty Murphy, "Bishop Dingman, 'Roast, Toasted,' *The Catholic Mirror*, 28 January 1984, 3.

90. John McCormally, "Dingman Shatters an Image," 23 January 1984, clipping from *Burlington Hawkeye* in Dingman Files, ADM.

Chapter 9—pages 335–57

1. "Future Is Secure," *The Catholic Mirror*, 19 October 1978, 1.

2. "Pope Draws Biggest Crowd Ever Gathered in Iowa," *Des Moines Register*, 5 October 1979, 15A (story continued from p. 1).

3. For a fuller discussion of the genesis and planning of the papal event, see Crisler and Mosle, *In the Midst*, 3–23. Also of help is the unpublished memoir of Monsignor Frank Bognanno. Personal copy given to author.

4. Phone conversation with Mr. Joseph Hayes, September 6, 2016. Hayes confirmed the details of this story of the letter and its presentation to Bishop Dingman. See also Paul Connelly, "Fences and Gifts," Memoir, 43–44, Paul Connelly Priest File, ADM.

5. Interviews with Monsignors Frank Bognanno and Stephen Orr.

6. William Simbro, "Why the Pope Chose D. M. for his 'surprise' visit," *Des Moines Register*, 3 October 1979, 3A.

7. "Proud Iowa Awaits the Pope," *Des Moines Register*, 30 August 1979, 1 & 4A. Another article highlighted Hayes, see Nick Lamberto, "Joe Hayes: The Man Behind the Pope's Visit," ibid., 1B.

8. An article noted that some of the people on the planning committee were new to the diocese. See William Simbro, "Newcomers to Area Catholic Posts Caught in Sweep of Papal History," *Des Moines Register*, 17 September 1979, 3A.

9. William Simbro, "Papal Fund-Raising Job, 'Challenging, Rewarding,'" *Des Moines Register* 5 September 1979, 3A.

10. Elizabeth Ballantine, "ICLU to Sue Over Holiday for Pope's Visit," *Des Moines Register*, 24 September 1979, 1; Elizabeth Ballantine, "Judge Lifts Ban on Polk County Holiday Today," *Des Moines Register*, 4 October 1979, 6A.

11. William Simbro, "Women Barred from Role in Papal Mass Communion," *Des Moines Register*, 8 September 1979, 1 & 5A.

12. Brian Owen, "D.M. Poles Feel Snubbed in Pope's Visit," *Des Moines Register*, 17 September 1979, 1B.

13. "D.M. Priest Named St. Patrick Pastor," *Des Moines Register*, 19 September 1979, 4A.

14. "John Paul and the Land," *Des Moines Register*, 4 October 1979, 14A.

15. Telephone interview with John Buscemi, October 7, 2016.

16. "Iowans Will Fashion Several Items Used in the Pope's Mass," *Des Moines Register*, 18 September 1979, 16A.

17. Nick Lamberto, "Venerable Oaken Timbers Will Form Pope's Altar," *Des Moines Register*, 17 September 1979, 3A.

18. Carol Pitts, "500 Attended Services to Pray for Pope," *Des Moines Register*, 24 September 1979, 5A.

19. William Simbro, "This Week His Heart Will Be in Iowa," *Des Moines Register*, 30 September 1979, 1. The *Register* issue of this day included a Papal Visit Guide and a tour of the Living History Farms.

20. "Surprises from John Paul," *Des Moines Sunday Register*, 30 September 1979, 1C.

21. Mary Kay Shanley, "Meet the Bishop," *The Iowan* 34 (Fall 1985): 4–9; 59.

22. Quoted in Crisler and Mosle, *In the Midst*, 23.

23. "What a Splendid Day," *Des Moines Register*, 6 October 1979, 12A.

24. Dingman to "Dear Bishop," n.d. Papal Visit Files, ADM.

25. Papal Visit, Press Release, December 17, 1979, Papal Visit Files, ADM.

26. "Rome Pilgrimage Recalls Papal Visit of Last Year," *The Catholic Mirror*, 28 September 1980, 1 & 12,

27. "Pilgrims Greet Pope in Rome," *The Catholic Mirror*, 2 October 1980, 12.

28. All of these recollections are taken from Tom Quiner, "Memories from the Iowa Visit: The Pope of the People," http://thepopeofthepeople.com/memories-from-iowa.cfm.

29. Walter E. Shotwell, "Bishop's Mansion on Auction Block," 21 April 1980, clipping from *Des Moines Tribune* in Dingman File. The house was first put up for auction and then finally listed with a real estate firm.

30. William Simbro, "D.M. Couple Buys Bishop's Mansion," 29 August 1980, clipping from *Des Moines Tribune* in Dingman Files, ADM.

31. "Bishop's House Finally Sold," *The Catholic Mirror*, 28 August 1980, 8.

32. "Two Sisters to Be Honored," *The Catholic Mirror*, 6 August 1981, 8.

33. Peter Dubec, "New D.M. Location for Diocesan Offices," *The Catholic Mirror*, 30 December 1982, 1 & 13.

34. Elizabeth Murphy, "Fewer Priests: More Parishes Without Pastors," *The Catholic Mirror*, 21 March 1985, 1 & 16.

35. Elizabeth Murphy, "Pastoral Administrator Plan Studied," *The Catholic Mirror*, 21 March 1985, 16.

36. Don Gard, "Diocesan Structure, Decision Making to Change on July 1," *The Catholic Mirror*, 13 June 1985, 1 & 16; Elizabeth Murphy, "New Focus for Decision-Making Bodies in Diocese," *The Catholic Mirror* 27 June 1985, 1 & 16.

37. "Bishop Announces Newspaper's Suspension," *The Catholic Mirror*, 6 March 1986, 6.

38. Don Gard, "Employee Layoffs, Paper Suspension to Address Deficit," *The Catholic Mirror*, 6 March 1986, 1 & 10.

39. Mary Ann Dorsett Dubec, "Treatment of Lay Employees Unjust," *The Catholic Mirror*, 20 March 1986, 11.

40. "Iowans Remember a Beloved Teacher, Shepherd, Friend," *The Catholic Mirror*, 20 February 1991, 6.

41. "Bishop Dingman Recuperating from Surgery," *The Catholic Mirror,* 20 August 1981, 1.

42. "Bishop Dingman Reports on Trip to Rome," *The Catholic Mirror,* 6 October 1983, 4.

43. Don Gard, "Services in Granger for Msgr. Ligutti," *The Catholic Mirror,* 12 January 1984, 1 & 16.

44. "Bishop Tells of Kidnap Ordeal," *Des Moines Register,* 10 October 1983, 1 & 22A.

45. Peter Dubec, "Bishop Dingman Released Unhurt after Abduction," *The Catholic Mirror,* 20 October 1983, 1 & 15.

46. William Simbro, "Bishop's Hard Month Ends," *Des Moines Register,* 16 October 1983, 1B & 3B.

47. Jerry L. Schmalenberger to Maurice Dingman, October 11, 1983, Dingman Files, ADM.

48. Orr interview.

49. Peter Dubec, "Bishop Recovering from Stroke," *The Catholic Mirror,* 1 May 1985, 1.

50. The following details of Dingman's last days are taken from Crisler and Mosle, *In the Midst of His People,* 227–46.

51. William Simbro, "Ailing Bishop Addresses Ecumenical Fest," 26 January 1987, clipping from *Des Moines Register* in Dingman Files, ADM.

52. Memorandum, n.d. (probably summer 1984) "When Should I Retire as Bishop of Des Moines?" Dingman Files, ADM.

53. Memo to Dingman's Jesu Caritas Group dated Pentecost 1984 asking the same question: "When Should I Resign as Bishop of Des Moines?"

54. Memorandum n.d. (summer 1984).

55. Daniel W. Kucera, OSB, to Maurice Dingman, January 28, 1985, Dingman Files, ADM.

56. William Simbro, "Dingman Considering Retiring," 26 June 1986, clipping from *Des Moines Register,* Dingman Files, ADM.

57. "Shepherd of His Flock," 18 October 1986, clipping from *Des Moines Register,* Dingman Files, ADM.

Index